THE
GREEK
SEARCH FOR WISDOM

THE
GREEK
SEARCH FOR WISDOM

MICHAEL K. KELLOGG

Prometheus Books

59 John Glenn Drive
Amherst, New York 14228-2119

Published 2012 by Prometheus Books

Cover image © 2012 Bigstock Photo
Cover design by Grace M. Conti-Zilsberger

Inquiries should be addressed to
Prometheus Books
59 John Glenn Drive
Amherst, New York 14228–2119
VOICE: 716–691–0133
FAX: 716–691–0137
WWW.PROMETHEUSBOOKS.COM

16 15 14 13   5 4 3 2

Library of Congress Cataloging-in-Publication Data

Kellogg, Michael K., 1954-
    The Greek search for wisdom / by Michael K. Kellogg.
        p. cm.
    Includes bibliographical references and index.
    ISBN 978-1-61614-575-0 (cloth : alk. paper)
    ISBN 978-1-61614-576-7 (ebook)
    1. Conduct of life. 2. Wisdom. 3. Philosophy, Ancient. I. Title.
    BJ1589.K45 2012
    880.9—dc23
                                                            2012004772

Printed in the United States of America on acid-free paper

For Mark Hansen, ἄνδρα πολύτροπον
Best friend and colleague for more than thirty years

Athena, goddess of wisdom:

καιρὸν δ᾽ ἐφήκεις: πάντα γὰρ τά τ᾽ οὖν πάρος
τά τ᾽ εἰσέπειτα σῇ κυβερνῶμαι χερί.

(You come just as I need you. Now and then
As heretofore, your hand shall be my guide.)

—Sophocles, *Ajax* 34–35

CONTENTS

8 CONTENTS

PREFACE

In a letter to Louise Colet, Gustave Flaubert wrote, "When I read Shakespeare I become greater, wiser, purer."[1] The same could be said of other writers and thinkers in the Western tradition—from Homer to Joyce, from Hesiod to Montaigne, from Aeschylus to Goethe, from Herodotus to Gibbon, from Aristophanes to Rabelais, from Plato to Nietzsche. Their works enrich our lives. They make us, through considered contact with them, "greater, wiser, purer."

How do they have this effect? And what wisdom do they teach us?

My goal is to consider these two interwoven questions as if they were—as I believe they are—the most important questions we could ask in our short time upon Earth. Through an exploration of what Matthew Arnold called "the best which has been thought and said in the world,"[2] I want to take the measure of human wisdom and the highest reaches of the human spirit.

Saul Bellow properly cautioned that we must not "take masterpieces and turn them into discourse."[3] The great works of Western civilization stand alone. They cannot be distilled into ideas; they cannot be summarized in prose (not even the prose ones). To know their transformative power, they must be encountered and experienced. They must be loved and appreciated. They must be read and reread. Only then do they effect what Samuel Johnson referred to as the enlargement of our sensibility.

But this enlargement of our sensibility can be enhanced by a thoughtful approach that respects both historical context and the intimate and indissoluble connection between form and content. In the process we can reach a deeper understanding of what each author has to tell us—through poetry, drama, prose narratives, essays, philosophy, or history—about our place in the world and how we should live our lives. The greatest geniuses gave the last ounce of their energy and the last drop of their blood in an effort to forge such a vision. If they cannot lead us to wisdom, then there is none to be found.

This volume covers the masterworks of ancient Greece. It begins with a historical and cultural introduction to the period, followed by chapters on individual authors and their most compelling writings. I hope in subsequent works to continue my exploration of the Western tradition down to the present day. Such an undertaking will inevitably invite, and suffer from, comparison to Will and Ariel

Durant's magisterial *Story of Civilization*, in eleven volumes, left incomplete at their deaths. But my focus is different. As Nietzsche noted, "In the mountains the shortest way is from peak to peak."[4] I lay no claim to being comprehensive. I want to focus rather on the highest peaks in our efforts to understand and give meaning to our lives.

I write with no preconception that there is a steady progress to be found among our greatest writers; rather the contrary. No later epic poet has surpassed Homer; no dramatist (not even Shakespeare) has eclipsed Aeschylus and Sophocles; no historian has bettered Herodotus and Thucydides; and no philosopher has come close to matching Plato and Aristotle in the depth, breadth, and subtlety of their thought. Each writer must be considered and judged on what he or she offers us, not just as a harbinger of a revised aesthetic or more refined thinking to come. Yet there is clearly an evolution, a changing conception of wisdom and the possibilities for poetry and prose and hence for the human spirit, that is also worth capturing.

Ultimately, there is no justification for my undertaking beyond a profound love for the great writers and thinkers of the Western tradition and a desire to spend my time among them, listening as they speak to us and to one another. If in the process I can inspire some renewed interest in imperishable classics, and perhaps even a sense that these dead authors still have something to say to us that is both urgent and necessary, so much the better.

To quote Flaubert again (when he was a miserable law student longing for a life of literature): "For me I can imagine nothing in the world preferable to a nice, well-heated room, with the books one loves and the leisure one wants."[5] That is unfortunately an aspiration out of the reach of far too many men and women on the planet, for whom the basic necessities of life are wanting. Yet even among those with both heat and leisure, the classics are too often a foreign land rarely visited. We must steal for them what time we can, for a life that has lost contact with our rich cultural and intellectual heritage and that ignores the wisdom of our forebears is a poor thing indeed.

I offer this work, in all humility, as a travel journal of sorts, in which I can at least point out those sites I most love and most want to share.

ACKNOWLEDGMENTS

I have not tried to document every source for the ideas in this book. But my extensive debt to generations of classical scholars and translators will be obvious to those in the field. Three in particular—Edith Hamilton, Bernard Knox, and Victor Davis Hanson—have long inspired in me the belief that sound scholarship can be combined with compelling prose. I have tried to list the books and articles on which I most relied, as well as those from which general readers would most benefit, in the Suggestions for Further Reading section. I also cite there, in full, the excellent translations of Robert Fagles, Richmond Lattimore, Apostolos Athanassakis, Philip Vellacott, Andrea Purvis, Richard Crawley, Paul Roche, and others, from which the quotations in the text are derived.

I was helped by many readers of the chapters in draft form. My brother Peter, an accomplished playwright, read each chapter as it unfolded and provided invaluable comments, encouragement, and humor. My friend and colleague Aaron Panner; my other siblings, Harry and Meg; and a talented young writer, Julius Taranto, each read a number of the chapters and helped me to shape their final form. Harry in particular checked the astronomical references in the Hesiod chapter and kept a close eye on my use of Greek and Latin terms and phrases. Kelly Murray and Eileen Sweeney—a philosopher at Boston College—provided much appreciated literary and philosophical conversation via e-mail.

I would like to offer special thanks to Helene Foley, now at Columbia University, who first taught me Greek at Stanford more than thirty-five years ago, and who graciously read my chapter on Aristophanes and offered many insightful suggestions. Victor Davis Hanson, Francis Fukuyama, Charles Fried, and Peter Huber read the finished manuscript and provided generous comments in support.

Darrin Leverette and Bernadette Murphy put the manuscript in its final form. Their intelligence, attention to detail, willingness to track down obscure sources, and sensitivity to the nuances of language were all indispensable. So, too, was my long-time assistant, Marilyn Williams, without whom my life would be in chaos.

Steven L. Mitchell of Prometheus Books has my undying gratitude for publishing my first book and then taking a chance on this one at such an uncertain time for traditional publishers. For more than forty years, Prometheus Books has been a model of the independent publisher, offering serious books for thoughtful readers on a range of subjects.

I would also like to thank Jade Zora Ballard for her meticulous editing, which improved the prose, sharpened the ideas, and saved me from many errors.

My discussion of Aristotle's *Nicomachean Ethics* draws upon chapter 5 of my earlier book, *Three Questions We Never Stop Asking* (Prometheus Books, 2010), and I drew some elements of my portrait of Socrates and my account of Plato's theory of forms from the preface and chapter 1 of that book.

I wish to thank the estate of W. H. Auden, which gave permission through Random House Publishing and Curtis Brown, Ltd., to quote a beautiful passage on Thucydides from his poem "September 1, 1939" (copyrighted 1940 and renewed 1968 by W. H. Auden, from *Collected Poems of W. H. Auden*, by W. H. Auden).

As always, my greatest thanks go to my wife, Lucy, and to my three children—Baird, Cole, and Camille—who supported and encouraged me throughout the writing of this book, and who endured my many digressions on why the ancient Greeks had so much to say about their own lives, as well as my many injunctions (depending on which chapter I was writing) that they should "drop everything and read [Homer]."

Introduction

THE GLORY
THAT WAS GREECE

On desperate seas long wont to roam,
Thy hyacinth hair, thy classic face,
Thy Naiad airs have brought me home
To the glory that was Greece,
And the grandeur that was Rome.
　　　　　　—Edgar Allan Poe, "To Helen"

[The Greeks] admit us to a vision of the earth unravaged, the sea
unpolluted, the maturity, tried but unbroken, of mankind. Every word is
reinforced by a vigour which pours out of olive-tree and temple and the
bodies of the young.
　　　　　　—Virginia Woolf, "On Not Knowing Greek,"
　　　　　　　　　in *The Common Reader*

Oh, those Greeks! They knew how to live. What is required for that is to
stop courageously at the surface, the fold, the skin, to adore appearance,
to believe in forms, tones, words, in the whole Olympus of appearance.
Those Greeks were superficial—out of profundity.
　　　　　　—Friedrich Nietzsche, preface to *The Gay Science*

GODS AND HEROES

Theseus, the legendary hero of Athens, rid the surrounding territory of its many bandits, including Procrustes, who placed his captives on an iron bed and ensured their proper fit by cutting or stretching as needed. But Theseus's most memorable exploit involved the Minotaur, a creature, half-human, half-bull, kept deep in a labyrinth at the palace of King Minos on Crete. Athens was compelled to send seven boys and seven girls each year as tribute to Crete, where they were devoured by the Minotaur. Theseus volunteered to join their number and—with the help of King Minos's daughter, Ariadne, and a ball of string—managed to kill the Minotaur, find his way out of the labyrinth, and flee in a ship with the other youths and with Ariadne (whom he promptly abandoned on the island of Naxos).

The story of Theseus and the Minotaur is one of many interwoven tales of gods and heroes that make up Greek mythology. Yet it turns out that this particular story has some grounding in historical events. Just over a century ago, Sir Arthur Evans excavated the palace of Knossos on Crete, a building originally five stories high, with hundreds of rooms and intricate passageways. He also uncovered a fresco showing youths vaulting over bulls in some elaborate and dangerous ritual. Archaeological evidence indicates, moreover, that the Minoans may have practiced human sacrifice.

The Minoan civilization, named after King Minos, emerged as early as 2200. (All dates in this book are BCE—before the Common Era—unless otherwise noted.) Minoans grew rich through agriculture and trade. They also had a powerful fleet that dominated the Greek world around the Aegean Sea, which included a fledgling Athens. The Minoans even had a written language, though it has never been deciphered. At some point, around 1400, Greeks from the mainland conquered Crete and took over the palace.

The "myth" of Theseus and the Minotaur appears to incorporate elements of this history, including the labyrinthine palace at Knossos, rituals involving a bull and human sacrifice, and the ultimate freedom of the Greeks from the domination of the Minoans. Somehow, through the centuries, history became myth, and yet elements of myth have since been returned to history through the efforts of archaeologists. In a similar vein, excavations by the wealthy German amateur, Heinrich Schliemann, at Troy, Mycenae, and Tiryns in the late nineteenth century CE revealed a world very much like that depicted in the epic poems of Homer, which had long been dismissed as pure fiction.

Through mythology, the Greeks made an effort to understand their world, their history, and the many inexplicable forces they could not control but with which they still had to contend. The Olympian pantheon of twelve gods was considered responsible for all natural phenomena, including disease, drought, storms, and even sudden surges of passion. The Greeks developed festivals and sacrifices to curry favor with, or at least appease, these divinities.

Equally significant was the pantheon of Greek heroes claimed as forebears of the many Greek city-states. In addition to Theseus, they included Perseus, who slew the snake-headed Medusa; Heracles, with his Twelve Labors; Jason and the Argonauts, who searched for the Golden Fleece; Oedipus, who inadvertently murdered his father and married his mother; and, most important of all, the heroes of the Trojan War: Achilles, Odysseus, and Hector, as well as Agamemnon, king of Mycenae, and his brother, Menelaus of Sparta, whose unfaithful wife, the beautiful Helen, precipitated the war.

Itinerant bards sang of the gods and heroes long before there was writing to record their stories. This oral mythology, which evolved over centuries and developed numerous variants, became the well out of which was drawn the astonishing array of Greek literature and thought. Myths about the Trojan War and its aftermath coalesced in the epic poems of Homer (ca. 725). Myths about the world's creation and evolution were synthesized in Hesiod's *Theogony* (ca. 700) and led to later scientific and philosophical speculation about the nature and origins of the universe. The tragedies of Aeschylus (525–456), Sophocles (496–406), and Euripides (480–406) were built around their own adaptations of ancient myths to fit contemporary concerns. Herodotus (484–425) freely mixed mythology with history, while his successor, Thucydides (460–395), felt compelled to draw a sharp line between the two. The comic poet Aristophanes (450–386) parodied the gods as liberally as he did men. Plato (427–347) created his own myths to explain his philosophy. Even Aristotle (384–322), that most rational of philosophers, thought the same sense of wonder led both to myth and to philosophy. He wrote from exile in his old age: "The more solitary and isolated I am, the more I have come to love myths."[1]

In short, all ten authors we will study in this book had an intricate, intimate relationship with mythology. We can never overestimate its importance in Greek thought. Nor should we overlook the power and beauty of Greek mythology in its own right.

THE MYCENAEAN PALACE CULTURE

Starting in 1900, the Greek peoples, in several tribal waves, migrated down from eastern Europe, through the Balkans, where they settled around the Aegean Sea, as Plato would later put it, like frogs around a pond. They had a common language of Indo-European origins (or at least dialects close enough readily to understand one another) and would develop and share a common cultural heritage, including their religion, their customs, and even their ideals. But they were never united as a people, except briefly, and even then only partially, in their conquest of the citadel of Troy (in Asia Minor, now modern Turkey) and much later in their defense against invasion by the Persian Empire. Throughout most of their history, the ancient Greeks fought with one another.

Scholars have long distinguished four main periods in Greek history. We will discuss relevant aspects of each period in the course of the individual chapters. But it will be helpful here to provide a short overview and briefly to mention events and writers not otherwise considered in the pages that follow.

The Lyric Age lasted from approximately 1600 to 1100. Powerful kings ruled and forged alliances from fortified palaces at Mycenae, Tiryns, Pylos, Thebes, and elsewhere. Mycenae was the dominant power, and, hence, we refer to the Mycenaean civilization. They were a warrior race, who made skillful use of bronze in constructing swords, spears, and knives, as well as ornate drinking cups and plates and even death masks.

The fall of Troy took place around 1125. It proved a hollow victory. Mycenaean civilization itself was destroyed shortly thereafter. According to tradition, Dorians (a tribe of Greeks said to be descended from Heracles) invaded from the north or perhaps, already present, staged an uprising from within. Regardless, the great palaces were sacked, and a dark age descended on Greece that lasted hundreds of years. Population dropped by as much as 80 percent through warfare, disease, and starvation. Whatever literacy had been derived from the Minoan civilization was lost. Small villages scraped out a poor living, often ruled by a local *basileus* (feudal lord), and piracy and pillaging were common. There is little wonder that the earlier Lyric Age continued to be celebrated through the dark age as a time of splendor and heroism in stories of gods and heroes passed down orally from generation to generation.

776 AND ALL THAT

The second period in ancient Greek history is known as the Archaic Age and is generally dated from 776 to 500. The Greeks obviously did not use our BCE dating system. For them, dates were geared to the Olympic Games held every four years. As a result, the year of the first Olympic Games (which took place by our reckoning in 776) has often been treated as the beginning of Greek history proper. Indeed, the classicist George Grote, with pardonable overstatement, dubbed 776 the beginning of Western history. The oracle at Delphi, where the Pythian priestess delivered prophecies inspired by the god Apollo, was established about the same time, as were various pan-Hellenic religious festivals. (The ancient Greeks referred to their homeland as Hellas, and themselves as Hellenes.)

Population was expanding. The use of iron (superior for tools and weapons alike) was more common. The *polis*, an autonomous, self-governing city-state that included a large city plus the surrounding territory and villages, dates from this period. Feudal lords and their arbitrary ways were gradually replaced by political institutions and the rule of law. The Greeks were heavily dependent upon agriculture for their livelihood, and the rocky, mountainous terrain both isolated and imposed severe limits on the size of the various *poleis*. An extensive period of colonization began, always preceded by an appeal to the oracle, as city-states sent their surplus populations to establish colonies on islands in the Aegean and on the coasts of Asia Minor, North Africa, and Italy. Trade by sea was difficult and dangerous but inexorably expanded, abetted by the use of gold and silver coins. The distinctive Greek black-figure vases, replacing an older geometric design, appeared throughout the Mediterranean.

With the rediscovery of writing, the restless energy of the Greek peoples found outlets in intellectual pursuits as well as in trade, colonies, and war. The Greeks adapted the alphabet of Phoenician traders in the eighth century and soon began to expand its use to refine and record the oral traditions that reconnected archaic Greece with its heroic past. In the late eighth century, Homer and Hesiod wrote their epic poems. They were succeeded by the unknown author(s) of the so-called *Homeric Hymns*, which presented stories of the individual Olympian gods in more detail.

Lyric poetry also thrived starting around 700, though unfortunately it survives only in tantalizing fragments. Archilochus of Paros penned the famous line "The fox knows many things, the hedgehog only one—but big."[2] Tyrtaeus urged his fellow Spartans to "fight for this land with all our heart, and for our children," for "to fall and die among the fore-fighters is a beautiful thing."[3] Others were more elegiac, such as Mimnermus of Smyrna in Asia Minor (now Izmir in modern Turkey):

But short-lived like a dream youth passes
in all its preciousness; and, grievous and unsightly,
old age immediately hangs over our heads,
hateful and dishonored alike, which makes a man unrecognizable
and ruins his eyes and mind as it pours about him.[4]

Semonides, from the island of Samos, was philosophical:

Understanding is not within men's grasp; from day to day
they live like animals, in no way knowing
how god will bring each thing to its fulfillment.
But hope and confidence encourage all of them
as they set their thoughts on unachievable things.[5]

Most beautiful of all, though, were the exquisite lyrics of Sappho, poet of Lesbos, who wrote of her love for a small group of female friends:

Come to me now as well; release me from
this agony; all that my heart yearns
to be achieved, achieve, and be yourself
my ally in arms.[6]

The eighth and seventh centuries also saw the growth of science and philosophy along the Ionian coast of Asia Minor, particularly in the colony of Miletus, where Thales was the first to predict an eclipse of the sun, and his pupil, Anaximander, posited a single underlying substance for all things, a substance in constant motion, giving rise to opposing properties. Pythagoras of Samos coupled sophisticated geometry with a belief in the reincarnation of souls and the mystical significance of mathematics and music. Xenophanes of Colophon portrayed religious beliefs as a function solely of custom and self-interest, and noted that if horses could draw, they would picture their gods as horses. Heraclitus of Ephesus claimed that all is flux and change, and that "it is not possible to step twice into the same river."[7]

Again, we have only fragments from these pre-Socratic philosophers (so called because they predated the Socratic dialogues of Plato, which were long taken to mark the beginning of formal philosophical thought). But, although their influence did not approach that of Homer, the pre-Socratics, along with the lyric poets, provided the essential intellectual background for the third period in ancient Greek history.

THE CLASSICAL AGE (500–323)

A history of the Classical Age is inevitably a history of Athens, the cultural and political center of ancient Greece. Aeschylus, Sophocles, Euripides, Thucydides, Aristophanes, and Plato were all Athenian citizens. Aristotle spent most of his working life there. Even Herodotus visited the city to read his *Histories* at public gatherings and was awarded a grant by the Athenian assembly.

Tragedy, comedy, and history were all invented in this period. Architecture, vase painting, and sculpture were brought to a perfection never surpassed and rarely equaled. Philosophy and science also flourished. Parmenides (515–ca. 450) argued that the world of change is an illusion and that true being is permanent and unchangeable; it neither comes into being nor passes away. His pupil, Zeno of Elea (490–430), posed paradoxes on the impossibility of change and motion, including that of Achilles and the tortoise: no matter how fast he runs, Achilles can never catch the tortoise because each time he reaches where the tortoise began, the tortoise will have moved forward, and so on, in an infinite series that will never allow Achilles to catch up completely. Democritus (460–370) claimed that all things were composed of minute "atoms," whose arrangement gives rise to the appearances of the everyday world: "By convention sweet, by convention bitter; by convention hot, by convention cold; by convention color; but in reality: atoms and the void."[8] Medicine, based on the researches of Hippocrates of Cos and his school, made dramatic advances. Itinerant teachers (the Sophists) taught rhetoric, politics, and ethics (for a fee). The first protouniversities were created at Plato's Academy and Aristotle's Lyceum.

Democracy was also invented in Athens. Draco, a quasi-legendary figure, gave Athens its first written code of laws in 621. The code was harsh, with the death penalty meted out for most offenses (hence our term *draconian*). Athens was then an oligarchy, controlled by aristocratic families and large landowners to whom others were indebted for their livelihood. Solon, who was the chief archon (or magistrate) in 594, ushered in fundamental reforms, including forgiveness of all pending debts and elimination of personal security for debt (which had led to the slavery of Athenian citizens).

A further expansion of political rights followed Solon, culminating in the democratic reforms of Cleisthenes in 507. Only adult male citizens could vote, but within that restricted group democracy grew increasingly direct and radical. The Athenian citizens themselves sat regularly in the assembly to debate and decide critical issues of foreign and domestic policy, as well as to elect the group of ten generals in command of the army and navy. Many offices were filled by lot rather than election, and they rotated regularly. Jurors and, later, even those attending the assembly were paid for their services so that all could afford to participate. The people (*demos*) ruled, and, to prevent any one person from obtaining too much power, ostracism was created (from *ostraka*, the shards of pottery on which voters wrote the name of the man they wanted banished for a period of ten years).

The democracy lasted—with brief interruptions—for almost two hundred years and played a critical role in the free and open exchange of ideas that was the Greek enlightenment. As we shall see, there are varying opinions as to how well it performed politically and militarily. But it survived two enormous challenges. The first was the Persian invasions of 490 and 480, chronicled in Herodotus, in which vastly outnumbered Greeks (led by Athens and Sparta) joined together to preserve their freedom against a foreign tyrant. The second was the Peloponnesian War of 431–404, recorded by Thucydides, in which the Greek city-states—divided roughly into democrats following Athens and oligarchs following Sparta—fought one another with a ferocity and brutality that belied the seemingly refined and enlightened culture of the Classical Age.

Sparta was the polar opposite of Athens. While Athens was open to new ideas and foreign influences, Sparta was closed to both. While Athens's institutions evolved, Sparta's remained rigidly the same. While Athens was democratic, Sparta was steadfastly oligarchic. While Athens devoted itself to commerce and the arts, Sparta focused solely on military training. While Athens's navy ruled at sea, Sparta's army was preeminent on land. While Athenians were restless, innovative, and garrulous, the Spartans were stolid, unimaginative, and so disinclined to surplus speech that our word *laconic* derives from the Spartans' homeland in Laconia.

The Spartans subjugated the peoples in Laconia, on the Peloponnesian peninsula, sometime around 950. Lycurgus, Sparta's own legendary lawmaker, established their oligarchic constitution in the eighth century. Vastly outnumbered by a large native population reduced to the status of *helots* (serfs to work the land), Sparta kept in a constant state of military readiness, even formally declaring war on the helots every fall.

The Peloponnesian War ultimately resulted in the defeat of Athens, but she rebounded quickly and restored her democracy after a brief, Spartan-imposed tyranny. Sparta was not so lucky. Decisively defeated by its former ally, Thebes, first at Leuctra in 371 and again at the battle of Mantinea in 362, the power of Sparta was broken forever by a rebellion of the helots.

The greatest beneficiary of this internecine warfare was Macedon, in northern Greece, where Philip II reigned from 359 to 336. After consolidating his hold over the leading families and securing his northern and western borders, Philip turned his attention to southern Greece. Despite vigorous warnings (known as *philippics*) delivered by the Athenian statesman and orator Demosthenes, there was little the weakened and still-quarreling city-states could do. The battle of Chaeronea in 338, in which Philip defeated the combined forces of Athens and Thebes, marked the end of Greek autonomy and the traditional polis. Philip's son, Alexander the Great, who ruled from 336 to 323, expanded his kingdom to the farthest reaches of the world, conquering Persia, Egypt, parts of North Africa, and Asia as far as the Indus River before his troops decided they had had enough of conquest and turned for home.

THE HELLENISTIC AGE (323–31)

The last phase of ancient Greek history lasted nearly three hundred years, from the death of Alexander in 323 to the beginning of the reign of Augustus, the first Roman Emperor, in 31. When Alexander died suddenly at the age of only thirty-three, there were no plans for his succession. His massive empire was split into three dynasties by his most powerful commanders. The Seleucids ruled from western Turkey to Afghanistan, though they were forced by neighboring powers to cede territory almost from the beginning, including in central and western Turkey where the Attalid dynasty ruled until 133, when Attalis III bequeathed his kingdom to the Roman Republic. The Antigonids controlled Macedon and Greece off and on until the Roman conquest in 168. The Ptolemies maintained their power in Egypt until Cleopatra, the last of the Macedonian rulers, was defeated by Augustus in 30 and chose to commit suicide by pressing an asp to her breast.

Little remains of the poetry and drama of this period. Apollonius of Rhodes, more scholar than poet, wrote an epic that still survives, the *Argonautica*, which tells the story of Jason and his quest for the Golden Fleece. But the Hellenistic Age was more focused on the private comfort of domestic life than on the overflowing, communal exuberance that found its expression in epic poetry, in tragedy, and in the great social, political, and intellectual comedies of Aristophanes. Menander (342–291) wrote plot-driven domestic comedies about thwarted lovers and wily slaves that were wildly popular with his contemporaries.

Science still flourished, and mathematics was brought to a hitherto-unknown perfection by Euclid, whose *Elements* (ca. 300) is a model of precision and elegance still read today with pleasure and profit. Archimedes (287–212) excelled in engineering, as well as math, and famously claimed that, given a lever long enough and a place to stand, he could move the world. Aristarchos of Samos (310–230) developed the first heliocentric model of the solar system.

Philosophy moved both literally and symbolically to the "garden" of Epicurus (341–270), where he preached a tranquil life focused on simple pleasures, and to the covered colonnade or walkway (*stoa*), where Zeno of Citium (334–262) emphasized control of the emotions and a life of virtue in harmony with nature. Pyrrho (360–270), the third great philosopher of this period, argued that every proposition can be met with its contradiction and that, since we cannot know things as they are in themselves, we should withhold judgment everywhere and always. These three schools—Epicureanism, Stoicism, and Skepticism—would exercise an enormous influence on Roman philosophy and are still studied, and sometimes embraced, today.

Perhaps the most significant contribution to culture in the Hellenistic Age, however, was the great library established by the Ptolemies at Alexandria in Egypt. By royal mandate, the library not only eagerly sought out works to purchase, but every visitor to the city carrying scrolls was required to turn them over to be copied. At its height, the library contained as many as five hundred thousand scrolls, and to it and other satellite libraries in Alexandria we owe the ultimate preservation of the works we have today from archaic and classical Greece. Scholars worked long hours preparing definitive editions and lengthy commentaries. They divided the otherwise continuous works of Homer, Herodotus, Thucydides, and others into "books" corresponding to the papyrus scrolls onto which they were laboriously copied and preserved. Most of these books were lost in the succeeding centuries, but enough survived by way of Rome and, after its fall, Constantinople to lay the foundations for the rediscovery of Greek culture in the Renaissance. So much was lost. The value of what remains is incalculable.

TEN GREEK AUTHORS

In search of the highest peaks of Western civilization, which provide the best perspective on all that is below, I have elected to limit this volume to ten Greek authors. Choosing those ten has been easy. No one could seriously dispute the finest exemplars of epic poetry (Homer, Hesiod), tragedy (Aeschylus, Sophocles, Euripides), history (Herodotus, Thucydides), comedy (Aristophanes), and philosophy (Plato, Aristotle).

The surviving works of the lyric poets and the pre-Socratic philosophers are too fragmentary for separate treatment of any one figure. Socrates never wrote anything of his own, and the Hellenistic philosophers, who left only fragments behind, are properly considered only along with their Roman counterparts. Despite recently discovered scrolls, Menander is still known mainly through his influence on Plautus and Terence, who adapted many of his now-lost plays to Roman times.

The only writers whose exclusion may merit protest are Pindar (522–443) and Xenophon (430–354). But Pindar's odes (which combine praise for a contemporary Olympic victor with mythological allusions and pithy maxims) are an acquired taste. Xenophon, though his merits are many and his interests wide-ranging, is not on a par with the others considered here.

In order to be faithful to the evolution of Greek thought, I have treated the ten authors in chronological order, with one exception. I placed Euripides before Herodotus (even though he was born five years later) because I wanted to keep the three tragedians and the two historians together.

Each chapter can be read as a stand-alone unit. Although Thucydides's detailed account of the Peloponnesian War comes after the chapters on Sophocles and Euripides, there is enough information about the war in those two chapters to explicate the plays. So, too, for the Persian Wars, chronicled in Herodotus, but essential to an understanding of Aeschylus. Since the intellectual milieu changed rapidly in the classical period, I preferred modest repetition to anachronism. Readers new to Greek history may find the abbreviated chronology at the back of the book useful in placing authors and events in context.

Chapter 1

HOMER AND
THE HEROIC IDEAL

The *Iliad* was written, according to the latest scholarly estimates, sometime between 750 and 700. It celebrates the last year of the siege of Ilium (the capital of Troy) by a Mycenaean Greek expeditionary force, a war that took place (if it happened at all) more than four hundred years earlier, between 1200 and 1100.

Four hundred years is a long time. It would be as if a contemporary poet sat down to write an epic on the defeat of the Spanish Armada by England in 1588. And yet it would be completely different. We have written records and firsthand accounts of the Spanish Armada. We know specific dates and the names of the individuals involved. We wish we knew much more; records of that time were spotty to begin with and often lost in the intervening years. But a poet writing today about the Spanish Armada would still have a wealth of detail both to fire and to constrain the imagination.

The Greek alphabet (adapted from the Phoenicians) did not even come into existence until the eighth century. An earlier, syllabic form of writing archaic Greek, known as Linear B, appears to have been used only for accounting records and lists of household stores. Linear A, from the Minoan civilization, has never been deciphered. Linear B was derived from Linear A and applied to the Greek language when the Mycenaeans conquered Crete sometime around 1400. Linear B in turn disappeared from the Greek world during the so-called dark ages between 1100, with the collapse of the Mycenaean civilization, and 776, the year of the first Olympic Games.

Homer, then, had no written sources upon which to rely for his account of distant Bronze Age battles. He did not even have the archaeological evidence available to us today. What he did have was an oral tradition, stories and poems handed down through the centuries, inevitably altered and romanticized according to the needs, interests, and customs of the various tellers of the tale. Itinerant bards sang of the fall of Troy at festivals and in princely houses. Two cycles of poems developed, telling not only of the war itself but also of the often-problematic return of the Greek heroes after the sack of Troy.

At some point, around 725, the *Iliad* was written down in the form we know it today, and it is surely fitting that its reduction to writing was among the first uses of the new alphabet. Some years later, a second poem, the *Odyssey*, was brought to term. Others in the cycles were presumably written down around the same time, but only the *Iliad* and the *Odyssey* have survived, and they survived due to their vital role as the collective bible of Greek culture. (The word *bible* itself originates from the Greek, *ta biblia*, meaning "the books," which is how the Hellenistic Jews referred to their sacred writings.) The *Iliad* and the *Odyssey* were *the* books for classical Greek education. The lost poems in the cycles were never accorded the same veneration.

The *Iliad* is not only the first written work in Greek, but it is the font of Western literature, a tradition that ultimately mixed uneasily, though fruitfully, with the tradition spawned by the Hebrew Bible, whose composition began around 950. Yet the *Iliad*'s origins in prehistory are shrouded in mystery and conjecture.

We do not know if the Trojan War actually happened, though some such event surely formed the kernel of the tales that begat the poem. Indeed, it would be surprising if the powerful, colonizing Mycenaean Greeks and the Trojans did not clash, given the latter's control over the entrance, through the Hellespont, to the trade and material riches of the Black Sea. And the wealthy city—or rather succession of cities—uncovered in 1871 by the amateur archaeologist Heinrich Schliemann, arguably shows signs of destruction by fire in the stratum corresponding to the relevant time period.

Nor do we know whether Homer—the legendary blind bard of Chios or Smyrna or any of half a dozen other cities that claimed him as their own—was the poem's author, though a single genius must ultimately have shaped the poem and created it in the form we have it today. It is not just an evolving oral poem, with spontaneous accretions and variations by a succession of anonymous singers through the centuries that some scribe wrote down from whatever performance he happened to hear once the alphabet made it possible to do so. It is a beautifully crafted, organic whole that far surpasses any oral tradition of which we can plausibly conceive. Many elements of that tradition were certainly incorporated into the written poem—including the familiar formulaic phrases (those rendered in English as "the wine-dark sea," "the rosy fingertips of dawn," "swift-footed Achilles," and so on) essential to the hexameter lines—but no unlettered oral tradition could approach the intricate architecture and subtle details of this lengthy work.

Homer may have dictated that poem to a scribe, rather than writing it down himself, but the *Iliad* is a poem with a single author responsible for its final form.

Nor, finally, do we know the related question of whether a single poet authored both the *Iliad* and the *Odyssey*, though, again, I believe that to be the case. The same consciousness pervades both poems, making them twin aspects of a complete worldview despite their differences in import and sensibility, just as Shakespeare wrote both *Macbeth* and *The Tempest*, and Stendhal both *The Red and the Black* and *The Charterhouse of Parma*. Indeed, the idea that two such surpassing geniuses happened to succeed one another yet were known by tradition under the same name seems eminently implausible.

Ultimately, however, these great questions of homeric scholarship pale before the astonishing beauty and power of the poems themselves. We read Homer, in the end, to understand ourselves and the greatness of our artistic heritage. As the art historian Bernard Berenson explained: "All my life I have been reading about Homer, philological, historical, archeological, geographical, etc. Now I want to read him as pure art only, as commensurate with the heart and mind while humanity retains both."[1] The *Iliad* comes to us as a sudden burst of light out of the darkness of prehistory and forever helps define the possibilities of being human.

THE RAGE OF ACHILLES

The *Iliad* does not tell the story of the fall of Troy. It does not tell the story of the causes of the Trojan War. It does not even tell us very much about the protracted siege of Troy. It assumes knowledge of, and alludes to, all three, but the poem itself focuses on only a few weeks in the ninth year of the war.

That in itself is a remarkable starting point. For nine years, the members of the Greek expeditionary force have been living in tents next to their ships, pulled up on the beach. They are a loose confederation of allies. Homer collectively calls them Achaeans, from a region in the north central part of the Peloponnese, but sometimes he also refers to them as Danaans or Argives—the Greeks had no single national identity in what archaeologists call the Mycenaean period. Agamemnon, hereditary king of Mycenae and head of the House of Atrides, is their acknowledged leader by virtue of the great power and central role of his city; he also has the most ships and the most men under his command, and he is strongly backed by his brother, Menelaus, king of Sparta. But there are many kings and princes among the Achaeans, each with his own domain, his own ships, and his own troops—and each jealous of his prerogatives and honor. They are a fragile coalition, made more so by nine years of living in an armed camp, seemingly no closer to their goal of sacking Troy.

Agamemnon, moreover, is deeply flawed as a leader. He is touchy and grasping, with bad judgment, an explosive temper, and little real knowledge of his men. On one occasion, he tests the troops by suggesting that they give up the siege and return home. Instead of roaring their dissent and insisting on pressing the attack, the rank and file give a shout of joy and head for the ships; only Odysseus's quick actions and harsh words turn them back to the assembly. On two other occasions, when the battle is going poorly, Agamemnon gives way to despair and genuinely suggests flight. Each time he is promptly and rudely rebuffed by one of his warlords, first by Diomedes and then by Odysseus, who says to him,

> "*You* are the disaster.
> Would to god you commanded another army,
> a ragtag crew of cowards, instead of ruling us."[2]

It is unsurprising, then, that under Agamemnon's leadership tensions boil over into a quarrel with deadly consequences. Plague has ravaged the camp, and Achilles, the greatest Achaean warrior, calls an assembly to determine what is to be done. The fact that Achilles must take the initiative is itself telling. Calchas, a seer and prophet, says the plague came upon them because Agamemnon spurned Apollo's priest, who sought to ransom his daughter, Chryseis. Chryseis had been awarded as a prize to Agamemnon in an earlier raid, and Agamemnon is predictably furious. Indeed, Achilles has already goaded Agamemnon by promising to protect Calchas even if Calchas names as the cause of the plague Agamemnon himself, who "claims to be, by far, the best of the Achaeans."[3] What Agamemnon claims is obviously not what Achilles believes, and he makes that clear to the entire assembly.

Homer brilliantly captures the steady escalation in angry rhetoric between the two men that leads to a decisive break. Much of the fault lies with Achilles, who—when Agamemnon demands an equal prize to replace Chryseis, "else I alone of the Argives go without my honor"—calls him the "most grasping man alive," "shameless," and "dog-face[d]," and suggests that Agamemnon lurks in the rear while the hard fighting is done and then steps forward to claim the lion's share of plunder.[4] At one point, Agamemnon tries to defuse the quarrel—

"Enough. We'll deal with all this later, in due time"[5]—by urging that they defer all other issues and immediately send Chryseis back to her father to appease Apollo. But the suggestion that Agamemnon may later commandeer another man's prize to take her place infuriates Achilles, and he insults Agamemnon so brutally that Agamemnon must reassert his preeminence. He does so by taking Achilles's own prize, his beloved Briseis, and Achilles returns to his ships resolved to fight no more for the Achaeans.

> "Someday, I swear, a yearning for Achilles will strike
> Achaea's sons and all your armies! But then, Atrides,
> harrowed as you will be, *nothing* you do can save you—
> not when your hordes of fighters drop and die,
> cut down by the hands of man-killing Hector! Then—
> then you will tear your heart out, desperate, raging
> that you disgraced the best of the Achaeans!"[6]

This dispute may seem almost childish on both sides. Yet at stake are nothing less than *kleos* (honor) and *timê* (the marks of public esteem), which are the ultimate values of the homeric hero. Achilles demands that his superior fighting skills be honored and recognized through the award of greater prizes and other indicia of public esteem. Agamemnon insists that his superiority as a king and leader be afforded the first place, and he disparages Achilles as a mere "spearman." This jockeying for honor and glory—this sense by each that *his* skills and *his* contributions are the most valuable—is a fundamental aspect of the Greek character in ancient times. Prowess in war and wisdom in counsel are the two most valued qualities of the homeric hero—to be "a man of words and a man of action too."[7] As Harold Bloom notes, "To compete for the foremost place was the homeric ideal."[8] Falling short of that ideal—failing to obtain the kleos and timê that one believes one deserves—was a source of shame, a shame so sharp and so great that (as told in the *Odyssey*) mighty Ajax killed himself when his fellow Achaeans, following the death of Achilles, awarded Achilles's armor to Odysseus rather than to him.

For Achilles, the demands of kleos and timê are all the greater because his goddess mother, Thetis, has told him that he can choose between two fates: he can fight and die at Troy and achieve imperishable glory (*kleos aphthiton*), or he can stay at home and live quietly and unheralded, dying in old age with his family around him. Achilles chooses Troy and immortal glory. Yet now he has been deprived even of the timê that is his due. He has been shamed by Agamemnon.

None of the other warlords, moreover, has supported Achilles in his dispute with Agamemnon, not even old Nestor, who merely urges calm and discretion on both men. Yet Achilles called the assembly and pressed Calchas for an answer for the benefit of all. Agamemnon tells Achilles that "others will take my side and do me honor,"[9] and the silence appears to bear him out. Afterward, when Achilles's absence leads to disaster on the battlefield, the other warlords claim that Agamemnon "took from his tents the girl Briseis, / and not with any applause from us, far from it."[10] But one must feel that their silence at the time was due not just to fear of Agamemnon but also to jealousy and annoyance at Achilles's arrogance and pride, and to their sense of their own worth. They undoubtedly respect his fighting skills, but the other warlords bear little affection for Achilles and almost seem eager to test their mettle against the Trojans without him.

Achilles in turn bears so little affection for his fellow Achaeans that he fervently wishes their deaths at the hands of the Trojans in order that his own worth and their need for him will be recognized. He appeals to his goddess mother, Thetis, to intercede with Zeus on his behalf and turn the tide of battle against the Greeks, and that is precisely what happens. So long as Achilles roamed the plains around Troy, the Trojans stayed largely within or close to their city walls. With him out of action, they press all the way to the camp by the sea and pin the Achaeans against their own ships.

Agamemnon's initial response, in the episode alluded to above, is to suggest flight. Instead, Nestor counsels him to send an embassy to Achilles to plead with him to rejoin the battle. Agamemnon chooses three emissaries—including Odysseus and Ajax—and recites at length the many splendid gifts he will give to Achilles as a "ransom paid for friendship."[11] These gifts include the return of Briseis (with a sworn oath that he has not touched her), seven women from Lesbos skilled in crafts, a dozen stallions, gold and silver, the pick of prizes from Troy, and his own daughter in marriage along with seven citadels and the men who live within them. "All this," Agamemnon says, "I would extend to him if he will end his anger." But Agamemnon ends his recital by reasserting his own supremacy over Achilles: "Let him bow down to me! I am the greater king, / I am the elder-born, I claim—the greater man."[12]

Odysseus, in his recital of these gifts to Achilles, wisely leaves off Agamemnon's last remarks, saying simply, "All this / he would extend to you if you will end your anger," and then adds that even if Achilles still hates Agamemnon he should take pity on "our united forces mauled in battle here," who will honor Achilles like a god if he returns to the fight.[13]

Achilles should be receptive to these overtures. Homer portrays him as raging grimly by his ships "yearning, always yearning for battle cries and combat."[14] And when the emissaries approach, they find Achilles playing the lyre and "singing the famous deeds of fighting heroes."[15] Clearly, the heroic ideal and the desire for kleos and timê are still strong within him. The many gifts and the acknowledged need of the Achaeans will augment both. He can return to battle in a much stronger position than before his dispute with Agamemnon.

Yet Achilles rebuffs the emissaries, saying that he and his troops will sail for home the next morning. He gives two reasons for that response. First, his anger at Agamemnon is unappeased, and he refuses to be patronized by him. Indeed, he picks up on Odysseus's artful elision and senses Agamemnon's continuing insistence on his supremacy. In prefacing his own speech, which he promises will be straight and true, Achilles says, "I hate that man like the very Gates of Death / who says one thing but hides another in his heart."[16] Achilles is the opposite in so many respects of Odysseus, the man of twists and turns, and the hero of Homer's second poem. Achilles neither dissembles nor adapts, and he can neither hide nor suppress his continued anger. Agamemnon has sent emissaries with bribes, but he has not come himself and has not proffered any apology.

Second, Achilles points out the irony of the whole expedition, which was ostensibly launched to win back the wife of Menelaus—the beautiful Helen, "with her loose and lustrous hair"[17]—who ran off with the Trojan prince, Paris. Having the two great civilizations locked in a death struggle over Helen makes for excellent poetry both in Homer and later, as Christopher Marlowe showed in *Doctor Faustus*:

> Was this the face that launch'd a thousand ships,
> And burnt the topless towers of Ilium?
> Sweet Helen, make me immortal with a kiss.[18]

Clearly, though, most of the Achaeans, including Achilles, are not there for Helen. They are there for glory and plunder or in obeisance to the superior power of Agamemnon. As Finley Hooper wryly remarked, "Helen's face may have launched a few ships but the rest are on a more practical mission."[19] Yet Achilles rightly protests that Agamemnon can hardly justify asking Achilles to fight for his brother's wife while simultaneously robbing Achilles of his own woman.

"Are *they* the only men alive who love their wives,
those sons of Atreus? Never! Any decent man,
a man with sense, loves his own, cares for his own
as deeply as I, I loved that woman with all my heart,
though I won her like a trophy with my spear."[20]

Yet neither of these reasons is a sufficient explanation of Achilles's refusal. He has been offered the restoration of the woman he claims to love and full recompense and more for the kleos and timê he has lost. Yet Achilles wonders aloud about the true value of kleos and timê, particularly because—as Agamemnon has shown—they are not actual guarantors of worth. If glory and esteem can be doled out or withheld by a worthless leader such as Agamemnon, why is it worth fighting and dying for them? Why should he not opt for the long life without glory promised by his mother? "The same honor waits / for the coward and the brave. They both go down to Death."[21]

Achilles is reaching here toward a sense of individual worth and the value of human life that transcends the heroic ideal. We see here the first hints of the Achilles who in the *Odyssey*, when Odysseus encounters him in the underworld, laments, "I'd rather slave on earth for another man— / some dirt-poor tenant farmer who scrapes to keep alive— / than rule down here over all the breathless dead."[22] The Achilles of the *Odyssey* has found that imperishable glory is a hollow consolation compared to the richness of even the most humble human life. But in the *Iliad* he is still conflicted and cannot bring himself to put aside his "yearning for battle cries and combat."[23] When simple, mighty Ajax appeals to Achilles on behalf of his comrades to "put some human kindness in your heart" and accept the emissaries "sent from the whole Achaean force," who "long to be your closest, dearest friends," he relents so far as to say that he will not sail away and will even rejoin the fighting if and when the Trojan hero Hector sets fire to the Achaean ships and batters his way to Achilles's own camp.[24] This is small consolation, perhaps, since Achilles's camp is at the end of the line, and Hector will need to engulf the rest of the fleet to reach it. But, in the end, it will suffice.

HECTOR, BREAKER OF HORSES

When Homer first reviews the Trojan forces, including their many allies from throughout Asia Minor, he begins with "tall Hector with helmet flashing."[25]

Hector, one of many sons of King Priam, is first among the Trojans, just as Achilles is first among the Achaeans. But there the similarity ends. Achilles is the Achaeans' best warrior, a man born for strife and killing. Hector is not just the best warrior but also the best man among the Trojans. Hector is at home with peace, as a member of a community, a husband, a father, a brother, and a dutiful son.

Hector stands in sharp contrast to the isolated Achilles, just as civilized Troy stands in sharp contrast to the armed camp by the sea. It is a place of sumptuous halls and rich customs; of women weaving, gossiping, gathering water from the well, and making sacrifices to the gods; of a wise and gentle king beloved by his people; of genuine affection between husband and wife; of old men sitting in the sun on the tower by the gates discussing the olden days and watching the war unfold before their eyes.

The Achaeans have known nothing but war for nine years. The Trojans seem better adapted for peace. But they must wage war to maintain their civilization. If they fail, their city will be sacked and destroyed, their men murdered, and their women (and whatever children survive) dragged off into slavery. The Achaeans are fighting for riches and glory and the figurative Helen. The Trojans are fighting for their very existence as a people.

In the end, only Hector stands between Troy and its fate. He understands his responsibility and bears it well. When a seer warns that various bird signs spell doom for the Trojans and suggests that they retreat, Hector angrily dismisses him. "Fight for your country—that is the best, the only omen," he says.[26] Fight he does, brilliantly and often savagely, setting aside his own feelings and concerns in a single-minded effort to drive the Achaeans from his shore. When his chariot driver is killed, Hector genuinely mourns for him and yet never stops to indulge his grief.

> There on the spot the man's strength and life collapsed
> and blinding grief for his driver overpowered Hector,
> stunned for his friend but he left him lying there,
> dead, and swept on, out for another hard driver.[27]

Hector knows only one way to save his city and his family, and that is to wage passionate war against the Achaeans. "Reckless one, my Hector," his wife Andromache tells him, "your own fiery courage will destroy you."[28]

In a series of scenes, we see Hector in many roles, and our admiration and affection for him grow with each. He is the brother of handsome, charming Paris, whose seduction of and elopement with Helen (and her magnificent jewels) when he was a guest in the home of Menelaus is the ostensible cause of the war. As the troops range for battle, Paris springs to the forward ranks, "lithe, magnificent as a god, / the skin of a leopard slung across his shoulders, / . . . challenging all the Argive best / to fight him face-to-face in mortal combat."[29] But when Menelaus marks him, "parading there with his big loping strides, / flaunting before the troops,"[30] Paris quails before him. Homer explains with cutting irony and a devastating simile:

> Backing into his friendly ranks, he cringed from death
> as one who trips on a snake in a hilltop hollow
> recoils, suddenly, trembling grips his knees
> and pallor takes his cheeks and back he shrinks.
> So he dissolved again in the proud Trojan lines,
> dreading Atrides—magnificent, brave Paris.[31]

Hector is shamed by his brother's cowardice and his shirking of a war that he brought upon his family and his people. Paris has the appearance of a fighter, "but you have no pith, no fighting strength inside you,"[32] Hector tells him. He chides Paris as a "curse to your father, your city and all your people, / a joy to our enemies, rank disgrace to yourself!"[33] Paris is suitably chastened and ashamed before his brother—a man who does have pith and fighting strength and is a credit to his father, his city, and all his people—and he offers to fight Menelaus, man-to-man, in front of all the troops, with Helen and her treasures as the prize, the rest to swear binding pacts of friendship and end the war. Hector strides into no-man's land between the lines, holding his spear aloft, and makes the proposal, which is joyfully accepted by both sides. He knows that his brother cannot defeat Menelaus but he sees a way to save his people from devastation.

Paris, of course, is quickly outmatched by Menelaus. But his protectress, Aphrodite, the goddess of love, saves him from death, wraps him in swirls of mist, and transports him back to his bedroom, to which she summons Helen and, "while the two made love in the large carved bed, / Menelaus stalked like a wild beast, up and down the lines."[34] Paris has let down his people once again, and a fool from the Trojan ranks breaks the truce by winging an arrow at Menelaus, wounding him. The entire episode repeats in capsule form the initial seduction and betrayal. Hector's effort to end the war has failed, and he returns to it with grim determination.

But Homer also shows us the domestic side of Hector. We see him back at Troy, speaking first with his mother, Hecuba; then with Helen; and finally with Andromache, his wife. He gently rebuffs Hecuba's anxious, motherly plea that he is wearing himself out and should stop to refresh himself with wine and build his strength. He speaks softly and kindly to Helen, with genuine affection, while asking her to rouse Paris and send him back to the fighting. As Helen later explains, she never heard a single reproach from Hector: "you with your gentle temper, all your gentle words."[35]

Hector declines all offers of rest: "My heart races to help our Trojans— / they long for me, sorely, whenever I am gone."[36] But he will make one stop he considers essential:

> "For I must go home to see my people first,
> to visit my own dear wife and my baby son.
> Who knows if I will ever come back to them again?—
> or the deathless gods will strike me down at last
> at the hands of Argive fighters."[37]

He finds his wife on the gate-tower of Troy, anxiously scanning the battlefield for signs of him. With her is Astyanax, "Hector's son, the darling of his eyes / and radiant as a star."[38] The conversation between husband and wife is beautifully rendered, realistic, and deeply affecting. She urges him to draw back from fighting in the open plains and make the protection of Troy his priority. Her father and seven brothers were all killed by Achilles, and her mother died of grief. She cannot bear another such loss.

> "You, Hector—you are my father now, my noble mother,
> a brother too, and you are my husband, young and warm and strong!
> Pity me, please! Take your stand on the rampart here,
> before you orphan your son and make your wife a widow."[39]

But Hector, too, is captive to the heroic ideal. He cannot shrink from battle but must fight in the front ranks and win glory for himself and his people. He would suffer shame otherwise. Moreover, he sees salvation for Troy only if he can drive the Achaeans from their shore. If he fails and Troy is fated to fall, he would prefer that the earth be piled over his dead body so that he never hears the cries of his wife, dragged off into slavery where she will spend her days "laboring at a loom, at another woman's beck and call" or "fetching water at some spring."[40]

Before he departs, Hector reaches for his infant son, who shrieks and cringes at the sight of his flashing bronze helmet with the horsehair crest. It is a rare and precious moment of levity, the only one allotted mortals in the entire poem. Hector and Andromache both laugh as he removes the helmet, sets it down, and raises his son, kisses him, and tosses him in his arms, praying to Zeus that he too will live to be a great warrior, first among the Trojans, greater even than his father, and a joy to his mother's heart.

Andromache smiles through her tears as she receives the child back from him.

> Her husband noticed,
> and filled with pity now, Hector stroked her gently,
> trying to reassure her, repeating her name: "Andromache,
> dear one, why so desperate? Why so much grief for me?
> No man will hurl me down to Death, against my fate.
> And fate? No one alive has ever escaped it,
> neither brave man nor coward, I tell you—
> it's born with us the day that we are born."[41]

Hector takes up his helmet, as Andromache makes her way home, glancing back at him again and again. Once home, she gathers her women together and they sing dirges for Hector, convinced that he will never come home from battle.

They are right, and with the death of Hector, the fate of Troy is also sealed. The reader knows that when Hector falls, so too will Troy; Hector's father will be murdered, his young son thrown from the ramparts onto the rocks below, and his wife and mother carried off into slavery. Not just a man but a civilization will be destroyed.

GENTLE PATROCLUS

Patroclus is the friend and comrade-in-arms of Achilles. He is the son of Menoetius, a king in his own right, but Patroclus is clearly in a subordinate position to Achilles. He was banished for murder as a boy (the result of a sudden quarrel that still haunts him) and sought refuge with Achilles's father, who raised him as a companion and aide to his son. When Patroclus beds down in the evening, it is with a consort given to him by Prince Achilles, and he soothes and defers to his volatile friend.

Despite his history and his own prowess as a warrior, Patroclus is a "gentle man, the soul of kindness to all."[42] He feels searing empathy for his hard-pressed Achaean comrades. Homer pictures him helping the wounded Eurypylus back to his shelter, arm around his waist, where he cuts out an arrow from his thigh, washes his wound, and covers the gash with healing herbs. Patroclus sits with Eurypylus, lifting his heart with stories and trying to soothe his pain.

Patroclus is beloved not just of the Achaean warriors but also of the captured servant girls in Achilles's camp. These women, wrenched from their homes and families, often after the slaughter of their husbands or fathers, have found a friend and protector in Patroclus, who treats them always with consideration.

Yet Patroclus is tall and magnificent, with a build close enough to that of Achilles himself that he can wear his armor. Indeed, when numerous Achaean champions have been wounded and the Trojans are threatening to fire the ships, cutting off the Achaeans from supplies and any hope of reaching home, Patroclus urges Achilles to let him don that armor and lead Achilles's troops into battle in hopes of giving the exhausted Achaeans some respite.

> "Breathing room in war is all too brief.
> We're fresh, unbroken. The enemy's battle-weary—
> we could roll those broken Trojans back to Troy,
> clear of the ships and shelters!"
> So he pleaded,
> lost in his own great innocence . . .
> condemned to beg for his own death and brutal doom.[43]

Patroclus chides Achilles for his intractable anger and his heart of iron, and Achilles gives way. He will not himself go into battle, because he promised not to do so until the Trojans reached his own ships. But he will allow Patroclus to go in his stead, wearing his armor and leading his troops so that, Achilles says, Patroclus can win great honor *for Achilles*, and the Achaeans will send Briseis back to him and shower him with the promised gifts.

In a remarkable passage, Achilles warns Patroclus only to drive the enemy from the fleet, not to carry the fight back to Troy, "not without *me*," for "you will only make *my* glory that much less."[44] The depths of Achilles's solipsism and megalomania, if there were any doubt on that score, are brutally clear.

> "Oh would to god—Father Zeus, Athena and lord Apollo—
> not one of all these Trojans could flee his death, not one,
> no Argive either, but we could stride from the slaughter
> so we could bring Troy's hallowed crown of towers
> toppling down around us—you and I alone!"[45]

Achilles's vision is of universal strife and slaughter in which only he and Patroclus are triumphant and win immortal glory.

But Achilles's vision goes terribly wrong. Patroclus does drive the Trojans from the ships and sends them into headlong flight back to Troy, slaughtering many of their finest warriors. But in his battle frenzy he ignores Achilles's warning and presses his assault to the very gates of Troy. The time for Troy's fall has not yet come. Stunned by a blow from the god Apollo, Patroclus is wounded by a spear thrust from Euphorbus and then, staggering back toward his own lines, falls easy prey to Hector, who rams a spear point straight through his bowels and out his back. As he dies, Patroclus prophesizes Hector's imminent death at the hands of Achilles. Driven by his own bloodlust, Hector dismisses the prophesy, brutally wrenching the spear from Patroclus's body and stripping him of the armor of Achilles.

> Hector, tearing the famous armor off Patroclus,
> tugged hard at the corpse,
> mad to hack the head from the neck with bronze
> and drag the trunk away to glut the dogs of Troy.[46]

A fierce battle ensues for the body of Patroclus, as Hector puts on the fatal armor of Achilles, armor that spells doom for him just as it did for Patroclus. The Achaeans with great effort and many losses gradually drag and carry Patroclus back toward the ships, while others fight a rearguard action to keep the Trojans at bay. But the issue is still very much in doubt when a runner is sent to tell Achilles of Patroclus's death.

Achilles reacts with overwhelming grief, guilt, and anger. He has allowed his dearest comrade to die unprotected while he sits by the ships, "a useless, dead weight on the good green earth."[47] He longs for death, forgetting his quarrel with Agamemnon and his lust for glory. "If only strife could die from the lives of gods and men," he says, "and anger that drives the sanest man to flare in outrage."[48] Yet it is anger that rouses Achilles from his grief and outrage at the threatened defilement of Patroclus's body that leads him to the ramparts, where his unarmed presence and unearthly, piercing war cry suffice to drive the Trojans to panic and flight. His craze for revenge, his desire to bring others grief that matches his own, is still inextricably mixed in his twisted mind with the battle feats that bring glory.

> "I'll lie in peace, once I've gone down to death.
> But now, for the moment, let me seize great glory!—
> and drive some woman of Troy or deep-breasted Dardan
> to claw with both hands at her tender cheeks and wipe away
> her burning tears as the sobs come choking from her throat."[49]

Achilles is in an inhuman state and will neither eat nor drink until Patroclus is fully avenged. Nor will he allow Patroclus to be buried, though the body is washed and anointed with oil and carefully laid upon its bier. Achilles would rush straightaway to war, yet he has no armor and the Achaeans are exhausted from the day's fighting. Odysseus urges him to wait while the troops eat and to allow for a ceremonious presentation of all the gifts promised him by Agamemnon. In words that will find their echo later in the work, Odysseus says,

> "We must steel our hearts. Bury our dead,
> with tears for the day they die, not one day more.
> And all those left alive, after the hateful carnage,
> remember food and drink—so all the more fiercely
> we can fight our enemies, nonstop, no mercy,
> durable as the bronze that wraps our bodies."[50]

Agamemnon at last makes his apology before the assembled troops and proffers his gifts to the now-indifferent Achilles. The Achaeans spend the night resting from the battle and singing dirges to Patroclus.

In the Trojan camp, Polydamas sensibly urges that they draw back to the city and fight from the shelter of its walls, now that Achilles will rejoin the fray. But Hector angrily dismisses this advice and promises to stand up to Achilles's grim assault, with fatal consequences for himself and so many of his Trojan warriors.

Once Achilles receives new armor from his goddess mother, he launches himself upon the Trojans with unimaginable fury. The rest of the Achaeans simply disappear from the poem. They are irrelevant to Achilles's devouring rage and the slaughter he wreaks. The catalogue of deaths (and detailed description of the fatal wounds he inflicts) is quickly numbing, as Achilles drives the Trojans back to Troy, where they stampede for the safety of the gates "like panicked fawns"[51]—all except Hector, who takes his stand outside the city, ignoring impassioned pleas

from his father and mother to take refuge inside the walls. Having rejected Polydamas's advice and led the army to disaster and rout, Hector is too ashamed to
face his fellow Trojans. He must take the chances of war—for "the god of war is
impartial: / he hands out death to the man who hands out death"—and face
Achilles instead.[52]

Yet Hector's nerve fails him when Achilles appears, like the god of war himself, shaking his great spear. He turns to run, and Achilles chases him three times
around the walls of the city, always cutting him off from the safety of the gate and
yet never gaining ground. In a beautiful image, as if painted on Keats's Grecian
urn, Homer describes the chase:

> endless as in a dream . . .
> when a man can't catch another fleeing on ahead
> and he can never escape nor his rival overtake him—
> so the one could never run the other down in his speed
> nor the other spring away.[53]

The actual fight is almost an anticlimax. When Hector recovers his nerve and
turns to face Achilles, knowing that he will die but hoping at least to win some
glory from the struggle, Achilles quickly cuts him down with a spear thrust
through the neck. Achilles angrily rejects Hector's dying request that his body be
ransomed to his parents and strips his body of its now-twice-fatal armor. With his
last breath, Hector prophesizes the imminent death of Achilles, just as Patroclus
foretold that of Hector.

While Priam and Andromache watch in horror from the gate-tower, the
other Achaeans come forward and stab the lifeless body of Hector. Achilles
pierces the heels, lashes them together with rawhide straps, and drags the body
face-down in the dust behind his chariot, parading before the city walls and back
to the ships. The cries of the Trojans—especially those of Andromache, drawn to
the tower by the others' screams of grief—sound in the distance.

With Hector dead, Achilles can finally bury Patroclus and pay him due
honors. In full armor, with fighters on their chariots and the infantry behind, they
carry Patroclus to the site appointed by Achilles. There the warriors cover his
body with locks of their hair and build a huge funeral pyre around him. They sacrifice sheep and cattle, and Achilles slaughters twelve captive Trojan youths. All
night long they keep the flames burning, as Achilles offers libations and weeps for
his lost friend. In the morning, they gather the bones of Patroclus in a golden urn

that will soon hold Achilles's remains as well. Achilles failed his friend by sending him out to battle alone, but he will escort him into the House of Death.

There follows a memorable scene in which funeral games are held for Patroclus. Achilles provides the prizes and presides over the various contests, which include a chariot race, running, boxing, wrestling, archery, shot put, and spear throwing. The Achaeans forget the war and even the loss of their comrade as they compete for first place—"the heart of each man raced, straining for victory"—and bicker like boys over the results.[54] There is a naive charm and simplicity in their delight in victory and the awarding of prizes. Better by far, one feels, that their love of contests—a constant in Greek history—take such a form rather than the deadly struggle that preceded and will follow this brief interlude.

When the games are finished, the other Achaeans turn their thoughts to food and sleep. But not Achilles; his anger and his guilt and his sorrow have not been assuaged, and he repeatedly drags Hector around Patroclus's tomb, as if that outrage on the body of his enemy could somehow help. It does not, and Achilles falls into a state of numbness in which he withdraws even from the now-returned Briseis. Only Achilles's most bitter enemy can rescue him from that inhuman isolation.

PRIAM'S GRIEF

Priam has lost many sons to Achilles, but none more dear to him and more important to his city than Hector. His grief does not inspire him to revenge; it crushes him. We see Priam in Troy, the powerful king, lord of many lands, collapsed in his courtyard, head and neck covered in dung that he has scraped from the ground.

Yet his grief ennobles as well as humbles him. Priam resolves to set off alone, with a single herald driving a wagon full of priceless gifts, to ransom Hector's body from Achilles and bring him home. He knows that the likely outcome is his own death, but he will not be dissuaded.

> "If it is my fate to die by the beaked ships
> of Achaeans armed in bronze, then die I shall.
> Let Achilles cut me down straightaway—
> once I've caught my son in my arms and wept my fill!"[55]

As he journeys toward the Achaean lines at night, he meets the god Hermes, disguised as an aide to Achilles, out scouting the plain in anticipation of the

morrow's renewed battle. Hermes guides him through the lines and straight to
Achilles's camp, where Priam slips past the astonished captains and kneels beside
Achilles, clasping his knees and kissing his "terrible, man-killing hands."[56]

In an impassioned and moving speech, Priam asks Achilles to remember his
own father, Peleus, at home and alone, waiting for news of his son. He asks for pity
for his own losses.

> "I have endured what no one on earth has ever done before—
> I put to my lips the hands of the man who killed my son."[57]

The emotionally spent Achilles responds with gentleness and compassion,
taking the old man's hand in his own, raising him from the ground, and seating
him in a chair. They both weep freely, and when they have their fill of tears,
Achilles speaks softly to Priam.

> "Let us put our griefs to rest in our own hearts,
> rake them up no more, raw as we are with mourning."[58]

In perhaps the most famous image from the poem, Achilles explains that, unlike
the immortal gods, men were born for sorrows. Two great jars, he says, stand in
Zeus's halls, one full of miseries, the other of blessings, and Zeus dispenses from
both. Our hope is to enjoy the blessings; our lot is to endure the sorrows.

Achilles orders the body of Hector to be bathed and anointed with oil, fearful
that if Priam sees it caked with blood and dust, the old man will flare in anger and
reignite Achilles's own rage. Once the body is cleaned and wrapped in linens,
Achilles himself carries Hector to a bier that comrades then place on the wagon.

In a bow to their humanity, Achilles and Priam eat despite their overwhelming grief. They are men and their hunger must be satisfied. Achilles speaks
words that echo those of Odysseus earlier in the poem. Having told the story of
Niobe, whose six sons and six daughters were slaughtered in her own halls, but
who after nine days of weeping turned her thoughts to food, Achilles urges:

> "So come—we too, old king, must think of food.
> Later you can mourn your beloved son once more,
> when you bear him home to Troy, and you'll weep many tears."[59]

Achilles promises to hold off further war for twelve days so that the Trojans
can bury Hector and do him proper honors. Achilles then has a bed prepared for

Priam outside, lest some visitor to Achilles's tent see him and report to Agamemnon. But Priam rises in the middle of the night and makes his way back through the lines to Troy, bearing his son in the mule-drawn wagon. The image of the old king, beaten down but full of dignity, traveling through the night with his melancholy burden and his overwhelming grief, is indelible.

Achilles, having recognized the limits of his humanity and reconnected with his fellows through compassion at their common fate, finally rests, "with Briseis in all her beauty sleeping by his side."[60] He will not have long to enjoy such blessings, for his own death, from an arrow shot by Paris, will soon follow the resumption of the war. The reader knows this, but Homer stops, as he should, with the burial of Hector and the end of Achilles's rage, which, as he said at the outset of the poem, "cost the Achaeans countless losses, hurling down to the House of Death so many sturdy souls."[61]

THEY KILL US FOR THEIR SPORT

The role of the gods in Homer is mystifying to the modern reader. Indeed, we do not even know how Homer himself felt about them. Some argue that the theology of the poem is to be taken literally, and that Homer and the Greeks saw the gods as actual, physical presences living on Mount Olympus and intervening in and overseeing human affairs. Others argue that the gods are purely metaphorical, representing aspects of the human psyche and natural phenomena that can all be explained in purely naturalistic terms.

As usual, the truth is more complicated. When Athena cautions Achilles not to draw his sword and kill Agamemnon during their initial quarrel, it is easy enough to see the personification of wisdom at work. When Aphrodite pushes Helen into bed with Paris, despite her initial reluctance, we can see the repetition of the sexual desire and moral weakness that led to her initial seduction. Even when the gods appear directly to mortals, it is often in the guise of others who might perfectly well have performed the acts in question themselves, as when Hermes guides Priam through the enemy lines or when Athena appears briefly outside the city walls disguised as Hector's brother Deiphobus, emboldening Hector to face Achilles but abandoning him when Achilles closes for the kill. The overall structure of the poem, which purports to chronicle "the will of Zeus . . . moving to its end," need reflect no more than a deep fatalism, which seems to run throughout Greek history.[62]

Yet other instances are not so easily explained away, as when Aphrodite rescues Paris by physically carrying him from the battlefield; or when Diomedes fights directly with, and wounds, Aphrodite; or when Apollo himself delivers a blow to Patroclus that so stuns him that he is virtually helpless, first against Euphorbus and, finally, fatally against Hector. These are all acts of direct intervention by the gods in human affairs that are not readily susceptible to naturalistic explanations.

Homer is neither a philosopher nor a theologian any more than he is a historian in the strict, modern sense of that term—as one who demands documented facts about the past. He is instead one of the profoundest students of the human condition we have ever known. The myths of the ancient heroes and the myths of the gods are intertwined, and he uses both to fashion his poem about the rage of Achilles. Homer clearly believes in his heroes. Whether he believes in his gods is not, I think, a question we can fruitfully ask. Nor is it particularly relevant to our appreciation of the poem or even to our understanding of Homer's worldview.

The questions we should ask, instead, are what roles do these gods play in the poem and how do they illuminate and deepen the stories of the mortal men who live and die within it? At least four such roles warrant mention, in order of increasing importance. First, the gods provide an appreciative audience for the events of the poem. The fact that the gods follow their favorite heroes and take the greatest interest in them lends a dignity and seriousness to the action that it might not have if it just unfolded on a remote shore with only the participants themselves there to witness it. The interest of the gods magnifies the greatness of the heroes and the import of their deeds. At the same time, the sacrifices made to the gods somehow—whatever one's own beliefs—sanctify and solemnify the proceedings. Sacrifices and petitions for success, however superstitious they appear, feed a fundamental human urge to invoke higher powers, to dress oneself in the armor of the gods. In the end, such armor saves no one, not Patroclus, not Hector, and not even godlike Achilles. But donning it is itself a mark of greatness.

Second, the gods provide an externalized substitute for psychological states. In Homer, as Erich Auerbach famously explained, everything is foreground and uniformly illuminated.[63] There are no dark recesses of the soul, no conception of internal mental forces that drive the action and that explain shifts in mood or motivation. Yet the gods themselves add that element of complexity. They can instill humans with sudden courage or inspiration or fear. They are even responsible for broader shifts of mood and momentum that govern an entire army, as when Athena sweeps through the Achaean forces,

lashing the fighting-fury
in each Achaean's heart—no stopping them now,
mad for war and struggle. Now, suddenly,
battle thrilled them more than the journey home,
than sailing hollow ships to their dear native land.[64]

To attribute such changes to divine forces is no less explanatory than to attribute them to "humours" or "drives" or "firing neurons."

Third, the immortal gods serve as a vital contrast to the all-too-mortal heroes of the poem. The squabbles and love affairs and mock battles of the gods provide a necessary element of comic relief in an otherwise tragic poem. It would be difficult to bear unrelenting strife and anger and suffering, without some such interludes (a lesson Shakespeare plainly took to heart). Even more important, though, as Eva Brann has explained, the "lightness" of their being gives weight to the homeric heroes.[65] Nothing is at stake for the gods. They are as arbitrary and willful as children. They can battle with one another and then retreat to Olympus for supper. When two humans battle, one generally dies and, in Homer, the afterlife is at best a shadowy, flitting affair, with no concrete existence and certainly no hope for resurrection in any form. Human life thus has both a pathos and a potential for glory that is lacking among the gods. One of the great themes of the poem is man's mortality and what it means for how he lives his life. What better way to explore that theme than against the background of a wholly different existence that knows not death and hence knows neither courage nor endurance nor true suffering.

Finally, and most critically, the gods are a representation of what Bruno Snell has called the "arbitrary forces and uncanny powers" that can destroy us in an instant.[66] Despite casual sympathy for a favored hero or two, the gods show an almost complete indifference to human suffering, including the destruction of human civilization and all the horrors of a sacked city: men slaughtered, women sold into slavery, babies cast from the battlements. At one point, Hera, in her eagerness to see the fall of Troy, offers Zeus three of her favorite cities in exchange.

"Raze them—whenever they stir the hatred in your heart.
My cities . . . I will never rise in their defense,
not against you—I'd never grudge your pleasure."[67]

The random hostility of the gods is a representation in Homer, as it is in Shakespeare, of the complete indifference of the universe to our fate. "As flies to wanton boys are we to the gods / They kill us for their sport," explains Gloucester in *King Lear*.[68] The core vision is the same, whether on the rain-swept heath of England or the windy plains of Troy: one of destruction and savagery, redeemed only by courage and the fragile connections mortal humans can forge with one another. Yet, in the end, the vision is not the same: for *King Lear*—with Cordelia hanged, Lear's heart given out, Gloucester blinded, and noble Kent off to commit suicide—is altogether darker and devoid of consolation; Homer faces the same indifferent universe full of violence and strife—with Patroclus and Hector dead along with countless other warriors and the death of Achilles and the destruction of Troy both imminent—and yet finds beauty and exquisite joy that somehow redeem and ennoble the whole. Reading *King Lear* is a profound and devastating experience. But reading Homer is, as Eva Brann remarked, "one of the purest, most inexhaustible pleasures life has to offer."[69]

HOMER'S "TERRIBLE BEAUTY"

In Robert Fagles's translation, the old men of Troy gaze at Helen moving along the ramparts and say to one another,

> "Who on earth could blame them? Ah, no wonder
> the men of Troy and Argives under arms have suffered
> years of agony all for her, for such a woman.
> Beauty, terrible beauty!"[70]

Fagles is echoing Yeats rather than translating Homer here. (In the Greek original the old men compare her to an immortal goddess.) But the phrase "terrible beauty" is wonderfully apt for Helen and, even more so, for the entire poem.

The Greek city-states were almost constantly at war, either with one another or with foreign invaders. War was not an unfortunate interruption of normal human life; it was a basic part of the human condition. The poem celebrates the heroic virtues and values of war, the exultation of its victors, and the pathos of its victims. It was a brutal world, and Homer never shrinks from portraying its brutality in the most matter-of-fact and direct way. He never sentimentalizes war and yet he recognizes its "terrible beauty," just as in his famous similes he recognizes the terrible beauty of a hungry lion separating a cow from a stampeding herd, or a wild boar turning savagely on its attackers, or a hawk swooping down upon a group of starlings. Warriors slaughtering one another is simply an extension of nature in its brute force and sublime indifference to suffering.

Homer does not sermonize. He does not analyze. He sings and celebrates. As Auerbach noted, the homeric style knows only "a uniformly illuminated, uniformly objective present."[71] The characters themselves are wholly present and complete in each moment. "Clearly outlined, brightly and uniformly illuminated, men and things stand out in a realm where everything is visible; and not less clear—wholly expressed, orderly even in their ardor—are the feelings and thoughts of the persons involved."[72] In the intensity of this presence, in the fullness of the passing moment, lies Homer's greatest genius. Joy and exuberance as well as grim death and heartbreak are to be found there together. As George Steiner puts it, "even in the midst of carnage, life is in full tide and beats forward with a wild gaiety."[73]

Yet Homer also sings of and celebrates custom and culture and the quiet and peaceful moments of men and women, moments on the ramparts of Troy or in the tent of Achilles. Homer knows the full cost of war and its destructive force. Not only will Troy fall, but the entire Mycenaean civilization and its great palaces at Mycenae, Tiryns, Pylos, and Knossos will soon be overthrown in a Dorian uprising (or invasion) sometime around 1100, and Greece will be cast into an unlettered dark age from which it will not begin to recover until the time of Homer.

The *Odyssey* is a natural continuation of the *Iliad*. The *Iliad*'s theme of the heroic ideal and its destruction of civilization and domestic life is transmuted into the *Odyssey*'s story of one exceptional warrior's attempt to reconnect with his civilization, his family, and his home. The theme of the *Odyssey* is one of reeducation. Just as Odysseus's son Telemachus must learn to fill his rightful place, Odysseus must relearn how to fill his own place as husband, father, son, and king and to reestablish peace and order in a chaotic and unheroic age. Mycenaean civilization failed that lesson.

The delicate balance between the heroic ideal on the one hand and the domestic ideal on the other is mirrored in the new shield forged for Achilles by Hephaestus (the god of fire and patron of all craftsmen). The shield depicts everyday life, the world that forms the backdrop of the endless destruction of the war. It shows a city at peace, with law courts and wedding feasts and a rich harvest under a blazing sun, boys and girls carrying wicker baskets of grapes while "a young boy plucked his lyre, so clear it could break the heart with longing."[74] Yet it also depicts a city under siege with clashing armies and violent death. Bringing all his art to bear, just as Homer does, the famous blacksmith fashions an entire world on the surface of the shield.

Ultimately, what we remember best from Homer is a series of such scenes, brilliantly crafted and placed in equipoise: the confrontation of Achilles and Agamemnon before the assembled warriors; the nighttime embassy; flamboyant Paris slinking back into the Trojan lines; the old men gazing at Helen in mingled admiration and resentment; Hector placing his blazing helmet on the grounds as he tosses Astyanax in his arms; the thousand watch fires of the Trojans camping close to the Achaean ships; Menelaus defending the body of Patroclus from a furious onslaught; Achilles loosing an unearthly scream from the ramparts; Achilles and Hector racing around the walls of Troy; the funeral games of Patroclus; and most of all, old Priam kissing the hands of the man who killed his son.

The overwhelming impression of such scenes is of the fragile beauty of human existence, the intensity of life on the verge of its destruction. Precisely because they cannot endure, these moments stand out with a vividness and pathos rivaled by few, equaled by none, in later literature. In book 12, Homer foretells the fate of the sturdy wall built by the Achaeans to protect their ships. After the fall of Troy and the deaths of so many, after the Achaeans have sailed for home, the forces of nature, driven by the gods, obliterate all traces of the scene.

> The Earth-shaker himself, trident locked in his grip,
> led the way, rocking loose, sweeping up in his breakers
> all the bastion's strong supports of logs and stones
> the Achaeans prized in place with grueling labor . . .
> He made all smooth along the rip of the Hellespont
> and piled the endless beaches deep in sand again
> and once he had leveled the Argives' mighty wall
> he turned the rivers flowing back in their beds again
> where their fresh clear tides had run since time began.[75]

Nothing remains of the armed camp by the sea. Troy has been destroyed. The voices of the warriors no longer echo on the plains, nor the lamentations of the women of Troy. Yet humankind endures.

> Like the generations of leaves, the lives of mortal men.
> Now the wind scatters the old leaves across the earth,
> now the living timber bursts with the new buds
> and spring comes round again. And so with men:
> as one generation comes to life, another dies away.[76]

So too does the beauty captured in art. After 2,700 years we still have this poem, and within its pages live the rage of Achilles; gentle Patroclus; Hector, breaker of horses; Helen's terrible beauty; and Priam's grief. In the *Iliad*, they have realized the heroic ideal of imperishable glory, but only because Homer has transformed man into myth and human life into poetry. In the process, all of our lives have been enriched and sanctified.

Chapter 2

HESIOD—
POET OF EVERYDAY LIFE

When Odysseus visited the underworld, the shade of Achilles announced that he would rather be the serf of a peasant farmer than rule over all Hades. Achilles's point was that even the lowest, most miserable existence on Earth was to be preferred to the insubstantial and shadowy realm of the dead.

It is precisely this low and miserable existence on Earth that Hesiod celebrated in the *Works and Days*. The contrast with Homer could not be starker. Both used the highly stylized literary language and the heroic diction—dactylic (long-short-short) hexameter—of epic poetry. Both were heirs of an oral tradition and incorporated many of the elements of that tradition in their poems. Both set forth the myths that were the foundation of later Greek religion and literature. And both composed at the dawn of the new alphabet and either wrote down their poems or dictated them to a scribe, allowing their works to be preserved for later generations in a form fixed by them. They were the first Greek authors, in the modern sense of that term.

But Homer sang of the mythical heroes of Greece's prehistory. He celebrated their wars, their deeds, and their deaths. Hesiod chose other scenes from the shield of Achilles. He sang of the peaceful existence of the small farmer in his own day, closely connected to the earth and the changing seasons. He celebrated hard-won wisdom in a life of unrelenting toil. The closest Homer came to portraying a peasant life was that of Eumaeus, the loyal swineherd of Odysseus, but even he was the son of a king, abducted at birth and sold into slavery. Homer's entire focus was on the aristocracy and their high-born virtues and tragic defects. Hesiod had the peasant's suspicion of the aristocracy and their autocratic ways, and he wanted nothing to do with their foreign wars and maritime adventures.

Hesiod thus replaced the heroic, aristocratic ideal of glory (Homer's *timê*) with injunctions to hard work, sobriety, and thrift. Hesiod's principle virtue was *dikê* (justice), which he viewed as a life in accordance with nature and the will of Zeus.

51

Hesiod had felt the arbitrariness of the aristocrats and the many "kings" left over from the homeric world, and he, like Greece, was ready to move out of its dark ages to a new, more ordered existence governed by law and custom. He was already anticipating the time of the great Greek law givers, Draco and Solon in Athens, Lycurgus in Sparta. Meanwhile, he expressed his ultimate faith in the regularity of a universe governed by the gods, a universe he described in detail in his other epic, the *Theogony*, and his highest ideal was a life lived in harmony with that order.

The *Works and Days* is often treated as a historical and sociological document. But it is far more than that. Just as Homer created poetry out of the aristocratic warrior's life of the twelfth century, Hesiod created poetry out of the small farmer's life of the eighth century. He invested that life with dignity, even heroism of a sort, without falsifying or romanticizing it. At the same time, he wrestled with ultimate issues of man's place in the cosmos and the value of just actions in a seemingly unjust world. Hesiod was a poet first, like Homer, but he was also a cosmologist, a protophilosopher, a proponent of individual rights and the rule of law, a nature writer, a compulsive giver of advice and collector of proverbs, and, most of all, a believer that wisdom is to be found in a simple, well-ordered life of hard work and just dealing. His poems are as much a part of Greece's (and, hence, our own) spiritual heritage as were those of Homer.

A PORTRAIT OF THE ARTIST

Homer, after invoking the Muse, disappears from his poems. The choice of scenes and the way he presents them of course tell us a great deal about the sensibility of the poet, but the poet himself is not a character in his own work. Hesiod, by contrast, is very much a presence in the *Works and Days*. He tells us about himself and his past life. That "self" is not yet the fully expressive self of the Greek lyric poets in the seventh and sixth centuries. But Hesiod's personality nonetheless intrudes directly upon the narrative in a way that Homer's never did. Indeed, there is no narrative in the *Works and Days* as there is in Homer's work—no story with a beginning, a middle, and an end. Hesiod's persona is the narrative device that gives a fragile unity to the many disparate elements of his own, much shorter poem. He offers us concrete details about his life as a prelude to, and a foundation for, the universal truths he seeks to draw from it.

Whether the autobiographical portions of the *Works and Days* are an accurate portrayal of Hesiod the poet is largely a fruitless question. Indeed, whether Hesiod even existed is still debated among scholars. According to Gregory Nagy, the name Hesiodos is derived from a generic description meaning "he who emits the voice" and hence could refer to an evolving line of oral poets, none of whom bears final responsibility for the poem as we know it.[1] I choose a middle ground here, believing in the poet Hesiod as I believe in the poet Homer, but recognizing that poetic autobiography is rarely to be trusted. The German poet Johann Wolfgang von Goethe would later subtitle his own autobiography *Dichtung und Wahrheit* (*Poetry and Truth*). The poetry comes first, and the truth arises from the poetry, not from strict fidelity to the facts. Our primary focus must be on Hesiod the narrator, the personality that anchors and informs the poem, while recognizing that the truth of poetry is not necessarily that of history.

Hesiod lived at the end of the eighth century. His works reflect a knowledge of, and reaction to, the homeric poems, leading most scholars to believe that he wrote (or orally composed) perhaps twenty-five years after Homer, around 700. Greece was then emerging from its dark ages, and the Greeks were actively establishing colonies throughout the Mediterranean world. Trade was flourishing and knowledge of other cultures was expanding. Greece was beginning its transition from a feudal society to the city-states of the classical era.

Hesiod's father was a seafaring merchant from Cyme, in northwestern Asia Minor. Despite growing trade, Hesiod's father failed at that profession and was forced by poverty to migrate. He moved with his family to the tiny village of Ascra in Boeotia, on mainland Greece, where he farmed a miserable plot of hilly land near Mount Helikon. Hesiod, who was nothing if not grumpy, had a lifetime hatred of the sea, and yet was hardly fonder of "the worthless village of Ascra, a place bad in winter, worse in summer, never good."[2]

The young Hesiod tended sheep, which he grazed on the slopes of Mount Helikon. There, he says, he encountered the Muses and was drawn to poetry. "It was they who taught Hesiod beautiful song as he tended his sheep at the foothills of god-haunted Helikon."[3] He even entered and won a poetry contest held during funeral games in nearby Euboea.

> I crossed over to Chalkis for the prizes
> in honor of wise Amphidamas, the many prizes proclaimed in advance
> by his magnanimous sons. And I claim that there
> I was the victor in a song contest and won an eared tripod,
> which I dedicated to the Helikonian Muses,
> where they first taught me mastery of flowing song.[4]

But poetry was not sufficient to earn Hesiod a livelihood. He continued to work the farm with his father and his brother, Perses. Despite the father's inauspicious start and poor choice of farmland, he was successful enough that his sons fought over the inheritance. Hesiod tells us that Perses brought a lawsuit and bribed the "gift-devouring kings" to obtain more than his fair share.[5] Yet Perses himself failed as a farmer through idleness and dissipated his inheritance. Hesiod, through constant work and careful attention, steadily improved his own holdings and even developed enough wealth to attract pleas for help from his wastrel brother. In lieu of material aid, Hesiod offers the advice that is the ostensible occasion for the *Works and Days*.

INVOCATION OF THE MUSES

Homer invokes the Muse (generally in the singular but occasionally in the plural) at the beginning of both of his poems, and in a few other places where a particular feat of memory is required. The invocations, however, are largely perfunctory. He asks the Muse (probably Mnemosyne, goddess of memory and mother of Hesiod's nine Muses) to sing of the rage of Peleus's son, Achilles, or of Odysseus, the man skilled in all ways of contending, and then moves on with the story. There is no reason to think that Homer views the Muse as anything more than a convenient metaphor for poetic (and mnemonic) inspiration; his invocation is a nod to piety and tradition at the commencement of an important task.

Hesiod's invocation of the Muses is altogether different. He begins his earliest extant poem, the *Theogony*, with an extended (115-line) hymn to the nine daughters of Zeus and Mnemosyne.

> I begin my song with the Helikonian Muses whose domain
> is Helikon, the great god-haunted mountain;
> their soft feet move in the dance that rings
> the violet-dark spring and the altar of mighty Zeus.[6]

The nine Muses are his personal source of knowledge and inspiration. He names each of them and places them on the slopes of his own Mount Helikon, where they dance and sing and glide through the night, veiled in mist.

Ah, my heart, begin with the Muses who hymn father Zeus
and in the realm of Olympos gladden his great heart;
with sweet voices they speak of things that are
and things that were and will be, and with effortless smoothness
the song flows from their mouths.[7]

Hesiod, the god-haunted shepherd, experiences the Muses as a genuine presence. They speak to him directly, award him a staff from a laurel tree (to hold in his hand as he recites his poems), breathe into him divine song that he might "spread the fame of past and future,"[8] and command him to "hymn the race of the deathless gods."[9] Hesiod's encounter with the Muses is clearly for him a religious, not just a metaphorical, experience, and, when he wins his eared tripod at Chalkis, he dedicates it at an altar to the Helikonian Muses, "where they first taught me mastery of flowing song."

The Muses tell the young Hesiod,
"We know how to tell many lies that pass for truth,
and when we wish, we know to tell the truth itself."[10]

Some scholars have seen these lines as a deliberate dig at Homer. Homer in his heroic tales of a bygone age tells lies that pass for truth, but Hesiod will offer us "the truth itself."

A better, more subtle reading is that the warning applies to his own *Theogony* in which Hesiod will speak of the origins of the cosmos and the race of the deathless gods, matters about which Hesiod the shepherd can only learn through the intermediary of the Muses. He has heard the Muses sing of these things, but they are beyond man's ken. He cannot vouch for their truth, only for their source and for the sincerity of his divine inspiration. By contrast, in the *Works and Days*, where he speaks of man's own place in the cosmos, Hesiod claims, "I will speak to Perses the naked truth."[11] In that work, his brief invocation of the Muses ("Come! Let us hear from you."[12]) is more in the Homeric style. The Muses still provide his inspiration, but the content is out of his own life experience, and he speaks of the way things are today.

An even more subtle but (I think) still justified reading is that the two-line warning from the Muses reflects the transformative power of poetry to invest experience with meaning. The very act of writing is a re-creation of sorts that must first "pass for truth" and may eventually become "the truth itself."[13] An author through the power of words provides an order and structure for his own cosmos and that of his listeners, just as Zeus in Hesiod's poems provides an order and structure in which human life unfolds. In the *Theogony*, Hesiod takes the disparate elements of an oral tradition, discarding some, transforming others, and forges a unified vision of the origins of the cosmos and the evolution of the divine order that now governs it. The shape and voice that he gives to that tradition are uniquely his own. It is an act of creation that transcends and displaces prior tellings.

The historian Herodotus, writing three centuries after Homer and Hesiod, explains that those poets effectively created the Greek religion.

> But the origin of each of the gods, or whether they always existed, and what they look like: all of this was unknown until just recently—only yesterday, so to speak. . . . Hesiod and Homer . . . were the poets who composed for the Hellenes the theogony, assigned to the gods their epithets, defined their particular honors and skills, and described what they look like.[14]

Hesiod, in his warning in the *Theogony*, recognizes that this is precisely what he is doing. Indeed, toward the end of his hymn to the Muses, Hesiod expressly equates Homer's mission and his own.

> Blessed is the man
> whom the Muses love; sweet song flows from his mouth.
> A man may have some fresh grief over which to mourn,
> and sorrow may have left him no more tears, but if a singer,
> a servant of the Muses, sings the glories of ancient men
> and hymns the blessed gods who dwell on Olympos,
> the heavy-hearted man soon shakes off his dark mood, and oblivion
> soothes his grief, for this gift of the gods diverts his mind.[15]

Homer sings the glories of ancient men. Hesiod sings of the blessed gods who dwell on Olympos. Each, through the power and beauty of his words, makes human life more bearable and closer to the divine. Each is involved in an act of creation that is the greatest and most genuine offering they can make to man and god alike. And each requires the Muses to forge the essential connections between past and present, between the divine and the merely human.

Even in the *Works and Days*, in which Hesiod speaks "the naked truth," the transformative power of poetry invests "the way things are today" with new meaning and significance. In celebrating the virtues of hard work, the rhythms of the seasons, and the struggle for justice, in the broader context of a cosmos ruled by Zeus, Hesiod creates a mythology of everyday life that transforms our experience and gives us comfort in the face of relentless toil. This is indeed a "gift of the gods."[16]

FROM COSMOLOGY TO MYTHOLOGY

At the end of the hymn to the Muses, Hesiod lays out his plan for the *Theogony* in short compass.

> Speak first of how the gods and the earth came into being
> and of how the rivers, the boundless sea with its raging swell,
> the glittering stars, and the wide sky above were created.
> Tell of the gods born of them, the givers of blessings,
> how they divided wealth, and each was given his realm,
> and how they first gained possession of many-folded Olympos.[17]

The most striking thing about this passage is that Hesiod will not tell us how the gods created the Earth, but how both came into being. Indeed, in Hesiod's cosmos, most of the gods come from the Earth rather than vice versa.

In the beginning there was only Chaos (the void), and out of Chaos came broad-breasted Gaia (the Earth), which contained within itself both the peaks of Olympos, seat of all the gods, and the depths of Tartaros (in the underworld), as well as the home of men. The fundamental force that came out of Chaos with Gaia was Eros (desire), which drives procreation and the evolution of the cosmos. Chaos gave birth to darkness and night, which in turn (in a parallel of the biblical light out of darkness) gave birth to Ether and Day. Gaia, in turn, gave birth to Ouranos (sky), and Ouranos ensures the fecundity of Gaia (through the rain that falls to earth).

On one level, the beginning of the *Theogony* reads like an ancient version of Steven Weinberg's *The First Three Minutes*, a description of the big bang and the gradual formation of the planets and stars and, hence, not only the beginning of time but also the separation of earth (Gaia) and sky (Ouranos) and the eventual development of life on earth, all through a massive initial release of energy (Eros). But Hesiod's own attempt to grapple with the mystery of the origins of the universe, like those of many since, involves religion. For Hesiod, Chaos and Eros, earth and sky, night and day, rivers, seas, and stars are not just physical realities;

they are divine presences. The mythological stories of the *Theogony* must therefore be understood on at least two levels: cosmological and pantheistic. The natural world and the divine world for Hesiod are but two sides of the same coin. Out of the *Theogony* came both the mythological tradition that dominated Greek and Roman religion for centuries, and the first stirrings of philosophy and science and their attempt to understand the origins of the world.

Our focus here will be on mythology but with a recognition that Hesiod is taking a number of ancient stories, in particular the succession myths of Egyptian and Mesopotamian cultures, and reworking them to show not only how the Hellenistic pantheon of gods came to displace the older, Eastern gods, but also to show how order and regularity were introduced into the cosmos and form the more or less stable backdrop against which human life now unfolds.

Hesiod tells us that Ouranos and Gaia gave birth to the Titans, six sons and six daughters, as well as the Kyklopes and three monsters with one hundred invincible arms and fifty heads. Ouranos was jealous of these offspring and fearful of his own overthrow and hence pushed each of them back into Gaia's womb and refused to let them return to the light. Gaia, however, made a huge sickle and conspired with her youngest son, Kronos (time). When next "Ouranos came dragging with him the night, longing for Gaia's love, / and he embraced her and lay stretched out upon her,"[18] Kronos hacked off his father's genitals and tossed them into the sea. Out of the drops of blood that landed on the earth sprang the Furies, goddesses of vengeance. Yet out of the foam of the sea, where Kronos cast the genitals, Aphrodite, the goddess of love, was born.

Kronos impregnated his sister Rheia, but fearing his own offspring "swallowed each child / as it moved from the holy womb toward the knees."[19] Rheia conspired with her mother, Gaia, to overthrow once again the repressive, domineering male, this time by substituting a stone wrapped in swaddling clothes for the infant Zeus, who was then hidden away in a cave on the island of Crete. When Zeus came of age, he displaced Kronos (though not so violently as Kronos dispatched Ouranos), and Gaia through cunning convinced Kronos to disgorge his remaining offspring. Zeus placed the stone, which was last swallowed and first disgorged, at Delphi "forever to be a marvel and a portent for mortal men."[20]

It was under the rule of Zeus that an evolving cosmos finally achieved stability, but not without struggle. Zeus and his siblings, the Olympian gods, first had to battle the Titans. Hesiod describes the battle in homeric terms, and indeed the two sides "fought incessantly for ten full years,"[21] the same duration as the Trojan War. At that point, Zeus enlisted the help of the "hundred handers," whom he had freed from their chains deep in the Earth, where they had been cast by Ouranos, and with their help and the power of his thunderbolts, the Olympian gods won out.

> And though the Titans' spirit was bold,
> they were vanquished and then hurled beneath the earth
> of the wide paths and bound with racking chains,
> as deep down below the earth as the sky is high above it;
> so deep down into the gloomy Tartaros they were cast.[22]

After a final battle against Typhoeus—the youngest child of Gaia when she lay in love with Tartaros—Zeus and the Olympian gods achieved supremacy, and Zeus was persuaded by Gaia "to rule over the gods, and he divided titles and power justly."[23]

Zeus himself, however, faced a final challenge, for it was foretold that his own son through his first wife Metis (wisdom/cunning) would overthrow him. Zeus this time enlisted Gaia to help him and at her urging he swallowed Metis (already pregnant with Athena), thereby combining male force and female cunning in himself, "so that of the immortals / none other than Zeus would hold kingly sway."[24] Zeus thus became the "father of gods and men,"[25] and he gave birth to Athena (goddess of wisdom and just war) out of his own head. He then took a succession of wives and mistresses, including Themis (established custom)—who gave birth to the Seasons, to lawfulness and blooming peace, and to all-important Dikê (justice)—and Mnemosyne (memory), who gave birth to the Muses, "nine daughters of harmonious mind, / carefree maidens whose hearts yearn for song,"[26] before finally marrying Hera. Hesiod then tells us briefly of the matings of gods and men and the race of heroes that emerged from these unions before the increasing separation of gods and men that marks his own world.

This, Hesiod tells us, was the dynamic, evolving, and violent process through which the cosmos achieved its current, relatively stable state and the gods of Olympos obtained their titles and spheres of influence. Along with the epics of Homer and the so-called *Homeric Hymns* (paeans to individual gods and goddesses that were almost certainly not by Homer), this was also the mythic backdrop against which the Greeks developed their culture. Tragic poets relied on these myths to add resonance and depth to their plays, and the visual arts (vase paintings, sculpture) consistently portrayed mythical subjects. History, science, and philosophy, too, all grew out of these ancient myths. Historians relied on the names, places, and events preserved (and of course transformed) in myths. The first philosophers speculated about the origins of the cosmos, and the first scientists sought to transform mythology into an explanation of the fundamental forces that have shaped our world. As the classicist Jasper Griffin explains, "From Homer to Attic tragedy, it is in terms of the myths that poets work out their deepest thoughts; both history and philosophy emerge out of mythical thought, and both poetry and visual arts remained always attached to mythical subjects."[27] Even psychology grew out of myth, as the anthropomorphic gods, who embodied particular human traits, were gradually transformed into internal aspects of the human soul.

Yet for Hesiod, the gods were still real presences, permeating all of experience, something we find hard to grasp in our own de-divinized, scientific world. But if we can imagine a prescientific world in which earthquakes and thunderbolts and storms at sea, the passing of the seasons, drought, famine and plenty, the irrational cravings of love and the stirrings of martial glory, not to mention the ultimate origins of the cosmos, have no mechanistic explanation, then it is easier to understand why the god-haunted Hesiod saw the divine hand everywhere. As creation myths go, Hesiod's was the most powerful and fecund in Western civilization until it was eventually overcome by the creation myth of the Hebrew Bible through the spread of Christianity.

THE SEPARATION OF GOD AND MAN

The focus of the *Works and Days* narrows dramatically from that of the *Theogony*. Hesiod is now intent on man: the communities in which he lives, the families he builds, his relations with others, and the ways in which he earns his living. Hesiod is always conscious of the role of the gods in these matters, but his perspective has changed from the divine to the merely human.

Indeed, the opening of the *Works and Days* tells us of man's increasing separation from the gods. We share a common descent, but Zeus deliberately weakened men and keeps them in straightened circumstances.

> The gods keep livelihood hidden from men.
> Otherwise a day's labor could bring a man enough
> to last a whole year with no more work.
> Then you could hang your oar over the smoke of your fireplace
> without a thought for the work of oxen and hardy mules.[28]

Hesiod gives us two stories to explain man's estrangement from the gods and his need to toil for his bread. One is the myth of the five ages of men. In the golden age, men "lived like gods, carefree in their hearts, / shielded from pain and misery."[29] They knew neither hunger nor the weakness of age; nor did they toil for bread, since the earth of its own accord produced rich flocks and a plentiful harvest, and they lived in peace and abundance, dear to the gods. They did not procreate, however, and eventually a sleeplike death subdued them, and they became holy spirits and benign protectors of mortals.

In the second age, the age of silver, men were much worse. They had a prolonged infancy and childhood, but a short adolescence and foolish life. They could not refrain from violence against one another and had no respect for the gods. Zeus buried them "because they denied the blessed Olympians their due honors."[30] Next came the race of bronze, fierce and mighty warriors, with bronze weapons and hearts tough as steel.

> With their hands they worked one another's destruction
> and they reached the dank home of cold Hades
> nameless. Black death claimed them for all their fierceness,
> and they left the bright sunlight behind them.[31]

Each of these three races comes prior to recorded history. But the next race is the race of heroes and demigods, sung by Homer, who "sailed to Troy for the sake of lovely-haired Helen"[32] and fought over the flocks of Oedipus at seven-gated Thebes. Many were killed in these wars, but others were transferred by Zeus to the blessed isles, where they still live in abundance, unburdened by cares.

Finally, Hesiod comes to the fifth and current race of men, the race of iron, and expresses his regret that he is counted among them. For this race must toil without rest and knows disease and pain. Currently, their lot is a blend of good and bad. But, like an Old Testament prophet, Hesiod predicts that Zeus will destroy this race of mortals, too, if injustice and selfishness prevail. He warns of a time in which love between friends and brothers will disappear, children will not respect their parents, the good will be harmed with false oaths, liars and scoundrels will be honored, "and all toiling humanity will be blighted by envy, / grim and strident envy that takes its joy in the ruin of others."[33] Then Shame and Retribution will flee to Olympos, while grief and pain linger among men, and they will be helpless against harm.

Myths of successive ages, showing the degeneration of man from a lost Eden to his present sorry state, are found in many ancient cultures. They reflect our longing for a better world. Perhaps more important, they embody our earliest reflections on why, in a universe governed by the divine, there is evil and suffering and ceaseless toil.

A second story of the separation of men from a divine state is found in the myth of the Titan Prometheus, which was already presented in the *Theogony* and was repeated in the *Works and Days* in shortened form. At a time when "the gods and mortal men were settling their accounts,"[34] Prometheus established a ritual of sacrifice to the gods that involved deception. He taught men to wrap the bones of an ox in glistening fat and offer these to the gods, while retaining the edible meat and entrails. Zeus accepted the sacrifice, knowing that he was being tricked, but in response he withheld the gift of fire from men, fire that was critical to warmth, to cooking, and to technology (especially the forging of weapons). Prometheus again defied Zeus, however, and stole fire for the sake of men, hiding a burning ember in the hollow of a fennel stalk.

This time, Zeus reacted with overwhelming anger. He shackled Prometheus to a remote pillar, where each morning an eagle swooped down upon him and devoured his liver, which regenerated itself each night, only to be devoured again the following day. Prometheus remained in this state until Zeus's son Heracles slew the eagle with his bow and broke the fetters binding the Titan.

For men, Zeus devised a different punishment in the guise of a gift. In possession of fire, men were formidable and potential allies of the Titans in their eventual battle with the Olympian gods. Zeus wanted to sideline men and weaken them so thoroughly that they would never think of doing battle with the gods. He accordingly directed Hephaistos, the divine blacksmith, to mix earth with water and fashion a lovely maiden with the grace of Aphrodite and the skills of Athena. But Zeus also caused to be "placed in her breast / lies, coaxing words, and a thievish nature."[35] She was called Pandora (meaning "all gifts").

> From her comes the fair sex;
> yes, wicked womenfolk are her descendants.
> They live among mortal men as a nagging burden
> and are no good sharers of abject want, but only of wealth.[36]

Pandora brought with her a *pithos*, a huge storage jar of the sort that can still be seen at the palace of Knossos on Crete. (This jar became "Pandora's box" through a mistranslation by Erasmus in the early Renaissance.) When she lifted the lid off the jar, all the evils and diseases of the world sprang forth. Forever after men would know pain and illness and suffering, and Zeus made the diseases mute so that they would steal upon men silently and without warning.

> Only Hope stayed under the rim of the jar
> and did not fly away from her secure stronghold,
> for in compliance with the wishes of cloud-gathering Zeus
> Pandora put the lid on the jar before she could come out.
> The rest wander among men as numberless sorrows,
> since earth and sea teem with miseries.[37]

There is obviously a strong element of misogyny in this myth of Pandora, akin to that of Eve, who tasted the forbidden fruit in the Garden of Eden and tempted Adam to their mutual downfall. But Pandora was not responsible for the evils and diseases that escaped from the jar. That was the will of Zeus and outside the control of man. There is no concept here of original sin. Rather, there is recognition that life has no unmixed blessings, including the fundamental sexual tension between men and women. Pandora's jar can be seen as a metaphor for intercourse, with hope—which can be either good or bad, either a life-sustaining enthusiasm or a dangerous illusion—still under the lid, forever beckoning and forever falling short of complete fulfillment. Zeus has not destined man for complete fulfillment. He has deliberately saddled us with ills and pains and the need to struggle for our daily existence. We occupy an intermediate state, between gods and beasts, and in that intermediate state men and women must forge an uneasy alliance.

JUSTICE AND HUBRIS

The central theme of the *Works and Days* is that we must be content with our intermediate state between gods and beasts, and neither pretend to a godlike existence nor descend to a bestial one. Hesiod marks these boundaries with two of the most critical concepts in Greek thought: *hubris* (overreaching, overweening pride) and *dikê* (justice). Much of Greek literature, especially classical drama in fifth-century Athens, is concerned with these two concepts and hence with characters who ignore the demands of justice or otherwise overstep the bounds of their humanity.

Hesiod illustrates both concepts in his discussion of his lawsuit with his brother, Perses. Hesiod treats this lawsuit not just as a dispute over property between two individuals but as a dispute over how to live one's life and even as a turning point in the evolution of Greece. As the great German classicist Werner Jaeger has written, "Just as Homer magnifies the struggles and agonies of his heroes into a drama played in heaven and on earth together, so Hesiod dramatizes his own little lawsuit into a battle between the powers of heaven and earth with justice at stake, and thereby raises an unimportant fact to the dignity and permanence of epic."[38]

At the time of Hesiod's lawsuit, the Greek city-states had not yet emerged with their more formalized institutions and laws. Petty nobles (Hesiod's "kings") and their autocratic ways were already in decline. Hesiod owned his own land and thus had a measure of independence. But there was no central government or rule of law to protect the common man from the whims and self-interest of the powerful. Hesiod's kings, acting as judges in areas over which they still held sway, had no written laws to guide them in resolving disputes; they had only established customs and an inchoate sense of justice and right dealing. Some of these kings spoke soft words and rendered "straight verdicts"[39] with knowing skill. They were a blessing on their communities. Others took bribes and favored the weaker case over the stronger. Hesiod calls the latter "fools" and says that "they know neither how the half is greater / than the whole, nor how asphodel and mallow nurture."[40]

These are curious proverbs, and much ingenuity has gone into deciphering them. The point of the first is not that half a loaf is better than none but rather that half a loaf is our allotted portion from the gods and that trying to grab a full one, through injustice, is a form of hubris that will incite their anger and jealousy. The point of the second is that asphodel and mallow are bitter plants that grow naturally in the wild; they will nurture but only barely, and no one would eat them willingly. If men want better fare they must cultivate it through their own labor, not by accepting bribes or, through the giving of bribes, taking what belongs to others. Only through justice will men fulfill the will of Zeus and realize their own fulfillment within the limitations set for them by the gods.

> He that wrongs another man wrongs, above all, himself,
> and evil schemes bring more harm on those who plot them.[41]

Several centuries later, Plato will develop the idea that injustice is a self-inflicted harm because it displaces the natural order and harmony of the human soul and hence can never lead to happiness and fulfillment. Without Plato's complex psychology, Hesiod must look for a divine sanction against injustice. Although the current social order appears to tolerate and even reward injustice, Hesiod states his belief that Zeus will ultimately punish the unjust. This very faith is, in fact, critical to the development of justice. Hesiod knows from his own case the futility of individual justice in an unjust world.

> As matters stand, may neither I nor my son
> be just men in this world, because it is a bad thing
> to be just if wrongdoers win the court decisions.
> But I do not believe yet that Zeus's wisdom will allow this.[42]

Hesiod notes that the community as a whole must be just in order to make justice worthwhile for the individual. Such a community will blossom and prosper, whereas the unjust community will descend into chaos. But the community as a whole will not become just until the gift-devouring kings renounce their bribes and give straight verdicts. Yet why would the kings forgo their bribes and submit to such a law in the first place?

Hesiod offers the kings a fable, in which a nightingale is seized by a hawk and raises a pitiful cry. The hawk chides her for complaining:

> "Lady, why all the screaming? You are your better's captive;
> you have to follow me, though you are a great singer,
> I can have you for dinner, or let you go, if I wish,
> for only fools oppose their betters in strength
> to suffer the pain of defeat topped with shame."[43]

The fable must be understood on at least three levels: the natural world, the current sorry state of society, and the more just civilization to come. In the realm of nature, violence and power prevail. Wild beasts and winged birds know no justice and so devour one another. In the current scheme of things, the kings are the hawks and Hesiod the poet is the nightingale. They have the power and he is helpless in their grasp, despite his song of protest. The kings are acting as if we were still in a state of nature, in which might makes right. Zeus, however, is the ultimate hawk, and, at the behest of his daughter Dikê, he will fall upon those whose judgments are crooked. They are fools to oppose his strength, for "the eye of Zeus sees all and perceives all," and the "kings whose slanted words twist [Dikê's] straight path" will themselves suffer "the pain of defeat topped with shame."[44]

Exactly when or how this punishment of the unjust is to occur, Hesiod does not explain. But it is an article of faith for him that it will happen and that we will either grow into a community governed by just laws or Zeus will destroy the fifth race of men and start over yet again. There is of course, in Hesiod, no sense of a Christian afterworld in which the good will be rewarded and the wicked punished. There is no afterworld whatsoever in Hesiod's cosmos, not even the shadowy existence portrayed in Homer. The will of Zeus must accordingly be realized on earth through the formation of a just society.

Our best fate is the life of struggle and toil allotted by Zeus to men. But a just society will at least allow us to lead that life and prosper within our human limitations rather than be subject to the arbitrary dictates of petty nobles and the false oaths of our fellow men. The evolution of established custom (*themis*) into a system of laws that promises impartial justice to citizens and strangers, to the noble and the poor alike, is Zeus's greatest gift to us. This evolution and the divine origins of our system of justice are symbolized in the birth of Dikê from the mating of Zeus and Themis. "Justice, the best thing there is, he gave to men."[45]

Yet Zeus's actions are still inscrutable, as the fable of the hawk and the nightingale reveals. Zeus is not answerable to our ideas of justice, nor need he act on any timetable or in any manner of our devising. Hesiod is grappling with the same problem as the biblical Job, the problem of suffering and injustice in a world ruled by a supposedly beneficent god. Just as Job must in the end simply bow before the greatness of his God, who made the heavens and the Earth, so too must Hesiod defer to "Zeus's wisdom."[46] As Bernard Knox has noted, "There *is* an ultimate justice in the world, he claims, and so labor is not a waste of effort; but the way that justice works, he cannot explain and for its existence he can offer no real proof."[47] Hesiod's faith in justice is a species of the ambiguous *elpis* (hope) trapped under the lid of Pandora's jar.

THE VIRTUE OF HARD WORK

The focus of Hesiod's work continues to narrow. From the origins of the cosmos to the birth and battle of the gods, to the hoped-for evolution of a just community of men living in accordance with the will of Zeus, Hesiod turns now to the hearth and home of the individual farmer.

He chooses farming not just because it is the occupation of Hesiod the narrator but because it is emblematic of the natural condition of man as decreed by

Zeus. Every other profession—indeed, all human life—is ultimately dependent upon the farmer and his ability to coax food from the soil. The soil in Greece was decidedly harsh, and the earth yielded her bounty only to hard, incessant work. Greece was not blessed with the broad, fertile plains of western Europe; there were mountains and narrow valleys and rocks everywhere, just as on Hesiod's own plot of hilly land near Mount Helikon.

But despite the fact that "the gods keep livelihood hidden from men,"[48] the Greek farmer was largely self-supporting, growing grain, raising livestock, planting olive trees and grape vines, and using the stones on his land for building and the clay for making pots. Through constant, back-breaking labor and careful planning, the farmer could achieve a measure of wealth and a degree of independence—even from the oppression and whims of gift-devouring kings—that was unknown in earlier times. And, if he chose carefully, his wife offered him companionship, shared his labors, and bore him children to care for him in old age and to inherit his property.

Hesiod does not romanticize the farmer's life, as later poets do. Indeed, he rather delights in portraying its harshness and fragility. Nor does he romanticize marriage. "Nothing is better for man than a good wife," he tells us, "and no horror matches a bad one . . . / who . . . needs no fire to roast / even a stalwart man and age him before his time."[49] Frankly, Hesiod does not much like his fellow man. Although "a good neighbor is a boon to him who has one," Hesiod cautions that "even with your brother, smile and get a witness, / for blind faith is as dangerous as excessive trust."[50] Stephanie Nelson notes in her wonderful book on Hesiod and Virgil: "As Hesiod sees hardship and suffering as an element inherent in farming, so he sees conflict and injustice as inherent in human relations."[51]

Yet Hesiod admires the farmer and his life of sturdy independence. He offers us a new vision of *areté* (virtue) in the hard work, quiet endurance, and righteousness of the farmer; he offers us, in short, a peasant hero to replace the aristocratic warriors of Homer. "Heroism is shown, and virtues of lasting value are developed," Werner Jaeger explains, "not only in the knight's duel with his enemy, but in the quiet incessant battle of the worker against the elements and the hard earth."[52]

Hesiod notes that there are, on this earth, two kinds of strife. The first is blameworthy and harsh and "fosters evil war and the fray of battle."[53] This is the strife of the homeric heroes, which leads to death and destruction or, in the context of civil life, to lawsuits, sharp dealing, and brawls in the marketplace. This form of strife seeks to get something for nothing by robbing another of the fruits of his labor.

But the second sort of strife is good for mortals and "stirs even the shiftless to work."[54] It is the strife that inspires a man to work when he sees his wealthy neighbor plowing and planting; it is the strife that leads one potter to outdo another, one singer to better another's song, and even one beggar to become a more enterprising beggar than his counterpart.

In short, the bad strife curbs one's zeal for work and seeks shortcuts to riches. The good strife builds wealth slowly through steady effort. Rather than indulging in bitter envy of the more successful or idle dreams of riches without effort, the good strife seeks to outstrip others through honest toil. "Turn your foolish mind / away from the possessions of your fellow men," Hesiod tells his brother, "to labor in the service of what is your own."[55] The house of misery and failure "lies near and the path to it is smooth."[56] But the path to wealth is long and steep. "If your heart is set on becoming wealthy, / do as I say and put more work on top of work."[57]

Hard work brings not just wealth but also virtue and glory among men. In perhaps his most seminal line, Hesiod writes: "The gods have decreed work for men!"[58] Not even the Protestant work ethic of John Calvin will draw a closer link between material success and spiritual grace. For Hesiod, the will of Zeus and the demands of nature are one and the same. The struggles of the small farmer are decreed by Zeus, and his success in those struggles is a measure of his excellence as a man within the scheme established by the gods. A "man must sweat / to attain virtue"[59] and realize his proper place in the cosmos.

THE FARMER'S ALMANAC

The Seasons were Zeus's first children with Themis. They are close relations with their sisters, "Lawfulness and Justice and blooming Peace, / who watch over the works of mortal men."[60] The Seasons are part of the divine order established by Zeus for man. Hesiod accordingly stresses the cycle of the farmer's year and the farmer's life, which requires constant application suitable to the current season and constant anticipation of the seasons to come. The gods are immanent in all things of nature, and to work as a farmer in harmony with the seasons is to honor and serve the gods. We must, as an act both of piety and of self-preservation, nurture and embrace "each of Demeter's gifts in the right season."[61]

In writing of the cyclical demands of the farmer's year, however, Hesiod is not so much offering practical advice on farming. Stephanie Nelson writes: "Hesiod is not teaching us how to farm. He is teaching us what the cycle of the year, with its balance of summer and winter, of good and evil, of profit and risk, of anxiety and relaxation, implies about the will of Zeus."[62] The *Works and Days* is a call to the work appropriate to each season in accordance with the will of Zeus. The farmer must never be caught unprepared, but always be laying the foundation for work ahead, lest hunger and want overtake him.

Hesiod accordingly pays close attention to the natural markers that indicate when each of the farmer's tasks should begin and end. By describing those markers he draws us into the life of the farmer and allows us to see it from the inside. He speaks to us as if we were fellow tillers of the soil. He tells us to start reaping when the Pleiades (a cluster of seven stars, clearly visible to the naked eye) first rises above the horizon (an event that occurs in late spring and marked the beginning of summer for the ancient Greek farmer). It is also the time when "the house-carrier" (snail) begins to climb from the ground onto plants. He tells us to thresh when Orion's brightest star (Betelgeuse) rises above the horizon (in the latter part of June). At the summer solstice, he reminds us: "Build barns! It will not be summer forever."[63] We should gather grapes when the dog star (Sirius) rises in the middle of the sky (mid-September). We must plow when the Pleiades and Orion set and the cranes begin their migration south (in October), and we must cut wood with the autumn rains, when the dog star is visible for only a brief part of each day. Even in winter, we must find tasks appropriate to the season.

> Walk past the smithy and its crowded lounge
> in winter when cold keeps men away from work
> —even then an industrious man can increase his fortune—
> so that in the grip of an evil winter's needy impasse
> you are not forced to rub your swollen feet with a scrawny hand.[64]

And "when the cuckoo's song is first heard among the oak leaves / to the delight of mortals throughout the wide earth"[65] and the swallow "flies up into the light,"[66] we must prune our vines in anticipation of "the coming of spring with its white blossoms and of rain in season."[67]

Hesiod emphasizes the constant hard work and never-failing vigilance of the farmer in a harsh environment. But there is also great beauty in his poetic description of the changing seasons. He is properly considered the first nature writer, and, in Apostolos Athanassakis's excellent translation, he rivals Thoreau, who also sought to describe over the course of a single year a simple life, stripped of all unnecessary luxury, in harmony with the seasons.

Hesiod's description of winter is justly famous. It is a time "cruel for men and cruel for sheep,"[68] when the "chilly wind pierces the shag that coats the breasts even of animals whose skin is covered with deep fur," and "sends an old man scurrying for protection," when "horned and hornless lodgers of the forest / . . . flee throughout the woodlands / and there is only one thought in their hearts: / they long to find shelter in windproof lairs / inside some hollow rock."[69] Even the young and hearty must "finish work and head for home, / wary of a dark cloud that swoops from the sky to envelop you / and soak your body and clothes until you are dripping wet."[70]

He offers an even more beautiful description of the summer months:

> When the thistle blooms and the chirping cicada
> sits on trees and pours down shrill song
> from frenziedly quivering wings in the toilsome summer.[71]

Then, even the stern and dour Hesiod counsels a rare period of relaxation and enjoyment.

> I wish you a shady ledge and your choice wine,
> bread baked in the dusk and mid-August's goat milk
> and meat from a free-roving heifer that has never calved—
> and from firstling kids. Drink sparkling wine,
> sitting in the shade with your appetite sated,
> and face Zephyr's breeze as it blows from mountain peaks.[72]

In Hesiod's cosmos, the life of the small farmer is not without its consolations, and, if industry combines with good sense and piety and a measure of luck, it can lead to wealth and a position of respect among men and favor among the gods. He cautions against overreaching, however. Success is a question of risk management, and there is always the danger of taking on too much risk in search of more reward. The sea is Hesiod's metaphor of choice for such hubris. Trade is a necessary evil for the small farmer, who must bring his wares to ready markets. For fifty days past the summer solstice, when the winds are mild and have a clear direction, he tells us, men can sail with safety. "But rush home as soon as you can; / come back before the new wine and the fall rains, / well ahead of winter and the violent gales of the south wind."[73] Otherwise, a man and his fortune are too

exposed and the greater potential rewards of trade are not worth the corresponding risks, as his own father's bitter experience showed. He tried for riches and
ended in grim poverty.

Hesiod is conservative in the most literal sense of that term. He shuns risk
and seeks to conserve what he has, building upon it slowly and surely, through
tried-and-true means, rather than venturing far into the unknown. It is an easy
transition from his description of the work appropriate to each season to a lengthy
series of proverbs and folk sayings that embody the wit and wisdom of the peasant
farmer. A man's priorities, he tells us, are a house, an ox, and a wife, in that order.
The proper age for a man to marry is around thirty, whereas a suitable bride is
closer to twenty and should be chosen from girls in the neighborhood so that one
has a clear idea of her character and can "check every detail."[74] He tells us that only
scoundrels change their friends, but if one of them wrongs you, "pay him back
doubly in kind."[75] Hire a seasoned hand for planting, rather than an easily dis-
tracted youth who will scatter your seed. And, on a personal level, a man should
be both straightforward and circumspect. "Your face should mirror what is in
your mind," but "a man owns no better treasure than a prudent tongue."[76]

From proverbs, Hesiod descends readily into ancient superstitions of
numerology and astrology, hardly surprising in one who finds the hand of Zeus
everywhere. He tells us what days of each month are propitious for shearing sheep,
sowing grain, offering sacrifices, giving birth to boys, and gelding boars. He even
warns us to watch for the bird signs that favor marriage, and he ends his poem
with a general injunction to follow his advice with care.

> Happy and blessed is the man who knows all this
> and does his work without offending the immortals,
> ever watching birds of omen, ever shunning transgression.[77]

THE CONTEST OF HOMER AND HESIOD

There is an ancient and almost certainly apocryphal tradition of a poetry contest
between Homer and Hesiod. Hesiod himself, as we saw, writes of crossing over to
Chalkis where he was the victor in a song contest and won an eared tripod. Hesiod
makes no mention of Homer in that passage, though an ancient variant of the text
refers to his opponent as "godlike Homer." Regardless, the temptation must have
been great to imagine the two epic poets face-to-face, leaning upon their staffs,

invoking the aid of the Muses, and crossing verses in a classical Greek *agon* (contest or struggle). According to the tradition, Homer was the popular favorite but Hesiod was declared the winner because of his more edifying subject matter (drawn from the farmer's almanac portion of the *Works and Days*).

Even if such a contest never occurred, we can certainly draw our own comparisons between the two poets. Indeed, Hesiod invites us to do precisely that, for he starts his journey to Chalkis from Aulis, "where once / the Achaeans weathered a grim storm and then with a great host / from holy Greece sailed over to Troy."[78] The gathered Achaeans waited at Aulis for a favorable wind, which did not come until Agamemnon sacrificed his own daughter, Iphigenia, thereby setting in motion not just the Trojan War but also a cycle of retribution killings told in Aeschylus's trilogy, the *Oresteia*, which is the subject of our next chapter. The homeric heroes thus began their journey with the brutal murder of an innocent young girl. They ended it with the brutal sack of a great city, killing all the men, casting babies from the battlements, and raping the women before hauling them off into slavery. Homer wisely omits both episodes from the *Iliad*, but the latter is foreshadowed throughout the poem and places the aristocratic, warrior ideals of the Achaeans in grim relief.

Hesiod hated war and foreign adventuring and he feared the sea. He sailed not to Troy, but to Chalkis in Euboea, the distance of a football field. Hesiod pokes mild fun at himself over this episode: "This is all I know about well-riveted ships," he tells us, but even so he will opine on sailing and the dangers of the sea because "the Muses taught me to sing and never weary."[79] Hesiod is at home in "holy Greece,"[80] and he writes of a life there that is in harmony with nature, with the gods, and, so far as possible, with his fellow men. Homer is the greater poet, to be sure, and certainly a grander poet in his subject matter. But Hesiod too should find a place in our hearts for his quiet wisdom and his powerful vision of man's place in the cosmos.

Chapter 3

AESCHYLUS AND THE INSTITUTION OF JUSTICE

A t his death in 456, Aeschylus was already acknowledged as the greatest of the tragic poets. He brought tragedy to a perfection that would not be equaled for two thousand years, if then, when William Shakespeare reinvented the genre and reshaped human consciousness with *Hamlet*, *Macbeth*, and *King Lear*. Yet Aeschylus's epitaph did not mention his plays at all. It focused on his service to Athens's fledgling democracy at the Battle of Marathon in 490, in which a small group of mostly Athenian soldiers defeated a much larger Persian force. Aeschylus was wounded and his brother was killed in that battle. Ten years later, Aeschylus fought again in the naval engagement at Salamis, which was an even more decisive defeat for the Persians and effectively ended their aspirations in Greece, thus ensuring the continued freedom of the Greek city-states.

It seems odd to us that Aeschylus would choose to emphasize his small role at Marathon over his paramount role as a writer of tragedies. But the great Athenian experiment in democracy and its successful defense of that experiment against the overwhelming autocratic might of Persia seemed both divinely inspired and a model for all Greece. John Winthrop's words about the fledgling America of 1630, echoing the Sermon on the Mount, have even more application to fifth-century Athens: "We must consider that we shall be as a city upon a hill. The eyes of all people are upon us."[1] The eyes of all people were indeed upon Athens. Thucydides rightly called Athens "the school of Hellas."[2] It was the political, intellectual, and cultural center of the Western world, and Aeschylus helped make it such, first at Marathon and then even more so in his work, which was a celebration of Greek independence, Athenian institutions, and the new democracy. Even today as one gazes up at the Acropolis (which in Greek means "[highest] edge of the city") and the noble ruins of the Parthenon and the Erechtheum, fifth-century Athens casts its light over our entire culture, serving as both beacon and warning.

Aeschylus modestly disparaged his own offerings as crumbs from the great homeric feast. In fact, tragedy was a worthy successor to epic, equally great in its creative achievement, equally comprehensive in its themes, and more intense in its impact. Aeschylus and his fellow tragedians explored Greece's mythic history in light of contemporary concerns, breathing new life into stories of the heroic age and at the same time providing depth and resonance to modern life. Aeschylus was a deeply religious thinker, but his primary focus was always upon the courage and strength of man to bring about a better and more just world. The British poet and critic Algernon Charles Swinburne called the *Oresteia* "the greatest achievement of the human mind."[3] More temperately, Werner Jaeger called it "the most powerful drama in the entire literature of the world."[4] The plays invite such superlatives. They are compelling, beautifully constructed dramas that are deeply moving on a personal level and, at the same time, celebrate the gradual coalescence of human and divine justice as a bulwark of civilization against violent chaos.

THE BIRTH OF TRAGEDY OUT OF
THE SPIRIT OF DEMOCRACY

The origins of tragedy, like those of epic, are obscure and shrouded in controversy. What is known is that Athens had annual festivals in honor of Dionysus, the elusive, appearance-changing god of wine and intoxication. The most prominent of these festivals, the City Dionysia, was held in late March in the sanctuary of Dionysus below the southern slope of the Acropolis.

This festival included processions, rituals, and sacrifices. Most important, it included dithyrambs (choral odes in honor of Dionysus), with dancing, music, and the use of masks. The exact nature of these early dithyrambs is known to us only in fragments, but they seem to have involved the retelling of myths in song and dance.

At some point, the leader separated himself from the chorus and spoke as a separate character. Tradition assigns this innovation to the poet Thespis (hence our word *thespian* for actor) in 534. It was both a brilliant and, in hindsight, an inevitable development. Athens already had a long tradition of contests in the recitation of Homer and other epic poets. Those narratives have intensely dramatic scenes, and reciters would already have perfected the art of speaking in the voices of the individual characters and presenting some scenes as minidramas.

Thus, having a single voice speak the words of individual characters against the background of a chorus must have seemed natural. But true *drama* (the Greek word meaning "action" or "performance") only became possible when Aeschylus added a second actor and hence made dramatic dialogue and confrontation possible. Again, the groundwork for such scenes was already laid in episodes from epic poetry, such as the confrontation of Achilles and Agamemnon at the beginning of the *Iliad* and of Achilles and Priam at its end. Sophocles, by tradition, added a third actor, making more complex triangles possible, and, as we shall see, Aeschylus made beautiful use of his much younger colleague's innovation.

According to Aristotle, writing two centuries later, dithyrambs evolved into tragedy, whereas phallic songs (performed at the same festivals) led to comedy. That explanation seems as good as any other that has been offered and more compelling than most. The Greek word for tragedy (*tragoidia*) means "goat song," though whether the poets were competing for the prize of a goat or the Dionysian festival involved the sacrifice of a goat or for some other reason is not known.

Friedrich Nietzsche, the nineteenth-century German philosopher, famously suggested in *The Birth of Tragedy: Out of the Spirit of Music* that the subject matter of all the early tragedies was the sufferings of the god Dionysus and that the tragic heroes were "mere masks of this original hero, Dionysus."[5] Dionysus is a god who breaks down boundaries and embodies elemental life forces that, unless properly channeled and expressed, lead to frenzy, a loss of control, and destruction. Nietzsche drew a dichotomy between the Dionysian will (dark, instinctive, subconscious, universal, ecstatic) and Apollonian individuation (enlightened, rational, conscious, measured, focused on appearance). He associated the former with music and intoxication and the latter with epic poetry and sculpture. Early tragedy, he claimed, arose when the two contrary impulses were united, and the Dionysian hero suffered the agonies of individuation and ultimately destruction as Apollonian beauty and repose were torn asunder by the blind universal forces that are essential to life and all creative achievement.

Nietzsche's analysis is brilliant, especially his discussion of the way in which beauty arises from and ultimately succumbs to chaos. (In Goethe's striking image, the spirit or energy of man is a waterfall—powerful, chaotic, pounding—and man's best creations are rainbows produced by the sun sparkling on the mist and spray.) But the agon (contest) of Dionysus and Apollo is too constricting a framework for understanding the birth of tragedy.

A more illuminating dichotomy is that between the myths of Greece's historical past and the realities of Athens's new democracy (from the Greek *demos,* meaning people, and *kratos*, meaning rule). The tragic poets were engaged in reenvisioning their myths in light of contemporary concerns. Ever since the fundamental reforms of Solon in the sixth century, which involved a cancellation of debts and an expansion of civic rights, Athens had been on a more or less steady path toward democracy. Even the tyrants (from the Greek *tyrannos*, meaning a single ruler who has seized power) who succeeded Solon tended to be reasonably benign and reform-minded, and they continued to expand political rights and political power beyond the old aristocracy.

The reign of Peisistratos, tyrant in Athens from 546 to 527, corresponded with the rise of Athens as a major military, economic, and cultural power. It was during this time that most scholars believe tragedies were originally presented at the City Dionysia. Peisistratos's sons, Hippias and Hipparchus, were less fortunate than their father: the latter was assassinated in 514 and the former was driven into exile by the aristocratic families, with the help of Sparta, in 510. But the populist Cleisthenes prevented the aristocrats from reestablishing themselves in power and pushed through further reforms that reorganized the citizen body around local units known as *demes*, thereby breaking the power of the older tribes.

With the reforms of Cleisthenes, Athens became a true democracy, which lasted—with brief lapses—for almost two hundred years. Participation was limited. There were only about forty thousand adult male citizens out of an overall population of more than three hundred thousand. Women, though technically citizens, had a very limited role in society (mostly confined to the home), and there were many slaves. Foreigners were generally welcome but could not become citizens; even the offspring of a citizen and a foreigner were excluded. Within the restricted group of citizens, however, democracy was direct and radical. The male citizens themselves sat in the assembly to debate and decide critical issues of foreign and domestic policy, as well as to elect the group of ten generals in command of the army and navy. Many offices, including those of jurors, were filled by lot rather than election and rotated regularly.

Following the Persian Wars from 490 to 479, the power and influence of Athens grew apace. Its wealth was fueled by contributions from the Delian League (initially a coalition of allies to combat Persia but increasingly an Athenian Empire), by rich silver mines (Athenian "owls" became the standard coinage throughout the eastern Mediterranean), and by key exports such as olives, olive oil, and pottery. This wealth led to the great building projects that gave shape to classical Athens and helped fund the theaters and Dionysian festivals at which tragedy flourished. It also attracted the fear and enmity of other city-states, especially Sparta and its Peloponnesian allies, which sought and ultimately succeeded in checking Athenian power at the end of the fifth century. All the tragedies we possess were produced in the period between the Persian Wars and the end of the Peloponnesian War in 404.

The growth of Athenian democracy laid the foundation for tragedy. Solon, who was a poet as well as a politician, articulated the ideals of a city governed by justice. His poetry became something of a model for later tragic speeches and choral odes. As Athenian democracy progressed, the citizens heard and partici- pated in lengthy debates on issues of policy in the assembly. Citizens would also sit in the law courts as jurors. And they would listen to the discourses of the sophists on issues of philosophy and rhetoric, in which they challenged traditional values and assumptions. Politics was itself theatrical as practiced in Athens; it is hardly surprising, therefore, that the theater was highly political.

The earliest full surviving play we have is Aeschylus's *The Persians*, performed in 472. It dealt with the reaction of the Persians on learning that their vast armies had met with defeat at the hands of the greatly outnumbered Greeks. At one point, Atossa, mother of the Persian king Xerxes, asks the chorus, "Who shep- herds [these Greeks]? What master do their ranks obey?"[6] The answer would have been sure to arouse the Athenian audience to a frenzy of pride: "Master? They are not called servants to any man."[7] At a 1976 performance of *The Persians* at the exquisitely preserved theater of Epidaurus, shortly after the ouster of the Greek military junta, it is said that the audience rose as one at these lines, cheering wildly and insisting that the scene be performed again and again.

Very few tragedies, however, dealt with recent events. The plays overwhelm- ingly retold stories from Greece's heroic past (the late Mycenaean period or the Bronze Age). Even within the realm of myth, moreover, the tragedies tended to focus on the Trojan War and its aftermath, on a few critical dynasties (the House of Atreus, Oedipus and his descendants at Thebes), and on the greatest mythical heroes (such as Heracles, Theseus, and Jason). The Greeks understood themselves and their past in terms of these stories and symbolic figures, and the tragedians rendered the ancient myths contemporary by including in their retelling religious, moral, and political themes being debated by the sophists, in the law courts, and at political assemblies, such as the dangers of tyranny, the conflicting demands of family and state, the nature of justice, man's relationship with the gods, and (always) the consequences of hubris.

At the same time, tragedy makes these myths personal in their concerns and direct in their impact. Despite the limited role of women in Athenian society, in tragedy (even more so than in Homer's epics) women are strong and vigorous and often drive the action. Intense family dynamics are crucial to the plots of most of the surviving tragedies. They offer us repeated examples of great families and characters whose fall from grandeur evokes pity and awe (to use Aristotle's terms). The result is a form of drama that was intensely alive for its contemporary viewers, that both connected them with their past and directly expressed their most pressing concerns and aspirations.

Despite the mythic context, the plays deal with men and women, not with the gods—except insofar as they affect men and women. Aside from the Prometheus cycle (in which Prometheus symbolizes man's relationship with Zeus in any event), there are no tragedies about the wars and marriages of the gods. The gods do function as parallel causes of events (thus universalizing those events), but their roles in the dramas are decidedly secondary—even, paradoxically, where it is outwardly crucial, as in the *Oresteia*—and they never displace human choice and character.

Religion for the Greeks was very different from later forms of piety. The gods were to be respected and appeased. But the gods were not eternal, infinite, unchanging beings. They were forces beyond human understanding and human control, forces that came into being and could evolve over time, but still forces with which humans must come to terms, through just action or propitiation (in the form of worship and sacrifice). Whether these forces were benign or horrific, or randomly one or the other, is one of the great themes of tragedy.

The audience already knew the basic plots of the myths that formed the raw material for tragedy. This shared heritage made possible the tremendous compression and straightforward power of Greek tragedy, which Aristotle canonized in his theory that drama should portray one main plot unfolding in a single physical space over the course of no more than a day. Such classical unities of action, place, and time were only possible because the tragedians did not have to develop a historical background and religious context for the audience. As the Swiss playwright Friedrich Dürrenmatt would later explain, "as soon as theater lost its religious, its mythical, significance, the unities had to be reinterpreted or discarded."[8]

But the myths themselves were not rigidly canonical; they were part of a largely oral tradition with often-substantial variations. The playwrights could choose the best version for their purposes or create a new version of their own (often explicated in the choral odes), and their choice of events and their method of rounding out and filling in the characters of traditional myths gave them ample scope for originality. The mythical context enhanced, dignified, and universalized the dilemmas and challenges of modern Athenian life, sometimes providing an ideal of character and action, sometimes providing a warning and example, but always embodying basic truths about the greatness and fragility of the human condition and human society.

THE STAGING OF TRAGEDY

From 776 on, athletes from throughout Greece gathered in Olympia every four years to compete for prizes. The tradition of such athletic contests dates back even further, to the funeral games depicted in Homer. It is hardly surprising, then, that tragedy too became an agon in Greek hands. There were already festival competitions in reciting Homer, and the presentation of tragedies followed a similar path. To participate in the City Dionysia, aspiring tragedians made application to the *eponymous archon*, a top civil official in Athens elected on a yearly basis and after whom the year in question was named. The archon chose three poets, each of whom would have a day set aside to present three tragedies plus a satyr play (a farce, often obscene, that seemed to serve a cathartic function after a long day of serious drama). The three plays did not have to be connected to one another, either in characters or themes, though Aeschylus often presented a true trilogy in which the action was carried through one play to the next. A fourth day was set aside for comedy in 486, with five different playwrights each offering a single play on the same day. Out of a pool of ten judges from the various demes, five were selected by lot to determine the prizes.

A *choregos* (chorus leader) was chosen to underwrite each set of four plays. He hired and trained the chorus and provided them with costumes and masks. There was no income tax in Athens, but acting as a choregos was considered a patriotic duty for wealthy citizens. It was also a source of great prestige for the winner. The young Pericles served as choregos for the prize-winning entry that included Aeschylus's *The Persians*.

Initially, when there was but a single actor, the poet himself played all the parts, changing masks (with wigs attached) as needed. When Aeschylus added a second actor, he had to pay that actor himself. Sophocles (who apparently had a weak voice) did not act in his own plays and hence had to pay for two actors plus the third that he subsequently added. The actors were highly skilled at projecting to an audience that might number between fourteen thousand and seventeen thousand. After 450, the city took over paying for the actors, all of whom were men and therefore played the women's parts as well.

The chorus was also all male. Most scholars believe the chorus numbered twelve initially, but was later increased to fifteen by Sophocles. They also wore masks. The chorus members were not professional actors but ordinary citizens who trained intensely for the part. They sang or chanted their lines and danced, accompanied by a flute (*aulos*) player. Both the dance steps and the music are unknown to us, but judging from the words, the rhythms were stately and solemn and the dances highly ritualized. The chorus played a key role in the dramas of Aeschylus, reflecting the origins of tragedy in the dithyrambs, but had a diminishing importance in Sophocles and especially Euripides.

The chorus would often have the first and last word in Greek drama. Following a prologue that set the stage, the chorus would enter with an opening song known as the *parados* (named for the corridors at the front of the stage through which the chorus entered). The chorus would then remain, commenting on the action and interacting with the characters, throughout most of the drama. The play would generally end with the *exodus*, the departure of the chorus members, as they chanted their final song.

Mostly, Greek drama was talk (or, at least, without the music and dance, that is what we have left). Any action generally occurred offstage. There were no sword fights or pitched battles as you find in Elizabethan drama. With a few notable exceptions, such as the suicide of Ajax in Aeschylus's play of that name, violence of any sort is rarely shown. Instead, it is described, often in a "messenger speech," in which an otherwise insignificant character arrives to relate actions that have taken place offstage. Perhaps this was due to convention, but more likely the dramatists believed that action has a greater impact when related rather than staged.

Certainly, much was left to the imagination of the audience. The plays were performed out of doors, in daylight hours, and the stage settings were very simple. There was an *orchestra* (or dancing place) where the chorus gathered and the characters delivered their lines. Behind the orchestra was a *skene*, originally just a tent where the actors could change their costumes, but later a wooden building that would often represent a palace or temple. The skene had a central door and a rollout platform (*ekkyklema*) that could reveal to the audience what was taking place within. Dead bodies were sometimes displayed on the ekkyklema along with the murderer who described and even exulted in the deed. Behind the skene was a sort of crane (*mechane*) that could be used to place actors (usually representing gods) above the action. Euripides in particular used the "god in the machine" (*deus ex machina*) to resolve some of his plots.

Theaters generally were located to take advantage of natural hillsides. Audience members initially sat on wooden benches or grassy slopes. Later, stone benches were constructed. The remains of the theater for the City Dionysia (which can still be seen today below the southern slope of the Acropolis) are from a reconstruction in early Roman times. As noted, perhaps fifteen thousand spectators attended the plays performed there. It is still hotly debated whether women and slaves were among them; the "evidence" either way is highly inconclusive. The acoustics in the Greek theaters were and still are a marvel. Sitting in the last row of the vast, beautifully intact theater of Epidaurus (which dates from the fourth century), one can hear a match struck in the center of the orchestra. But the actors still had to be skilled in projection to make themselves understood by the entire audience. The size of the theater precluded any reliance on facial expressions or subtle gestures, and their faces were covered by masks in any event.

The festival at the City Dionysia, held each spring, was perhaps the most significant event on the Athenian calendar and a showcase of Athenian power and importance. The City Dionysia helped both to define and display Athens's civic, democratic identity. It lasted five days, beginning with a procession that included young men whose fathers had been killed in military service to Athens and who were being raised at public expense, as well as a display of monies collected from the Delian League. It also included sacred rituals, sacrifices, dithyrambic (choral) contests, the three days of tragedies, and the day set aside for comedies. Important political and military leaders were prominently in attendance, and spectators gathered from throughout the Greek world. A fund established by Pericles allowed all Athenian citizens to attend the theater free of charge.

The festival at Lenaea (also honoring Dionysus) took place in late January or early February. It was a more local affair, with less pageantry. It was less a display of Athenian greatness than a reaffirmation of Athenian unity. Few foreign guests attended. Tragedies and comedies were produced as part of the Lenaea beginning around 440. Similar festivals occurred throughout Greece and led to the rapid spread of drama and the building of theaters. In the fourth century, groups of players traveled throughout the Greek world, and theaters were built even in the smallest city-states to accommodate them. The possession of a theater was a defining fixture of Greek communities.

The total number of plays composed and performed during this golden age of tragedy is subject to debate but probably totaled more than one thousand. Alas, few have survived. We have tantalizing lists of titles and victors from ancient sources but few complete texts. Aeschylus wrote at least eighty-two plays, of which we have only seven (one of which, *Prometheus Bound*, may actually be by his grandson). Sophocles wrote at least 118, of which we also have seven. Euripides was more fortunate: we have seventeen (possibly sixteen if *Rhesus* is by another hand) of his ninety-two tragedies. We have titles and fragments from at least ten other dramatists, but nothing approaching complete plays. Thus, only thirty-one more or less complete tragedies have survived out of more than one thousand. There is also one satyr play, *Cyclops*, by Euripides. Not a single work from any other tragic playwright has survived intact.

AESCHYLUS'S EXTANT PLAYS

Aeschylus was born around 525 in Eleusis, a deme of Athens with a sanctuary for Demeter and an annual festival in her honor that initiated aspirants from throughout the Greek world into the Eleusinian mysteries. He died in 456 in Sicily.

Aeschylus wrote eighty-two plays for which we have titles, and possibly as many as ninety-two overall. That is approximately one tetralogy (three tragedies plus a satyr play) every other year for forty-two years. Given the lead time required for plays to be chosen and prepared for production, poets rarely competed in consecutive years.

Aeschylus's debut at the City Dionysia was in 498, and his first victory in 484. After that, he won almost every time he competed, except in 468, when the young Sophocles won in his debut performance. Aeschylus had thirteen total victories; twenty-eight if you count later, posthumous revivals, which were presented with increasing frequency in the fourth century.

Aeschylus tended to write connected trilogies, telling the continuous story of a family, such as the House of Atreus or the daughters of Danaus. Such trilogies allowed Aeschylus in the two subsequent plays to explore the consequences of actions taken in the first. It also allowed him to paint on a broader canvas and portray historical developments and changing mores and to offer a deeper perspective on divine purposes.

The earliest extant play we possess, however, was not part of a unified trilogy but rather a stand-alone drama. *The Persians* was performed in 472, less than eight years after the Persian invaders were finally driven from Greece. The play is set at the palace of Xerxes in 480, shortly after the critical sea battle at Salamis, in which a much smaller Greek fleet overwhelmingly defeated the Persians. The following year, the remnants of the Persian army would be destroyed in a land battle at Plataea and a further naval engagement at Mycale. A chorus of councilors to the king awaits news from the army, amid a growing sense of foreboding: "Our hearts / Heave in our breasts, clamouring prophetic fears."[9]

Their fears prove fully justified. Xerxes, the absolute Persian monarch, has been guilty of hubris in his invasion of Greece, symbolized in the bridge of boats he constructed across the Hellespont (a narrow strait separating Europe from Asia Minor) for his army to cross upon. Xerxes believed he could yoke both continents together and "bind the Hellespont with fetters like a slave."[10] But Zeus punishes such arrogance, and using the Athenian-led Greeks as his agents he "swept from sight / The boastful pride of Persia's vast array."[11] A messenger arrives to give us the only eyewitness account we have of the battle of Salamis: "Sirs, I was there; what I have told I saw myself; / I can recount each detail of the great defeat."[12] Aeschylus the poet (who may himself have played the part of the messenger) was indeed there, and he recounts for us each detail that he saw of the great victory. It is priceless reading, especially in conjunction with the longer, but thirdhand, account in Herodotus.

The theme of the play is remarkably straightforward and straight out of Hesiod: "Zeus, throned on high, / Sternly chastises arrogant and boastful men."[13] Xerxes in his pride and godless insolence reaped only ruin and untold pain. The defeat of Persia by the Greeks shall forever bear witness, in Aeschylus's play,

> that man is mortal, and must learn to curb his pride.
> For pride will blossom; soon its ripening kernel is
> Infatuation; and its bitter harvest, tears.[14]

The dangers of hubris and the punishment it engenders is a constant in Greek tragedy. But the simplified vision of this early play, in which an orderly cosmos ruled by Zeus exacts a just punishment, gives way to a much darker, more complex vision in Aeschylus's later plays.

Seven against Thebes, presented in 467, gives us the first hint of a tragic hero (possibly influenced by Sophocles's debut the year before). Xerxes was simply the embodiment of hubris. Eteocles is more interesting, a courageous but flawed leader who feels compelled to play out the curse of his father, Oedipus. We will discuss the play in the chapter on Sophocles, who in his three Theban plays (produced in different years but all dealing with Oedipus and his children), provides such a definitive treatment of the myth that even Aeschylus's play was later altered to fit it.

The Suppliant Maidens was long considered Aeschylus's earliest extant play because of the prominent role of the chorus, the limitation to two actors, and the simplicity of the staging, with no need for a skene building. But in a caution to scholarly conclusions based solely on internal evidence, a later-discovered papyrus fragment revealed that the play was not presented until 460. It is the first of a trilogy telling the story of the fifty daughters of Danaus, fleeing from the prospect of marriage with their fifty Egyptian cousins. In this play, the Danaids are received as suppliants by the people of Argos in the Peloponnese. According to the myth, which we must assume Aeschylus followed in general terms in the two following plays, the cousins arrive and force the marriages regardless. Danaus exacts a pledge from his daughters to kill their husbands on their wedding nights and all but one of them obey. Hypermestra opts instead for love, and the fruit of their union includes the future kings of Argos and, ultimately, Heracles, the greatest of the Greek heroes and the rescuer of Prometheus.

Some scholars question the authorship of *Prometheus Bound*. They argue, based on staging, plot, and a detailed verse analysis, that the play was composed much later, perhaps by Aeschylus's grandson of the same name. We have seen that internal evidence can be a misleading basis for such conclusions; a better explanation may simply be that it was composed quite late in the author's career. Otherwise, we must conclude that Aeschylus's grandson was also a playwright of genius, for *Prometheus Bound* is a play of great power and significance. Its theme is man's heroic struggle for civilization, his acceptance of suffering as the price of creativity, and his refusal to submit to arbitrary force. Werner Jaeger has rightly called Prometheus an "imperishable symbol of humanity."[15]

The play follows the outline of the myth twice told by Hesiod. Prometheus is dragged to a remote mountaintop by Strength and Violence, where he is chained and nailed to a rock. His sin was the theft of fire, which he gave to men as "their grand resource"[16] and "a teacher in every art."[17] He has thus thwarted the will of Zeus, who had planned to annihilate men and create another race. In their misery, men were living in holes and sunless caverns, "their every act was without knowledge,"[18] and they "passed like shapes in dreams, confused and purposeless."[19]

The gift of fire is symbolic of man's gradual struggle out of this darkness into the light of mind and reason. "All human skill and science was Prometheus' gift,"[20] and in a beautiful passage Prometheus recounts the gradual accretion of such knowledge, as man learned to mark off the seasons, to live in "brick-built, sun-warmed houses,"[21] to acquire mathematics and writing, to harness beasts under a yoke, to build ships, to mix healing herbs, to make tools, and to honor the gods.

Prometheus is unrepentant for saving the human race "from being ground to dust."[22] His suffering is the price of man's advancement; indeed, such suffering is the wellspring of inventions that allow men to cope with their harsh environment and live in dignity. The gods have no need of science and creativity. When the chorus tells Prometheus he is wrong to defy Zeus, he responds, "Wrong? I accept the word. I willed, willed to be wrong!"[23] The chorus replies, "You are defiant, Prometheus, and your spirit, / In spite of all your pain, yields not an inch."[24] "I must endure as best I can,"[25] concludes Prometheus. "I'll drink my painful cup / To the dregs."[26]

The character of Zeus in this play is violent, arbitrary, and tyrannical. But that will change. Prometheus will outwait him, for Prometheus knows that Zeus must change or he is destined to be overthrown. As first told in Hesiod and foretold here, only when Zeus combines within himself both strength and wisdom will his lasting rule be assured and an orderly cosmos attained. For that, even Zeus depends on the prophetic knowledge of Prometheus and will ultimately be reconciled to him.

We have nothing but titles and the barest fragments from the two other plays in the trilogy, *Prometheus Unbound* and *Prometheus the Fire-Bringer*. But we know the story of Heracles's rescue of Prometheus, shooting the eagle that feeds daily on his liver and breaking the chains that bind this "imperishable symbol" of human intellect, artistic creativity, philosophical genius, and heroic endurance.

THE HOUSE OF ATREUS

The *Oresteia* is the one surviving trilogy by an ancient playwright, though even here we are missing the accompanying satyr play, *Proteus*. The *Oresteia* won first prize in 458, when Aeschylus was sixty-seven, only two years before his death. It deals with the precipitous decline of the House of Atreus and provides an excellent example of the use of mythological materials to explore contemporary issues. Aeschylus would have assumed knowledge of the background myth by his audience.

The House of Atreus ruled in the territory of Argos in the Peloponnese, which included Mycenae, Tiryns, and other ancient strongholds. (Hence, in Homer, the Greek warriors are sometimes called the Argives.) Tantalus, the first in this line of hereditary kings that move from myth into history, so abused his friendship with the gods that they devised a unique punishment for him in the underworld, where he stands forever in a pool of inviting water with bounteous fruit trees overhead. Yet whenever he stoops to drink the pool recedes, and whenever he reaches for the fruit it eludes his grasp. Hence, our word *tantalized*.

His son Pelops (for whom the Peloponnese is named) was more fortunate, though no more virtuous. He sought the love of Hippodamia, whose father, Oenomaus, had a unique way of vetting suitors. He challenged them to a chariot race, and if they lost—which they inevitably did because of Oenomaus's magnificent horses—he killed them. Pelops, leaving nothing to chance, bribed Oenomaus's charioteer, Myrtilus, to replace the linchpins of the chariot with wax. During the race, the wax melted, and the chariot fell apart, killing Oenomaus. Pelops rewarded Myrtilus by throwing him off a cliff, but the falling charioteer cursed Pelops and his descendants, and the gods heard him.

Pelops's two sons, Atreus and Thyestes, contested for the kingship. Thyestes proposed that the son who could produce the fleece from a golden lamb should rule. Atreus, who had just such a fleece stored in a chest, readily agreed. But his wife, Aerope, was having an affair with Thyestes, and she stole the fleece. When Thyestes produced it and claimed the kingship, however, the omens from the gods were so adverse (the sun set in the east) that Atreus became king and banished Thyestes. Later, after learning of Aerope's adultery, Atreus proposed reconciliation and invited Thyestes to a feast. The stew was made of the flesh of Thyestes's sons. In his search for an instrument of vengeance, Thyestes fathered another son, Aegisthus, by coupling with his own daughter.

Atreus's two sons were Menelaus (king of Sparta) and Agamemnon (king of Mycenae, but identified simply as Argos in the *Oresteia*). They married, respectively, Helen and her half-sister, Clytemnestra. The subsequent abduction of Helen by Paris was an affront to family honor as well as a violation of *xenia*, the guest-host relationship sacred to the Greeks. Agamemnon, the elder brother, accordingly organized the expedition to retrieve Helen and to sack and plunder the rich city of Troy.

The massive Greek fleet gathered at Aulis on the coast of Boeotia. There, however, the goddess Artemis blocked their passage with unfavorable winds and demanded the sacrifice of Iphigenia, the daughter of Agamemnon and Clytemnestra. Agamemnon, faced with a choice between abandoning the expedition to recover a wanton woman who willingly left her husband for a younger lover and murdering his innocent daughter, chose the latter course. While he was away at Troy, Clytemnestra took his cousin Aegisthus for a lover and together they plotted the murder of Agamemnon upon his return.

The trilogy begins with the sack of Troy and the return of Agamemnon. But the history of the House of Atreus and its repeated cycle of adultery and kindred family murder form the true background.

AGAMEMNON

The play opens with a watchman perched on the roof of the palace of Agamemnon. His job through long years, winter and summer alike, has been to look for a signal fire indicating that Troy has fallen. Clytemnestra has established a series of beacons all the way from Troy so that she will have almost instant notice when the city is taken and Agamemnon will soon return. "To such end," the watchman mutters, "a lady's / male strength of heart in its high confidence ordains."[27]

The watchman would be fully at home in Shakespeare; he is a harbinger of Shakespeare's vivid, comic minor characters (grave diggers, valets, constables), sketched in a few lines of dialogue, as he grumbles about leaning upon his elbows dog-wise on this hard bed drenched with dew and the danger of tumbling from it should sleep close his eyes. But he also sounds the first note of foreboding in the play. He would weep with pity, he says, for everything is upside down in this house. He longs for the chance to take his king's hand once again within his own; the rest he will leave to silence.

> The house itself, could it take voice, might speak
> aloud and plain. I speak to those who understand,
> but if they fail, I have forgotten everything.[28]

When he finally sees the "flare burning from the blackness in good augury"[29] and cries the news to Agamemnon's queen, he hails the victory, yet even more he hails what he hopes will be a return to the old ways of order and right behavior in a house governed by a king.

The chorus of elders, which enters as the watchmen exits, is yet unaware of the news from Troy. These men were too old even ten years earlier to join the expedition and were left behind "to prop up / on staves the strength of a baby."[30] They have a darker view of their king, who dragged the youth of Argos off to fight and die "for one woman's promiscuous sake."[31] They regard the sacrifice of Iphigenia as "sacrilegious, utterly infidel"[32] and the sign of a warped will that stops at nothing.

According to the chorus, even Agamemnon recognized that he was wrong to spill his daughter's innocent blood. But he was unwilling to fail in his self-chosen role as leader of the expedition. His vanity and lust for war would not allow it. The way to Troy lay through the blood of his own daughter. It was a price he ought not to have been willing to pay. Yet he hardened his heart and sacrificed his daughter, just as he would sacrifice the innocent inhabitants of Troy in his quest for military glory and vengeance for the outraged honor of his family.

> Her supplications and her cries of father
> were nothing, nor the child's lamentation
> to kings passioned for battle.[33]

Aeschylus's psychological insight is profound in this passage as he recognizes that the very act of choosing changed Agamemnon, numbing his conscience and making him a more brutal leader. At the same time, Aeschylus views this single human action through multiple filters, as directed by the gods, as a free choice, as "necessity's yoke,"[34] and as a horrible crime for which atonement must be paid. Aeschylus appreciates the ambiguity and complexity of human action in a way no author has yet done, not even Homer. The chorus, however, throws up its hands in incomprehension:

> Zeus: whatever he may be, if this name
> pleases him in invocation,
> thus I call upon him.
> I have pondered everything
> yet I cannot find a way,
> only Zeus, to cast this dead weight of ignorance
> finally from out my brain.[35]

Zeus, whatever he may be and by whatever name he wishes to be called, presumably has purposes and reasons that give a deeper meaning and coherence to human events. The sacrifice of Iphigenia—itself insisted upon by a god as a condition of attacking Troy—is outside the ken of the chorus. But Aeschylus sees and develops in the full trilogy a broader pattern of a cosmos evolving, through suffering, toward a more just order.

When Clytemnestra appears and announces that Troy has fallen that very night, the chorus is skeptical and dismisses her womanish fancies. But Clytemnestra is very much in control, and she offers a searing vision of the midnight slaughter and loss of freedom for those who survive. She also expresses the false-pious hope that the victorious Argives will honor the gods and not indulge in needless outrages lest (as she already plans) the despoilers "be despoiled in turn."[36] The chorus echoes this sentiment, without conscious irony, when it says that Paris was punished because he "trampled down the delicacy of things inviolable."[37] The chorus also reminds us of the heartbreaking misery and secret muttering of many Argive households that sent forth fighters and received urns and ashes in return or whose sons "keep / graves deep in the alien soil."[38]

Agamemnon's arrival is preceded by a herald who revels in the very outrages that Clytemnestra said would call forth the wrath of the gods ("Gone are their altars, the sacred places of the gods / are gone."[39]). In a speech of consummate hypocrisy, Clytemnestra tells him to hurry Agamemnon home where he will "find a wife within his house as true / as on the day he left her,"[40] one who has kept herself chaste and faithful to him alone. The chorus ineffectually hints to the herald that something is amiss in the house, but the herald blithely reassures them that all will be right soon with the return of Agamemnon.

Agamemnon finally appears, riding in a war chariot accompanied by Cassandra, daughter of Priam, who was awarded to him as a prize of war. Agamemnon boasts of the sack of Troy and claims that the gods were partners in his enterprise. He expresses no remorse for the city's destruction, though Cassandra's silent presence is a vivid reminder of the outrages perpetrated there. Yet there is a certain dignity in Agamemnon's manner that is not wholly unappealing, and that will contrast sharply with the later behavior of Aegisthus. Even the chorus hails his victorious return.

Clytemnestra greets him with too extravagant protestations of her love, her fears for him at Troy, and how much the state needs his guiding hand, even as she throws in a reminder of the murder of Iphigenia: "Let none bear malice; for the harm that went before / I took, and it was great."[41] She has her servants spread delicate fabrics of crimson for him to walk upon so that his feet will not touch the earth. Agamemnon immediately protests that he is not some oriental potentate; he should be reverenced as a man, not a god. He fears the wrath of the gods if he so forgets himself as to trample down these lovely things.

But of course he is a man who has already at Aulis and again at Troy "trampled down the delicacy of things inviolable,"[42] as the chorus said of Paris. And in a test of wills, he is no match for his wife, who appeals to his vanity and pride and who insists that he walk upon the crimson fabrics, a symbol of the path of blood that Agamemnon has already followed to his own destruction. He compromises by removing his sandals and, as he walks into the house, casually enjoins his wife to be kind to Cassandra, "flower exquisite from all my many treasures."[43]

The chorus is full of dark forebodings as it waits outside the palace with the silent Cassandra. Clytemnestra reappears and invites Cassandra into the house to partake of the sacrifices to mark Agamemnon's return, but Cassandra simply stands mute upon the chariot, lost in her own wild thoughts. With the actor who played Agamemnon gone into the palace and Clytemnestra back on stage, the audience would have thought that Cassandra was a purely silent role. That assumption is dramatically shattered when Clytemnestra returns to the palace. Cassandra, in the first known use of a third actor by Aeschylus, descends from the chariot and utters a howl of protest against Apollo, who gave her the gift of prophecy but then, when she spurned his love, condemned her never to be believed. She foresees the death of Agamemnon and her own imminent murder, but the chorus can make nothing of her prophecies. She calls the House of Atreus a house that God hates, a house dripping with blood of the children fed to their own father and soon to be the scene of more kindred carnage. Yet Cassandra is resigned. Her family and city have been destroyed: "I too will take my fate."[44] As she walks slowly and with tremendous dignity into the palace, she prophesizes the coming vengeance to be taken by Orestes and Electra, and asks only "that they avenge as well / one simple slave who died, a small thing, lightly killed."[45]

Almost immediately, Agamemnon calls out from the house that he has been struck a deadly blow. When he cries out a second time, the chorus recognizes his voice but cannot decide how to react. The previously unified chorus fragments into a confusion of separate voices: some urge that they immediately rush the palace, others counsel caution, still others further investigation of "how it stands with Agamemnon."[46]

Their ineffectual babbling is cut short when the palace doors open and Clytemnestra appears on the ekkyklema with the bodies of Agamemnon and Cassandra. She is defiant and in full glory, the strongest female character in all of drama. Harold Bloom has compared her to Lady Macbeth and to Goneril and Regan. But Clytemnestra did not, as Lady Macbeth did, send a man to do her killing. And she has more cause than the two older daughters of Lear, who are vile rather than magnificent.

She notes that she has out of necessity disguised her feelings in "seeming tenderness."[47] But she is now free of all constraint and will accept no shame. With a repeated emphasis on the word "I," she describes how, like a fisherman casting a net, she entangled Agamemnon in robes while he was in his bath, and then struck him through those robes with her sword. Twice she struck him and twice he screamed out and then fell silent, and she plunged her sword a third time into the now-lifeless corpse. She exults over the blood that spattered upon her, comparing it to a life-giving rain on garden buds.

The chorus reacts with horror at her obscene vaunting, but she readily dismisses them:

> You try me out as if I were a woman and vain;
> but my heart is not fluttered as I speak before you.
> You know it. You can praise or blame me as you wish;
> it is all one to me.[48]

When the chorus says she must be cast out and driven homeless from the land for her crime, she turns fiercely upon them. Where were they when Agamemnon killed Iphigenia? Did they hunt him down? Did they condemn him? No. It was left to her to seek justice for her daughter's blood.

> The flower of this man's love and mine,
> Iphigenia of the tears
> he dealt with even as he has suffered.
> Let his speech in death's house be not loud.
> With the sword he struck,
> with the sword he paid for his own act.[49]

It is clear, however, that the sacrifice of Iphigenia was not the sole cause of her actions. She was born to command, not to be commanded, and she has freed herself from her putative lord and master. She has grown used to power in the ten-year absence of Agamemnon, she has found a new companion for her bed whom she can dominate, and she has avenged as well the humiliation of Agamemnon bringing his captured concubine so blatantly into the palace.

In response to this bold explosion of repressed feelings, the chorus is cowed and declines to judge between the claims of Agamemnon and those of Clytemnestra. But the chorus does ask a critical question: "He who has wrought shall pay; that is law. / Then who shall tear the curse from their blood?"[50] Clytemnestra sees no such dilemma. Just as Agamemnon thought that bloodshed was behind him when he returned home, so, too, Clytemnestra believes she can now "swe[ep] from these halls / the murder, the sin, and the fury."[51]

After Clytemnestra has killed Agamemnon with her own right hand and quelled a potential rebellion by neutralizing any opposition from the chorus, Aegisthus arrives with his bodyguard to crow over Agamemnon's body and claim credit for the deed. "It was I, in my right," he says, "who wrought this murder"[52] in revenge for Atreus's slaughter of his younger brothers. The chorus snaps out of the stupor to which Clytemnestra has reduced them and calls him vile and a woman who did not have the courage to act in his own right. Aegisthus threatens the chorus with all the tools of the tyrant: imprisonment, starvation, torture, and death. But Clytemnestra, not Aegisthus, is in control, and she quickly pacifies him and dismisses the chorus: "forget them, dearest; you and I / have the power; we two shall bring good order to our house / at least."[53]

Clytemnestra believes that the killing is at an end and that they (with Aegisthus nominally the tyrant but in fact ruled by her) will restore order to the House of Atreus. They consider themselves instruments of divine justice in killing Agamemnon, just as he did in sacking Troy. But there is no end yet in sight to the chain of hubris, violence, and *nemesis* (retribution). Left hanging at the end of this most powerful of all plays is the chorus's question: "who shall tear the curse from their blood?"[54]

THE LIBATION BEARERS

Eight years have passed. The city is a grim tyranny. Clytemnestra, like Lady Macbeth, is haunted by bad dreams—not dreams of what she has done, but dreams of retribution to come. She dreams she has given birth to a snake, and when she gives it suck, the snake bites her breast and draws in blood along with milk.

Shaken, she decides to offer libations at the tomb of Agamemnon and sends her daughter Electra and a group of female attendants to perform the rites. Already at the tomb, however, is Electra's brother, Orestes. Clytemnestra had sent him away shortly after Agamemnon left for Troy. She told Agamemnon, upon his return, that she did it out of concern for an uprising during his absence. But a more likely explanation is that she wanted him out of the way to give herself free rein and, perhaps, to save him from being murdered by Aegisthus.

Orestes has finally made his way home, at the behest of the god Apollo, to avenge his father's murder and to take over his proper inheritance. He and his friend Pylades have stopped at the tomb of Agamemnon (outside the city walls) to offer their respects and Orestes leaves a lock of his hair. They withdraw as the procession of women approaches. Electra and her attendants speak freely of their hatred for Aegisthus, and they offer prayers to Agamemnon not on behalf of Clytemnestra but for the return of Orestes and the exaction of a just revenge.

In a recognition scene that is later justly parodied by Euripides, Electra discovers the lock of hair and a footprint left by Orestes and finds that they match her own. And when Orestes steps before her, he shows her some weaving done by her own hand before he left Argos. Together, they plan to kill Aegisthus and Clytemnestra. Electra prays: "grant that I be more temperate / of heart than my mother; that I act with purer hand."[55] Orestes in typical Aeschylean fashion recognizes a more complicated set of motives:

> Here numerous desires converge to drive me on:
> the god's urgency and my father's passion, and
> with these the loss of my estates wears hard on me.[56]

Electra, too, expresses her fury at being dishonored and cast apart like a slave while Aegisthus and Clytemnestra live in luxury, and she later admits that she and her brother are "savage born from the savage mother."[57] Yet it is clear that Orestes and Electra are different from Clytemnestra and Aegisthus. They are not acting out of hubris or illicit passion. There is humility in their manner as they call upon the gods and the spirit of their father to guide their actions. Agamemnon is portrayed very differently in this play. The murder of Iphigenia and his brutal sack of Troy go unmentioned. He is remembered only as a noble king and heroic warrior, treacherously slain by his adulterous wife and her womanish, conniving lover.

As the chorus sings out its hope that "blood stroke for the stroke of blood / shall be paid,"[58] Orestes and Pylades go to the back gate of the palace disguised as strangers from Phocis, an area in central Greece near Mount Parnassus. One can walk today in the fading daylight from the tomb of Agamemnon up to the dark, narrow back gate of the huge and brooding ruins at Mycenae, with its massive stone walls. The setting perfectly captures the mood of the play:

> O hearth soaked in sorrow,
> o wreckage of a fallen house.
> Sunless and where men fear to walk
> the mists huddle upon this house
> where the high lords have perished.[59]

Orestes and Pylades pretend to bring news of the death of Orestes. Clytemnestra in turn pretends to be devastated ("Oh curse upon our house . . . to strip unhappy me of all I ever loved."[60]), yet when she sends Orestes's old nurse, Cilissa, to fetch Aegisthus, her instructions are that he should bring his body-guard. There then occurs a rarity in Greek tragedy. The chorus, whose role is to comment upon rather than influence the action of the play, actively intervenes and convinces the truly devastated nurse (who has seen the smile behind the sad face put on by Clytemnestra) simply to tell Aegisthus to come as quickly as he can.

As the chorus members wait, they express their hope that Orestes will not fail in nerve and that "innocent murder"[61] will somehow wash out the blood of old murder in the house and rekindle the flame of liberty. Aegisthus arrives and rushes into the palace, eager to question the messengers and verify that this threat to his power has been removed. His death cry is quickly heard from inside the palace.

Clytemnestra returns to the stage and to her old magnificence. Immediately realizing what has happened, she calls for a man-killing ax and promises, literally, to go down swinging and take Orestes with her. But Orestes and Pylades appear before she can arm herself, so she takes a different and potentially more effective tack. She bares her breast, the very breast she says that so often gave him nourishment as a baby, and asks his pity. Since we have just heard a lengthy description from Cilissa of how she nursed Orestes, the irony of this plea is not lost on the audience. But Orestes hesitates before the shameful reality of killing his own mother. Here, Aeschylus once again makes dramatic use of the third actor. The hitherto silent Pylades reminds Orestes of the oracle of Apollo and of Orestes's own sworn oaths to avenge his father: "Count all men hateful to you rather than the gods."[62]

Pylades's words—spoken as from the gods themselves—harden Orestes's resolve, and Clytemnestra's various appeals, justifications, and in the end, curses, all fall before the simple truth to which Orestes clings: "You killed, and it was wrong. Now suffer wrong."[63] He leads her into the house to strike her down over the body of Aegisthus so that they can be forever joined in death.

When Orestes displays the two bodies on the ekkyklema, the parallel with *Agamemnon* is deliberate. He has repeated the cycle of violence with an act that is on one level justified and necessary and on another level a horrific crime. Yet Orestes's reaction contrasts sharply with that of Clytemnestra eight years earlier. He does not crow over the bodies: "I have won; but my victory is soiled, and has no pride."[64] As justification for his matricide, he displays the very robe in which Clytemnestra entangled Agamemnon and through which she stabbed him. And he cites the oracle of Apollo in his defense. But he recognizes he must in life wander as an outcast and in death bear the name of what he has done. He is overtaken by the madness of the Furies, ancient avengers of blood guilt, that only he can see:

These are no fancies of affliction. They are clear,
and real, and here; the bloodhounds of my mother's hate.[65]

As Orestes leaves the stage to seek sanctuary at the temple of Apollo at Delphi, the chorus has the last words, echoing again from *Agamemnon*:

Where
is the end? Where shall the fury of fate
be stilled to sleep, be done with?[66]

THE EUMENIDES

In the third play, Aeschylus finally answers the question posed in the first two: "Where shall the fury of fate / be stilled to sleep, be done with?" The cycle of violence and revenge is finally broken, to be replaced by the new institutions of a democratic Athens. The ancient Furies, older than Zeus, forces of darkness and brutal vengeance, are co-opted into a regime of justice blessed by the current race of Olympian gods.

The play opens at Delphi, where the Furies have pursued Orestes into the temple of Apollo. A horrified priestess describes them as "black and utterly repulsive,"[67] with foul breath, tattered rags, and eyes dripping ooze. We in the audience do not expect to see them, since they were invisible to all but Orestes in the prior play. But in a stunning piece of stagecraft, Aeschylus renders them as "clear, and real, and here" as they were to Orestes, and tradition has it that audience members fainted and pregnant women miscarried at the sight of the Furies swarming in their first chorus.

Just how this effect was created, unfortunately, is unknown to us. At the play's opening, the Furies have been literally stilled to sleep by Apollo, who promises to stand by Orestes and tells him to travel to Athens and seek there a judgment from Athena on the rightness of his conduct. The ghost of Clytemnestra appears to rebuke the Furies, rousing them from their slumber and urging them to follow Orestes and hunt him down. In their opening chorus, the Furies reassert their primeval right to avenge the shedding of kindred blood and point out that Zeus and the Olympians have but recently won by unconditional force a throne reeking with blood.

Athena, goddess of wisdom, knows that she cannot simply dismiss these ancient forces, as Apollo would do. But she tells them that their side is "only half the argument"[68] and that a proper trial must "make clear where in this action the truth lies."[69] Confident in their case, the Furies agree. Thus begins the first courtroom drama in literature.

Athena selects the finest twelve citizens as jurors. She also dictates that the Furies will begin, "for it must justly be the pursuer who speaks first / and opens the case, and makes plain what the action is."[70] The key elements of our justice system—a jury of twelve peers and the burden of proof upon the prosecution—are thus laid down. (It is a remarkable fact that our contemporary criminal jury corresponds to the standard size of the chorus in ancient drama.)

The case for the prosecution is simple and direct. On questioning, Orestes readily admits that he killed his mother: "with drawn sword in my hand I cut her throat."[71] The Furies are not interested in reasons or excuses. The shedding of kindred blood must be avenged; otherwise, all the laws will be overthrown and "every man will find a way / to act at his own caprice."[72] The fear of punishment "must keep its watchful place / at the heart's controls."[73] The Furies threaten to "let loose indiscriminate death"[74] and a "life of anarchy"[75] if their claims are denied.

Apollo speaks on behalf of Orestes. His basic plea is that the murder of Clytemnestra was justified by her more heinous murder of her lawful king and husband. To the Furies' protest that the shedding of kindred blood can only be assuaged by more blood, Apollo responds that only the father shares blood with the child; the mother is but a repository and nursery for the seed planted by the father. As proof of his point, Apollo cites the example of Athena, born directly from the head of Zeus. (Greek biology did not yet understand the role of the mother's egg. But Apollo's argument still seems a lawyer's trickery—a pattern, alas, for centuries of lawyers to come.)

The jury is equally divided. Athena casts the deciding vote. She acknowledges the critical role of fear in a just order, for "what man who fears nothing at all is ever righteous?"[76] But she opts to protect the lawful king and the sanctity of marriage by acquitting a man who vindicated both, even at the cost of killing his own mother. Orestes makes a gracious speech expressing his relief and, with promises of lasting loyalty and friendship to Athens, returns to his native land and disappears from mythology and history alike. The curse of the House of Atreus has played itself out.

But Athena must still deal with the outraged Furies, who see the ancient order overthrown and threaten to let loose vindictive poison on the land. Instead of dismissing these primeval forces, Athena seeks to incorporate them into the new order in which justice is determined not by individual revenge but by a fair ballot. She offers the Furies new positions as goddesses of the hearth with honor for the rest of time and devotions from the citizens of Athens: "no household shall be prosperous without your will."[77] After much cajoling, the Furies accept and become Eumenides (kindly ones) who bestow blessings and fertility upon the land and its people. The trilogy ends in a torchlight processional in which the former daughters of night pray that Athens—"civilized as years go by, / sheltered under Athena's wings, / grand even in her father's sight"[78]—shall find peace and meet its destiny.

Athena's vote for acquittal is not a vindication of Orestes's matricide but rather of the social order embodied in the democratic *polis*. It is a vote to break the ancient cycle of violence and retribution, of hubris and nemesis. Murder must still be punished, but not through individual, flawed human agents, such as Agamemnon and Clytemnestra, who are themselves guilty of hubris and destroyed in turn. A neutral court takes upon itself the task of vengeance or acquittal. The rule of law must incorporate the reverence and fear of the old gods in support of new institutions that administer justice impartially.

These civic institutions may themselves be flawed. But Aeschylus possesses a deep faith that divine forces underwrite our lives. "Zeus, whatever he may be,"[79] allows us to draw wisdom and justice out of chaos and violence. A divine order transcends the apparent contingency of human life and even the horror of savage violence. Our lives are not merely random. That does not mean we can fully understand them or that the universe corresponds exactly with our own sense of justice and morality. But it does mean that we can learn wisdom through suffering and move toward a civilization that seeks justice in accordance with the will of the gods.

The gods of Aeschylus, like those of Hesiod, have themselves evolved from their primal state of arbitrary and tyrannical violence. Zeus and the Olympians conquered the older gods by force and violence, but Zeus himself had to learn wisdom in order to remain in power and impose a new order upon the cosmos. The suggestion that the gods have evolved is shocking to a modern religious sensibility (though who could deny that the god of the New Testament is quite different from the more archaic, and frankly more interesting, god of the Old Testament?). But it is a natural concept if you believe, as Aeschylus did, that the universal principles of justice that govern human life developed gradually out of chaos and darkness. The *Oresteia* is his prayer that Athens may flourish within the context of this imperfectly understood divine scheme.

Perhaps it is fitting, then, that Aeschylus's epitaph features his role in the Battle of Marathon. The *Oresteia* embodies the hope and confidence of Athens, fresh from its defeat of the Persians, at the height of its military and financial power, and in the midst of its great and radical democratic experiment. The *Oresteia* is a profession of faith in what Robert Fagles has called man's "rite of passage from savagery to civilization."[80] Through the institutions of a free polis, and under the guidance of a divine will, man has moved out of the darkness of prehistory into the light of an ordered democracy.

Chapter 4

SOPHOCLES— THE THEBAN PLAYS

The most striking difference between Sophocles and Aeschylus is that, while the latter presents connected trilogies, the former writes individual plays meant to stand on their own. The trilogy format allows Aeschylus to connect events over time with a divine plan that gives meaning to the suffering of individuals. Sophocles's focus is much tighter, on a single dominant character and his fate. Gods almost never appear, and, while a divine order is assumed, it is incomprehensible and of limited consolation to the men and women who suffer in his dramas. As Bernard Knox, the greatest critic of Sophocles, explained, "the Sophoclean hero acts in a terrifying vacuum, a present which has no future to comfort and no past to guide, an isolation in time and space which imposes on the hero the full responsibility for his own action and its consequences."[1]

Aeschylus offers us a vision of progress, as man and his institutions evolve in accordance with the will of the gods. Athens in particular is treated as a city of God, a symbol of man's achievements and divine favor. Sophocles, though by all accounts a pious man, makes no attempt to justify the ways of God to man; nor does he suggest that divine favor is ever more than fleeting, not for man and certainly not for Athens, as the disastrous Peloponnesian War would soon make all too clear.

Sophocles paints a darker and yet, paradoxically, more inspiring vision of man than Aeschylus. His universe is terrifying, lonely, and largely incomprehensible, made wonderful only by the courage and intelligence of individuals who refuse to recognize their necessary human limitations. At the moment of supreme crisis in their lives, they feel abandoned by gods and men alike. Yet they angrily reject any suggestion of compromise or moderation. These individuals bear the consequences of their actions and decisions without flinching. They may be flawed in various respects, but their suffering is not a just punishment. They suffer because fate is unaccountable and because humans are not gods, immune from time,

99

change, and death. Their suffering has no meaning, except insofar as it is borne with dignity and heroic courage and hence serves as an example, however transitory, of the greatness of which man is capable.

THE ATHENIAN CENTURY

Sophocles was born just outside Athens in Colonus, the setting of his last play. He came from a noble family and was said to be exceptionally handsome. In 480, at the age of sixteen, he was the lead dancer in a chorus celebrating the Greek victory at Salamis.

Sophocles was active in political as well as artistic affairs. He was conservative and aristocratic in outlook, though he supported and participated in the democracy. Sophocles served as treasurer and was later twice elected as one of the ten generals for the Athenian Empire, though Pericles is said to have remarked: "good poet, poor general."

He was also one of ten emergency magistrates appointed to guide Athens after the expedition to Sicily ended in disaster in 413. And he played an important role in establishing at Athens the cult of Asclepius, the god of medicine and healing, and in founding the first hospital there.

The span of Sophocles's life, from his birth in 496 to his death in 406, covers a time during which, despite the broadening efforts of more recent scholars, Greek history and culture still largely equate to Athenian history and culture. Athens was the center of the universe as Rome would later be, and as Paris, London, and New York would each aspire to be at different times. But Athens surpassed them all in the richness of its creative outpouring.

Sophocles's life completely embraced what we know of classical drama. He was twenty-four when the first extant tragedy, Aeschylus's *The Persians*, was produced. He lived through all seven of Aeschylus's extant plays and the eighteen or nineteen of his younger colleague, Euripides. Sophocles led his chorus in mourning for Euripides in 406, the year of his own death. Ironically, the only extant tragedy that Sophocles did not live to see was *Oedipus at Colonus*, written when he was ninety and produced five years after his death.

What we know of classical comedy was also largely contained in his lifetime. The first extant comedy dates to 425, and all but two of Aristophanes's eleven surviving plays were produced before 406. Herodotus wrote his *Histories* and Thucydides most of his *The Peloponnesian War* in the same period. Many of the sculptures, temples, and friezes, as well as the black-and-red figure vases we possess date to this time. The legendary sculptor Phidias made his huge statues of Zeus and Athena, both unfortunately destroyed, and the shining example of classical architecture, the Parthenon, was completed in 431. To find a comparable period of creativity in the fine arts and literature, one would have to look to the ninety years in western Europe as a whole from the maturity of Leonardo, Michelangelo, and Raphael in the early sixteenth century through the careers of Montaigne, Cervantes, and Shakespeare.

This golden age of Athens also saw the separation of philosophy and science and remarkable advances in both. Hecataeus of Miletus wrote extensively on geography and refined Anaximander's map of the world. The followers of Pythagoras of Samos developed his work in mathematics and astronomy, as well as his mystical belief in the power of numbers and the harmony of the spheres. Empedocles of Sicily postulated that all matter is composed, in varying degrees, of four elemental substances (earth, air, fire, and water). Democritus of Thrace went even further, positing only atoms and the void and insisting upon strict scientific explanations for observable phenomena. Advances in electricity and magnetism and the development of biology, botany, zoology, and anatomy all paved the way for the Aristotelian synthesis to come. Hippocrates of Cos (author of the Hippocratic oath, which still guides many physicians today) was the father of medicine as a science, taking it away from the dark ages of amulets, sorcerers, and divine forces. A vast collection of texts, published under his name, focused on careful observation of patients, their symptoms, and their responses to various treatments.

Most of these scientific developments did not originate in Athens. They were spread throughout the Greek-speaking world. But Athens took particular pride in embracing the new scientific, rational spirit. This spirit is reflected in the teachings of the Sophists, who brought philosophy to Athens, where it became—along with democracy, drama, and history—one of the city's lasting legacies.

The Sophists were itinerant teachers who purported to prepare the youth of Athens for public life in a democracy. Unlike their sixth-century, protoscientist predecessors, they were interested in moral and political issues, not cosmological speculation. They taught skill in argument for substantial fees. Protagoras of Thrace (ca. 490–421), who moved to Athens around 450, was the most famous of the Sophists. He is best remembered for three statements. First, "man is the measure of all things,"[2] by which he seems to have meant that man can know the world only from his own limited perspective and that he creates the "measures" against which he judges all things. Second, "there are two opposing arguments concerning everything," and it is possible, through skill and training, "to make the weaker argument the stronger."[3] In this, he has fashioned a motto, for better or worse, for our modern legal system, as well as that of Athens. Third, "concerning the gods I am unable to know either that they are or that they are not, or what their appearance is like."[4] Here, he is echoing Xenophanes, who a century earlier wrote that if horses could draw, their gods would look like horses, and who suggested that "no man has seen nor will anyone know the truth about the gods."[5]

The spirit of the Sophists was one of rational argument and persuasive rhetoric. But it increasingly harbored a disdain for inherited values and religious beliefs. Their rational humanism was at odds with Greece's mythological and religious past. They saw moral values as mere conventions subject to change or distortion by clever speakers. They considered the gods unknowable and therefore irrelevant to human affairs. Even truth itself was beyond human comprehension or at least beside the point in crafting a persuasive argument.

Athenian conservatives of the late fifth century hated the Sophists for corrupting the youth by encouraging them to question received religion and traditional values. (Sparta banned Sophists for just this reason.) They were concerned that such inquiries would tear apart the mythological and religious tradition that held them together as a people and that the resulting impiety would offend the gods and risk the divine favor that had heretofore nurtured and sheltered Athens. Perhaps they were not far wrong.

The light of divine favor did appear to dim in the latter half of the Athenian century. Jealous of the expanding Athenian Empire, Sparta and its allies launched the equivalent of a civil war in Greece in which the various city-states were compelled to take sides. As chronicled by Thucydides, a series of missteps (both moral and political) and misfortunes (including a deadly plague that killed Pericles) led to Athens's eventual defeat in the Peloponnesian War. In 404, Athens was compelled to surrender. Spartan forces dismantled the "long walls" that provided Athens with a secure connection to the critical port of Piraeus and installed a pro-Spartan, antidemocratic oligarchy (the Thirty Tyrants) to rule the city. Their brutal reign of terror lasted less than a year before democratic forces took to the streets and regained power. The democracy was restored, but Athens was crippled militarily and financially.

Sophocles died two years before Athens's surrender to Sparta, but the outcome of the war was already clear at that point. The Athenian century was at an end, and so too was the golden age of tragic drama.

EXTANT PLAYS

Sophocles defeated Aeschylus with his very first tetralogy, produced in 468 when he was just twenty-two. He went on to write more than 120 plays, approximately thirty productions over a sixty-year creative life. He won at least twenty victories.

As with Aeschylus, we possess only seven of his plays, and none at all from his first twenty-plus years in theater. Most of his plays we can date only within a five-year period, if that. He introduced a number of innovations, including the third actor (which Aeschylus himself promptly adopted) and some sort of scene painting and more elaborate sets. He also increased the chorus from twelve to fifteen. And, as noted, he wrote stand-alone plays rather than trilogies, though we assume that the three tragedies he would produce on a single day had overlapping and interweaving themes.

His three Theban plays (dealing with the life and descendants of Oedipus), which will be the focus of our discussion, were each written separately. *Antigone*, last in the mythological chronology, was the first produced, circa 440. *Oedipus the King*, produced circa 425, begins the story; and his final play, *Oedipus at Colonus*, fits in the middle. Yet the three together form a remarkably coherent and powerful unit, despite some plot patches that Sophocles needed in *Oedipus at Colonus* to fit them together. Since our main interest is in the development of Sophocles as a playwright and thinker, we will deal with them in the order of their composition (after a brief discussion of the four other extant plays, which sound many of the same themes).

The earliest play we possess, *Ajax*, dates to the mid-440s, when Sophocles was already fifty. It derives directly from an incident noted in Homer. After the death of Achilles, the Greek army voted to give his arms to Odysseus. Ajax, the mightiest of the Greek warriors after Achilles, was so humiliated by this slight to his honor that he killed himself. In Sophocles's retelling, Ajax resolves to murder the chiefs of the Greek army, including Odysseus and the two sons of Atreus, Agamemnon and Menelaus. But he is driven mad by Athena and attacks a herd of livestock instead, thinking he is wreaking slaughter upon the Greeks. When he finally comes to his senses, he finds no recourse for his shame but suicide.

> Here I am, the bold, the valiant,
> Unflinching in the shock of war,
> A terrible threat to unsuspecting beasts.
> Oh! what a mockery I have come to! What indignity![6]

Ajax is deaf to the pleas of the followers who depend upon him and even to those of Tecmessa, the mother of his son, whom he won as a prize after razing her city. "What fatherland," she asks him, "shall I ever have but you?"[7] She has lost much but retains her life and her son and her capacity for love. He brusquely rebuffs her, and yet she plants in his mind a seed—of kindness given and dependents who warrant protection—that bears at least some ambiguous fruit. When he reenters the stage, sword in hand, his mood is softened by pity for his wife and child. It even appears, at first, that he has changed his mind and will not kill himself but rather will submit to the sons of Atreus. In a magnificent meditation on the inevitability of change, he notes,

> Winter's hard-packed snow
> Cedes to the fruitful summer; stubborn night
> At last removes, for day's white steeds to shine.
> The dread blast of the gale slackens and gives
> Peace to the sounding sea; and Sleep, strong jailer,
> In time yields up his captive. Shall not I
> Learn place and wisdom?[8]

But the very thought of such softening brings bitterness and resolve. Ajax's code recognizes neither time nor change. It certainly does not recognize compromise and submission. "Enough," he says, "Now I am going where my way must go."[9]

Kent will unconsciously echo these words with the same intent two millennia later in *King Lear* when he departs the scene of carnage saying, "I have a journey, Sir, shortly to go. / My master calls me, I must not say no."[10] Ajax's master is no mortal man. It is an ideal of heroic honor and constancy from a bygone age. Ajax cannot give way to Tecmessa even when he wants to do so. He is too much committed. He thinks he has learned wisdom but cannot profit from it, for he has not learned that common humanity can trump personal pride and an ancient code of honor.

Odysseus has learned that lesson. He feels pity for Ajax from the outset and, though Ajax has become his enemy, will treat him as his friend.

> I think of him, yet also of myself;
> For I see the true state of all us that live—
> We are dim shapes, no more, and weightless shadow.[11]

After Ajax kills himself, Agamemnon and Menelaus would forbid his burial, leaving his body exposed to the beasts and birds as a lesson to others. But Odysseus dissuades them from seeking "unworthy triumphs"[12] in violation of the gods' law, and urges them to honor Ajax for his past greatness and bravery.

Ajax is the last hero of a vanished archaic age, living according to an inflexible code that values personal honor above all: "Let a man nobly live or nobly die."[13] He has even shunned the help of the gods for fear it would detract from the greatness of his own achievements. Ajax considered himself like a god, unchangeable, unconquerable, and immune to the weaknesses of common men. He "kept no human measure."[14]

Odysseus, by contrast, takes the full measure of human limitations. He is a modern man, attuned to the vagaries of fate and the changes of time and fortune. He knows that permanence is an illusion for man. Odysseus is clever, persuasive, and adaptable, full of the practical wisdom that Ajax lacks. As such, he is the perfect citizen of a modern *polis*, something Ajax, with his fierce independence, could never be. Yet Odysseus honors Ajax, for with his passing and that of the heroic age he embodied, the world is a smaller, meaner place.

❧

Sophocles's *Electra* was produced circa 415, some forty to forty-five years after the *Oresteia*. This is the only subject (the murder of Clytemnestra and Aegisthus by the children of Agamemnon) on which we have extant plays by all three tragic poets.

In Aeschylus, Electra was an incidental character in a larger tableau of moral and political evolution. She was the chief libation bearer, but she was eclipsed by her forceful mother and even by her conflicted, but otherwise colorless, brother. She was not even present when Clytemnestra and Aegisthus were killed. Sophocles, however, has made her the focus of his play. In his hands she becomes a tragic heroine in her own right, though one so consumed by hate that we can neither love nor admire her. Ajax, rigidly bound by his archaic code of honor, still softens sufficiently for us to understand the love and affection he inspires in his wife and his followers. But Electra never softens. As Virginia Woolf has noted, Sophocles's Electra "stands before us like a figure so tightly bound that she can only move an inch this way, an inch that."[15] She is married to her grievance. "My bed is witness to my all-night sorrowing / dirges for my unhappy father,"[16] she tells the chorus of Mycenaean women. She has no husband. She is beyond childbearing years. Her hatred and desire for revenge are so all-consuming that her life can have no other meaning. "Never shall I give over my sorrow,"[17] she says with pride.

There are several plot differences from *The Libation Bearers* that help maintain the focus on Electra. The myths were an oral tradition, in which versions varied and many details were left unspecified. As a result, the poets could, within common constraints, shape them to their own purposes. In Sophocles's version, Aegisthus, not Clytemnestra, has killed Agamemnon. This serves two purposes. There is less focus on the character of Clytemnestra and the anticipated matricide. And there is more of an explanation for Electra's lack of action until Orestes arrives. The Electra of Sophocles's play seems a fair match for the Clytemnestra of Aeschylus, but with Aegisthus as a stronger character than he appears in *The Libation Bearers*, she can only wait and hate.

Another plot difference in *Electra* is that Orestes was still living at home at the time of his father's murder, and it was Electra herself who snatched him up and sent him away with an old, trusted servant to keep him from being murdered. Orestes, moreover, is diffident, even dawdling. As Electra complains, "he is always longing to come, but he does not choose to come, for all his longing."[18] Finally, Sophocles's Electra has another sister, Chrysothemis, living at home who in her passivity and willingness to yield to authority provides a useful contrast to and foil for Electra.

Despite her feeling of complete isolation, Electra defines herself by her relations to others. Electra simply *is* her grief for her father, her hatred of her mother and Aegisthus, her longing for Orestes, and her fierce impatience with her sister. She has forfeited her very being at its core. There is a telling moment in which Orestes arrives, disguised as a stranger from Phocis, pretending to bear the ashes of Orestes in an urn. Electra takes the empty urn, a potent symbol of her existence, in her arms and delivers to it a lengthy speech of mourning.

Once the recognition scene occurs and brother and sister are united, their speeches of joy and anticipations of revenge are so protracted that Paedagogus, the servant who carried Orestes away and has been his companion ever since, must chide them into action.

> Have done once and for all
> with your long speeches, your insatiate
> cries of delight! And in with you at once.
> As we are now, delay is ruinous.
> It is high time to have done with our task.[19]

Even then they delay for another forty-five lines, during which the tension mounts. This delay is characteristic of Orestes. But one also senses that the culmination of Electra's revenge fantasies will leave her completely at a loss, with no more purpose in her life. She draws out the moment for fear of the abyss beyond.

Orestes finally enters the palace. When Clytemnestra cries out that she is struck, Electra shouts in chilling words, "If you have strength—again!"[20] And when Aegisthus arrives a short while later, she lures him inside with the promise of seeing Orestes's body. But the shrouded corpse is that of Clytemnestra, and once Aegisthus uncovers it, Orestes leads him offstage to his own death. Electra's accompanying words, her last in the play, are equally fierce:

> Kill him as quickly as you can. And killing
> throw him out to find such burial as suit him
> out of our sights. This is the only thing
> that can bring me redemption from
> all my past sufferings.[21]

Electra has her revenge but enjoys no redemption. There is no hint in this play, as there was in Aeschylus, of a future in which the cycle of violence is resolved. There is no happy ending for Electra, as there was none for Ajax. She lives on, but, without the passionate hatred that has kept her going, she will be like the empty urn of Orestes.

Sophocles's judgment of Electra is clear when she urges that Aegisthus's body be cast out unburied, an affront to the gods and to humanity. In *Ajax* and *Antigone*, the exposure of a corpse is treated as a grievous wrong. "Past the bounds of sense you dwell in grief,"[22] the chorus tells her, "breeding wars in your sullen soul."[23] In another image from *Antigone*, Electra's sister tells her, "You shall live out your life in an underground cave."[24] That is indeed the case. For Electra has cut herself off from her own humanity. "I wait and wait and die,"[25] she says at one point. She is now done with waiting. There is nothing left to her but death.

The Women of Trachis, produced circa 413, is Sophocles's most puzzling and uncharacteristic play. It deals with the death of Heracles, the greatest of the Greek heroes, son of Zeus and Alcmene, a mortal woman. Heracles was the strongest man alive, impossible to defeat in battle. He had appetites, emotions, self-confidence, and good humor in abundance, but limited intelligence and almost no self-restraint. He was harried throughout his life by Hera, the wife of Zeus, and blundered into horrendous crimes which he expiated, in all humility and penitence, through his stupendous labors.

His wife, Deianira, endures long absences and serial infidelities. She compares his treatment of her to "a farmer working an outlying field, / who sees it only when he sows and when he reaps."[26] But Heracles is finally returning home after a long absence. His herald precedes him accompanied by a group of captive women from a city in Euboea, which Heracles has recently sacked. Among them is Iole, daughter of King Eurytus. The herald offers an elaborate explanation for why Heracles bore a legitimate grudge against Eurytus. Another officious messenger, however, insists that Heracles was driven solely by his passion for Iole. Deianira is far from pleased.

> So now the two of us lie under the one sheet
> waiting for his embrace. This is the gift my brave
> and faithful Heracles sends home to his dear wife
> to compensate for his long absence![27]

She decides to try a remedy given her by the centaur Nessus, who had once tried to rape her but had been killed with a poisoned arrow by Heracles. Before he died, the centaur told Deianira that his blood was a love charm that would prevent Heracles from looking at any other woman and loving her more than Deianira. She spreads this blood on a cloak, which she carefully packs away and sends to Heracles for him to wear upon his triumphant return.

No sooner has the herald departed with the cloak, however, than she has misgivings. Why, after all, would the centaur want to help her? And, of course, he did not. For when Heracles puts on the cloak, it clings to him like a second skin and he is burned with an unimaginable, searing, and inescapable pain. Deianira, cursed by their son Hyllus for what she has done, walks off the stage in silence and retreats to their marital bed where she plunges a double-bladed sword into her side.

Heracles himself, who cannot bear the pain, insists that a huge funeral pyre be built and that he be burned alive upon it as the only respite from suffering available to him. According to myth, as the flames mount, Heracles is rescued by Zeus and transformed into a god. But in Sophocles's version, there is no hint of this apotheosis, but only the expectation of a "terrible death / and agonies, many and strange."[28] The moral the chorus seeks to draw is that man's fate is always uncertain and that those who know joy also know its loss: "If anyone / counts upon one day ahead or even more, / he does not think. For there can be no tomorrow / until we have safely passed the day that is with us still."[29]

The play is uncharacteristic because it lacks the typical Sophoclean hero who presses an ideal (or a fixation) beyond the limits of human endurance and yet faces disaster with courage and a refusal to compromise. Deianira is noble in her own way; she strives for goodness, shows kindness even to her rival Iole, and, when her plans lead to disaster, she faces her own death with a courage made all the more chilling by her silence and absence of complaint. But her character is too bland to sustain the interest of the play. Nor is Heracles, despite his superhuman appetites, emotions, and prowess a standard tragic hero. His buffoonery is more often the subject of comedy. Here he does not even appear onstage until he is already suffering beyond endurance. He welcomes death as the only escape open to him.

Yet the play is also puzzling because, despite the somewhat pedestrian moral drawn by the chorus, it has a powerful impact. In part, this is because we sense that Deianira is not so simple after all; her decision to use the centaur's blood can be characterized, without too great anachronism, as a subconscious means of revenge on her unfaithful husband. Her purpose, after all, has been achieved—the "charm" will prevent Heracles from loving another. Deianira can hardly be compared with Aeschylus's Clytemnestra, despite the parallel of the silent concubine brought home by the long-absent husband, or with Euripides's Medea, who used a poisoned robe to similar effect. But Deianira illustrates how readily despair can drive even good people to foolish actions that are bound to end in disaster. There may be "nothing here which is not Zeus,"[30] as Hyllus concludes—there may, that is, be a divine plan past our comprehension—but the fulfillment or frustration of human hopes is also inextricably bound up with our human limitations and the ambiguity of our motives.

$$\clubsuit$$

The *Philoctetes* is one of the few plays of Sophocles that we can accurately date. It was produced in 409, when Sophocles was eighty-seven. The play is closely connected to the myth of Heracles, because Philoctetes was the only one willing to light the funeral pyre on which Heracles had placed himself. In gratitude, Heracles gave Philoctetes his great bow, a bow that never missed.

Philoctetes was recruited for the expedition to Troy. But during an island stop on the voyage he inadvertently trespassed on the unmarked sanctuary of a god and was bitten by a snake. His wound festered, leaving him a cripple with savage pain. Unable to bear his cries or his rank smell, his companions simply abandoned him on another island, Lemnos, and sailed to Troy without him.

For ten years, Philoctetes has remained on Lemnos in miserable conditions, surviving only by the accuracy of his bow. Occasional visitors flee from him; none will accept him on their ship and remove him from the island. But when a prophet foretells that Troy will not be taken without Philoctetes and his bow, the Greeks send Odysseus and Neoptolemus, the son of Achilles, to fetch him.

Their choices are three: they can persuade Philoctetes to come, they can force him to come, or they can use deception and trick him into coming. Odysseus quickly rejects the first two options. They cannot force Philoctetes so long as he possesses the bow of Heracles. But neither will they be able to persuade him. Philoctetes's wound is not the only thing that has festered for ten years; so, too, has his hatred for the Atridae and Odysseus, whom he holds responsible for his abandonment. He will not willingly help them, even at the cost of saving himself and winning immortal glory. Odysseus, therefore, readily settles on craft as the sole means of success.

But he must first persuade Neoptolemus that expediency warrants treachery. Neoptolemus adheres to the heroic creed of his father and Ajax, a creed that spurns all deception. Neoptolemus, however, is still young and therefore pliable in the hands of an older, more experienced warrior. He himself is destined to lead the sack of Troy, but without Philoctetes and his bow, that will not happen, which would deprive him of the success denied even his great father. Odysseus appeals to his desire for victory and claims that men will honor him for his wisdom and his loyalty in addition to his prowess if he can "ensnare / the soul of Philoctetes with [his] words":[31]

> I know, young man, it is not your natural bent
> to say such things nor to contrive such mischief.
> But the prize of victory is pleasant to win.
> Bear up: another time we shall prove honest.
> For one brief shameless portion of a day
> give me yourself, and then for all the rest
> you may be called most scrupulous of men.[32]

Neoptolemus easily tricks Philoctetes, who, despite his prior betrayal, still trusts easily. Philoctetes is touchingly eager for human contact and affection, especially from the son of his old friend Achilles. Neoptolemus claims that he has left Troy in anger and disgust because the Atridae gave his father's armor to Odysseus instead of to him. It is a story cynically calculated to appeal to Philoctetes, who believes he has found an ally in his hatred of the Greek leaders. When Neoptolemus appears to yield to Philoctetes's pleas to carry him home, Philoctetes is so overwhelmed with gratitude that he gives the boy the bow of Heracles to hold while a fit descends upon him. But Neoptolemus cannot carry through the deception. He is disgusted with his own betrayal of his better nature. When Philoctetes recovers, he tells him the truth and returns the bow to him.

Neoptolemus then seeks to persuade Philoctetes to come with him willingly. According to the prophecy, Philoctetes will be cured at Troy and then, with his bow, kill Paris and take the city at the side of Neoptolemus. He will be rid of his island and his disease and, at the same time, win immortal glory and a route home to his aging father—all things of which he has dreamed for so long. But Philoctetes refuses because it would mean helping his enemies. Odysseus and the Atridae callously abandoned him, and he will not help them even if doing so is the sole means of release from his suffering. Neoptolemus chides Philoctetes for his intransigence:

> Men that cling willfully to their sufferings
> as you do, no one may forgive nor pity.
> Your anger has made a savage of you.[33]

Philoctetes hesitates but will not yield. He prefers death to the humiliation of crawling back to those who entombed him on this island. Instead, it is Neoptolemus who yields and agrees to fulfill his promise and take Philoctetes home. He will sacrifice his own glory in loyalty to another.

But Troy is destined to fall, and Philoctetes is destined to be cured there. In a rare instance, Sophocles brings a god upon the stage to resolve this impasse. The now-immortal Heracles appears and directs Philoctetes to follow Neoptolemus to Troy, where he will achieve all that Neoptolemus has promised to him. Philoctetes quickly agrees:

> Voice that stirs my yearning when I hear,
> form lost for so long,
> I shall not disobey.[34]

The ambivalence of Philoctetes is clear. He yearns for the redemption that will restore him to humankind. Yet he fears it also. The yearning is deeply buried; it has been held in close check and must be stirred to life. For ten years, Philoctetes's wound has been his sole companion, a visible symbol of his contact with the divine and of his isolation from his fellow men. It is not easy for him to let go of that, just as it was not easy for Electra finally to realize the revenge she had long sought.

But Philoctetes has been touched by the divine for better as well as for worse. His skill with a bow is a gift that makes him indispensable to his fellows. Even more important, he has never lost his basic dignity and his willingness to reach out to others in friendship. "I would have you know what I have lived from," he tells Neoptolemus, "how tough the spirit that did not break."[35] The bond forged between Philoctetes and Neoptolemus is unique for a Sophoclean hero. It tells us that life holds blessings as well as wounds.

Edmund Wilson makes of *Philoctetes* a portrait of the artist, nurturing his private wound, shunned by society, and yet "also the master of a superhuman art which everybody has to respect and which the normal man finds he needs."[36] In his work, the artist finds his own redemption and his own connection and thereby confers his blessing on others.

H. D. F. Kitto and Bernard Knox offer equally thought-provoking, political readings of the play based on the repudiation of Odysseus. In *Ajax*, Odysseus was pragmatic but still compassionate. He was modern political man at his best. But *Ajax* was written when Athens was still at the height of its power and the promise of its young democracy seemed bright. By 409, Athens was in the hands of demagogues spouting sophistic doctrines that seemed to justify any expediency. Athens had lost its moral compass, was beset by treachery, and lurched from one disaster to another, a course that would culminate in its loss of the Peloponnesian War. The Odysseus of the *Philoctetes*, like the demagogues of Athens, is amoral and unattractive. He embodies not just a pragmatic softening of the heroic virtues, as he did in *Ajax*, but their complete antithesis; he even proves a coward in the face of Philoctetes's bow. "As the occasion / demands, such a one am I," says Odysseus, "What I seek in everything is to win."[37] But his counsel is false and will never lead to victory. His advice is not just morally wrong, it is politically disastrous. Redemption for Athens, like the capture of Troy, will require a renewed allegiance to justice and respect for the will of the gods. If words and acts "are just," says Neoptolemus, "they are better than clever."[38]

Both readings are limited, which is not to say invalid, but merely that they do not exhaust the play. We are all touched by the divine, Sophocles seems to be saying. All of us carry wounds. But we cannot nurse those wounds in isolation. We must reengage with our fellow men. We must reconnect with our own common humanity.

Philoctetes bids a tender farewell to his island and his comfortless cave, the scene of ten years of misery and loneliness. He has retained his purity of spirit, and he has refused to compromise the ideals of just dealings and fellowship that were betrayed by the Atridae and Odysseus and that Neoptolemus has restored to him. That does not necessarily suggest, as Kitto argues, that there is a "beneficent world order,"[39] but only that blessings are sometimes granted as well as withheld. The "spirit that did not break"[40] allows Philoctetes to embrace those blessings and to go forth again to the world of men.

ANTIGONE

Antigone, Sophocles's first foray into the House of Oedipus at Thebes, dates to the late 440s, shortly after *Ajax* but some fifteen to twenty years before *Oedipus the King*. The story of Oedipus is undoubtedly familiar to most readers, if only from the Freudian gloss. Oedipus and Jocasta (the mother he inadvertently married after unknowingly killing his father) had two daughters, Antigone and Ismene, and two sons, Polynices and Eteocles. *Oedipus the King* deals with the hero's efforts to find the truth about the murder of the former king and his discovery of his own identity as parricide, regicide, and incestuous husband. *Oedipus at Colonus* deals with the last wanderings of the self-blinded exile who has been cast out of Thebes as a pollution to the city.

In *Seven against Thebes*, produced at least twenty years before *Antigone*, Aeschylus focused on an intermediate episode. The two brothers contended for the throne of Thebes (which had been in the hands of Jocasta's brother, Creon, as regent until they reached maturity). Eteocles, the younger brother, seized power and banished Polynices. But Polynices found help at Argos and returned with an army to attack the city. Six mighty warriors and Polynices himself each were assigned to storm one of the seven gates of Thebes. Eteocles sent champions of his own to the first six gates and himself to the seventh, despite learning that Polynices was at that gate. Both brothers had been cursed by their father, Oedipus, for abandoning him to exile, and Eteocles goes to meet Polynices with a sense of fatality. "To this ritual," he says, "my own father's wicked curse / Appoints me."[41] He rejects all pleas to switch to another gate. His father's son to the end, he says, "My will is set; not all your words can blunt it now."[42] The attack is repulsed and Polynices's six champions are killed, but so too are Eteocles and Polynices, who have killed one another with their sword thrusts.

Antigone—which Hegel called "one of the most sublime, and in every respect most consummate works of art human effort has ever brought forth"[43]—begins where *Seven against Thebes* ends. Creon has declared himself king and ordered that Eteocles, the savior of Thebes, be buried with full honors. But Polynices and his champions must lie unburied, without funeral rites or dirges for their repose. Antigone, driven by a mix of family loyalty, piety for the demands of religion, and an intense, instinctive aversion to the thought of Polynices rotting in the open air and being torn by dogs and pecked at by birds, resolves to defy the law and bury her brother. (In a revival presented well after the death of Aeschylus, the ending of *Seven against Thebes*, in the only version we now possess, was altered to mesh with the beginning of *Antigone*, showing how strongly the latter play had by then imprinted itself in the minds of Greek playgoers.)

The city of Thebes has just won a narrow victory, at a time when defeat could mean the murder of the male citizens and the slavery of its women and children. The chorus of Theban elders celebrates their deliverance and hails Creon as "the new man for the new day."[44] Creon in turn emphasizes the critical importance of the city-state, the "ship of state,"[45] he calls it, upon which all depend and to which all personal connections must defer. No one, he says, should place a friend or family member above the good of his own country. Nor has Creon done so himself; one of his two sons, Megareus, was killed in beating back the assault.

> Remember this:
> our country *is* our safety.
> Only while she voyages true on course
> can we establish friendships, truer than blood itself.
> Such are my standards. They make our city great.[46]

The chorus leader supports Creon but is plainly uneasy with the decree that Polynices lie unburied. "The power is yours, I suppose," he acknowledges, to make and enforce laws "for the dead and all of us, / the living."[47] But Creon, of course, has no power over the dead. That is the realm of the gods, and his rash initial decision—a decision he will feel obliged to defend with increasing intransigence—will end in disaster for himself and his city.

The immediate instrument of that disaster is Antigone, daughter (and half-sister) of Oedipus. Antigone's own intransigence is more than a match for Creon's. She is determined to bury Polynices and seeks to enlist her sister in the plan. But Ismene (like Chrysothemis in *Electra*) counsels submission. She will not defy the law or the men who are in power. "Remember we are women, / we're not born to contend with men."[48] She chides Antigone for rushing to extremes and, in a wonderful phrase that captures the essence of the Sophoclean hero, being "in love with impossibility."[49]

Antigone angrily dismisses her sister and makes two attempts to bury Polynices. The first is done in secret. She covers the body with a layer of dust and performs what funeral rites she can to honor Polynices and permit his proper repose in the land of the dead. When one of the soldiers guarding the body claims to have seen nothing, the chorus leader suggests that the burial might be the work of the gods. But Creon grows furious and, in the first sign that the "new man for the new day" is headed toward tyranny, speaks of dark conspiracies (as leaders who feel affronted are wont to do, from that time to this).

> From the first there were certain citizens
> who could hardly stand the spirit of my regime,
> grumbling against me in the dark, heads together,
> tossing wildly, never keeping their necks beneath
> the yoke, loyally submitting to their king.
> These are the instigators, I'm convinced—
> they've perverted my own guard, bribed them
> to do their work.[50]

The imagined conspirators, however, resolve themselves into a single girl. After Polynices's corpse is brushed clean, Antigone makes a second attempt to bury her brother, this time in broad daylight in view of the now-vigilant guards. When she is taken before Creon, he offers his niece a ready excuse by suggesting that she was not aware of his decree forbidding the burial on pain of death. But she angrily rejects any mitigation of her offense. The laws of the gods, she tells him, are more important and more to be feared than the laws of men. Creon, a mere mortal, cannot override "the great unwritten, unshakeable traditions."[51] Given the pains she has already suffered—the suicide of her mother; the disgrace, exile, and death of her father; and the deaths of her brothers at each others' hands—her own death seems a small thing compared to the agony of allowing "my own mother's son to rot, an unburied corpse."[52]

Antigone has reached a state of such fierce and exalted pride that anything short of death would be deflating. She calls Creon a fool to his face and mocks his wounded pride in front of the citizens of Thebes. He reacts predictably by vowing to break her stubborn will as he would break a horse. He is particularly offended that his role as lord and master has been challenged by a woman.

> I am not the man, not now: she is the man
> if this victory goes to her and she goes free.[53]

Creon condemns Ismene as well as Antigone, assuming the two have acted together. Ismene accepts the charge and is willing to die with her sister, but Antigone—both protecting and brutally excluding her sister—insists that she acted alone and prefers to die alone.

> Never share my dying,
> don't lay claim to what you never touched.
> My death will be enough.[54]

Creon's other son, Haemon, who is engaged to Antigone, tries to persuade Creon to relax his anger. Haemon is exceptionally diplomatic, flattering and promising to obey his father and be guided by him in all things. He never mentions his love for Antigone but acts as if his sole concern were for his father. He suggests that the citizens of Thebes are now indeed murmuring in the dark, that they believe Antigone is acting heroically, and that it is wrong to "trample down the honors of the gods."[55] Haemon urges his father to take counsel and not "assume the world is wrong and you are right."[56]

But Creon has reached a point at which he cannot back down. He insists that when a man is in authority "his orders / must be obeyed, large and small, / right and wrong."[57] Any softening of his decree would invite anarchy. "Am I to rule this land for others—or myself?"[58] he asks rhetorically, and then provides his own answer: "The city *is* the king's—that's the law!"[59] He will condemn Antigone because he can, as a show of his authority and a balm to his wounded pride. Creon the tyrant has been fully revealed, and his son parts from him in horror and disgust.

Creon then orders that Antigone, but not Ismene (he has changed his mind in that, at least), be sealed in a rocky vault, with minimal provisions, so that she will die without active participation by, and hence pollution of, the city. In her final speech, Antigone no longer offers a religious justification for her actions; she even notes that she would not do the same for a lost husband or child, since they could be replaced. But with her mother and father dead, she can never replace her brothers, and she prays only that they will embrace her warmly when she "descend[s] alive to the caverns of the dead."[60]

It is a deeply moving scene, and reminds us what a young girl Antigone is (perhaps no more than fourteen). Some critics consider it marred by the bizarre argument that she feels a greater duty to her brothers than to any future husband

and children because "a husband dead, there might have been another. / A child by another too, if I had lost the first."[61] But Antigone will never know the joys of marriage and children. The husband and child she is never to see are mere abstractions to her now. Indeed, she has had no sign of support from her fiancé, for she was kept bound inside the palace while he pled for her life. She feels abandoned by men and gods alike. She has been stripped of all defenses and therefore clings to the one palpable reality of her life, her parents and her brothers, all of whom are now dead and therefore cannot fail her. She clings to the one fundamental connection that is immune to the vagaries of fate, the whims of a tyrant, and the apparent cowardice of a fiancé.

The denouement follows rapidly upon Antigone's exit. The prophet Tiresias tells Creon that the altars of the city have been polluted by his refusal to bury Polynices and the other six champions. The gods are rejecting their sacrifices. In an astonishing display of impiety, Creon announces that even a direct sign from Zeus would not lead him to permit the burials, and he berates Tiresias as a liar who prophesizes for money. Goaded into speaking more than he intended, Tiresias tells Creon that before the sun sets his only remaining son will be dead, "a corpse for corpses given in return,"[62] and that Creon has doomed his city to a devastating attack of revenge by the cities "whose mutilated sons / the dogs have graced with burial."[63]

Finally shaken, Creon asks the chorus of elders for advice and agrees to free Antigone and raise a mound for Polynices. But he is too late. As a messenger later explains, by the time Creon had buried Polynices with due rites and entered the vault, Antigone had hanged herself. Haemon was there already, clinging to and howling over the corpse. He tried to run Creon through with his sword but, when Creon escaped, fell upon it himself, joining his would-be bride in death. Eurydice, Creon's wife, listens to the messenger and then silently enters the palace, where she stabs herself and dies cursing Creon. The play ends with Creon as a "wailing wreck of a man"[64] who announces, "I don't even exist—I'm no one. Nothing."[65]

How different his ending from the possibilities set forth in the magnificent choral ode that accompanied Creon's accession to power. In a paean to man that echoes Prometheus's great speech on the conquest of the Earth and the growth of civilization, the chorus sings, "Numberless wonders / terrible wonders walk the world but none the match for man."[66] Man is the crosser of seas, the plower of the earth, the tamer of horses, the master of beasts and birds, the speaker of words, and, most important of all, the builder of cities and the creator of the rule of law. Only death conquers man. When he weaves together the laws of his land and the laws of the gods, he rises to greatness. Yet, the chorus warns, the "man who weds himself to inhumanity"[67] is a disaster for himself and his city. Man, the measure of all things, can become as nothing in a moment: "Man the master, ingenious past all measure / past all dreams, the skills within his grasp— / he forges on, now to destruction / now again to greatness."[68] Creon aspired to greatness but he perverted and dehumanized the very accomplishments of man: he vowed to break Antigone as he would break a horse; he brutally suggested that his son, deprived of Antigone, should plow in other fields; he made the dogs and birds masters of unburied corpses; and he treated the ship of state as the vessel of his own aggrandizement and ran it upon the shoals. Most egregiously, he ignored what Antigone calls "the great unwritten, unshakeable traditions" that join the laws of man with the justice of the gods and thereby ensured his own downfall and that of the city he swore to preserve.

Yet Creon is not the tragic hero of this play. His goals, in the end, are not lofty enough, and his will is broken when events spin out of control and his son, his city, his wife, and the gods all turn against him. The play is rightly named for Antigone. Her will remains unbroken. Her sister, her king, and, apparently, the gods, the city, and her fiancé all abandon her. Yet she perseveres with fierce conviction. And she is proved right in the end, for "the great unwritten, unshakeable traditions" are vindicated with terrible force and even Creon must acknowledge that "it's best to keep the established laws / to the very day we die."[69]

Yet Antigone, too, "weds [herself] to inhumanity." She, like Creon, sees only one side of an equation that must combine the laws of the land and the justice of the gods. She simply dismisses the claims of the polis and assumes a posture of utter defiance against her ruler and the male head of her family. You are, the chorus tells her with a mixture of admiration and admonishment, "a law to yourself, alone."[70] Ismene, faced with the same situation and some of the same feelings, is more prudent. She lacks the pride and will and fortitude of Antigone. But she also lacks the exalted sense of self that drives Antigone forward, the sense that the dictates of her individual conscience trump all other considerations. Antigone is not just abandoned; she deliberately severs all her existing connections with the living in favor of her past ties to the dead. She herself forces Creon's hand and forfeits her life not only to realize an ideal of heroic conduct but also to punish others and apotheosize herself. Antigone ensures that Creon cannot change his mind by putting herself beyond any hope of rescue, beyond any remaining connection with humanity.

She is magnificent, and she is terrible. "Numberless wonders / terrible wonders walk the world but none the match for man."[71] Certainly, none is a match for Antigone, except perhaps her own father (and half-brother), Oedipus.

OEDIPUS THE KING

Oedipus the King was produced around 425, almost twenty years after *Antigone*. Its theme is again the wonders and terrors of human life. But the vision it imparts is even darker. Oedipus, like Creon, is repeatedly described in terms of the great ode from *Antigone*. He is the pilot of the ship of the state, the plowman, the hunter, the master of land and sea. Mathematical, medical, and philosophical terms also abound: Oedipus is the measurer, the healer, and the relentless seeker of truth. Unlike Creon, however, he has not distorted the tasks of men. He has brought them to a glorious fulfillment and represents the pinnacle of man's material and intellectual progress. Yet the abyss opens at his feet, and all his accomplishments, all his vaunted knowledge, are as nothing. Creon's words at the end of Antigone—"I don't even exist—I'm no one. Nothing."—apply equally here. As Bernard Knox explains, man in this play "is not the measure of all things but the thing measured and found wanting."[72]

If *Eumenides* was the first courtroom drama, *Oedipus the King* is the first detective story, but with a twist: hunter and hunted turn out to be one and the same. All of Oedipus's great intelligence, courage, determination, and love of truth serve only to disclose his own pollution from two of the gravest crimes imaginable: he has killed his father and married his mother. These events were done in ignorance, long before the play even starts. But they are uncovered in a plot of astonishing tautness and power, driven by the will and character of Oedipus.

Oedipus's parents, Laius and Jocasta, were king and queen at Thebes. The oracle of Apollo at Delphi revealed that their newborn son would kill his father and marry his mother. Accordingly, they handed the baby over to a shepherd with instructions to pierce his feet, bind them together, and expose him on a mountain between Thebes and Corinth. But the shepherd pitied the child and instead gave him to a shepherd he knew from Corinth. The king and queen of Corinth, Polybus and Merope, learning of this rescue and being childless themselves, took in the baby and raised him as their own. When Oedipus was a young man, a drunk at a banquet taunted him with his illegitimacy. Polybus and Merope vigorously denied the charge, but the slander spread and Oedipus went secretly to ask the oracle at Delphi if they were indeed his parents. Instead of answering that question, the oracle replied that he was fated to kill his father and marry his mother.

Oedipus immediately fled from Corinth in order to give the lie to the oracle. At a lonely spot in the mountains where three roads meet—roads to Delphi, to Corinth, and to Thebes, a place you can still look down upon from the modern road to Delphi—he encountered an old man in a wagon with several servants. Brusquely knocked aside by the driver, Oedipus struck him and was then set upon by the others. In the ensuing fight (the first recorded case of road rage), he killed the man and all but one of his servants. Oedipus then made his way to Thebes, where a sphinx (half lion, half woman) terrorized those who sought to enter or leave the city. The sphinx posed a riddle: What creature walks on four feet in the morning, two feet in the afternoon, and three feet in the evening? Those who failed to answer the riddle were devoured, but Oedipus promptly answered: "man," who moves on all fours as a baby, on two feet as an adult, and uses a cane in old age. The sphinx, her riddle solved, threw herself off a cliff. Thebes was thus delivered and in gratitude rewarded Oedipus with the hand of the queen, whose husband had recently been killed by a band of robbers.

When the play opens, Oedipus's astonishing rise from stranger to king is many years in the past. He is a beloved and respected leader, and he and Jocasta already have four children. But a plague has descended upon Thebes, and the people pray to Oedipus, "first of men,"[73] to deliver them from this plague as he once delivered them from the sphinx. The situation is fraught with irony: defeating the sphinx required him to solve the riddle of man; defeating the plague will, though he does not yet know it, require him to solve the riddle of his own identity.

Oedipus sets about the task with his customary decisiveness. Whenever a course of action is suggested (whether it is sending Creon to consult the oracle or calling upon the prophet Tiresias), he has already done it. As a consequence, events move quickly to their devastating conclusion. Creon announces that Apollo has commanded the city, if it is to be cured of the plague, to uncover the murderer of Laius and drive him from the land. Oedipus vows to do so, as if Laius were his own father, and places a curse on the murderer and anyone who harbors him:

> Banish this man—
> whoever he may be—never shelter him, never
> speak a word to him, never make him partner
> to your prayers, your victims burned to the gods.[74]

When the blind prophet Tiresias is brought before him but refuses to speak out, Oedipus accuses him of involvement in the murder and threatens him. Stung, Tiresias tells Oedipus, "You are the murderer you hunt," and "You and your loved ones live together in infamy."[75] Oedipus responds furiously, mocking Tiresias as a false prophet who could not solve the riddle of the sphinx. He accuses Tiresias of conspiring with Creon to drive him from Thebes by blaming him for the death of Laius. Tiresias warns Oedipus that

> the double lash of your mother and your father's curse
> will whip you from this land one day, their footfall
> treading you down in terror, darkness shrouding
> your eyes that now can see the light![76]

Despite this warning, Oedipus presses ahead with his inquiry, and the pieces of the puzzle come together with sickening rapidity. Jocasta, in trying to convince him that prophecies have no power and cannot penetrate the future, notes that Laius was supposedly destined to be killed by his own son, but his son was exposed on the mountainside as a baby and Laius was killed by robbers on the way to Delphi "at a place where three roads meet."[77] She describes the party exactly as Oedipus encountered it, but the stories do not jibe because the sole survivor, a shepherd and servant of Laius, claimed that they were set upon by an entire band of thieves, and Oedipus clings to this one fact: "I cannot be the killer. One can't equal many."[78] He sends for the shepherd to solve the equation.

A messenger from Corinth arrives to tell Oedipus that his father, Polybus, is dead and that Oedipus is now king of Corinth. Oedipus fears returning, though, because his mother is still alive and the prophecy could yet be fulfilled, especially if Polybus could be said to have died of grief at his absence. The messenger reassures him. Oedipus is not the son of Polybus and Merope, but was found abandoned on a mountainside at birth, with his ankles fastened together. The messenger himself received the baby from a shepherd of Laius, who pitied the child. That shepherd and the survivor of the attack on Laius, who arrives next, turn out to be one and the same. Oedipus himself has become the point at which three roads meet. The oracle of Delphi, the messenger from Corinth, and the shepherd of Thebes come together to destroy him utterly. Yet even facing the abyss, Oedipus does not hesitate. "I'm at the edge of hearing horrors, yes, but I must hear!"[79]

Jocasta does not need to hear more. She now knows, and she hangs herself over their marriage bed. Oedipus enters the palace, lays his wife and mother gently on the bed, and, using the brooches that bound her gown, gouges out his own eyes. Imperious to the last, Oedipus commands Creon to banish him from the land, a pollution on the Earth to be shunned by all. The chorus of elders chants his epitaph:

> People of Thebes, my countrymen, look on Oedipus.
> He solved the famous riddle with his brilliance,
> he rose to power, a man beyond all power.
> Who could behold his greatness without envy?
> Now what a black sea of terror has overwhelmed him.
> Now as we keep our watch and wait the final day,
> count no man happy till he dies, free of pain at last.[80]

Yet the play is not simply a commentary on the chance reversals of fortune, which cast down even as they raise up. Certainly chance has seemed to play a huge role in the events of Oedipus's life: his survival through the kindness of a shepherd, the drunken words at the banquet, his crossroads encounter with Laius, his challenge by the sphinx. There are also many reversals of fortune: the homeless wanderer becomes king; the savior of the city becomes the cause of its plague; the abandoned child is restored to his mother only to lose her forever; and Oedipus discovers his true home and his rightful place as hereditary king only to become again a homeless wanderer.

But there is an underlying pattern to it all, which has been foretold by the gods. Jocasta, in her increasing desperation, had disparaged oracles and any concept of a divine order:

> What should a man fear? It's all chance,
> chance rules our lives. Not a man on earth
> can see a day ahead, groping through the dark.
> Better to live at random, best we can.[81]

But even as she spoke, the iron circle of fate was closing around them both. If the oracles are not true, the chorus asks, "why join the sacred dance?"[82] Why, that is, should we honor and fear and celebrate the gods? What need for religion? What need even for tragedy? If all is random chance, there is only melodrama and its close cousin, comedy, recounting man's frantic efforts to cope with an absurd and meaningless universe.

But all is not random chance. The oracles are true. The gods do know the future that man, with all his foresight, cannot penetrate. Sophocles and his chorus affirm their faith in a divine order beyond our comprehension. It is not, however, a comforting vision. In this incomprehensible divine order, man counts as "nothing." Aristotle, who considered *Oedipus the King* to be the most perfect of Greek tragedies, said that the purpose of tragedy is to evoke both pity for the sufferings of the hero and fear for our own human vulnerabilities in a universe whose purpose and meaning we cannot fully grasp. Aristotle, the archetype of rational man, loved and appreciated tragedy and this play above all for what it says about the limitations of human thought.

If there is divine justice—and piety and reverence cling to the belief in such justice—it is beyond our capacity to measure. On the level of rational thought, Oedipus is not guilty of any crime. His parricide (committed in self-defense) and his incest were both done in ignorance of their true nature. He, like Jocasta, is a victim of that ignorance. Yet a rational assignment of responsibility offers no protection against archaic, deep-seated feelings of guilt, pollution, and remorse. The slender currents of human enlightenment are swamped by what the chorus calls "a black sea of terror."

Yet man can retain his freedom and his dignity. Divine foreknowledge does not mean that human actions are predetermined, that man is not a free agent. Oedipus himself drives the action of the play, persevering in the face of grave warnings and insisting that he will know the truth at whatever cost. No man has perfect knowledge of himself, his circumstances, or his future. Indeed, man's freedom *is* his lack of knowledge, his ability to choose in the face of uncertainty. Sophocles conveys this freedom by having all the prophesied events occur long before the play even starts. In the play itself, Oedipus's every action is a product of his own will and his own indomitable character, a point on which he grimly insists:

> Apollo, friends, Apollo—
> he ordained my agonies—these, my pains on pains!
> But the hand that struck my eyes was mine,
> mine alone—no one else—
> I did it all myself![83]

Oedipus offers us an ideal vision of man at his most magnificent and his most vulnerable. He has a powerful intellect and a commanding presence; he is decisive, courageous, and deeply loyal to his city and its people. But all his qualities cannot save him from forces beyond rational human understanding. From the perspective of men, he is the embodiment of all that is great. From the perspective of the gods, he is blind and insignificant. Yet we, as men, admire in particular his relentless pursuit of the truth. "I must know it all," he says, "must see the truth at last."[84] The greatest of all tragic heroes tears the veil from every illusion and faces the "black sea of terror."

OEDIPUS AT COLONUS

It is reported that in 406, when Sophocles was ninety, he was brought into court by the son from his first marriage, who sought to have him declared incompetent to manage his own affairs. In his defense, Sophocles simply recited a choral ode from his new play, *Oedipus at Colonus*. He won the suit, of course, as he had won so many prizes in the theater of Dionysus, but he died soon after and the play was not performed until 401. In the interim, Athens surrendered to Sparta, which dismantled Athens's empire, its protective walls, and its democracy.

It is not surprising that Sophocles decided to revisit his most famous character as his own life wound down. What is surprising is the softening of his tragic vision. Even as the early hope of Athenian democracy turned to despair, and the city was beleaguered and threatened with extinction, Sophocles himself found a new hope beyond the "black sea of terror" that washed over his early plays. In the *Philoctetes*, from 409, the Sophoclean hero finds it possible to reconnect with his fellow men and to trust again in the good faith of others. In *Oedipus at Colonus*, the blind and aged Oedipus is granted a final resting place at Colonus through the kindness of Athenian strangers and reconnects with the gods who once ordained his agonies.

There is a Job-like quality to this ending. But in the Book of Job, the long-suffering hero is given a new family to replace the one destroyed by God and new material possessions that dwarf his initial wealth. There are no such replacement goods in *Oedipus at Colonus*. The only recompense is spiritual, which is more satisfying and more respectful of the earlier sorrows.

Oedipus arrives in Colonus at the sacred grove of the Eumenides—the ancient Furies, daughters of darkness, who became the kindly guardians of Athens—on the arm of his young daughter Antigone. She describes to him the holy ground, "bursting / with laurel, olives, grapes, and deep in its heart, / listen . . . nightingales, the rustle of wings— / they're breaking into song."[85] Oedipus recalls that the ancient oracle that spelled his doom also said he would find a haven in just such a place and become a blessing to his hosts. There Oedipus is welcomed by Theseus, the legendary king of Athens, who promises him asylum and protection. There Oedipus remains, notwithstanding the violent efforts of Creon (on behalf of Eteocles) and the pleas of Polynices that he make common cause with one against the other, for the oracle has said that his support would be decisive in the coming battle for Thebes. Oedipus curses them both and himself prophesizes with the assurance of an oracle their coming destruction at one another's hands.

Summoned by lightning and thunder, Oedipus moves with new confidence and without need for guidance toward the sacred grave promised him by the gods. His last words to Theseus and the citizens of Athens are a blessing and a prediction of their future greatness. The gods call out to Oedipus to join them, speaking no longer through omens and oracles, but directly to the much-enduring hero. Theseus alone remains, "shielding his eyes, / both hands spread out against his face as if— / some terrible wonder flashed before his eyes and he, / he could not bear to look."[86]

Critics have long seen *Oedipus at Colonus* as a valedictory to Athens itself. It was increasingly apparent that Athens would lose the war and perhaps be destroyed utterly, its buildings razed, its men killed, and its women and children sold into slavery. Athens had done as much to other cities. Yet even if destroyed, Athens would live on in glorious memory of its golden age, an age of hope and youth and an artistic outpouring never before seen and never since surpassed. Bernard Knox writes, "The old Oedipus of this play is like the exhausted, battered Athens of the last years of the war, which, though it may be defeated and may even be physically destroyed, will still flourish in immortal strength, conferring power on those who love it."[87]

Knox's interpretation surely has more than an element of truth and aesthetic beauty. But it is not, in the end, what interests us most about this play or its predecessor, *Oedipus the King*. We see those plays most clearly in a more personal dimension. In *Oedipus the King*, the hero was a model of intelligence, courage, and decisiveness; he reached the pinnacle of social, material, and political power, and yet a yawning chasm opened beneath his feet. In *Oedipus at Colonus*, "despised old age overtakes him, / stripped of power, companions, stripped of love— / the worst this life of pain can offer,"[88] and yet, as William Wordsworth would later write, he finds "strength in what remains behind,"

> In the primal sympathy
> Which having been must ever be;
> In the soothing thoughts that spring
> Out of human suffering;
> In the faith that looks through death,
> In years that bring the philosophic mind.[89]

There are "great mysteries"[90] that lie beyond the reach of words. Man must accept those mysteries and even "the worst this life of pain can offer,"[91] and still find joy in what remains. "O light of the sun," Oedipus calls out, "now for the last time I feel you warm my flesh."[92] The great choral ode of *Oedipus at Colonus*, whose recitation showed Sophocles's undiminished powers, celebrates the Colonus of his boyhood, a place of deep green shadows, where horses are a glory and nightingales sing, a place rich with laurel and olive trees, where the springs never sleep and never fail,

> quickening life forever, fresh each day—
> life rising up with the river's pure tide
> flowing over the plains, the swelling breast of earth.[93]

Oedipus at Colonus is a valedictory to life itself, which is always passing away and yet retains its splendor in experience, in memory, and in art. "Only the gods can never age," the chorus notes, "all else in the world / almighty Time obliterates, crushes all / to nothing."[94] But there is a "power that age cannot destroy,"[95] the power of beauty, the power of faith, the power of truth, the power of art. Those are the blessings that Sophocles, in the person of Oedipus, bestows on Theseus, on Athens, and on us.

> Come, my children, weep no more,
> raise the dirge no longer. All rests
> in the hands of a mighty power.[96]

Chapter 5

EURIPIDES AND THE TWILIGHT OF THE GODS

Sophocles is reputed to have said that, whereas he shows men as they ought to be, Euripides shows men as they are.[1] There is, in truth, a steady lowering of tone (though not of quality) from Aeschylus through Sophocles to Euripides. Aeschylus depicts a universe in which justice is part of the divine plan and man is its ultimate instrument. Sophocles despairs of understanding the fate decreed by the gods but presents us with a heroic ideal of fortitude and truth and loyalty that somehow redeems the whole. In Euripides, fate has become mere chance—random, destructive, and wholly indifferent to human suffering—and the heroic ideal is simply a blind for selfish ambition, violent aggression, and unbridled passion.

Aeschylus and Sophocles, each in his own way, invest modern life with the power and significance of myth. Euripides goes in exactly the opposite direction, reinterpreting myth in light of the insignificance and harshness of everyday life. He strips away the romantic illusion from Greece's glorious past in search of a more realistic understanding of its present.

Much of Euripides's work can be viewed in terms of his often explicit contest (*agon*) with his greatest predecessor, Homer. Euripides portrays the Trojan War, the defining event of Greek history and mythology, as an unjust war for a wanton woman, opened with the shameless sacrifice of an innocent young girl and ending with the mindless destruction of an entire civilization—the slaughter of its men, the enslavement of its women, the needless murder of Hector's infant son, and the shameless sacrifice of yet another innocent young girl. All the homeric charm is gone. In its place is a dark, superstitious brutality.

Yet Euripides's refusal to romanticize aggression or to grant reality to the heroic ideal allows him to put in its place a quieter ideal of compassion for our common humanity, battered by forces (from without and within) that we can never fully understand or control. Men are men; they are not demigods, but neither need they be beasts. There are no heroes in Euripides, at least not in the traditional sense. Nor are there any beneficent forces looking out for us or guiding our actions. Yet Euripides clings to certain core moral values, and his plays are a continuous plea for peace, for justice, and for understanding on a purely human level. In steadfastly defending these fragile ideals, Euripides shows his own heroic qualities, and it is only fitting that Sophocles led his chorus in mourning for his younger colleague who predeceased him by less than a year.

LIFE AND WORK

Euripides was born in Athens around 480, making him forty-five years younger than Aeschylus and sixteen years younger than Sophocles. By some accounts, he came from a noble family; by others, his mother sold vegetables in the market. The truth is we have little reliable knowledge of his background or his life. Euripides was not, like Aeschylus, a veteran of the Persian Wars, which ended the year of his birth. Nor, like Sophocles, did he take part in military and political affairs during the Peloponnesian War (except insofar as his plays themselves made a political statement). He lived largely as a recluse with an extensive library. He is said to have married, but to have divorced his wife when she had an affair with one of his friends (though that may simply be a tale to account for Euripides's alleged cynicism and misogyny). He died in 406, at the court of Archelaos in Macedon, having left Athens on the eve of her defeat in the Peloponnesian War. Some find significance in this symbolic transfer of the torch from Athens to a new regime that would ultimately overwhelm the Greek world.

Euripides's debut at the City Dionysia dates to 455, the year after Aeschylus's death. But his first victory was not gained until 441. Although he wrote as many as ninety-two plays (twenty-three groups of four), he won only four victories in his lifetime, and a fifth posthumously with a presentation that included *The Bacchae* and *Iphigenia in Aulis*. Despite the paucity of prizes, Euripides was the most popular and most often revived of the three great tragedians in the century following his death. The mood and outlook of Athens had by then caught up to his tragic vision.

Most of Euripides's extant plays are from his later years; the earliest we possess (*Alcestis*) dates to 438, when he was already forty-two. Through astonishing good fortune, we have a total of nineteen plays attributed to him (eighteen if we exclude *Rhesus*, which many scholars doubt he wrote). In addition to a medieval edition of his "selected plays" (comparable to the selections we possess for

Aeschylus and Sophocles), there is also a manuscript volume, presumably from a lost edition of his complete works, that contains nine plays in roughly alphabetical order.

There is far more variety among the nineteen extant plays of Euripides than among the seven each of Aeschylus and Sophocles. Aristotle called Euripides the "most tragic" of poets because of the dark vision of suffering that imbues so many of his plays.[2] But Euripides experimented with different genres and incorporated into his plays many of the elements that would later be seen in melodrama and modern comedy: mistaken identities, domestic scenes, sudden reversals of fortune, rekindled romances, last-second rescues. Euripides wrote tightly plotted tragedies in *Medea, Hippolytus*, and *The Bacchae*. But plays such as *Helen, Alcestis*, and even *Ion* are more like the late romances of Shakespeare than anything by Aeschylus or Sophocles. *Electra* and *Orestes* start out in the world of Aeschylus and end up in that of *Pulp Fiction*.

As that last comparison suggests, Euripides is the *enfant terrible* of Greek theater, an iconoclast and rebel. He brashly reenvisions traditional myths. He deliberately flouts and sometimes parodies the dramatic conventions of his predecessors. He incorporates the cutting-edge thinking of the Sophists. (Socrates was always in attendance at his plays.) He marginalizes the tragic chorus. His characters are vacillating and uncertain where they are not cruel and remorseless. His plays, too, often swing between the comic and the serious, between pathos and revulsion, between the profound and the frivolous. They are, in other words, rather like life.

From Aristophanes to Nietzsche, writers have claimed that Euripides "killed tragedy" by devaluing myth, overvaluing rational thought, and portraying men and women realistically. It is certainly true that Euripides deliberately shook the foundations of classical tragedy. But I would suggest that in the process he saved drama from a heroic, mythic tradition that had been mined to exhaustion and that no longer spoke to contemporary audiences. Euripides was forging a new, more complex vision of human life and human wisdom—a vision so multifaceted, indeed, that he is difficult to pin down on almost any issue. Each of the three criticisms leveled by Aristophanes and Nietzsche tell only part of the story.

For example, Aristophanes claims, with good reason, that Euripides was an atheist. The anthropomorphic gods of Homer are exposed in his plays as vain, willful, and often-vicious children. Aeschylus and Sophocles are extremely sparing in bringing the gods on stage; Euripides, however, seems to delight in introducing them whenever he needs some particularly ugly or irrational force to destroy characters, such as Hippolytus or Pentheus, whose sins do not warrant destruction, or to rescue others, such as Medea and Orestes, who do not deserve rescuing. Sometimes, like Apollo in *Ion*, they are too embarrassed by their own bad behavior (in that instance, the rape of a young girl) even to appear at all, and they send a surrogate in their place. The gods, in Euripides, are not impartial dispensers of justice. They are walking refutations of their own divinity, and his characters continually call their existence into question: if there were gods, they would not behave like this; therefore, there are no gods.

But disdain for received religion is not inconsistent with natural piety. Contemporary religious belief was a jumble of irreconcilable ideas. In rejecting the Olympian deities with their all-too-human foibles and hatreds, Euripides is not necessarily rejecting religious belief altogether. Just as he saved drama from classical tragedy, Euripides may have been trying to save religion from the gods of classical mythology and even from the Aeschylean vision of divine providence (echoed in a much-darker key by Sophocles). Certainly, Euripides shows no consistent faith in a divine order that rewards virtue and punishes wrongdoing. He does not seem to believe in fate at all, only in blind chance. But that is not the same as being an atheist. It is rather a recognition that human concepts and human values are inherently limited and have no application to the cosmos as a whole. Whether Euripides affirms some unknown and unknowable deity beyond those concepts and values is frankly unclear—different readers have reached and will continue to reach different conclusions.

Nor can Euripides properly be accused of overvaluing rational thought. Critics have cited the highly intellectualized speeches of many of his characters and accused him of displacing tragedy with philosophy. But no other Greek poet so carefully probes the power of the irrational. In Euripides, we do not need external powers to destroy us because we carry the seeds of such destruction within ourselves: violence, pride, ambition, and unbridled passion, all of which are nurtured and cultivated by the ancient heroic ideal. Euripides recognizes the necessary role of emotion and passion in human life. They are forces that cannot simply be ignored or suppressed. Accordingly, there is a constant agon in his plays between the rational and the irrational and, in the end, neither takes pride of place. Euripides may have been a humanist, but he was also obsessed with the limitations of humanism, as is shown in plays such as *Hippolytus* and *The Bacchae*.

Finally, Euripides is not an unrelenting realist. Stripped of their mythic covering, his characters are more recognizably human than the heroes of Aeschylus and Sophocles. He is often called the first psychologist because he explores his characters' internal motivations. He even gives us a soliloquy, in which Medea verbalizes her struggle between maternal instinct and the desire for vengeance. But his ultimate interest is not in the realistic portrayal of individual characters or situations. Euripides always has a more abstract focus on the ways in which psychological, social, and political forces conspire to destroy our tenuous hold on a humane existence. Gods and humans alike often simply embody these forces in his plays. Hence, the plays have a schematic, intellectual structure that detaches us from individual characters in favor of more universal lessons. In Sophocles, we enter deeply into the fates of Antigone, Philoctetes, and Oedipus. But, aside from the special case of Medea, there are no tragic heroes in Euripides, only tragic victims, and even they are simply representatives of our constantly besieged and imperiled humanity.

Athens in the late fifth century was a world of war and violence, in which demagogues and Sophists alike dismissed traditional moral values as naive and ungrounded. It was a world of doubt, uncertainty, and looming catastrophe. Even more than his two great predecessors, Euripides was always writing about the present, despite the mythological setting of the plays. He was writing about the vast, unbridgeable gulf between humankind's desire for justice and the reality of contemporary life. It is a dark vision, but never despairing. There are rays of light amid the gloom. The central tragedy of man is that he cannot live up to the best that is in him. But that is not, for Euripides, a reason not to try.

EURIPIDES CONTRA HOMER

Euripides wrote ten plays on the Trojan War and its aftermath. Only one, *Rhesus*, deals with the war itself, and even that one concerns only a peripheral incident. Euripides was not interested in reenvisioning homeric scenes—though *Cyclops*, a satyr play, does just that for an episode in the *Odyssey*. Euripides treats the Trojan War as paradigmatic of war generally and wants to explore its nature and its consequences. Most of all, he wants to strip from it any homeric luster that has survived the grim years of the Peloponnesian War.

Iphigenia in Aulis is chronologically the first of his Trojan War plays, though it was the last written. It deals with the sacrifice of Agamemnon's daughter Iphigenia to ensure favorable winds on the voyage to Troy. The incident is not discussed in Homer, but in Aeschylus it forms part of Clytemnestra's motivation to kill her husband. Euripides employs it to very different effect.

One thousand ships have gathered at Aulis only to be marooned there in a dead calm. The prophet Calchas claims that the goddess Artemis will allow the Greeks to proceed and to sack Troy only if Iphigenia is killed on her altar. When the play opens, Agamemnon has already written to Clytemnestra asking her to send Iphigenia to Aulis under the pretext that she will be married to Achilles. Beset by anguished second thoughts, he writes again to tell Clytemnestra the truth. He gives the letter to a loyal old servant and urges him to intercept Iphigenia and send her back home.

The chorus, unaware of this development, delivers a stirring ode—with clear echoes from book 3 of the *Iliad*—reviewing the Greek forces, and foremost among them "Menelaus, the yellow-haired / And Agamemnon, nobly born."[3] The transformation of life into myth is occurring before our eyes. "My vision of the marshaled ships / Will live in memory," the chorus concludes.[4] It is indeed a dream vision, a literary transformation of reality. The contrast with what follows could not be starker.

Menelaus, who has been watching for any weakness on his brother's part, intercepts the messenger and forcibly takes the letter from him. He then confronts Agamemnon in a scene in which our respect for either man is quickly and permanently dissipated. In bemoaning his fate, Agamemnon has said that the leadership of the expedition was thrust upon him. Menelaus points out that he lobbied hard and even toadied to the rank and file to get the position and then, as soon as he was chosen, became arrogant and unapproachable. When the absence of wind threatened his dreams of glory, he welcomed Calchas's prophecy and happily sent for the daughter, who, through her death, would ensure his success as captain. Only now, with Greece ready to vindicate its honor against the barbarians, are his will and his leadership failing him.

Agamemnon's reproaches to Menelaus are equally telling. Besotted with an unfaithful wife that he was incapable of looking after, he is willing to sacrifice his brother's innocent daughter, as well as thousands of Greek lives, to get her back. Such an enterprise, Agamemnon assures him, cannot "prosper against all justice."[5]

Their quarrel is interrupted by the announcement that Iphigenia has arrived with Clytemnestra. Agamemnon bursts into tears at the prospect of having to face his daughter and his wife, who will "find me out the author of this evil."[6] Menelaus, surprisingly, does a complete about-face. He acknowledges the horror of the impending sacrifice, the claims of kinship, and the inadequacy of the cause, and he urges Agamemnon to disband the army and save his daughter. But Agamemnon insists that it is too late: "A compulsion absolute / Now works the slaughter of the child."[7] The army, seized with a passion to sail on Troy, would force the sacrifice and kill anyone who tried to prevent it. Agamemnon accordingly enlists Menelaus in hiding the truth from his wife and daughter until the sacrifice can be arranged.

Both Agamemnon and Menelaus, then, get what they have wanted all along: Agamemnon will appease his lust for glory and Menelaus his lust for an unfaithful wife. Their changes of mind and their shifts in emotion may be genuine on one level, but they are also self-serving—where not self-deluding. They indulge feelings that they know will not change the planned sacrifice. In the end, they distance themselves from the murder of Iphigenia as if it were an event outside their control, a "compulsion absolute," for which they bear no responsibility.[8] "I want no part in it," says Menelaus, figuratively washing his bloody hands.[9] "We are weak and of no account before this fated thing," says Agamemnon, leader of men.[10]

Achilles adopts a more heroic attitude but also does nothing in the end. He is more annoyed that his name has been used to lure Iphigenia to Aulis without his permission—a permission he admits he might well have granted—than he is at the imminent slaughter of the young girl. He considers the whole business an "insult and injury" to him![11] "I cannot bear my part in it," he says, varying only slightly Menelaus's formula.[12] He offers, with great pomp, to defend Iphigenia to the death as a salve to his wounded pride. Yet he explains to the girl and her mother that such a course will be hopeless, leading to his own death as well as that of many Greek warriors.

Only Iphigenia seems to play a noble part in this drama. She pleads with her father at first in a deeply moving speech "not [to] take away this life of mine before its dying time."[13] But in the end she too changes her mind. She embraces her sacrifice for Greece and resolves to die "well and gloriously" so that Greeks can conquer barbarians and avenge the abduction of Helen.[14] "To Greece I give this body of mine. / Slay it in sacrifice and conquer Troy."[15]

Yet Iphigenia is the most deluded of all. The arguments she gives in favor of the war are transparently bad ones. They are typical of warmongering propaganda from time immemorial. The barbarians, she says, ravish Greek women and drag them from their homes. They seek to rule Greece, she claims. All this because one woman willingly ran away from her husband! As Nietzsche will later write, "How good bad music and bad reasons sound when one marches against an enemy!"[16]

Iphigenia is the youth of humankind sacrificed to war with her own consent. She believes her death to be glorious, for God and country, as have soldiers from the Trojan War down to World War II. Such wars are always dressed in heroic terms. Sometimes, Euripides tells us in plays such as *The Suppliant Women* and *The Heracleidae*, war may be a necessary evil and serve a just cause. Even then, noble words often disguise dubious motives and ambiguous situations. Yet it is so much worse when those in power manipulate genuine nobility in an ignoble cause.

"After the sacrifice of your child," Clytemnestra asks her husband, "what prayer can your mouth utter?"[17] The answer clearly is none. If there are gods, they cannot "joy in human blood."[18] But "if there are none, / All our toil is without meaning."[19] The Trojan War is indeed toil without meaning, human innocence slaughtered on the altar of a "terrible passion."[20]

This message is bitterly reinforced in *Helen*. The conceit of the play (derived from the sixth-century lyric poet Stesichorus and elaborated in Herodotus) is that Helen never actually went to Troy. Only a phantom accompanied Paris. The real Helen was swept off to Egypt by Hera, where she virtuously awaited a reunion with her Menelaus. Their rediscovery of one another as a middle-aged couple and their subsequent escape from Theoclymenus, the Egyptian king who has been importuning Helen to marry him, is the stuff of romantic comedy. But the subtext is clear: the Greeks and Trojans spent ten years fighting for an illusion, for a cloud image with a name but no substantial reality. Nineteen years into the Peloponnesian War, it might often have seemed to Euripides's contemporaries that the Athenians and Spartans were doing the same. Their reasons for continuing the war were increasingly obscure. They were at war because they did not know how to make peace.

Helen was produced in 412, shortly after the disastrous defeat of the Sicilian expedition, a defeat that would lead to the ultimate surrender of Athens. In 425, Euripides had already dealt with the consequences of such a defeat in *Hecuba*. The Trojan women are gathered in a separate camp where they are to be divided among the conquering Greeks. Hecuba, the wife of King Priam, is "shorn of greatness, pride, and everything but life," facing an old age of slavery and bitterness.[21] Her husband was killed by the son of Achilles while praying at an altar built by Apollo; Hector, Paris, and all but one of her other sons have died in battle. Yet her sorrows are not at an end. The ghost of Achilles appears to the Greek troops, demanding that his grave be honored with the living blood of Hecuba's daughter Polyxena, and the Greeks, at the urging of Odysseus, agree. Polyxena welcomes the prospect of death over slavery and regrets only that she can offer no continuing comfort to her mother. She goes to her death so nobly that even the Greeks are "torn between pity and duty" before they slash her throat.

Hecuba's remaining son, Polydorus, "the last surviving anchor of my house," is the next victim.[22] During the war, he was sent to Thrace to live with a family friend, King Polymestor, along with a quantity of gold to safeguard from the Greeks. Once Troy fell, Polymestor murdered Polydorus and cast his body into the sea. But the body washes ashore near the women's camp, and the women cleaning Polyxena for burial discover it. Hecuba's devastation is now complete; all human feeling in her has been brutalized. Having known no pity, she will show no pity. She lures Polymestor and his two children to their camp on the promise of more hidden treasure, and she and her women set upon them, murder the children, and gash out Polymestor's eyes with their brooches. Polymestor's innocent children are of no account to Hecuba (as her own children were of no account to others); they are simply instruments of her exquisite revenge. Our common humanity is the ultimate victim, as violence breeds violence and erases the last traces of fellow feeling.

The Trojan Women, produced in 415, just weeks before the launch of the Sicilian expedition, is equally bleak and equally prophetic of the disaster soon to befall Athens. Euripides was plainly looking back to the year before, when Athens insisted that the neutral state of Melos join its alliance against Sparta. Melos refused, and Athens besieged and ultimately conquered the city, after which it killed the men, enslaved the women and children, and populated the city with its own inhabitants. As portrayed in Thucydides, the Athenians never even attempted to defend their actions on moral grounds and were wholly deaf to the Melians' pleas for justice. Their argument in the famous Melian dialogue is simple and brutal: the strong do what they will, and the weak bear what they must.

Certainly, the latter portion of that message is underscored in *The Trojan Women*. Once again, Hecuba and the Trojan women are gathered together, this time against the backdrop of a partially demolished and still-burning Troy. The Greeks have desecrated the temples of the gods, killing Priam in one, raping Cassandra in another. The play begins with a prologue in which Athena, previously an ally of the Greeks, urges Poseidon to attack the Greek ships with lighting and thunder, with "tripled wave and spinning surf," and to fill the sea with floating dead "so after this Greeks may learn how to use with fear / my sacred places, and respect all gods besides."[23] Yet no god lifts a hand for, or heeds the cries of, the Trojan women. The gods' concern is not for the murder of innocents but for their own honor. They symbolically depart the stage and, in a series of scenes, misery is heaped upon misery: Hecuba sprawled in the dust; Cassandra raving in her madness; the sacrifice of Polyxena to appease a dead Achilles; Andromache, wife of Hector, driven off in a cart to be the concubine of the son of Achilles; and, worst of all, the senseless murder of their infant son, Astyanax, who is thrown to his death from the battlements of Troy, lest he grow up to avenge his father. Andromache is not even allowed to bury him before she is driven off. It is clear, moreover, that the cause of this misery, Helen, will escape any harm. Menelaus at first resolves to kill her but then defers the deed until he returns home, by which time he will have fallen again under her spell.

The Greeks in these two plays are not wholly evil. They often show sympathy. Even the mass of men feels pity and admiration for Polyxena. But they are easily swayed by the demagogues among them. Their leaders are calculating and pragmatic and care only for their own advancement. They are, as Hecuba calls them, "politicians / who cringe for favors from a screaming mob."[24] They are not homeric heroes. They are the very type of men who destroyed Melos and who dispatched an imperialist expedition to conquer Sicily. They have lost their moral compass.

The question raised by these plays is whether an external moral compass even exists. Hecuba, before she finally breaks and attacks Polymestor and his sons, insists that there must be "some absolute, some moral order" that stands over gods and men alike: "Upon this moral law the world depends; / through it the gods exist; by it we live, / defining good and evil."[25] But Talthybius, the Greek herald, is not so sure.

> O Zeus, what can I say?
> That you look on man
> and care?
> Or do we, holding that the gods exist,
> deceive ourselves with unsubstantial dreams
> and lies, while random careless chance and change
> alone control the world?[26]

ALL AGAMEMNON'S CHILDREN

In *Electra* and *Orestes*, Euripides goes beyond the direct effects of war and explores the fruits of long years of violence and nihilism on the next generation. These two plays are melodramas; even calling them soap operas would not be harsh. Yet they have a universal appeal and power that stem precisely from the felt absence of fixed values and heroic virtues. Electra and Orestes are alienated and confused. Their lives are, as Electra notes, "a casualty of war," every bit as much as were those of Iphigenia and Astyanax.[27]

When Orestes first appears in *Electra*, he is lurking at the edge of town, ready to flee at the slightest threat. He accosts Electra, pretending to bear a message from her brother. But he maintains this pretense far longer than he need do and only acknowledges his identity when he is recognized by the old man who had rescued him from Aegisthus as a child and smuggled him to foreign lands.

Euripides goes out of his way to mock the recognition scene from Aeschylus in which Electra matches her hair to the lock left by Orestes, compares her footprint with that of her brother, and recognizes some weaving she had done for him. The old man, who has been weeping at the grave of his former master, Agamemnon, comes to Electra with the news that someone has been making sacrifices there and urges her to go make just those comparisons that were decisive in Aeschylus. Electra ridicules him: hair color alone would show nothing, she says; the rocky ground would not hold prints and, in any event, a man's foot would be bigger than a girl's; and it is not possible that any piece of weaving done for a growing boy would still fit a man.

In part, Euripides is simply being clever at his great predecessor's expense; he is not above that. But he is also underscoring his own realism and his refusal to adopt the mythic formulas of earlier drama. Once the old man encounters Orestes directly, he immediately recognizes him from a scar above his eye. This echoes the most famous recognition scene in epic poetry, in which Odysseus's old nurse knows him from the scar on his leg, the result of a wound he received as a boy during a boar hunt. But the contrast could not be greater: Odysseus killed the boar with a spear thrust even as he was being gored. Orestes fell while chasing a fawn in his father's courtyard. The contrast is endearing in Orestes's favor and humanizes him. But we are a long way from Homer.

Electra, too, is a very human, if unattractive, character, with "filthy locks" and "robe all torn into slavish rags."[28] She has been married off to a farmer by Aegisthus, lest she have a noble son who avenges his grandfather. But the farmer, a kind and gentle man with innate nobility, refuses to force himself upon her. The marriage accordingly deprives her of sex, children, and social position. She is as much an exile as Orestes. But she wallows in her abject condition, refusing better clothes and doing menial chores that her "husband," with whom she is churlish, would gladly spare her. "I am not forced," she says. "I chose this slavery myself / to illuminate Aegisthus's arrogance for the gods."[29] Her prime complaint seems to be that she has been deprived of her rightful place as a princess in a palace life of wealth, luxury, and social prominence. She therefore perversely (but quite humanly) accentuates the contrast in her present condition.

The case for the punishment of Aegisthus and Clytemnestra is powerfully stated, every bit as much as in Aeschylus. Clytemnestra even admits that she planned the murder of Agamemnon not because of the sacrifice of Iphigenia but because of her savage rage at his bringing Cassandra to their home: "two brides being stabled in a single stall."[30] Nor does she deny Electra's accusation that she was primping for a lover the moment Agamemnon left for Troy. ("Women are fools for sex, deny it I shall not."[31]) Aegisthus is painted in even darker tones. He not only killed Agamemnon with his own hand but also sought to kill Orestes and, after the old man spirited the boy away, put a price on his head in hopes that someone else would do the deed for him. He would even have killed Electra but for Clytemnestra's intervention. She balked at murdering her children but otherwise shows little concern for them.

In mythological terms, the crimes of Aegisthus and Clytemnestra warrant punishment. But reality steadfastly refuses to correspond to mythology. Even if there is justice in the cause, revenge is a tawdry reality. The murder of Aegisthus is opportunistic and brutal. He is conducting a religious ceremony outside the city walls, and all Orestes and Pylades need to do is walk past where he can see them. The hospitable Aegisthus immediately invites the "most welcome, strangers" to join in the sacrifice and the ensuing feast.[32] As told by a later messenger (since violence is almost never shown directly on the Greek stage), Orestes strikes a savage blow as Aegisthus bends over the sacrifice, breaking his spine as if he were an animal: "Head down, his whole body convulsed, he gasped / to breathe, writhed with a high scream, and died in his blood."[33]

Electra plans the death of their mother, luring her to their farmhouse with the false claim that she has recently given birth. Her mother comes to check on her condition and make sacrifices to the gods in honor of the new child. She has clearly never visited her daughter's home before, and she expresses surprise at her poverty and sympathizes with her condition. In response to Electra's reproaches, she says simply, "I am not so happy / either, child, with what I have done or with myself."[34] Orestes does not want to kill his mother, but Electra orders him not to play the coward and fall into weakness. When Clytemnestra exposes her breast and clings to him, pleading for mercy, Orestes covers his eyes with his cloak and strikes out with his sword as Electra guides his hand.

Orestes and Electra don't correct the evil of the earlier murders, they repeat it. "Justice has claimed [Clytemnestra]," the mythical Dioscuri (Helen's brothers) note, "but you have not worked in justice."[35] Their actions are sordid and criminal, not heroic, and they are immediately beset by guilt and remorse at "this work of blood and corruption."[36] It is in their remorse that Orestes and Electra are most sympathetic and most pathetic. They seem to have believed that vengeance would set everything right in their lives. But it has not done so. Their mother bought herself a lover with their inheritance and gave to him the love that rightfully should have been theirs. But killing her has not restored the mother's love they never knew. It has not filled the gaping voids in their own hearts. They both are even more lost than they were before, and Clytemnestra's words apply equally to her children: "O god, how miserably my plans have all turned out."[37]

Orestes takes place six days after the murder of Clytemnestra. Orestes cannot face the hideous reality of his crime, any more than Raskolnikov will be able to do in Dostoevsky's *Crime and Punishment*. He falls ill, collapsed on a pallet in the anteroom of the palace, alternately raving and weakly lucid. Some token mention is made of the Furies, but it is clear that the forces attacking Orestes are psychological, not mythological. Or perhaps the better way to put it is that Orestes cannot bear the burden of a mythological past that has no visible connection with his sordid present. That is a gulf that cannot be bridged, and all apparent meaning lies on the far side of that gulf.

The people of Argos, urged on by Aegisthus's supporters and by Tyndareus, the father of Helen and Clytemnestra, have declared Orestes and Electra to be matricides and plan to decide their fate that very day in the assembly. Their sole hope lies in Menelaus, who has finally made his way home from Troy. Helen has been smuggled into the palace at night, lest she be stoned by those who lost their sons at Troy. But Menelaus makes a triumphant daylight entry hailed by the chorus for his "glory and success."[38]

Menelaus, the homeric hero, proves cautious, petty, and scheming. He listens, with expressions of concern but no commitment, to Orestes's plea that—out of love and gratitude for his dead brother, who led the expedition to restore Menelaus's honor—Menelaus should use his influence and power to sway the assembly in their favor. In the end, Menelaus does nothing—his eye is already on his brother's former throne—and the assembly condemns both Orestes and Electra; the sole concession is that they may kill themselves rather than be stoned to death.

At this point, chaos ensues. Pylades, who resolves to die with his friend rather than desert him, proposes that they murder Helen, thereby punishing Menelaus and winning the gratitude of all Argos and possibly a reprieve. Electra suggests that they also kidnap Hermione, the daughter of Menelaus and Helen, and hold her hostage to use as a bargaining chip and buy time. The initial revenge plot of mythology spins totally out of control. Orestes attempts to cut Helen's throat (though as the sword descends she magically disappears), and the three fugitives then drag Hermione to the roof of the palace, neutralizing Menelaus and an angry crowd below by threatening to kill her and set the palace in flames.

Remarkably, this standoff ends happily, in certainly the most bizarre *deus ex machina* conclusion in all Greek drama. Apollo, accompanied by Helen, whom he snatched from Orestes's sword, descends at last to deal with the consequences of his oracle commanding Orestes to avenge his father. He announces in rapid succession that Helen is now a goddess and will be enthroned forever in the sky; Menelaus is to remarry and reign as king in Sparta; Electra will marry Pylades; and Orestes, who will reign in Argos, is to marry Hermione, "the girl against whose throat [his] sword now lies."[39] It is a Gilbert and Sullivan moment. "Let each one go to his appointed place," says Apollo.[40] Electra and Pylades embrace, Orestes lays down his sword, and Menelaus bids a hearty farewell to Helen, while handing Hermione over to Orestes as his betrothed. The chorus offers a final song of triumph and everyone files off stage.

The bitter irony in this absurdist ending cannot be missed. Apollo does not bridge the gap between myth and reality; he widens it. His intervention is a fantasy wish fulfillment that attacks the traditions of tragic drama at their core. As William Arrowsmith notes, Euripides "deliberately inverted the *deus ex machina* to show precisely that no solution was possible; not even a god could halt the momentum of these forces in their sweep toward inevitable disaster. . . . The discord outlasts both the coda and the concert."[41]

Yet there is a hint of harmony in this play, to be found in the genuine love and devotion that the three alienated, rejected delinquents show for one another. No such loyalty is found among the greatest generation that fought at Troy. "My poor father," Orestes laments, "even in his grave, deserted by his friends."[42] But Pylades refuses to desert his friend and is willing to die with him. Orestes and Electra share "loving words," and "sweet embraces," as they touchingly care for and comfort one another.[43] Real life may bear no relation to the irrational hopes nurtured by the mythic tradition. The degenerate offspring of Homer may not be able to align right motives and right actions with an elusive, perhaps illusory, scheme of divine justice. But they can reaffirm their vital connection to one another. "Love is all we have," concludes Orestes, "the only way that each can help the other."[44] Perhaps it is, in the end, enough.

But is tragedy still possible in such a diminished, chaotic universe? Recall Henry James's famous, and only partly tongue-in-cheek, list of items lacking in American life as fodder for a novelist: "No sovereign, no court, no personal loyalty, no aristocracy, no church, no clergy, no army, no diplomatic service, no country gentlemen, no palaces, no castles, nor manors, nor old country-houses, nor parsonages, nor thatched cottages, nor ivied ruins; no cathedrals, nor abbeys, nor little Norman churches; no great Universities nor public schools—no Oxford, nor Eton, nor Harrow; no literature, no novels, no museums, no pictures, no political society, no sporting class—no Epsom nor Ascot!"[45] We can hear, through the millennia, Euripides muttering to himself about contemporary Athens: "No Zeus, no Apollo, no Hermes; no Theseus, nor Perseus, nor Heracles; no Minotaur, no Medusa, no Twelve Labors, no Golden Fleece; no heroic code, nor divine scheme of justice; no Troy, nor rocky Ithaca, nor sandy Pylos; no Helen, nor Achilles, no Ajax, nor Odysseus; no bronze-greaved Achaeans; no black-hulled ships; no wine-dark sea." Yet, just as James would create novels by introducing his American characters to the artificial, seductive world of Europe, Euripides creates tragedy by introducing his contemporary characters to the artificial, seductive world of the Greek tradition and finding therein basic truths about human nature and the human condition. James's three greatest novels, *The Portrait of a Lady*, *The Ambassadors*, and *The Golden Bowl*, are fruits of the former encounter. Euripides's three greatest tragedies, *Medea*, *Hippolytus*, and *The Bacchae*, are fruits of the latter.

SEX, LIES, AND MURDER

The central conflict in *Medea* is straightforward. Jason has decided to abandon his foreign wife, by whom he has two children, and marry instead the virgin daughter of the king of Corinth. Medea reacts with bitterness and rage, and she delivers a marvelous speech, often anthologized in feminist works, about the injustices to which women are subjected: they must buy themselves a master, in the guise of a husband, who has total dominion over their bodies, their fortunes, and their lives; they must adapt themselves to the manners and behavior of their new household; if they are lucky and careful, they may live in modest harmony; if not, their home becomes a living hell. Whenever a husband tires of his wife, moreover, he will seek company elsewhere, whereas she remains utterly trapped. Men suggest that women have it easy staying at home while they do the fighting in war. "How wrong they are!" says Medea. "I would very much rather stand / Three times in the front of battle than bear one child."[46]

Medea laments that her position is particularly difficult because, as a foreigner, she has no family to support her, "no mother or brother, nor any relation / With whom I can take refuge in this sea of woe."[47] At this point, the audience knows that

Euripides has more in mind than a feminist manifesto. Her indictment of Greek patriarchy does not lack force. But this is no ordinary wronged woman. Medea has no family to turn to because she betrayed them to Jason, and she has no brother to defend her because she murdered him in a particularly grisly fashion.

Euripides's audience is thoroughly familiar with the story of Jason and his quest for the Golden Fleece, a foundational myth (like those of Theseus, Perseus, and Heracles) that predates the Trojan War. Jason was the rightful heir to the throne of Iolchis. Pelias, who had deposed Jason's father, promised to cede him the throne if he would first retrieve the famous Golden Fleece, guarded by a sleepless dragon in the barbarian land of Colchis. Jason recruited the finest youth in all Greece to join his quest. In its surviving version, the story was set down in the *Argonautica* by Apollonius of Rhodes in the third century.

Medea, the daughter of King Aeëtes of Colchis, fell passionately in love with Jason and helped him fulfill the various tasks set by her father, including plowing a field with fire-breathing oxen, sowing dragon's teeth (that sprouted into warriors) in the plowed field, and drugging the otherwise sleepless dragon that guarded the fleece. In exchange, Jason promised to marry Medea and take her with him. Chased by her father's fleet, they avoided capture only because Medea killed and dismembered her brother, Absyrtus, and scattered the parts in the ocean. Her father stopped to collect them for burial. That is why Medea cannot return to her family and has no brother to protect her.

Back in Iolchis, the elderly King Pelias still refused to yield the throne. Medea convinced his daughters that she knew the secret of restoring his youth. She took an old ram, cut him into pieces and boiled them in a cauldron, out of which sprang a young ram. When the sisters did the same with their father, however, no young Pelias sprang forth, and the people of Iolchis drove Jason and Medea from their land.

The character of Medea, then, is fixed in the audience's mind before the play even starts. She combines a fierce sexual attraction for Jason with complete egocentrism and an utter lack of moral constraint. She herself remarks that, although in many ways a woman is weak and defenseless, "when once she is wronged in the matter of love, / No other soul can hold so many thoughts of blood."[48] The traditional suppression of violence and aggression in women causes those forces, when they do break forth, to do so with shocking ferocity.

Jason tries to calm her fury, but in a manner calculated only to augment it. He tells her that she has received more from their relationship than he did because she, a barbarian, is now able to live in civilized Greece under the rule of law, and, besides, he has made her famous for her cleverness. He explains, moreover, that his new marriage would have benefited her and their children by putting him in a position to provide for them and "draw the families together and all be happy."[49] But Medea has spoiled it with her sexual jealousy and her threats, and, as a result, the king has ordered her and the children to be banished.

Medea then recognizes that she must dissemble and appear meek and submissive to achieve her revenge. She beguiles the king to delay her sentence of exile for one day, a day that will prove fatal to him and his daughter. She arranges a secure refuge in Athens. She even pretends to her husband that he has convinced her that what he is doing is wise—"I should have helped you in these plans of yours, / Have joined in the wedding, stood by the marriage bed, / Have taken pleasure in attendance on your bride"—and that she now seeks only to allow her children to remain in Corinth while she is banished.[50] To that end, she sends the children to her husband's fiancée with gifts of a beautiful robe and gold diadem, hoping to warm her heart.

The gifts, however, are poisoned, and both the fiancée and the king, who tries to strip them from his daughter, die a horrible death. Medea then kills her own children, leaving Jason utterly destroyed, with no bride and no heirs. In the process, she has destroyed her own happiness, but that is secondary to her need for vengeance. In a remarkable soliloquy (with no counterpart in earlier drama, and no imitator until Shakespeare), Medea verbalizes her internal struggle between a mother's love and a wronged wife's fury.

> Oh, arm yourself in steel, my heart! Do not hang back
> From doing this fearful and necessary wrong.
> Oh, come, my hand, poor wretched hand, and take the sword,
> Take it, step forward to this bitter starting point,
> And do not be a coward, do not think of them,
> How sweet they are, and how you are their mother.[51]

Medea may be the most shocking and subversive of all Euripides's plays, and it is hardly surprising that it initially won only a third-place finish. Medea justifies her revenge in terms of the moral code of Homer, which the Greeks of the time still widely accepted: she wants to be "one who can hurt my enemies and help my friends; / For the lives of such persons are most remembered."[52] Medea envisions herself as a tragic hero, an Ajax or an Achilles, and is concerned only with shunning any sign of weakness: "Do I want to let go / My enemies unhurt and be laughed at for it? / I must face this thing."[53] Medea sees only "the wrong they dare to do me" and must therefore wreak a terrible revenge to establish her status and command respect.[54] The sufferings of the king, his daughter, and her own innocent children are all secondary to Medea's perverted ends, just as Ajax would have slaughtered the Greek commanders in a fit of wounded pride, and just as Achilles let thousands of Achaean warriors go to their deaths as he nursed his quarrel with Agamemnon. Even "my grief is gain," she tells Jason, "when you cannot mock it."[55] This is what the "heroic ideal" brings us to, Euripides seems to say. The fragile ties we have to one another are broken by pride and destructive passion.

Jason calls Medea a "woman most utterly loathed by the gods."[56] So should she be. Yet, at the end of the play, Medea appears above the house, with the bodies of her two children, in a chariot drawn by dragons. Just how this was accomplished on the Greek stage is unclear. The important thing is that Medea appears in a place traditionally reserved for the gods. She has become, through the ferocity of her passion and her indifference to human suffering, like a god, an aspect of human life that must be reckoned with and somehow appeased, just as Aphrodite will be in *Hippolytus* and Dionysus in *The Bacchae*. Medea's effective divinity on stage is a repudiation of traditional Greek mythology and yet, at the same time, a profound psychological recognition of the overpowering and implacable forces that so often make human life a misery.

Phaedra, one of four principal characters in *Hippolytus*, is also consumed by an overpowering and implacable force. Aphrodite has taken offense that Hippolytus, the son of Theseus and the deceased Amazon queen Hippolyta, disdains her. Hippolytus has a "maiden soul"[57] and worships Artemis, goddess of the hunt and of virginal young girls. He spends his time in the forests and fields with like-minded young men and "will none of the bed of love nor marriage."[58] For this offense to her honor, Aphrodite will destroy him, using Phaedra, the current wife of Theseus, as her instrument. Aphrodite announces her intentions at the outset of the play and brusquely dismisses (in words that could easily have been spoken by Medea) any concern that Phaedra will necessarily suffer as well.

> Her suffering does not weigh in the scale so much
> that I should let my enemies go untouched
> escaping payment of that retribution
> that honor demands that I have.[59]

Aphrodite inspires in Phaedra a passionate sexual attraction for her stepson. Phaedra is determined to keep silent, preferring to waste away and die rather than to act dishonorably. But her old nurse extracts the secret from her and then undertakes to act as go-between with Hippolytus. Phaedra both fears and desires disclosure to Hippolytus. Hence, although she protests, she lets the nurse act in her stead. Hippolytus is predictably shocked and outraged and delivers an uncontrolled diatribe against the wickedness of women that Phaedra overhears. Fearing that he will betray her to Theseus, despite promising the nurse not to do so, Phaedra hangs herself and leaves a note claiming that Hippolytus had raped her. Theseus banishes Hippolytus, ignoring his claims of innocence (which are hindered by his vow of silence), and calls down upon him the curse of his mythical father, the sea-god Poseidon. As Hippolytus is driving his chariot, a bull emerges from the sea, terrifying the horses. Hippolytus is thrown from the chariot and dragged to his death. Artemis ends the play by telling Theseus of Phaedra's false letter and Hippolytus's innocence. She expresses her regret at the loss of her acolyte but notes that she was powerless to prevent the actions of another god. The only consolation she offers is that she will find some mortal dear to Aphrodite and punish him in recompense.

The bookend speeches of the two gods are hardly necessary to the human action of the play. The characters and their motivations are perfectly plausible without any divine intervention. Phaedra, concerned with maintaining her own honor at all costs, falsely accuses another and forever dishonors herself. The nurse, concerned with finding a pragmatic solution for her mistress, destroys where she most wishes to help. Hippolytus, who deliberately cuts himself off from the full range of human emotion and experience, is cursed for a sexual crime wholly antithetical to his nature. Theseus, the man of action, kills his son and his own reputation in a rush to judgment. Each of the characters acts out of ignorance, with effects totally different from those they intended. Their combined flaws—moral, emotional, and intellectual—lead to the tragic outcome, in which two lives are lost and two others forever blighted.

But the role of the gods is still critical to the overall impact of the play and the sense that forces we do not understand and cannot control conspire to shatter us. That is the essence of Euripides's tragic vision. There is no central tragic hero in *Hippolytus*, as there was in *Medea*. But there is a central force, sexual passion, that engulfs and destroys all the characters. Whether Aphrodite is really a "god" or just the embodiment of a force beyond human control is a question Euripides leaves to the philosophers. In terms of her impact on human life and her indifference to human suffering, Aphrodite is real enough. Human ignorance and human weakness are readily overwhelmed by such a force. Yet, as he lies dying, Hippolytus forgives his father and absolves him of all guilt. "I sorrow for you in this more than myself," he says.[60] In that forgiveness, in that still-unbroken connection between father and son, Euripides finds human value in an inhuman world.

THE WAGES OF REPRESSION

Euripides wrote *The Bacchae* in Macedon shortly before his death in 406. It was presented posthumously in Athens, along with *Iphigenia in Aulis* and the lost *Alcmaeon in Corinth*. The acclaim that had so often eluded Euripides during his lifetime was fully accorded these plays, which won first place at the City Dionysia festival. *The Bacchae* is generally regarded as Euripides's masterwork. But its theme is hardly what one would expect of this irreverent iconoclast: "Let me go the customary way," the chorus intones, "the timeless, honored, beaten path of those who walk / with reverence and awe beneath the sons of heaven."[61] The play is conservative in tenor and consistently confounds those who see Euripides as an atheist, for even if the god Dionysus is reduced to metaphorical and psychological terms (which he readily can be), the reader still cannot escape the deep religious feeling—of reverence, awe, and humility—that pervades this work.

It is almost as if Euripides decided to take stock at the end of his life and feared the wages of his earlier impiety. Almost, but no; Euripides is always more subtle than that. *The Bacchae* poses the same basic question with which Euripides grappled in all his plays: Where is wisdom to be found? The answer he offers to that question has not changed in its fundamentals, even if some of the coloring is different.

The play opens with the god Dionysus insisting that he receive due recognition and honors from the citizens of Thebes, who must be initiated into his mysteries and observe his rites. Dionysus has one of the more outlandish birth stories among the Olympian gods. His mother, Semele, was visited secretly and in darkness by Zeus. At the urging of the jealous Hera, disguised as an old beggar woman, Semele extracted a promise from Zeus to grant her one wish. When he did so, she asked to see him in his full glory as a god. Since mortals cannot bear such a sight, she was consumed in lightning and flame. But Zeus rescued his prenatal son and sewed him into his own thigh, from which the god Dionysus was subsequently born.

Dionysus is the only one of the original Olympian deities with a mortal parent. He is portrayed as beardless, soft, and effeminate, dressed in a fawn-skin and carrying a thyrsus (a fennel wand topped with ivy leaves). But this twice-born, languid, androgynous god is at once "most terrible, and yet most gentle, to mankind."[62] He is the god of wine and intoxication, of theater and disguise. Most fundamentally, though, he is the god of the collective life force itself that spills over into sex and joyous exuberance on the one hand and uncontrollable violence and frenzy on the other. His female acolytes (the "Bacchae" or maenads) are "endowed with mantic powers" and dance for hours in the forest.[63] They are shown alternately suckling baby wolves and gazelles and tearing grown animals apart with their bare hands and devouring the flesh.

It is hardly surprising, then, that Dionysus is unwelcome in Thebes. He is a foreign and destabilizing influence for any civilized society. He represents forces that must be carefully controlled and channeled if not fully extirpated. But the situation is complicated by the fact that the former ruler of Thebes, Cadmus, is the father of Semele and hence, technically, the grandfather of Dionysus. The current king, Pentheus, is the son of Semele's sister, and therefore Dionysus's first cousin. Cadmus urges Pentheus to accept Dionysus as a god, whether he actually is or not, "for Semele will seem / to be the mother of a god, and this confers / no small distinction on our family."[64] But Pentheus angrily rejects this "madness."[65] Semele, he says, was blasted by lightning for her lie that she lay with Zeus, and any child in her womb was destroyed with her. Dionysus, then, is simply an imposter. Worse, he is a source of "obscene disorder"[66] and has induced the women of Thebes, including Pentheus's mother, Agave, and her sisters "to frisk in mock ecstasies among the thickets on the mountain."[67]

In *As You Like It*, Shakespeare depicts the forest of Arden as an idyllic refuge from the corruption of court and city life to which his characters repair to restore their souls and find fellowship and love. The mountain thickets outside Thebes are a much-darker place, where the amoral stirrings of nature overwhelm the slender restraints of reason and the rule of law, and we realize how thin is the veneer of civilization that we struggle to maintain. In the forest of Dionysus, we find unconstrained instinct, a celebration of the sensual, an elimination of the boundaries of individuation and conscious thought, an expansion beyond the everyday limitations of class, gender, and age.

Pentheus, however, is determined to uphold the restraints of self and the *polis*. Like his cousin Dionysus, Pentheus is young and beardless. But Pentheus is the self-appointed emblem of order and the rule of law. He believes that reason can and should control irrational behavior and eliminate customs and practices that have no place in a civilized society. He lays violent hands upon Dionysus and seeks to imprison him. He threatens to send soldiers to overwhelm and corral the

Bacchae. But of course Dionysus is a god and cannot be constrained by man. The chains fall from his arms. He destroys Pentheus's palace with an earthquake. Most important of all, he preys on Pentheus's own "excited and disturbed" fascination with the very rites and mysteries that he would suppress.[68]

Dionysus convinces Pentheus to don women's clothes and steal forth into the mountains to observe the Bacchae firsthand. When he arrives and climbs a tree for a better look, however, Dionysus exposes Pentheus as an unbeliever who has mocked their holy mysteries. The frenzied maenads uproot the tree and literally tear Pentheus to pieces. His own mother, "foaming at the mouth, and her crazed eyes rolling with frenzy," is oblivious to his identity and his cries for mercy.[69] When the "pitiful remains lie scattered," she picks up his head and impales it on her thyrsus, believing it to be that of a mountain lion she has hunted with her bare hands.[70] She descends the mountain in procession with her sisters and the others, "gloating over her grisly prize."[71]

In a scene of utmost subtlety and pathos, Cadmus gradually brings Agave out of her trance and leads her to recognize, with steadily increasing horror, what she has done. Her slow awakening, even as she averts her eyes from the head she carries until finally forced to confront it, is chilling. "All our house / the god has utterly destroyed," Cadmus laments, as he gazes at the remains of his only male heir, the child who hugged him, touched his chin, and called him grandfather.[72]

The lesson Cadmus draws from these events is that one must believe in and honor the gods. But Euripides is not embracing traditional religion, at least not in a simplistic way. Euripides deliberately chooses a wild and outlandish myth—the birth story of Dionysus—to make into a talisman of belief for his characters. Although the literal terms of that myth are impossible to credit, the reality underlying it cannot be denied. Dionysus, the god of theater and the mask, allows us to lose ourselves in an illusion that somehow conveys truth.

Pentheus was killed because he presumed to deny and even mock a force that he thought antithetical to rational order and civilized behavior, a force that cannot be suppressed without devastating consequences. In this, Euripides anticipates Freud, and particularly his book *Civilization and Its Discontents*. Freud's thesis is that the growth of civilization requires men, and even more so women, to suppress many of their most basic instincts, which accordingly turn inward and find their expression in individual neuroses and mental conflicts, as well as "mass delusions," among which he counts the religions of humankind.

Euripides recognizes that men and women must find outlets for their instincts, which will otherwise tear them and their society apart. Escape from everyday existence must, paradoxically, be part of everyday existence. Otherwise the tensions mount too high and the rules of society, the conventions of daily life, cannot fully constrain us. At times we must escape from our own selves, in the theater, in the rites and mysteries of religious worship, and in a communion with our animal natures that can be at once most gentle and most terrible. Dionysus represents a source of deep power and strength, both physical and spiritual. He is as liberating and exhilarating as music, dance, and wine; he is as terrifying as mass frenzy that ends in a riot of violence.

The goal for Euripides, as for his contemporary, Socrates, is self-knowledge. But Socrates seeks such knowledge through the application of reason alone. Socrates even believes that to know the good is to do the good; that is, that rational thought is sufficiently powerful to overcome emotion, instinct, and the other nonrational determinants of human behavior. In *The Bacchae*, Euripides decisively rejects that view. Man has a double nature as citizen and savage, as civilized and wild. Pentheus cannot change that double nature any more than he can wage war with a god. "You do not know the limits of your strength," Dionysus tells Pentheus.[73] "You do not know who you are."[74] Pentheus has no appreciation of his own limitations or the forces that excite and disturb him and lead him to his own destruction.

Where, then, is wisdom to be found? The ubiquitous prophet Tiresias tells us that "we are the heirs of customs and traditions / hallowed by age and handed down to us / by our fathers. No quibbling logic can topple *them*, / whatever subtleties this clever age invents."[75] This seems a highly conservative message. The archskeptic, Euripides, the cutting-edge sophistic thinker, in the year of his death embraces ancient myth as the embodiment of a higher truth that eludes rational thought. He does so in a play that is itself a throwback to the tragedies of his great predecessors, a play with a tight, formal structure and a vital role for the chorus.

But this is no sudden turn for Euripides. As Bruno Snell explains, Euripidean man still "stands alone in a precarious and confusing world" without fixed standards to guide him.[76] Myth does not present us with a picture of divine order; to the contrary, it underscores the senseless disorder of the universe and the random violence that have been constant themes in Euripides's plays. Yet it also casts the whole in the light of beauty, just as the "customs and traditions / hallowed by age"[77] allow us to "garner day by day the good of life."[78] Euripides's core values remain the same: moderation, kindness, and the courage to endure—not the intransigent courage of the Sophoclean hero, confident in his or her heroic ideal of right conduct, but the courage to sustain a myth, a mass delusion, of order and civilization and human connection.

> All is change; all yields its place and goes;
> to persevere, trusting in what hopes he has,
> is courage in a man.[79]

Chapter 6

THE INQUIRIES OF HERODOTUS OF HALICARNASSUS

The first great prose work in the Western canon opens with the following lines:

> Herodotus of Halicarnassus here presents his research so that human events do not fade with time. May the great and wonderful deeds—some brought forth by the Hellenes, others by the barbarians—not go unsung; as well as the causes that led them to make war on each other.[1]

The parallels with Homer are deliberate; the differences, equally so. Both seek to tell of the deeds of men in warfare, so that their memory will be preserved. Both tell of a war between Greeks and the non-Greek peoples of Asia Minor. (The former are called Hellenes by Herodotus and their land Hellas. The latter he signifies by the word *barbaros*, which simply meant those who do not speak Greek but instead use unintelligible foreign words sounding to Greek ears like the drone of *bar bar*.) Both treat the non-Greek, *barbarian* opponents in this war with remarkable sympathy and nuance. Both see war as a constant in human life and yet celebrate the quiet moments of peace as well. The words Herodotus gives to Croesus, king of Lydia—"no one could be so foolish as to prefer war to peace: in peace sons bury fathers; in war fathers bury sons"[2]—echo throughout his work. Yet Homer could easily have given those same words to Priam, king of Troy.

But Herodotus is not the "prose Homer," as claimed by his native city of Halicarnassus (on the Ionian coast of what is now western Turkey, a day's drive from Troy). Homer starts in the middle of the action and focuses on a few critical days of rage and combat. Herodotus wants to explore the causes of the war and hence delves deeply into the historical background of both antagonists. Homer's Greeks and Trojans are largely indistinguishable; Hector and Priam appear to share the same customs, values, and gods as Achilles and Agamemnon. Herodotus, by contrast, repeatedly stresses the unique culture of the Persians from Asia Minor, who already control most of the known world and are seeking to add mainland Greece to their empire. For Herodotus, moreover, pyramids, bridges, canals, and monuments are themselves great and wonderful deeds to be celebrated in his work. So, too, are the unique stories, traditions, and customs that make up each ethnic group and unite them as a people.

Perhaps most significantly, Herodotus nowhere invokes the Muses to sing through him the story of the Persian invasion. He relies upon *historiē* (research or inquiries) to construct his narrative. Herodotus must forge his own understanding out of myths, tales, conjectures, oral traditions, inscriptions, eyewitness testimony, and, where necessary, "through hearsay alone."[3] He weighs the evidence, gives alternative explanations, and acknowledges his own uncertainty and ignorance. He even raises the problem of the reliability of his sources: "I may be obliged to tell what is said, but I am not at all obliged to believe it. And you may consider this statement to be valid for my entire work."[4] There is no omniscient, god-inspired bard narrating the *Histories*; it is a thoroughly human and self-consciously fallible work.

Many have suggested that Herodotus combines an *Odyssey* with an *Iliad*, though that is also said, perhaps with more justice, of Virgil's *Aeneid*. In the first four books (of a work divided into nine books by later scholars), Herodotus uses the expansion of Persian power as a device for a tour of the known world, while the final five books focus more specifically on the Persian invasion of Greece. His principal narrative covers a period of almost seventy years, from the defeat of Croesus in 546 by Cyrus the Great, founder of the Persian Empire, to the final repulse of the Persians by the Greeks in 479. But his interests and aims extend far beyond the arc of the narrative itself. As he rather mildly explains, "My account goes searching from the start for extra material."[5] Nothing is outside the scope of his interests, and he takes obvious delight in telling a good story or describing a curious practice or retailing some marvel of which he has heard. His seeming digressions irritate some readers (particularly his immediate successor, Thucydides). For Herodotus, they are not digressions but building blocks in his overarching and comprehensive effort to understand the world in which the Persians built an empire that so inevitably and so dramatically clashed with the Greek desire for autonomy. His great themes—East versus West, tyranny versus freedom, the corruption of power, and, most of all, the mutability of human fortune—are constantly reinforced by the stories he tells and the customs and beliefs he describes.

Herodotus's inspiration springs not from the heroic age sung by Homer but from the intellectual milieu of sixth- and fifth-century Greece, in which ideas were rapidly changing and traditional mythology was being replaced by a more rigorous and systematic attempt at understanding the world. Herodotus shares many of his themes with the great trio of Greek tragedians. He was a friend and younger contemporary of Sophocles, who borrowed material from Herodotus for both *Oedipus Rex* and *Antigone*. Even more so, Herodotus is literally at home among the natural philosophers from Ionia (along the Aegean shore of Asia Minor, where Halicarnassus and other Greek colonies flourished). Thales, Anaximander, Anaximenes, and others from nearby Miletus wrote prose works (fragments of which survive) on cosmology, astronomy, philosophy, and the nascent physical sciences. Hecataeus of Miletus even attempted a geography of the world.

Herodotus shares with these writers the project of using prose for the serious investigation of the world. But he wholly transcends them in the length of his work, the scope of his interests, and the subtlety of his narrative. Herodotus moves Western thought from an oral tradition of myth and poetry into the realm of prose as the medium for the transfer of knowledge. He was rightly called, by Cicero, the "father of history." Indeed, less than a century after the death of Herodotus, Aristotle in his *Poetics* had already adopted the word *historiē* to indicate something akin to our modern sense of "history." Herodotus gave birth to a new and unique form of inquiry—as Montaigne would later do with his *essais* (or "attempts")—and all future writers laboring under that rubric have had to come to terms with him, either through imitation or rebellion.

HERODOTUS, THE TRAVELER

Little is known of Herodotus's life. The focus of his writing was on the world around him rather than upon himself. His "biography" is mostly a reconstruction after sifting through tall tales and slanders (as he himself so often had to do in writing the *Histories*). Herodotus was born around 484 in the port city of Halicarnassus, in Caria, a region of Ionia. Greeks from Athens and the Peloponnese had established a number of significant colonies in this area, including Miletus and Ephesus. These Ionian cities have through the centuries been battered and subjugated any number of times by greater powers, starting with Lydia, then Persia, Athens, Sparta, Persia again, Macedon, the Roman Empire, the Byzantine Empire, and the Ottoman Empire, all the way down to the early twentieth century when, following World War I, Greece tried to seize them again in pursuit of a deluded idea of restoring the "greater Greece" that existed 2,500 years earlier, and the new Turkish state responded with massacres and mass deportations. The measure of human suffering in this one small area of the Ionian coast is incalculable. Halicarnassus is now Bodrum, a Turkish beach town overrun in the summer months by vacationing Germans and Brits.

Herodotus came from a prominent family of mixed Greek and Carian heritage. At the time of his birth, Halicarnassus was ruled by the warrior queen Artemisia, whom Herodotus would later make famous in his work. At some point, Herodotus was involved in a revolt against her grandson and spent a period of exile on the nearby island of Samos. There may have been a later, more successful revolt. But, for whatever reason, Herodotus was no longer welcome in his home city and embarked on a series of travels, probably earning his living through trade, but mainly gathering material for his life's work, which he began writing around 450.

"Many cities of men he saw and learned their minds," as Homer said of Odysseus.[6] Herodotus traveled to various points along the Black Sea coast, throughout Asia Minor, to Persia, Babylon, Phoenicia, Egypt, North Africa, and into Europe, including mainland Greece, Macedon, and Italy. By 447, he was in Athens, where he gave readings from his works and was awarded a grant by the Athenian assembly. Sophocles and Euripides were then both active in the theater, though their greatest plays lay ahead. The length of his stay in Athens is subject to dispute. He also visited Sparta (known to Herodotus as Lacedaemon), Delphi, and Olympia. There is a nice, if likely apocryphal anecdote of his giving a reading of the *Histories* during the Olympic Games to rapt attention by an audience that included the young Thucydides. Appropriately, though, there is a variant on the story, in which he declined to start his reading until clouds covered the blazing sun and he had lost most of his audience. "Herodotus and his shade" became a catchphrase for a missed opportunity.

Herodotus later migrated to Thurii, a pan-Hellenic colony (aided by Athens but accepting settlers from anywhere in the Greek world) in southern Italy. The latest reference in the *Histories* that can be dated with any certainty is 430. He died sometime in the next decade, though whether in Thurii or at a Macedonian court where he received patronage, or whether he returned to Athens and died there in the plague during the early years of the Peloponnesian War, is a subject of conjecture and dispute.

What is known is that the *Histories* was his life's work and embraced the full scope of his interests and his insatiable curiosity. It was the repository for all his inquiries, thoughts, travels, reflections, and knowledge. In it, he rejects Hecataeus's map of the world—portrayed as a disc surrounded by the circular river "Ocean," with Europe and Asia in perfect symmetry—as too tidy and inconsistent with eyewitness accounts. Herodotus wants to know how things actually are, not how some philosopher thinks they should be. He charts the courses of rivers, describes canals, buildings, and monuments. He comments on weather patterns and their effect on health. He speculates (intelligently, if ultimately wrongly) on the possible causes of the Nile's annual flooding and the manner of building the pyramids. He tells of remarkable trees in India (presumably cotton trees) that produce wool "which surpass[es] sheep's wool in beauty."[7] He describes crocodiles, lions, hippopotamuses, and other strange creatures (sometimes accurately, sometimes quite amusingly not so), as well as noting "what they claim"[8] about mythological creatures such as the phoenix and winged serpents.

Geography, geology, zoology, meteorology, and engineering are all within the scope of his charter. But most of all, in the first four books, he is concerned with ethnography, a description of the various peoples of the world: their histories, customs, folk tales, food, clothing, drinking parties, and rituals for sacrifice. It is a discipline that Herodotus appears to have invented and that was not fully embraced again until the early twentieth century. Herodotus conveniently follows the Persian conquests (and defeats) as a means of covering the entire known world, and he pauses to say something about every nation and every people about whom he could obtain information, including, among others, Babylonians, Egyptians (to whom he devotes an entire book), Scythians, Libyans, Ethiopians, and Indians.

Herodotus takes it as a given that related customs must come from a common source, and he is constantly inquiring as to the origins of various practices and beliefs. He reports on an interesting attempt to determine whether the Phrygian or the Egyptian peoples were the earliest humans. In the seventh century, Psammetichos of Egypt put two newborn children in an isolated shepherd's hut and gave instructions that the shepherd should feed them and tend to their needs but that no one was to utter a word in their presence. When the children were two years of age, one of them began to cry out "*bekos*," which means "bread" in the Phrygian language, thereby establishing (at least to the satisfaction of the king) that the Phrygian language was the oldest language from which all others must originate and that, therefore, the Phrygian peoples were older than the Egyptians.[9]

Herodotus is particularly interested in religious observances and burial rights.

He offers a detailed description of Egyptian mummification, including the three different price options available.[10] He notes another experiment of sorts, this one conducted by Darius of Persia, in which he summoned a group of Greeks, who ritually burn their dead parents, and asked them how much money they would take instead to eat the bodies of their dead fathers. They answered that they would not do so for any amount of money. He then brought in a group of Kallatiai Indians, who consider it pious to eat their dead parents, and asked them how much money they would accept to burn them instead. The horrified Indians were outraged and demanded that the king not offend the gods with such a suggestion. "Well, then," Herodotus mildly comments, "that is how people think, and so it seems to me that Pindar was right when he said in his poetry that custom is king of all."[11] As he elsewhere explains, "If someone were to assign to every person in the world the task of selecting the best of all customs, each one, after thorough consideration, would choose those of his own people, so strongly do humans believe that their own customs are the best ones."[12] Herodotus's interest in, and broad tolerance of, the customs of all peoples was without precedent.

Marriage customs and sexual practices hold his most consistent interest; Herodotus knows what sells. In Agathyrsoi, he notes, males "share their women in common for the purposes of intercourse, in order that they will all be brothers to one another."[13] In Nasamones, "it is customary for [the] bride to have intercourse with all the guests at the feast in succession, and for each of these guests to then present a gift he has brought from home."[14] In Scythia, no virgin may marry until she has slain a male enemy.[15] In Lydia, daughters of the common people work as prostitutes to earn their dowries.[16] In Babylon, by contrast, wives were auctioned in the marketplace, and the money earned by the most desirable was then used as dowries in a reverse auction "to help marry off the unattractive and crippled."[17] Herodotus calls this "their finest custom" and laments that it is no longer observed.[18] He is critical, by contrast, of "the most disgusting of all Babylonian customs" by which every woman must, once in her life, sit in the sanctuary of Aphrodite and have intercourse with the first man to throw a silver coin into her lap.[19] Tall and beautiful women leave quickly, he explains, perhaps superfluously, but others must wait a long time to fulfill their obligation.

Herodotus's methodology, like his curiosity, is all-encompassing. "My entire account is governed by the rule that I write down precisely what I am told by everyone, just as I heard it."[20] He will distinguish "information for which I have certain knowledge"[21] or that is "the result of my own observation, judgment, and research."[22] But he will report other stories or explanations "just as I heard them,"[23] though sometimes prefacing or concluding them with qualifiers such as "though it sounds incredible to me,"[24] or "although I find it difficult to believe."[25] Sometimes he is dismissive—"I think they were talking total nonsense when they said this";[26] sometimes supportive—"which I, at any rate, found convincing";[27] and sometimes strictly neutral—"Whether or not this is true I do not really know; I am only writing what is said."[28]

At times he will give two or even three versions of the same event or explanations for the same phenomenon, either expressing his own preference for one or leaving it to the reader to "believe whichever one you prefer."[29] At times he seems naively credulous, as when he finds it "convincing" that Egyptians have particularly thick heads because they are shaved from childhood and the "bone then thickens with exposure to the sun," or when he accepts his fast-talking guide's suggestion that certain writing on the Great Pyramid of Cheops details the amount of radishes, onions, and garlic consumed by the workers who built it.[30] At other times he is more discerning, as when he rejects a suggestion that an island in the Nile delta floats, noting, "I myself did not see it float or move and frankly, whenever I hear that an island actually floats, I wonder if it can be true,"[31] or when he dismisses as nonsense a story, based on a set of statues of concubines without hands, that a king of Egypt raped his own daughter and his wife cut off the hands of the serving women who surrendered the girl to her father. Herodotus wryly notes: "I myself saw that the images' hands had simply fallen off with time and were still plainly visible to me at the feet of the statues."[32]

Herodotus's willingness to report precisely what is said is invaluable to the preservation of oral traditions and our understanding of the state of knowledge in his day. Sometimes it even provides a telling detail to confirm what Herodotus himself doubts, as when he does "not find credible, though someone else may," a claim that the Phoenicians circumnavigated Africa because they said that "the sun was on their right side as they went."[33] As they rounded the Cape of Good Hope in the Southern Hemisphere, the sun would in fact be on the Phoenicians' right side, thus supporting their account and underscoring Herodotus's faithful reportage.

Most important, though, Herodotus's methodology means he never has to pass up a good story, even as he distances himself from it. Herodotus is a master of the good story.

HERODOTUS, THE STORYTELLER

In Michael Ondaatje's *The English Patient*, the already-married Katharine Clifton (played in the movie by Kristin Scott Thomas) inflames the passions of a Hungarian geographer/archaeologist (Ralph Fiennes) at a camp in the Sahara Desert by telling the story of Kandaules, king of Lydia, who was so besotted with his wife that he wanted to show her off naked to his trusted bodyguard, Gyges, to convince Gyges that she was the most beautiful woman in the world. Gyges resisted, but Kandaules would not be deterred, and he positioned Gyges behind the door in her bedroom one night to watch her undress. She saw Gyges when he later tried to slip from the room, and the next morning confronted him with a choice: either die for the affront to her decency or kill Kandaules, have her as a wife, and become king of Lydia.

Needless to say, Gyges became king of Lydia and married the freshly widowed queen. Things turn out less well for Katharine and her explorer/lover, despite the fact that he carries with him, everywhere, a volume of Herodotus, in which he pastes photos and drawings and scribbles innumerable notes. Herodotus's history of the world reduces to the history of his own life and, ultimately, to the stories swirling in his consciousness.

Aristotle called Herodotus a *mythologus*, a teller of tales. And so he is. He collects oral tales and presents them in an utterly spellbinding way. The impossibly beautiful Katharine, standing in the light of a campfire on a desert night, telling an ancient story that would become in part her own, is a fitting image of the power of the mythologus. It is a power that some later historians found antithetical to their mission, and they dubbed Herodotus "the father of lies." We can only be grateful that Herodotus took a broader, more inclusive approach to his historiē.

The story of Kandaules and Gyges, one of the earliest in the book, is followed by a veritable *Arabian Nights* scattered through the text. He tells of Arion, the lyre player, who was forced to jump overboard by sailors intent on his money but rode to shore on the back of a dolphin;[34] of a clever Egyptian thief who so outwitted and astounded the king that, instead of punishing him, the king gave him his daughter in marriage;[35] of Democedes of Croton, the reluctant physician to the Persian king Darius who so longed to return to his homeland that he convinced Darius to invade Greece so that he could lead a reconnaissance mission and then jump ship to seek refuge among his countrymen;[36] of Thrasyboulos, tyrant of Miletus, who advised a fellow tyrant on how best to maintain control of his city by walking through a grain field and cutting off any stalks that extended above the others;[37] of Peisistratos, who regained the tyranny of Athens in "the silliest scheme I've ever heard of," by dressing up a tall, beautiful peasant girl as the goddess Athena, placing her in a chariot, and having heralds proclaim that Athena herself was bringing Peisistratos back to his rightful place in the city;[38] and of Hermotimos, the eunuch, who, having obtained a position of influence, found the man who had castrated and sold him, lured him and his family by promising to treat him as well as he had treated Hermotimos, and exacted a grisly revenge.[39]

These and innumerable other stories punctuate the historical narrative. Some stories reinforce the moral themes in the book; some illuminate important characters. But others are just wonderful tales, which Herodotus delights in telling. One of my favorite stories combines all these elements. Amasis, sent by a brutal king to put down a rebellion among his Egyptian subjects, went over to the rebels. Summoned by the king's messenger, Amasis, who "was not at all a serious man,"[40] raised himself in the saddle, broke wind, and told the messenger to take that response back to the king. Upon further demand, he assured the messenger that "he was going to be there with the king forthwith and would be bringing others, too."[41] Once installed in the king's place, however, Amasis's subjects failed to pay him proper respect since he was not from a prominent family and had a reputation for riotous behavior. So he took a golden basin, broke it into pieces, and had the pieces reworked into a statue of a divinity and placed in a prominent location. When the Egyptians became accustomed to worshiping the statue, "he summoned them and revealed that the statue had come from the foot basin into which they had previously vomited, urinated, and placed their dirty feet, but now they were worshiping it with reverence. Then without further ado, he told them that he himself had turned out just like the foot basin: he had been a common man before, but now he was their king. And that is how he won over the Egyptians."[42]

HERODOTUS, THE MORALIST

Herodotus describes his overarching storyline as one of:

> recounting cities both lesser and greater, since many of those that were great long ago have become inferior, and some that are great in my own time were inferior before. And so, resting on my knowledge that human prosperity never remains constant, I shall make mention of both without discrimination.[43]

That "human prosperity never remains constant,"[44] or, alternatively translated, "human happiness never abides," is pretty much the definition of history for Herodotus. History is a narrative of changing fortunes, for better and for worse. Nothing remains as it is. The prosperity of individuals and states is either augmenting or falling. Stasis is the opposite of history.

This theme—or moral, if you will—is constantly reinforced not only in his narrative of events but also in many of the stories he chooses to tell. Perhaps the most important of these is the fictional encounter between Croesus, king of Lydia, and Solon, the great Athenian lawgiver who, after setting in place a series of reforms in 594–593 that would eventually lead to Athenian democracy, spent ten years traveling the world. The encounter is necessarily fictional because Solon was dead well before Croesus came to power in 560. Yet the dialogue between them is of critical importance in setting the stage for what follows. (Those who are shocked that Herodotus would manufacture a dialogue out of whole cloth should recall that "reconstructed" dialogue has been a staple of narrative histories down to the present day, and Herodotus, who is often vague on dates, may have genuinely believed that the two men could have crossed paths.)

Croesus had expanded his realm throughout Asia Minor. When Solon visited him at his magnificent capital at Sardis, Croesus was eager to display his great riches to the wise man. Croesus then prompted him by asking whether in his travels he had "seen anyone who surpasses all others in happiness and prosperity."[45] Solon, who was no flatterer, answered, "Tellus the Athenian,"[46] and explained that Tellus was a moderately well-off citizen of a famous city who had noble children, lived to see his grandchildren, and died in glory on the battlefield, where he was buried with great honors. Pressed for a second best, Solon cited the case of Cleobis and Biton, two young athletes of modest means who, when their mother needed to attend a festival at the shrine of Athena and the oxen were still in the field, hitched themselves to the cart and hauled her five miles to the sanctuary. There—in response to their mother's prayer that they be granted "the best thing a human being could have"—they fell asleep and never woke again.[47]

Croesus was annoyed at this disparagement of his own happiness, but Solon explained that "the gods are jealous of human prosperity and disruptive of our peace."[48] Great wealth will not protect us from misfortune, and no man can be judged happy until he is dead. "We must look to the end of every matter to see how it will turn out. God shows many people a hint of happiness and prosperity, only to destroy them utterly later."[49] Croesus would remember Solon's words in later days, when first his beloved son and then his entire kingdom were taken from him.

Solon's words, which echo throughout the book, take on a more fatalistic (and fantastic) tinge in the story of Polykrates, tyrant of Samos. Noting Polykrates's extraordinary good fortune, his ally Amasis (of the golden basin) wrote to him about the importance of occasional failure: "For I have never yet heard of anyone enjoying good fortune in all things who did not ultimately die in total disaster."[50] Amasis advised him to counterbalance his perpetual good fortune, and thereby appease the gods, by selecting his dearest and most valuable possession and throwing it away. Thinking the advice sound, Polykrates chose a cherished signet ring and had himself rowed far from shore, where he cast it into the sea. But the ring was swallowed by a huge, beautiful fish, which was in turn caught by a poor fisherman, who presented the fish as an offering to the king. When the fish was cut open for serving, there was the ring, restored to him. Learning of these events, Amasis immediately broke off their alliance, and Polykrates did indeed come to a bad end. He could not turn aside the disaster decreed by the gods.

This theme of changing fortune and cosmic balance, presented in terms of divine jealousy and retribution for *hubris*, is a constant in Greek thought. As Artabanos, who counsels Xerxes against invading Greece, warns: "The god strikes with his thunderbolt those creatures that tower above the rest, and does not permit them to be so conspicuous, while those who are small do not at all provoke him."[51] Yet equally important, at least in Herodotus, is the notion that men are driven to their fate by forces they cannot evade. Xerxes himself has second thoughts about his invasion, but he is visited with dreams warning him that, if he fails to campaign at once, "as high and mighty as you have become in a short time, so low will you fall again and just as quickly."[52] Artabanos dismisses the dreams as mere reflections of "what one is thinking about during the day."[53] Yet Xerxes knows their truth: stasis is impossible; if his empire is not to be destroyed from within, he must direct those internal forces toward its expansion. Artabanos may be right that "it would be evil to teach the heart to always pursue more than it already has,"[54] but such was the fate of the Persian kings and of all those who would conquer and rule over their fellow men.

ORACLES, OMENS, AND DREAMS

Herodotus is remarkably subtle on the subject of religion. He notes with apparent approval that the Persians, unlike the Hellenic Greeks, "do not believe that the gods have human qualities."[55] Even for the Greeks, he explains, "the origin of each of the gods, or whether they always existed, and what they look like: all of this was unknown until just recently—only yesterday, so to speak."[56] Noting accurately that Hesiod and Homer "lived no more than 400 years before my time," Herodotus credits them as "the poets who composed for the Hellenes the theogony, assigned to the gods their epithets, defined their particular honors and skills, and described what they look like."[57] In other words, they simply made it up. They provided colorful trappings and stories for an underlying religion that transcends any particular culture. "I believe that all people understand these things equally," proclaims Herodotus.[58] The particular form taken by religious observance is simply one more aspect of his all-encompassing ethnography. It tells us a great deal about the people being studied but very little about the gods.

Yet Herodotus is undoubtedly pious. He decries sacrilege and the mockery of religious customs. He repeatedly declines to reveal the details of secret religious ceremonies. He tells stories of divine vengeance for the sacking of temples and other shrines. In part, this seeming piety is simply a reflection of his respect for different cultures. But he clearly means it when he asserts that "the gods manifest their resentment against humans who execute vengeance violently and excessively,"[59] and he evidently shares Solon's belief that "the gods are jealous of human prosperity and disruptive of our peace."[60] Herodotus, however, manages to infuse his work with a more generic, generalized sense of the divine, while avoiding any offense to his Greek patrons and audience.

Greek religion is itself a complicated subject, with its focus on rituals, festivals, and sacrifices rather than doctrines. Even the Olympic Games and other pan-Hellenic festivals had strong religious overtones, and truces were rigorously observed to allow warring Greek peoples to attend together in peaceful competition. Oracles and other shrines were also important and were regularly consulted. The oracle at Delphi was the most famous, but there were perhaps a dozen others in the Greek-speaking world. Omens and dreams were taken seriously by Greeks and Persians alike, who made critical military decisions with their guidance.

To say that Herodotus takes these portents with a grain of salt would be too strong. But he does manage to have it both ways by "writing what is said" without necessarily endorsing any miraculous predictions. In Herodotus, many reported oracles prove true, but others are calculatingly ambiguous, so as to prove correct on either outcome. For example, when Croesus was wondering whether to challenge the growing might of Persia, he first tested many oracles to determine which was the most accurate. Settling on Delphi, which he lavished with gifts, he was told "that if Croesus were to wage war against the Persians, he would destroy a great empire."[61] The oracle proved true, but the empire he destroyed was his own.

Herodotus notes instances in which the oracle at Delphi succumbed to bribes, and other points where the oracle simply shifted with the changing political winds during the Persian Wars. Mardonios, the war-hungry cousin of Xerxes, collected numerous oracles regarding the proposed invasion of Greece but suppressed any unfavorable ones, reciting "only those that predicted the most fortunate outcomes."[62] Omens, too, can be ambiguous, as when an eclipse of the sun was hastily reinterpreted by Persian soothsayers as a sign that the Greeks, for whom the sun was a prophetic symbol, were being abandoned by their gods. In hindsight, of course, one can say that every omen was correct, but simply misinterpreted by those who saw in it what they wanted to see. Herodotus, as noted, also articulates a quite modern approach to dreams—as mere reflections of "what one is thinking about during the day"—while still allowing for the possibility that dreams are divine messages, for good and for evil, whose true import is clear only in retrospect.

Direct divine intervention in human events, though common in Homer, is rare in the *Histories*, and almost invariably is presented as something claimed by others. Divine apparitions are reported at both Marathon and Salamis, underscoring the miraculous nature of those victories. Croesus is saved from being burned alive by rain providentially sent by Apollo. Crocsus probably was burned alive, however, or otherwise killed following the battle in question; Herodotus keeps him alive for his own narrative purposes as a sort of one-man Greek chorus to link and comment upon unfolding events.

The *Histories* reports the inquiries of one man into the doings of all men, including their religious doings, without making a doctrinal commitment to any. It reflects a broad tolerance of disparate religious views and a curious mixture of skepticism and piety, all within a strong moral framework in which the mighty are brought low and hubris is invariably punished.

THE RISE OF THE PERSIANS

The Persian Empire was founded by Cyrus the Great by way of a revolt against the Medes in 550. The Persians were a tribal people in what is now Iran. The neighboring Medes, who were ethnically related to the Persians, had joined their villages into a state around 700, and managed to conquer much of Assyria and to exercise control over the Persians.

In 584, Astyages, the Median king who had married his daughter to a Persian, became frightened when a dream revealed that his daughter's son would replace him as king. Herodotus recounts an Oedipus-like story (which Sophocles adapted for his own purposes), in which the infant Cyrus was condemned to die, and one of Astyages's generals, Harpagos, was charged with the task. Rather than kill the child himself, however, Harpagos handed him over to a herdsman with orders to expose the baby in a remote area. The herdsman exposed his own stillborn infant instead, and he and his wife raised Cyrus as their own. Some years later, when Astyages learned that Cyrus was still alive, he exacted a grisly revenge on Harpagos by inviting him to dinner and serving him the roasted flesh of Harpagos's own son. But, wrongly informed by his seers, the Magi, that Cyrus no longer posed a threat to him, Astyages sent him back to Persia to live with his true parents. There, when Cyrus grew older, Harpagos encouraged him to revolt. Cyrus gathered together the many Persian tribes and marched on the Median capital of Ecbatana. Harpagos and most other Medes went over to the rebels, and the remaining resistance quickly collapsed. Astyages barely had time to impale the Magi who had advised him to send Cyrus away before he was himself captured.

Cyrus expanded the power of Persia (from this point in his narrative, Herodotus uses the terms Medes and Persians almost interchangeably) by conquering Lydia. Croesus, a descendant of Gyges (who killed Kandaules, married his wife, and usurped the throne), had built Lydia into a wealthy power, where he reigned from 560 to 546 from his capital at Sardis. But his oracle-driven decision to challenge the growing might of Persia proved his undoing. Cyrus was a greater tactician, and Croesus ended up lashed to a pyre, where he despondently called out Solon's name as the flames began to kindle. Questioned by Cyrus as to the meaning of his outburst, Croesus explained his encounter with Solon. Cyrus, reflecting that "nothing is really secure and certain for human beings," "changed his mind about committing a living man to the fire, a fellow human being who had been blessed with happiness no less than he."[63] But the Persians were unable to extinguish the fire, and Croesus would have perished had Apollo not sent a sudden rain storm.

According to Herodotus, the Persians were a straightforward people. A man's worth depended on his valor in battle and his ability to father many sons. "From the age of five to the age of twenty, they teach their sons just three things: to ride horses, to shoot the bow, and to speak the truth."[64] Cyrus added the ancient kingdoms of Babylon and Assyria to his realm. But his efforts to expand deeper into Asia toward the Caucasus Mountains and the Caspian Sea met a bloody end at the hands of the Massegetai, a warrior people ruled by Queen Tomyris, who promised to slake Cyrus's thirst for blood if he persisted in invading her land.

Cyrus, who had hitherto enjoyed unrelieved good fortune and believed his army invincible, was decisively defeated, and his severed head was thrust into a wineskin filled with the blood of his own soldiers.

The career of Cyrus's son, Cambyses, had a similar arc. After expanding his father's realm through the conquest of Egypt and the surrender of Libya, his attempt to press deeper into Africa was defeated by poor planning. Meanwhile, a bizarre plot involving his brother, Smerdis, threatened Cambyses's hold on power. As reported by Herodotus, Cambyses had his brother murdered because a dream indicated that Smerdis would seize the throne. But later a Magus also named Smerdis pretended to be the true Smerdis and assumed power while Cambyses was in distant Ethiopia. In hurrying home, Cambyses suffered an accident—in divine retribution for his mockery of what was sacred to the Egyptians—and died.

Since Cambyses was childless, seven senior Persian officers decided to depose the false Smerdis. (Most historians believe that the real Smerdis was on the throne and that the Magus story was put out by the conspirators to justify their actions.) They bluffed their way past the palace guards and, after a brief struggle, dispatched the alleged imposter and led a widespread slaughter of Magi. Faced, then, with establishing a new government, they debated among themselves on the best course of action. One argued in favor of democracy, noting that absolute power corrupts and leads to reckless arrogance, whereas the "rule of the majority . . . has the most beautiful and powerful name of all, equality."[65] Another argued for oligarchy, because "the best men are most likely to make the best decisions,"[66] whereas "nothing can be both more unintelligent or insolent than the worthless, ineffectual mob."[67] The third, Darius, argued that oligarchy leads to instability and bloodshed and ultimately monarchy, and thus it is better to start by choosing the best man to rule: "Since we were freed by one man [Cyrus], we should preserve that form of government" and "not let go of our ancestral traditions."[68]

It is a fascinating exchange, clearly influenced less by Persian history than by fifth-century philosophic currents that would later coalesce in Aristotle's *Politics*. Darius's views prevailed, and he himself then prevailed (through trickery) in the contest to become king. He proved a worthy one, however, beginning his reign in 522 by marrying the daughters of Cyrus and the true Smerdis, among others. He consolidated his empire and organized the bureaucracy, creating twenty separate provinces, or *satrapies*, each ruled by an administrator answerable directly to Darius. He built roads throughout the empire and regularized the payment of tribute, thus becoming known as the shopkeeper king. Herodotus gives a survey of all the twenty provinces controlled by Persia and the tribute paid by each.

Darius expanded his empire in Asia as far as the Indus River, solidified his holdings in North Africa, and moved into Europe with the conquest of Thrace and the payment of tribute by Macedon. Like his predecessors, though, Darius went a bridge too far; specifically, a bridge of boats he built across the Ister River (the modern Danube) in order to invade Scythia in 513. The Scythians, a fierce nomadic people, adopted a tactic that the Russians would later find invaluable against Napoleon. They simply retreated before Darius's massive force, drawing him deeper into the country, thinning his supply train, and harassing his men with hit-and-run raids. When Darius finally gave up and turned back, the Scythians sought to destroy the bridge of boats, thereby trapping the Persians. But Darius's Ionian troops, who had been left to guard the bridge, ignored their chance to leave Darius's army at the mercy of the Scythians and free Ionia from Persian rule. It was a decision they would soon come to regret.

THE ROAD TO WAR

Herodotus begins his account of the causes of the war between East and West with a series of mythological abductions: of the Greek princess Io by the Phoenicians; of the Colchian princess Medea by Jason and the Argonauts; and of Helen by Paris. He notes, however, that he has "no intention of affirming that these events occurred thus or otherwise."[69] Instead, he quickly bypasses mythology for history: "I do know," he assures the reader, "who was the first man to begin unjust acts against the Hellenes."[70] That man was Croesus: "Before the reign of Croesus, all Hellenes had been free."[71] Croesus brought under his control the Greek cities along the Ionian coast—which were wealthy from trade but isolated from the protection of mainland Greece—and required them to pay tribute. When Croesus's Lydia was conquered by Persia in 546, the Ionian cities were part of the spoils, and Cyrus easily put down an incipient rebellion.

In 499, however, the Ionian cities revolted again, led by Aristagoras of Miletus, who overthrew a number of the Ionian tyrants installed by Persia and replaced them with popular governments. He then went to Sparta, urging them to "rescue the Ionians from slavery,"[72] and disparaging the Persians' prowess in war in an effort to convince the Spartans that they could easily conquer all of Asia and reap its riches. The Spartans, however, were unmoved by the prospect of distant riches in a war far from home and sent Aristagoras on his way. That way led to Athens, where he faced a better reception. The false promise of easy conquest, the idea of spreading democracy and freedom among fellow Greeks, and the fact that Darius had given refuge to Hippias, Athens's former tyrant whose ouster led to her present democratic government, all coalesced in a vote of the assembly to dispatch twenty ships (with perhaps two hundred men per ship) to help the Ionians. Eretria, a neighboring city-state, sent five additional triremes, since Miletus had previously helped them in a war.

The allies met with immediate success, marching on Sardis, the former capital of Lydia and now the most important of the western Persian cities. They took the city without resistance and, whether by accident or design, burned it to the ground, including a local religious sanctuary, whose destruction later became an excuse for similar Persian sacrileges. But the Persians proved better soldiers than advertised and soon drove the Ionians and their allies back. The Athenians learned, moreover, that Aristagoras was playing a double game, promoting his own interests ahead of his coalition. They promptly sailed home and ignored all further pleas for assistance.

But the damage had been done. Darius resolved to take revenge against the Athenians. Indeed, "he appointed one of his attendants to repeat to him three times whenever his dinner was served: 'My lord, remember the Athenians.'"[73] But first he dealt with the Ionians and various other distractions in the empire. The once-great city of Miletus was sacked in 494; its men were either killed or deported, and its women and children became slaves to the Persians. The other cities and neighboring islands were also brutally subjugated; the most handsome boys were castrated and sent off as eunuchs to the Persian court, while the most beautiful virgins were added to the king's harem. Recognizing that resentment of the Persian-sponsored tyrants had fueled the rebellion, Mardonios, the king's son-in-law, deposed the remaining tyrants and established democracies in their cities. He then pressed on across the Hellespont and into Europe. He reconquered Thrace but was badly wounded in the process, and his accompanying fleet was wrecked in a storm while sailing around the Mount Athos peninsula, which juts far into the Aegean Sea. The invasion of mainland Greece was thus further delayed to 490.

The destruction of Miletus, a former Athenian colony, depressed the Athenians. When the playwright Phrynikos produced a tragedy on the capture and destruction of Miletus, the audience was so moved that they fined him heavily "for reminding them of their own evils."[74] Yet the Athenians would face their own evils soon enough. Persia, having put its empire in order, was set to advance, and the iconic battles of Marathon, Thermopylae, and Salamis—battles that would preserve Greek freedom and alter the course of Western civilization—lay ahead.

THE PUNITIVE EXPEDITION: MARATHON

In 490, six hundred triremes set sail from Ionia under the combined command of Artaphrenes and Datis, with the avowed aim of punishing Eretria and Athens. "Those two cities," Herodotus explains, "were the professed goals of the expedition, but what the Persians really intended was to subjugate as many Greek cities as they could."[75] Hippias sailed along with them, hoping to be reinstalled as tyrant of Athens. Avoiding the coastal route around Mount Athos, the expedition hopped from island to island, subjugating each as it went. The Persians also sent heralds far and wide, demanding from the Greek cities earth and water as tokens of submission to Darius (tokens that would be followed by the payment of tribute and the provision of troops to swell the Persian ranks). Many acquiesced. But Athens and Sparta, the two most powerful Greek city-states, responded by throwing the heralds, respectively, down a pit and into a well, thereby literally complying with the request for earth and water.

The Persians invested Eretria, on the island of Euboea. For six days, they assaulted the city and were repelled at the walls. But on the seventh day, the city was betrayed from within and surrendered to the Persians, who proceeded to plunder and set fire to the sanctuaries, "exacting vengeance for the sanctuaries burned down in Sardis, and as Darius had instructed, they enslaved the people."[76]

The Persians then moved on to Attica, the homeland of Athens, landing their troops and their cavalry on the plain of Marathon, about twenty-five miles from Athens. A resolution to "take provisions and march" was passed by the assembly, and nine thousand Athenian hoplites—heavily armed troops with bulky bronze-covered shields; long, bronze-tipped spears; helmets; body armor; and short swords—went forth to meet the invaders.

At the same time, an Athenian messenger Pheidippides ran to Sparta (a distance of at least 140 miles) to seek assistance. He later reported that "the god Pan fell in with him"[77] during his run, and the Athenians erected a shrine to Pan along the route after the war. Arriving the next day, Pheidippides found the Spartans celebrating a religious festival and claiming that they could not march against the enemy until some days hence when the moon was full. Only tiny Plataea, a neighboring city-state, long under the protection of Athens, sent troops. Plataea's one thousand fighters constituted almost their entire adult male population; women, children, the aged, and the infirm remained behind.

The Athenians and Plataeans were heavily outnumbered. The Persians, joined by troops pressed into service from Ionia and other subject states, had perhaps twenty-five thousand fighters. But the Persians were more lightly armed than the Greeks. They had wicker or leather shields and leather vests that held little protection against thrusting spears, and their short swords and daggers were outmatched by the long spears carried by the hoplites. Their bows were useful at a distance, but not in up-close fighting. Hoplites, moreover, were rigorously trained to fight in a closely packed phalanx, in which each solider depended in part on the shield of the soldier to his right. The Persians, though valiant and fierce warriors, were not similarly drilled.

There were ten Athenian generals, each commanding a regiment. Their votes split evenly on whether to attack the Persians or to retreat behind the Athenian walls. Kallimachos, the polemarch (war leader), held the decisive eleventh vote, but an impassioned speech by Miltiades, the first of the great Athenian war heroes, presented him with a stark choice: "If this city prevails," he argued, "it can become the first among all Greek cities. . . . If we fail to fight now, I expect that intense factional strife will fall upon the Athenians and shake their resolve so violently that they will medize" (that is, go over to the Persian cause).[78] His sense of urgency was increased by intelligence from defecting Ionians that the Persians had loaded their cavalry and some troops back on their ships to sail for Athens and establish a position between the hoplites and their city.

Kallimachos was convinced, and all the generals voted to cede command to Miltiades, who organized his troops in an unconventional manner. Instead of massing them at the center where the best Persian troops were deployed, he lengthened the line to equal that of the larger Persian force, thinning out the center and strengthening his wings. Then, to minimize the effect of Persian archery, he advanced his troops to just out of arrow range (probably no farther than 450 feet, though Herodotus says it was "about a mile"), where "they charged at a run toward the barbarians."[79] The Persians at the center pushed back the attack and went on the offensive, but their wings quickly folded and broke. Instead of pursuing the fleeing Persians at each wing, the Athenians, showing great discipline, wheeled to the center and attacked both flanks of the remaining Persian forces. After intense fighting, the remaining Persians also broke and ran. Some perished in a nearby swamp. Others fled to the ships, which the Athenians sought to seize in order to prevent their escape. It was thus that Kynegeiros, brother of the playwright Aeschylus, who also fought in the battle, died, "for while seizing the sternpost of a ship, his hand was chopped off by an axe."[80]

The polemarch Kallimachos was also killed in the fighting, but remarkably few other Athenians were—only 192, plus 11 Plataeans. By contrast, 6,400 of the enemy were killed. But the Athenians could not rest. The fleeing Persians sailed around Cape Sounion to join the rest of the fleet in an assault on Athens. So the Athenian soldiers marched back as quickly as they could, arriving just in time to forestall an attack. The Persians "held their ships there for a while, and then sailed back to Asia."[81]

At the full moon, two thousand Spartans marched to Athens in great haste, arriving in Attica on the third day out of Sparta. They were too late for the battle, but they visited the scene of the fighting at Marathon. "Then they praised the Athenians for their achievement and went home."[82] They would do their part in the next encounter with the forces of Persia, a decade later.

Miltiades dedicated the helmet he wore at Marathon as an offering to Zeus at Olympia, where it can still be seen today. But, in Athens, acclaim was often fleeting. Miltiades was given ships and men to exact reparations from medized Greek states. After an unsuccessful siege of Paros, in which he suffered a wound in the thigh, Miltiades was indicted on a capital charge of deceiving the Athenian people. Convicted, he was spared a death sentence but ordered to pay a large fine. Soon after, he died of his festering wound, less than a year after the Battle of Marathon, a warning to future Athenian leaders.

THE SECOND INVASION: THERMOPYLAE

In the wake of his failed invasion, Darius immediately began gathering a much larger army to try again. This time his objective was total domination of the Greek world and the utter destruction of Athens. But the heavy taxes—in men and materials—that he imposed led to a rebellion in Egypt in 486, and he was forced to turn his attention there. Darius died before he could pacify Egypt or launch a new invasion of Greece. He had ruled the Persian Empire for thirty-six years. His son Xerxes—a name that would become synonymous, thanks to Herodotus, with a willful, cruel, luxury-loving despot—became king.

Xerxes crushed the revolt in Egypt, but he did not share his father's intense desire to punish the Athenians and subdue Greece. He had to be persuaded by Mardonios, who was eager to become satrap (governor) of Greece. Once convinced, however, he devoted enormous resources to the task. He sent men, "laboring under the whip and working in relays,"[83] to cut a channel across the Mount Athos peninsula so that his invasion fleet would not have to sail around it and risk violent storms. He arranged for food and other supplies to be deposited in suitable locations for his troops marching overland. Like his father, he also gave the Greek cities—except Athens and Sparta—the chance to offer earth and water as tokens of submission. As before, Herodotus tells us, many Greek states were "eager to medize."[84]

Herodotus estimates the initial strength of Xerxes's mixed army of Persians and their allies at more than 1.7 million men. That is surely far too high, and contemporary scholars suggest that Herodotus may have confused the Persian terms *chiliarch* (1,000) and *myriarch* (10,000), thereby swelling the number by a factor of ten. Yet even at 170,000, this was a more formidable force than the world had ever seen, and Xerxes added to its numbers from every subject state through which he passed. Herodotus recounts that Greek spies were captured trying to survey the Persian forces. Instead of executing them, Xerxes had them shown around the entire camp and then released, expecting the Greeks to realize that any resistance to so large a force was hopeless.

The overland expedition began symbolically in Sardis, the town once burned by the Ionians and their Athenian allies. There, Pythios, a loyal subject of Xerxes, asked the monarch if the eldest of his five sons might be excused from service and remain at home with him. Furious at this impertinence, Xerxes had the boy cut in two, and the army marched between the halves as they left Sardis. Xerxes rode in splendor, standing in a chariot, but once out of Sardis, and "whenever he thought it prudent to do so,"[85] he would dismount and ride in a covered wagon, which is how women and children traveled. A massive throne was brought along so that he could sit upon it at strategic points to review his troops and watch unfolding battles. During one such review, Xerxes wept at the sheer magnificence of his army, explaining to his uncle Artabanos: "I was suddenly overcome by pity as I considered the brevity of human life, since not one of all these people here will be alive one hundred years from now."[86] Many, in fact, would not survive the year.

The Persians built two bridges of boats across the Hellespont—the boats were lashed side by side, secured by strong cables, and covered with planks and soil, with a fence to keep the horses and other animals from falling into the sea— but a violent storm broke them both apart before they could be crossed. Xerxes ordered his men to throw shackles into the water and to deliver to it three hundred lashes, and he "instructed his men to say barbarian and insolent things as they were striking the Hellespont."[87] Perhaps with more effect, he also beheaded the engineers who had supervised the initial bridges.

After the replacement bridges were secured, Herodotus says it took a week for the army to cross into Europe. The army marched overland, shadowed by the fleet, through Thrace and Macedon, drinking the rivers dry as they went. Each city through which they passed was required to give a feast for the king and his men and a luxurious tent for Xerxes to use as his quarters. The next day, they would leave with the tent, the plates, and more troops, all pressed into service of the Great King.

Thessaly tried to convince the rest of Greece to send a sufficient force to stop the Persians before they invaded. The Greek allies initially voted to do so but soon realized the position was indefensible and retreated. The abandoned Thessalians "medized with no further hesitation."[88]

The Greeks now decided to make their initial defense below Thessaly, at a narrow pass known as Thermopylae, where the track, with mountains on one side and the sea on the other, was "wide enough for only a single wagon."[89] The Greeks sent an advance guard of at most four thousand troops to guard this pass, including three hundred elite Spartan warriors, all under the command of Leonidas, one of the two kings of Sparta. A larger Greek force was promised to follow promptly behind them. The rest of the Spartans were celebrating yet another religious festival, "but they intended to go as soon as they had concluded it."[90] Neither they nor the additional Greek forces ever arrived. Accordingly, a small contingent of Greeks faced perhaps 250,000 troops of the Great King (though Herodotus here puts the number at 2.6 million!), a significant number of whom had been recruited in the march through Europe.

The Battle at Thermopylae was perhaps the most glorious loss in military history. For three days, with fresh contingents constantly rotating to the front, Leonidas and his long-speared, disciplined troops fought the Persians to a standstill. Even the ten thousand Immortals—Xerxes's elite Persian guard—could not break the Greek line in this confined space, in which the Persians were unable to derive any decisive advantage from their superior numbers. An increasingly frustrated Xerxes watched as Persian bodies piled up in front of the Greek line, which showed no signs of cracking.

There is no telling how long this impasse would have lasted, but a local Greek, hoping for a large reward, told Xerxes of a path through the mountains that would allow him to send troops to the rear of the Greek position. A large contingent of Persians set off in the night, guided by the traitor. Troops from nearby Phocis, who had been sent by Leonidas to guard this pass, were literally caught napping and quickly fled. Realizing that his position was now untenable, Leonidas sent the allies away before the trap was complete. The three hundred Spartans remained, along with some hoplites from Thespiae who also refused to depart.

Since their rear was about to be overrun, the Spartans attacked to the front "with reckless desperation and no regard for their own lives,"[91] slashing and stabbing, driving many barbarians into the sea while others were trampled alive. It was here that Leonidas fell, and the Spartans fought furiously over his body. After a violent struggle, they managed to drag the body of their king back to the narrow part of the road where they had built a defensive wall. At this point, they were completely surrounded. Told that the Persian archers were so numerous that their arrows would block out the sun, the Spartan Dienekes welcomed the news: "Very well, then, we shall fight in the shade."

The Spartans were buried where they fell—all but two of the original three hundred, since one had been sent off as a messenger and the other was in a neighboring town recovering from a serious eye disease. (A third, Eurytos, similarly blinded, put on his armor and ordered his servant to lead him to the fighting, where he "charged into the raging battle and was killed."[92]) Both survivors were held in disgrace: the former hanged himself while the latter found a measure of redemption at Plataea, where he threw himself into the front of the fighting and was killed.

The Spartans and other allied troops were betrayed and outflanked. But they killed twenty thousand of the enemy, Herodotus reports, and their heroism bought crucial time for the rest of Greece to prepare. Two monuments were later erected on the spot. The first was dedicated to the troops generally who fought against such superior numbers. The second was dedicated to the Spartans alone and was inscribed:

> Tell them in Lacedaemon, passer-by,
> That here obedient to their command we lie.

THE SECOND INVASION: SALAMIS AND PLATAEA

Herodotus tells us that the Persian army was accompanied by more than 1,200 triremes. Although the actual number was probably no more than eight hundred, and possibly as low as six hundred, it was still a formidable armada. That the Greeks were able to counter it at all was due to the fortuitous discovery in 483 of a rich new vein of silver at Laureion, in Attica near Cape Sounion. The Athenian statesman Themistocles convinced the assembly to use the money from the Laureion silver mines to build new ships. His pretext was an ongoing war with neighboring Aegina. But Themistocles kept his eye on the greater threat from Persia. As a result, the Athenians had 250 ships available by the time of the second Persian invasion.

Yet despite providing almost two-thirds of the vessels and even more of the naval expertise, Athens ceded command at sea, as well as on land, to Sparta. The Athenians "considered the survival of Hellas of paramount importance, and they knew that if they quarreled over the leadership, Hellas would be destroyed."[93] As a consequence, the Spartan admiral Eurybiades nominally led the Greek fleet, but Themistocles in fact controlled strategy and was the mastermind of the Persian defeat. "So anyone who said that the Athenians proved to be the saviors of Hellas," Herodotus explained, "would not have strayed from the truth."[94] Without their Laureion-built ships, no amount of Spartan valor could have stopped the Persians.

At the same time troops were dispatched to defend the pass at Thermopylae, the Greeks also sent a fleet of perhaps 270 ships to nearby Artemision. The Persian fleet settled opposite them on the coast of Magnesia, without any large protective harbor. Heavily outnumbered, the Greeks prayed to the wind god Boreas for a storm that would wreak havoc upon the exposed Persian fleet. That is what they got. For three days a violent tempest cast Persian ships on the rocks or sank them at sea. Herodotus reports that "no fewer than 400 ships were destroyed"[95] and then dryly adds: "But at last the Magi, by offering sacrificial victims and singing incantations to the wind . . . , brought about an end to the storm on the fourth day—or perhaps it abated of its own accord."[96]

Even with the Persian fleet battered and much reduced, the Greeks were still outnumbered. Themistocles had to bribe other commanders to stay and fight. But fight they did, in a running sea battle that spanned the same days as the fighting on land. The Greek fleet was badly mauled and lost many ships but sank even more of the Persians before finally withdrawing when the Greeks learned that the pass at Thermopylae had fallen. It was not a victory, but it evened the odds for the climactic battle ahead and, like Thermopylae, proved that the Persians were not invincible.

Themistocles convinced Eurybiades to gather the entire Greek fleet (380 ships, according to Herodotus) in the sheltered bay between Attica and the nearby island of Salamis. There they debated their best course. The Greek land forces, led by the Spartans, had retreated to, and were fortifying, the isthmus of Corinth (a narrow strip of land separating the Peloponnese from the rest of Greece). Boeotia and Attica were thus left to their own devices, defenseless against the fast-moving Persian army. The Greek fleet was prepared to pull out as well. Only Themistocles kept them in place.

According to the oracle at Delphi, "a wall made of wood" would save the Athenians. Three interpretations were offered for this prophecy: that the Athenians should fortify the old wooden fence around the Acropolis and make their stand there; that the navy (a wall made of wood) would defeat the Persians; and that the Athenians should abandon Athens altogether and sail in their ships to a new colony. Interpretation of the oracle was complicated by yet another ambiguous line: "O Salamis Divine, the children of women you will yet destroy."[97] Themistocles convinced the Athenian assembly that all ambiguity was in their favor and that they would win a decisive naval victory against the Persians at Salamis.

Athens was accordingly abandoned by all but a few conservatives who prepared to fight on the Acropolis. The women, children, stock animals, and whatever possessions could be carried were ferried across the bay. The old, the infirm, and the household pets were left behind. The Persians soon swept into Athens and burned it—and its sanctuaries—to the ground. After brief resistance, they slaughtered the handful of Athenians remaining on the Acropolis. Xerxes was so delighted with the fulfillment of his father's ardent wish that he sent the news back home by a relay of fast riders, of whom Herodotus writes (in words that would later be adopted as the unofficial motto of the US Postal Service): "And neither snow nor rain nor heat nor dark of night keeps them from completing their appointed course as swiftly as possible."[98]

With Athens burning and the Persian fleet gathering outside the bay, Eurybiades and the other non-Athenian commanders wanted to sail to the isthmus to remain close to the army. But Themistocles convinced them that fighting in the narrow straits on either side of Salamis would neutralize the enemy's superior numbers and provide other tactical advantages to the Greeks. More bluntly, he threatened:

> If you refuse to do as I say, we shall pick up and leave with our families, and without further ado go off to Siris in Italy, which is still ours from ancient times, and which the prophecies say we are destined to colonize. Then, when you find yourself left alone without allies like us, you will remember my words.[99]

For the time being, the Greek fleet remained in place.

Artemisia, queen of Halicarnassus, advised Xerxes against fighting a sea battle, citing the superior seamanship of the Greeks, and urged him instead to press his advantages on land against a fragile alliance of Greek city-states. "The Hellenes are incapable of holding out against you for very long; you will scatter them, and each one will flee to his own city."[100] She was probably right, but Xerxes followed the view of the majority of his commanders. Although he sent his army toward the Peloponnese, he also prepared to engage the Greek fleet.

The Greeks, however, were having second thoughts about being trapped in a small bay. Concerned that the fleet would depart, Themistocles sent a messenger in secret to Xerxes to tell him that the Greeks were terrified and planned to flee in the night and to urge Xerxes to encircle Salamis and block both of the narrow outlets. Whether Themistocles was seeking to force the fight contrary to the wishes of the other Greeks, as Herodotus claims, or whether his message was an agreed-upon strategy to lure the Persian fleet into the narrow confines of Salamis is still debated. Regardless, the ruse worked, and the Persians spent the night on an exhausting patrol. In the morning, a group of Greek ships simulated flight, further drawing in the Persians. The rest of the Greeks backed water in apparent panic and then turned on the pursuing Persians with unexpected ferocity.

Xerxes watched in increasing horror from his throne on nearby Mount Aigaleos as line after line of Persian ships, unable to navigate in the narrow waters, ran afoul of the ships in front of them and were rammed and disabled or sunk by the Greeks. The Persians fought bravely but quickly dissolved in mass confusion, with some trying to retreat and others to come up, while the Greeks maintained their ranks and their discipline. Most of the Persian fleet was destroyed in a single morning.

The Greeks cleared away the wreckage, quickly saw to their own ships, and "prepared for another naval battle, expecting the king to use those of his ships that had survived intact."[101] But Xerxes had had enough of Greece. His principal concern was to maintain the bridges across the Hellespont so that his army would not be trapped in Europe. He accordingly sent his remaining ships to guard the bridges and prepared to march back the way he had come. Mardonios suggested that Xerxes take the bulk of the army with him but allow Mardonios to "select 300,000 troops from the army and deliver Hellas to you when it has been completely enslaved."[102] Pleased with this advice, which corresponded with his own desire to flee, Xerxes set off and was back in Sardis, with his much-diminished forces, within two months.

The threat to Greek freedom was not over, however; Mardonios still had a substantial army at winter quarters in Thessaly, though it was probably closer to fifty thousand, including twenty thousand medized Greeks, than the three hundred thousand projected by Herodotus. The Spartans remained huddled behind their fortifications at the isthmus, and no amount of Athenian pleading seemed likely to bring them forth to fight. Mardonios offered Athens terms of friendship if they would sideline their fleet. Athens angrily rejected the overture and was, in 479, sacked and burned a second time, while its citizens floated offshore. One Athenian councilman, who recommended that they accept peace with Persia, was stoned to death by an angry mob, and his wife and children were then stoned by the Athenian women.

The Spartans, finally recognizing that their fortified isthmus was useless without the Athenian fleet to prevent a landing in the Peloponnese, sent their army north under Pausanias. Hoplites from Athens and other Greek allies soon joined them outside the small town of Plataea, at the edge of Boeotia, near Attica. The two sides faced each other for days, neither eager to make the first move. But delay favored the Greek army, whose ranks swelled "as more and more Hellenes streamed in to join it,"[103] and Mardonios was finally induced to attack on unfavorable ground that neutralized his cavalry. The result was almost as one-sided as Marathon: "The Persians were not inferior in courage or strength," Herodotus explains, "but they did not have hoplite arms, and besides, they were untrained and no match for their opponents in tactical skill."[104] Once Mardonios was killed, along with his most formidable division, the remainder of the army gave way in a rout. A small contingent, led by Artabanos, held back from the fray and marched as quickly as possible back to the Hellespont. The rest were slaughtered, and the Persian threat to mainland Greece was at an end.

"On the very same day," Herodotus claims, the Greeks enjoyed another victory across the sea at Mycale, where Greek sailors under the Spartan king Leotychidas disembarked and defeated a superior force of Persians, thus driving them from Ionia and freeing the cities and islands from Persian rule and incorporating them in the Hellenic alliance.[105] Herodotus suggests, as one of "many clear proofs that the divine is present in what happens,"[106] that rumor of the victory at Plataea somehow reached the sailors at Mycale, buoying their sprits and redoubling their zeal in the final charge against the Persians.

THE TRIUMPH OF A FREE PEOPLE

In a stirring speech reported by Herodotus, the Athenians rejected Persian overtures that they make a separate peace before their city was burned a third time.

> It would not be fitting for the Athenians to prove traitors to the Greek people, with whom we are united in sharing the same kinship and language, with whom we have established shrines and conduct sacrifices to the gods together, and with whom we also share the same way of life. So understand this now, if you have not learned it before: as long as even one Athenian still survives, we shall make no agreement with Xerxes.[107]

Yet, curiously, it was Persia that largely gave the Greeks their identity. The Hellenic peoples of the Mediterranean did share a common language, a common racial heritage, a common religion with pan-Hellenic shrines and festivals, and a common cultural heritage. But the city-states were independent of one another and frequently at war. They descended from mixed racial and linguistic subgroups, with their separate dialects. They each sought their own advantage. It was only the threat of Persia that led them to see themselves, for a brief period, as one people, united against a common foe.

Of course, even then they were not truly united. Many city-states medized and fought for the Persians. Moreover, the unity of the Greek-speaking world against the barbarians was short-lived. Internal power struggles broke out almost immediately. Athens developed an empire that extracted tribute from a far-flung group of Greek allies, who traded the threat of Persian dominance for a home-grown version. Sparta and her allies, fearful of Athenian intentions and jealous of her power and wealth, formed the rival Peloponnesian League. A civil war that would engulf Greece was all but inevitable.

That is the history to be told by Thucydides, picking up where his great predecessor ended. But it is fitting to pause, first, and reflect upon how much we owe to that glorious moment in Greek history, when a small, otherwise divided people fought for their freedom against a foreign tyrant with vastly superior resources. The Athenians in particular cast a shining light for all future democracies: they met directly in the assembly; they debated issues of the gravest import; they made wise decisions under the guidance of brilliant leaders; and then, having voted to do so, they marched or sailed forth against the foe. Herodotus directly attributed to the Athenian democracy the prowess that defeated the Persians: "The Athenians, while ruled by tyrants, were no better in war than any of the peoples living around them, but once they were rid of tyrants, they became by far the best of all."[108]

The British philosopher John Stuart Mill suggested that, even as an event in British history, the Battle of Marathon was more important than the Battle of Hastings. There is truth in that claim. Marathon and its successor battles at Thermopylae, Salamis, and Plataea preserved the autonomy of the Greek city-states, and a resurgent Athens, buoyed by its victory, proceeded to lay the cornerstones of Western civilization. Perhaps most important, as Herodotus stressed, the Persian Wars showed that a free people could, against overwhelming odds, fight fiercely against the forces of tyranny and maintain their fragile democracy. What Herodotus himself showed is the vital importance of chronicling such events as a guide and lesson for future generations.

Chapter 7

THUCYDIDES—
POWER AND PATHOS

"Thucydides, an Athenian, wrote the history of the war between the Peloponnesians and the Athenians..."[1] Thus begins the second great work of history in the Western tradition, identifying author and subject just as Herodotus did. But there the resemblance appears to end. While never naming him directly, Thucydides is at pains to distinguish his own procedure from that of his predecessor. He is dismissive of those who take "so little pains... in the investigation of truth" that they "accept readily the first story that comes to hand," and who render their compositions "attractive at truth's expense."[2] Thucydides himself aspires to more exacting standards, judging the accuracy of his reports "by the most severe and detailed tests possible,"[3] a procedure that he notes, with mock regret, may make his history less superficially appealing.

> The absence of romance in my history will, I fear, detract somewhat from its interest; but if it be judged useful by those inquirers who desire an exact knowledge of the past as an aid to the understanding of the future, which in the course of human things must resemble if it does not reflect it, I shall be content. In fine, I have written my work, not as an essay which is to win the applause of the moment, but as a possession for all time.[4]

The evident disdain for Herodotus is largely feigned: Thucydides not only starts his history where Herodotus left off—itself a form of tribute—but builds upon the narrative techniques used so effectively by Herodotus in his account of the key battles of the Persian Wars. What Harold Bloom would call "the anxiety of influence"[5]—the need felt by each writer to distinguish and thereby disparage his most important models—is very ancient indeed.

Yet there are, in truth, significant distinctions between the two writers. History for Thucydides is an exclusively human affair. He has no use for oracles or portents. There are no divine interventions in, or supernatural explanations for, events. Of the great plague that devastated Athens, he states bluntly that it made no distinction between those who worshipped the gods and those who did not.

His focus, moreover, is narrowed to political, military, and diplomatic issues. Charming anecdotes, digressions on ethnography and geography, descriptions of monuments and customs—none of these has a place in his often-dry narrative. Thucydides thereby sets the tone for the writing of history—which became synonymous with the fate of nations and the machinations of the powerful—for more than two millennia, until Fernand Braudel and his *Annales* school discovered that what Thomas Gray called "the short and simple annals of the poor" were neither short nor simple and did not deserve their "destiny obscure."[6]

Most significant, Thucydides wants "exact knowledge of the past as an aid to the understanding of the future."[7] His premise is that human nature is largely constant and that patterns of behavior—"such as have occurred and always will occur as long as the nature of mankind remains the same"[8]—will emerge from a close study of events. He seeks the universal in the particular, and he considers his work a possession "for all time," because the proper study of the past will tell us about our present and our future. George Santayana would later say, "Those who cannot remember the past are condemned to repeat it."[9] Thucydides has perhaps a darker view: that we are already by nature condemned to repeat the past, but should at least strive to understand it and thereby ourselves.

Thucydides is heavily influenced by the growth of science and, in particular, by the remarkable progress made by Hippocrates of Cos and his school in the study of medicine. He approaches the Peloponnesian War like a physician detailing the progress of a disease or like a scientist gathering data upon which theories are to be formed. The procedure requires strict attention to accuracy, for if the data are wrong, the theories will be as well, and the whole point of the enterprise will be defeated. His prose is precise, exacting, and unsentimental.

Thucydides creates a new way of studying man. Eschewing both the imaginative reconstructions of the poets and the abstractions of the philosophers, he seeks to gather historical facts into predictive laws. History, for Thucydides, is a tool for analyzing human nature and understanding human experience. As a result, he has long been hailed as the first scientific historian: objective, dispassionate, and even clinical, with an unwavering commitment to the power of reason to reveal the patterns of human behavior.

Yet, ironically, Thucydides is the most passionate of historians, far more so than the genial but somewhat detached Herodotus. He is appalled by the callous slaughter and widespread suffering brought on by the war and by the resulting degradation in character. "In peace and prosperity," he explains, "states and individuals have better sentiments, because they do not find themselves suddenly confronted with imperious necessities; but war takes away the easy supply of daily wants and so proves a rough master that brings most men's characters to a level with their fortunes."[10] Elsewhere he has an Athenian envoy note that the three motives driving men are "fear, honor, and interest," and that "the cry of justice" is only that, a cry "which no one ever yet brought forward to hinder his ambition when he had a chance of gaining anything by might."[11] In a time of war, Thucydides says, "words had to change their ordinary meaning and to take that which was now given them."[12]

In the face of this debasement of both values and language, Thucydides finds it a moral imperative to weigh his words with care and to speak the truth, clearly, directly, and unsparingly. He rarely editorializes, but his moral viewpoint is implicit in his selection, presentation, and juxtaposition of events. There is no such thing as a purely scientific historian: all choices are, in the end, moral ones. His two great themes—the inexorable expansion of power until checked by counterforces and the pathos of war—alternate in his account. Thucydides defies convenient labels. He is a realpolitik cynic redeemed by his own sentiments of decency and decorum. He is a believer in the power of human reason to predict and understand events, who demonstrates how easily events defy expectations and spin out of control. He posits predictive laws of human behavior but refuses to compromise the complexity of his account of actual motives and events. He is a child of the Greek enlightenment who despairs at the heart of darkness within men. Thucydides is always more subtle and more subversive than one would first imagine, both of received opinions and even of his own apparent opinions. His loyalty, first and foremost, is to the truth. It is a moral commitment, and he demands that we ourselves examine the data and draw our own tentative conclusions, subject always to further analysis and revision. Only in this last sense is the label "scientific historian" an accurate one.

A LIFE IN EXILE

Thucydides was born in Athens around 460. He came from a wealthy, aristocratic family and had mining interests in Thrace. Little is known for certain about his life beyond what he tells us in *The Peloponnesian War*, which is very little. He was in Athens in 431, when the war began. He suffered from the plague but survived.

Presumably he fought in a number of early battles (though which ones is a matter of speculation). In 424, he was elected one of the ten generals who guided Athens's military affairs. He was posted to Thrace, where his main responsibility as commander of the naval forces in the area was to protect the strategically located and wealthy city of Amphipolis. But, for reasons he never explains, he and his ships were a day's sail away when the city capitulated to a surprise Spartan attack. Thucydides was convicted of treason and exiled for twenty years. He spent much of that time living in the Peloponnese and traveling to other venues where the war was being fought. Turning necessity to advantage, he notes that "being present with both parties, and more especially with the Peloponnesians by reason of my exile, I had leisure to observe affairs more closely."[13]

He does not, however, rely solely on his own, first-person recollections. "With reference to the narrative of events," he explains, "far from permitting myself to derive it from the first source that came to hand, I did not even trust my own impressions, but it rests partly on what I saw myself, partly on what others saw for me."[14] Most difficult is the reconciliation of often-conflicting accounts: "My conclusions have cost me some labor from the want of coincidence between accounts of the same occurrences by different eyewitnesses, arising sometimes from imperfect memory, sometimes from undue partiality for one side or the other."[15]

One place where Thucydides takes more license (and in this respect is often followed by later narrative historians) is in the reporting of speeches. They are the most fascinating part of his narrative. He sets the stage—a meeting of the assembly on a critical issue, a funeral oration, a debate among rival diplomats—and allows his historical characters to expound upon their motivations, their strategic considerations, and even their ideals (or lack thereof). Some of these speeches Thucydides heard himself; others were reported to him. "It was in all cases," he acknowledges, "difficult to carry them word for word in one's memory." Accordingly, "my habit has been to make the speakers say what was in my opinion demanded of them by the various occasions, of course adhering as closely as possible to the general sense of what they really said."[16] In this way, Thucydides can editorialize upon events without seeming to do so. Deciding which speeches to report, how to present them, and where to insert them are his most important (and subjective) narrative choices. In them, he takes the reader from the heights of democratic ideals to the basest displays of power politics.

W. H. Auden captured this aspect of Thucydides in his poem "September 1, 1939," which Auden wrote on the eve of World War II:

Exiled Thucydides knew
All that a speech can say
About Democracy,
And what dictators do,
The elderly rubbish they talk
To an apathetic grave;
Analysed all in his book,
The enlightenment driven away,
The habit-forming pain,
Mismanagement and grief:
We must suffer them all again.[17]

When Thucydides died around 395, he left his life's work unfinished, breaking off midparagraph, his account stalled forever in 411, with seven more years of war and the ultimate defeat of Athens still to write. Yet we need not mourn the loss overmuch, for the vision of the world and of man embodied in his book was already fully formed.

SPARTANS AT HOME

Thucydides begins his history with a short account of how political order first developed in Greece, stressing the importance of military security to economic growth and expansion. While noting that "events of remote antiquity . . . could not from lapse of time be clearly ascertained,"[18] he explains that the early Greeks were a tribal people vulnerable to incursion, frequently migrating in the face of superior forces. There were no settled population centers, and agriculture was at a subsistence level since greater productivity inevitably invited plunder. There was no commerce, whether by land or by sea; there was limited communication and no accumulation of capital. Communities first settled inland, with geography to protect them from seaborne marauders. Only with the gradual development of sea power and the suppression of piracy did cities develop and expand along the coast, protecting their seaports, increasing their agriculture and trade, building walls for security, and sending their excess populations to colonize additional cities. Paradoxically, however, this increased security and wealth led inexorably to clashes among rival powers, culminating in the war that Thucydides is to relate, which he considers greater and more worthy of study than any that preceded it.

Thucydides offers only the merest sketch of these "events of remote antiquity," but in doing so he serves notice that Greece's mythical past of gods and heroes has no place in his history. His account will focus on military and economic power and how such power expands until checked by still stronger forces. As a result, wars have become greater and more terrible with time. He notes that the war with Persia, "the greatest achievement of past times, yet found a speedy decision in two actions by sea and two by land."[19] The Peloponnesian War, by contrast, lasted twenty-seven years and was orders of magnitude more deadly. "Never had so many cities been taken and laid desolate . . . ; never was there so much banishing and bloodshedding, now on the field of battle, now in political strife."[20] Thucydides undertakes to explain why and how the war developed as it did.

Thucydides thus starts his history proper where Herodotus stopped, with the failure of the second Persian invasion. From there he traces the continued rise of the two great powers in Greece: Athens, with her naval might, and Sparta, with her superior land forces. Once the Persians were driven from mainland Greece, Pausanias—the Spartan leader at Plataea—led the allied forces in an effort to expel the Persians from Asia Minor and to liberate the Greek colonies along the Ionian coast and nearby islands. But Pausanias, freed from the austerity of his native Sparta, soon fell in love with wealth and luxury, adopted Persian ways, and so violently controlled the newly "liberated" populations that "his conduct seemed more like that of a despot than of a general."[21] The Ionians complained bitterly to the Spartans and sought leadership from the Athenians instead.

Eventually, the Spartans recalled Pausanias and decided not to send anyone else in his place, thereby washing their hands of distant entanglements. Such isolationism was in keeping with Spartan traditions and Spartan necessities. They had enjoyed a stable form of government for more than three hundred years, from the time of their legendary lawmaker Lycurgus, largely by focusing on interests close at hand. The Spartans had a very small citizenship, usually no more than ten thousand male citizens with full rights. Yet they ruled over Laconia and neighboring Messenia, with a population as large as three hundred thousand. These subject peoples, known as *helots*, worked the land in rigorous servitude to the Spartans, and fear of a helot rebellion dictated most Spartan policy decisions.[22] Indeed, every autumn the Spartans ritually declared war on the helots, controlling them with violence and terror. Pausanias, upon his recall, intrigued with the helots, promising them freedom if they would join him in an insurrection. But the plot was exposed, and Pausanias sought refuge in a temple where he was entombed and ultimately died of starvation. Thucydides reports another occasion during the war when the Spartans offered freedom to the helots who had fought with the greatest distinction for Sparta. Two thousand were selected. They were feted, paraded, and then murdered to the last man to eliminate this potential threat.

Sparta was an oligarchy, ruled by two hereditary kings, one of whom had to remain always at home, while the other led armies into the field. There were five *ephors*, chief officers of the state, elected annually, and a senate of thirty members who were chosen from aristocratic families and held office for life. The most distinctive feature of Spartan life, however, was its rigorous military focus. Weak or defective male infants were exposed to die. For the rest, military training began at the age of seven and continued to adulthood. At the age of twenty, males joined messes and lived in barracks, where they followed a bleak and austere diet until age thirty, when they could set up households of their own. Since they were supported by the labor of the helots, they could devote themselves to perfecting the arts of war, and no one could equal a Spartan army on land. But the Spartans were reluctant to roam far for fear that the helots would seize the opportunity and revolt. Instead, they cultivated alliances with nearby city-states, forming and dominating what we now call the Peloponnesian League, as a land-based counterweight to the Athenian naval empire.

GROWTH OF THE ATHENIAN EMPIRE

The Athenians were the irresistible force to Sparta's immovable object. When Sparta returned to its own concerns after the Persian invasion was thwarted, Athens eagerly led the effort to free the Greek cities and islands along the Ionian coast. Eventually, 150 to 200 cities joined what became known as the Delian League, because its treasury was kept on the island of Delos. Two members, Lesbos and Chios, contributed ships. But the others were happy to pay money instead, leaving the shipbuilding and fighting to Athens. That was fine by Athens, which thus became the only great naval power in the region and was happy to use that power to advance its own interests.

Over time, the Delian League became a de facto Athenian Empire to which the member states paid tribute. Defections were not permitted: a siege, capitulation, and increased tribute were their only fruits. The treasury was moved to Athens for "safekeeping" in 454, and a portion of the funds was dedicated to the great building projects of classical Athens, including the Parthenon and other buildings on the Acropolis.

Athens had been quickly rebuilt after its second sack by Persia. At the urging of Themistocles—the Athenian hero of Salamis—long stone walls were constructed around the city and all the way down to the port of Piraeus, which was fortified against attack. The Spartans, who had no need of walls, protested these measures but were stalled by Themistocles until their complaints became moot. Themistocles himself, however, fared less well. Thucydides claimed that he "surpassed all others in the faculty of intuitively meeting an emergency,"[23] but when the Spartans implicated him in Pausanias's flirtations with the Persians, he had to flee to escape arrest. He died of illness shortly thereafter at the court of the Persian king, Artaxerxes. Thus, the heroes of the second invasion—Pausanias and Themistocles, "the most famous men of their time in Hellas"[24]—met the same fate as Miltiades, the hero of Marathon. Before the cheering even had time to fade away, they were all accused of treason and arrested, fined, or banished by the cities they saved. It was a pattern that the Athenian democracy would continue and would come to regret.

The Athenians met in assembly on the Pnyx, a hill leading down from the Acropolis, several times each month. As many as six thousand would attend to debate and vote upon every issue of importance to the city. Many administrative positions were assigned by lot. Other officials, such as the ten generals who governed military affairs, were elected yearly by a direct vote of the citizens. It was the most radical democracy in Greece and, perhaps, that the world has ever seen, within the limitations imposed on citizenship, which were admittedly severe. Only the child of an Athenian mother and an Athenian father could become a citizen. There were about 40,000 male citizens at the outbreak of the war, out of 300,000 residents, including 100,000–150,000 slaves and perhaps 25,000 free foreigners. The Athenians also had three hundred warships, a vast fleet of merchant vessels, and plenty of skilled rowers, all of which made Athens the wealthiest, most powerful city in Greece, a city with boundless ambition and immense self-confidence.

Athens was thus the antithesis of Sparta in so many respects: a naval power rather than a land power; a democracy rather than an oligarchy; an open and expansive society rather than a closed and insular one. These differences are reflected in the characters of the two peoples. In a famous speech reported by Thucydides, a diplomat from Corinth draws a sharp contrast between the two cities while urging the Spartans to meet the growing threat from Athens.

> The Athenians are addicted to innovation, and their designs are characterized by swiftness alike in conception and execution; you have a genius for keeping what

you have got, accompanied by a total want of invention, and when forced to act you never go far enough. Again, they are adventurous beyond their power, and daring beyond their judgment, and in danger they are sanguine; your wont is to attempt less than is justified by your power, to mistrust even what is sanctioned by your judgment, and to fancy that from danger there is no release. Further, there is promptitude on their side against procrastination on yours; they are never at home, you are most disinclined to leave it, for they hope by their absence to extend their acquisitions, you fear by your advance to endanger what you have left behind. They are swift to follow up a success, and slow to recoil from a reverse.[25]

These differences, which clearly reflect Thucydides's own estimation of the two cities, are borne out in the events that follow. His summary of the Athenians in particular is telling: "To describe their character in a word, one might truly say that they were born into the world to take no rest themselves and to give none to others."[26] This restlessness was the source of their greatness and would be their undoing.

CASUS BELLI

Athens and Sparta had already clashed in a "first" Peloponnesian War that lasted off and on from 460 until 446. This running series of conflicts and skirmishes was largely fought over changing alliances, particularly when Megara, a state strategically located between Corinth and Attica, joined the Delian League. The expansion of Athenian influence right to its borders infuriated Corinth, one of Sparta's most important and bellicose allies. In 446, Athens and Sparta nonetheless agreed on a "Thirty Years' Peace," which recognized the independent spheres of influence of Athens and Sparta. Megara was returned to the Peloponnesian League, and the states in each alliance were forbidden to change sides to avoid precipitating another war. Current neutrals could choose to join either alliance, and any further disputes between Athens and Sparta were to be submitted to arbitration.

Despite the carefully designed treaty, various "grounds for complaint" continued to arise, culminating in three incidents described by Thucydides. First, in 433, Corcyra and Corinth fought over Epidamnus, a colony far up the western coast of what is now Albania. Athens had no direct interest in this dispute, but Corcyra nonetheless appealed for her support. The speech of the Corcyraean ambassador is telling. He notes that, after Athens, Corcyra is the strongest naval power in Greece. If Corcyra falls to Corinth, and her fleet comes under Corinthian control, the balance of naval power will be upset. By contrast, an alliance between Corcyra and Athens will greatly enhance Athenian power and influence. "It will be urged," the ambassador acknowledged, "that it is only in the case of a war that we shall be found useful."[27]

> To this we answer that if any of you imagine that the war is far off, he is grievously mistaken, and is blind to the fact that the Spartans out of fear of you want war, and that Corinth is influential with them—the same, remember, that is your enemy, and is even now trying to subdue us as a preliminary to attacking you.[28]

The Corinthian ambassador counters that "the coming of the war ... is still uncertain, and it is not worthwhile to be carried away by it into gaining the instant and declared enmity of Corinth."[29] The Athenians, feeling "that the coming of the Peloponnesian War was only a question of time" and wishing to gain every possible advantage, entered into a defensive alliance with Corcyra and, accordingly, sent a small fleet to aid her in repelling a Corinthian attack.[30]

The second incident concerned Potidaea, a Corinthian colony that was nonetheless an ally of Athens. Persuaded that it would enjoy the protection of Corinth and Sparta, Potidaea revolted in 432 and was besieged by Athens. The siege would last for years, depleting the Athenian treasury, before Potidaea was finally starved out in 429. The third incident involved border disputes with Megara, which led Athens to exclude Megara from trading at the markets in Athens and from using any of the harbors in the Athenian empire.

With these grievances in mind, members of the Peloponnesian League met in Sparta in the fall of 432 to urge war against the Athenians. Athenian envoys who were conveniently present "on other business" also spoke.[31] They first reminded the assembled states of Athens's superior service against the Persians; not only did she supply the vast majority of ships, but "we left behind us a city that was a city no longer, and staked our lives for a city that had an existence only in desperate hope, and so bore our full share in your deliverance and in ours."[32] Athens acquired her empire because Sparta was unwilling to carry on the fight and "because the allies attached themselves to us and spontaneously asked us to assume the command."[33] Athens could hardly be expected to decline such an advantage, "for it has always been the law that the weaker should be subject to the stronger," and Athens has proved worthy of its position.[34] The Athenian envoys urged the Spartans to settle any treaty differences according to their agreement rather than risk what was sure to be a painful and protracted war: "Consider the vast influence of accident in war, before you are engaged in it. As it continues, it generally becomes an affair of chances, chances from which neither of us is exempt, and whose event we must risk in the dark."[35]

Archidamus, one of the two Spartan kings, also spoke in favor of peace, contending that the Spartans could not beat Athens on land alone: "Unless we can either beat them at sea, or deprive them of the revenues which feed their navy, we shall meet with little but disaster."[36] But the Spartans voted that the treaty had been broken and that war must be declared, "not so much because they were persuaded by the arguments of the allies, as because they feared the growth of the power of the Athenians."[37]

PERICLES

Despite this dramatic declaration of war, Sparta continued to send envoys to Athens to try to avoid it. At first the Spartans sought various unacceptable concessions, but in the end they made clear that war would be averted if Athens simply lifted the Megarian decree. Yet Athens, at the behest of its most prominent statesmen, Pericles, declined. Pericles urged the assembly to hold to "the principle of no concession to the Peloponnesians,"[38] because any such concession would be taken as a sign of weakness and simply invite further demands. Athens, with her long walls, her vast treasury, and her unrivaled navy was in an all but impregnable position, provided she did not engage in a traditional, full-scale land battle with the highly trained and numerically superior Peloponnesians. Sparta and her allies might march with impunity into Attica and lay waste to the land, but the people would be safe behind the city walls and well supplied through the port at Piraeus. "We must cry not over the loss of houses and land but of men's lives; since houses and land do not gain men, but men them."[39] Moreover, "if they march against our country we will sail against theirs," with hit-and-run reprisals in the Peloponnese that will do even more harm there.[40]

Provided, Pericles warned, "you can consent not to combine schemes of fresh conquest with the conduct of the war," the Athenians could expect the Spartans soon to realize that continued warfare was self-defeating. "Out of the greatest dangers," he concluded, "communities and individuals acquire the greatest glory." Their fathers fought off the Persians with far fewer resources: "We must not fall behind them, but must resist our enemies in any way and in every way, and attempt to hand down our power to our posterity unimpaired."[41] Pericles thought he could limit both the damage and the cost of the war. It was a perfectly rational calculation that turned out to be terribly wrong because of what his own envoys had called "the vast influence of accident in war."[42]

In March 431, Thebes, a Spartan ally, launched a surprise attack against tiny Plataea, a member of the Athenian alliance. Two months later, the Spartans marched through Corinth and Megara and began their first invasion of Attica. The war had officially begun, and Thucydides follows it chronologically, "by summers and winters," as the various campaigns unfold.

Pericles's strategy worked at first. The Athenians from the countryside brought their families and what they could carry of their goods within the long walls, where they were out of reach of the Spartan forces. But "deep was their trouble and discontent at abandoning their houses and the hereditary temples of the ancient state, and at having to change their habits of life" and crowd into the city, where they either stayed with friends or relatives or made do as best they could in the open spaces.[43] Moreover, as they watched the Spartans ravaging the territory with impunity, "the determination was universal, especially among the young men, to sally forth and stop it."[44] But aside from cavalry raids to keep the Spartans from the city and to pick off isolated groups of marauders, Pericles would not permit the Athenians to do battle, and, "confident of his wisdom in refusing a sally, would not call either an assembly or a meeting of the people, fearing the fatal results of a debate inspired by passion and not by prudence."[45]

Instead, Athens exploited its sea power, hitting Spartan interests in the Peloponnese and elsewhere, including a raid led by Pericles that ravaged Megara. Athens also kept a tight rein on its own allies, whose payments were critical to Athens's survival. The Spartans soon withdrew from Attica and returned home. Spartan interests had probably suffered more than Athenian, but it should now have been clear to both sides that there would be no ready end to the hostilities.

In the first winter of the war, when military operations were curtailed by the season, the Athenians held a state funeral for those who had fallen so far. Pericles gave the oration, and it is among the greatest speeches in antiquity, for in it he articulates the ideals of civic order and individual fulfillment that animated Athens and shaped her citizens. In doing so, he draws a sharp contrast between Athens and the closed and oppressive society of Sparta, making clear how much is at stake in this war.

Pericles argues that Athens is the "school of Hellas," because her constitution forms a pattern for others. It favors "the many instead of the few," and the laws "afford equal justice to all in their private differences." Moreover, "advancement in public life falls to reputation for capacity, class considerations not being allowed to interfere with merit; nor again does poverty bar the way, if a man is able to serve the state, he is not hindered by the obscurity of his condition."[46]

This political freedom is accompanied by an unrivaled personal freedom. A man in Athens may do as he likes in his private life without sanction or disapproval from his neighbors. Yet "all this ease in our private relations does not make us lawless as citizens."[47] Athenians obey the magistrates and the laws, particularly those that protect others from injury, "whether they are actually on the statute book, or belong to that code which, although unwritten, yet cannot be broken without acknowledged disgrace."[48]

The Athenians, moreover, have a genius for leisure and "plenty of means for the mind to refresh itself from business," including games, sacrifices, and festivals celebrated all the year round.[49] "We throw open our city to the world," attracting the ideas and energy as well as the produce of other countries.[50] "We cultivate refinement without extravagance and knowledge without effeminacy."[51] In politics, "instead of looking on discussion as a stumbling block in the way of action, we think it an indispensable preliminary to any wise action at all."[52] In education, "where our rivals from their very cradles by a painful discipline seek after manliness, at Athens we live exactly as we please, and yet are just as ready to encounter every legitimate danger."[53]

This last point is the most important for Pericles. The open, democratic government of Athens that accommodates private leisure and freedom, that cultivates the mind as well as the body, leads to the finest citizens, "with habits not of labor but of ease, and courage not of art but of nature,"[54] citizens who combine "daring and deliberation, each carried to its highest point,"[55] who are motivated "by courage, sense of duty, and a keen feeling of honor in action,"[56] and who can think and act for themselves and for the greater glory of their city. "I doubt if the world can produce a man, who where he has only himself to depend upon, is equal to so many emergencies, and graced by so happy a versatility as the Athenian."[57]

It is an idealized portrait, to be sure, and it would be sorely tested in the years ahead. Indeed, Thucydides immediately juxtaposes Pericles's speech with an account of the plague that devastated Athens the following summer and quickly made a mockery of some of the ideals he espoused. Yet the Athenians were indeed equal to many emergencies, this one among others, and showed a resiliency and daring that is nothing short of astounding.

PLAGUE

The Spartans returned the following summer, and the Athenians duly retreated to the city. Again, the Spartans did little real harm outside the walls. But this time, crowded and unsanitary conditions within proved a breeding ground for a plague said to have come from Africa by way of Egypt. In the *Iliad*, of course, the plague would have been sent by Apollo in divine retribution for one transgression or another. Thucydides will have nothing to do with such unscientific speculation. Finding himself unequal to documenting the origins and causes of the plague, he says, "I shall simply set down its nature, and explain the symptoms by which perhaps it may be recognized by the student, if it should ever break out again." He adds, quite dispassionately, "This I can the better do, as I had the disease myself, and watched its operation in the case of others."[58]

There follows a gripping and gruesome description of the progress of the disease, from violent heats in the head, through "discharges of bile of every kind named by physicians," pustules, unquenchable thirst, sleeplessness, and violent ulceration of the bowels, culminating in internal inflammation so severe and a weakness so profound as to be generally fatal.[59] Thucydides notes that even beasts shunned the dead bodies, and birds of prey disappeared from the skies of Athens. Physicians could not treat the plague; indeed, they themselves died most thickly, as they visited the sick most often. "Supplications in the temples, divinations, and so forth were found equally futile, till the overwhelming nature of the disaster at last put a stop to them altogether."[60]

Modern science still does not agree on the exact nature of this disease. But that Thucydides survived makes him one of the lucky ones. The plague devastated Athens for two consecutive summers, in 430 and 429, and it returned again in 427. The long walls and fortified harbor were worse than useless against such a pitiless enemy. As many as eighty thousand in total died in Athens. The plague, moreover, proved an indifferent reaper, taking in equal measure the strong along with the weak, the just with the unjust, the beloved as well as the neglected. It engendered despair among those who felt themselves sickening and a callousness born of fear in those who had not yet succumbed. The recently recovered were immune to a second attack and thus showed the most compassion. Others, "not knowing what was to become of them, became utterly careless of everything, whether sacred or profane."[61] Even burial rites, so important to the Greeks, were neglected. Men did as they pleased, without shame, "regarding their lives and riches as alike things of a day."[62] The principles of honor and piety lauded by Pericles themselves fell victim to the plague:

Fear of gods or law of man there was none to restrain them. As for the first, they judged it to be just the same whether they worshipped them or not, as they saw all alike perishing; and for the last, no one expected to live to be brought to trial for his offenses, but each felt that a far severer sentence had been already passed upon them all and hung ever over their heads, and before this fell it was only reasonable to enjoy life a little.[63]

This depletion of manpower and erosion of moral courage obviously had a profound impact on Athenian attitudes toward the war, though fear of the plague at least sent the Spartans scurrying back to the Peloponnese. The Athenians began to blame Pericles as the author of the war and hence of all their misfortunes. Against his advice, they even sent ambassadors to seek peace, but Sparta would make no concessions. In the face of this uproar, Pericles made the third and last of his speeches reported by Thucydides (at each of which Thucydides was undoubtedly present). In it, he urges the Athenians "to a calmer and more hopeful state of mind."[64]

Pericles makes no apologies for leading Athens to war, still believing that no other course is consistent with her past greatness and future glory. The current reverse is both terrible and sudden, he admits, while the future advantage is remote and obscure. But he chides the Athenians for "the infirmity of your resolution" and for being "too much depressed to persevere in your resolves."[65] Pericles reassures them that their naval power is still unrivaled and may be exercised at will. They control a vast and wealthy empire and their walls are yet unbreached. In short, their position has not materially changed since the outset of the war. In any event, "to recede is no longer possible. . . . For what you hold is, to speak somewhat plainly, a tyranny; to take it perhaps was wrong, but to let it go is unsafe."[66] He urges the Athenians to be worthy of their fathers. Never before has Athens "bent before disaster"; that is the source of her past greatness and her future glory.

> Make your decision, therefore, for glory then and honor now, and attain both objects by instant and zealous effort: do not send heralds to Sparta, and do not betray any sign of being oppressed by your present sufferings, since they whose minds are least sensitive to calamity, and whose hands are most quick to meet it, are the greatest men and the greatest communities.[67]

Pericles convinced the citizens to reapply themselves to the war. But their feelings still found outlet in removing Pericles from office and imposing a heavy fine upon him on a trumped-up charge of embezzlement. "Not long afterwards, however, according to the way of the multitude, they again elected him general and committed all their affairs to his hands."[68]

Pericles himself soon fell victim to the plague. Thucydides's brief but heartfelt epitaph of "the best man of all for the needs of the state"[69] attributes most of Athens's subsequent misfortunes to this loss. Pericles was a man of judgment, integrity, and foresight who led rather than flattered the people, and who "enjoyed so high an estimation that he could afford to anger them by contradiction."[70] Those who came after him, each eager to grasp at supremacy through an appeal for popular support, "ended by committing even the conduct of state affairs to the whims of the multitude,"[71] resulting in a host of blunders that squandered the abundant resources Pericles had sought to husband. It is a harsh judgment against the democracy, but it is largely borne out by Thucydides's account of subsequent events.

COLLATERAL DAMAGE

In the fourth summer of the war, much of the island of Lesbos, led by the city of Mytilene, revolted from Athenian control. With the two main combatants at a virtual stalemate in their series of raids and retaliations, prying loose allied states became an important third front, though often with deadly consequences for the states in question.

The Athenians, concerned that such revolts might spread and their empire disintegrate, reacted swiftly and forcefully to the Mytilene defection. They sent forty ships to Lesbos, established fortified camps on both sides of the city, and blockaded both its harbors. Mytilenian ambassadors convinced the Spartans to invade Attica again, by both land and sea, in hopes that Athens might feel compelled to raise its siege. But Athens had ample resources to meet both challenges and separately to attack the Peloponnese with thirty ships. The siege continued, and relief ships promised from the Peloponnese never arrived. By the following summer, the Mytilenian people refused any longer to obey their leaders, who were forced to surrender the city to Athens.

The Athenian general Paches sent the leaders of the revolt as prisoners to Athens and sought instructions on the further treatment of Mytilene. The Athenians debated the issue in the assembly and "in the fury of the moment determined to put to death not only the prisoners at Athens, but the whole adult male population of Mytilene, and to make slaves of the women and children."[72] They dispatched a trireme to Paches with those instructions. Yet, Thucydides explains, "the morrow brought repentance with it and reflection on the horrid cruelty of a decree which condemned a whole city to the fate merited only by the guilty."[73]

There follows a remarkable debate, in which Cleon, "the most violent man at Athens, and at that time by far the most powerful with The People," argues in favor of the original sentence as a necessary sign of firmness. Indeed, he chides the Athenians for their compassion and clemency, which are "full of danger to yourselves, and bring you no thanks for your weakness from your allies; entirely forgetting that your empire is a despotism and your subjects disaffected conspirators, whose obedience is insured not by your suicidal concessions, but by the superiority given you by your own strength and not their loyalty."[74] The counterspeech, by the otherwise unknown Diodotus, follows an equally pragmatic line, immediately dismissing any concerns about justice as suitable only for the law courts. Perhaps cowed by Cleon's vehement insistence that compassion also be discarded, he argues that, while the Mytilenians have no claims to their indulgence, Athens's own future interests require a more moderate policy that would not "exclude rebels from the hope of repentance and an early atonement of their error." If "surrender is out of the question," sieges will be more costly, and destruction of such cities will reduce "the revenue-producing powers of our dependencies."[75]

Diodotus's argument carried the day, and a second trireme was sent bearing the reprieve. The rowers in the second ship—on a happier mission than those in the first—took their meals as they rowed and slept by turns while others were at the oars. They arrived just as the sentence was being read out by Paches. On Cleon's motion, however, the Mytilenian prisoners in Athens, numbering more than one thousand, were put to death, and the land on Lesbos, aside from that of one loyal ally, was divided among Athenian shareholders. The Lesbians essentially became serfs on their own island, working the land for Athenian overlords.

Tiny Plataea, which fought with outsized courage against the Persians for the benefit of all Greece, met an even harsher fate. It successfully repelled the surprise attack launched by Thebes at the outset of the war. But in the summer of 429, the Peloponnesians and their allies attacked Plataea instead of proceeding on to Attica. The Plataeans protested that, when their city and territory were restored after the successful battle against the Persians, they were declared "independent and inviolate against aggression or conquest,"[76] and that, in recognition of their patriotism and service, the Spartans and others swore a solemn oath to protect them against any future attack. The Spartan king, Archidamus, brushed the oath aside, claiming that Plataea had forfeited its protection by allying with the Athenians, and he proceeded to invest the city.

The Plataeans managed to send women, children, and the elderly to relative safety in Athens before the full encirclement was completed. They held out against the siege for two more years, and even managed a dramatic winter breakout, in which half the remaining men escaped. But in 427, shortly after the Mytilene surrender, the Plataeans too gave way. Athens could no more protect its landlocked ally than Sparta could protect the island of Lesbos. No debate took place in any Spartan assembly. No compassion (whether pragmatic or genuine) was displayed. The Spartans simply asked each of them "whether they had done the Spartans and allies any service in the war; and upon their saying that they had not, took them out and slew them all without exception."[77] After this, neither side would give quarter, and small, often reluctant allies were increasingly swept from the board as so many dispensable pawns. Yet the words of the Plataeans continue to echo: "Our lives may be quickly taken, but it will be a heavy task to wipe away the infamy of the deed."[78]

CLASS WARFARE

In addition to outright attacks, the rival powers often fomented or inspired revolution in the cities outside their existing spheres of influence. Popular leaders sought help from democratic Athens, while oligarchs looked to Sparta. Differences that might have been resolved civilly, or at least with a minimum of bloodshed, in a time of peace were suddenly magnified by the ability of competing factions to call upon outside assistance to hurt their adversaries and advance their own interests. The result was a new and especially virulent form of class warfare that spread like an epidemic and convulsed the Hellenic world.

As he often does, Thucydides picks out and describes in detail one example of this trend to illustrate his broader point. He chooses the island of Corcyra, whose fight with Corinth and alliance with Athens helped precipitate the war. With the help of Corinth, the oligarchic party seized power in the fifth summer of the war and declared Corcyra's neutrality. The dispute started small, with competing prosecutions, but soon escalated to assassination and a takeover of the assembly, followed by street battles, in which the people (*demos*) "had the advantage in numbers and position, the women also valiantly assisting them, pelting with tiles from the houses."[79] The oligarchs, fearing total destruction, set fire to part of the town to bar their adversaries' advance and took refuge in the temple of Hera.

Athenian attempts to restore calm were disrupted by the arrival of a large Spartan fleet, until a still-larger Athenian fleet appeared. Each party was in turn emboldened and then fearful during these reversals, each of which occasioned further bloodshed until the violence was universal. For a seven-day period, "the Corcyraeans were engaged in butchering those of their fellow citizens whom they regarded as their enemies," usually for political reasons, but sometimes also in settlement of private quarrels.[80] Moderates, too, perished, caught between the two extremes like small cities whose neutrality could not be tolerated. "Death thus raged in every shape; and, as usually happens at such times, there was no length to which violence did not go."[81]

Complete and brutal anarchy thus prevailed until the slaughter ran its course as the plague ultimately had done in Athens. All moral considerations and even ties of blood were cast aside in the name of party faction. With revolution spreading from city to city, moreover, the level of cunning and atrocity increased, as the combatants were schooled in what had been done elsewhere. "In the confusion into which life was now thrown in the cities, human nature, always rebelling against the law and now its master, gladly showed itself ungoverned in passion, above respect for justice, and the enemy of all superiority."[82] The breakdown of *nomos* (law and custom) in favor of unbridled *physis* (nature) was almost complete.

Thucydides is at particular pains to trace the abuse and degradation of language along with that of morals. Anticipating George Orwell's famous essay, "Politics and the English Language," he writes:

> Words had to change their ordinary meaning and to take that which was now given them. Reckless audacity came to be considered the courage of a loyal supporter; prudent hesitation, specious cowardice; moderation was held to be a cloak for unmanliness; ability to see all sides of a question, incapacity to act on any. Frantic violence became the attribute of manliness; cautious plotting a justifiable means of self-defense.[83]

In the face of this collapse, Thucydides's restrained and painstaking style is itself an act of moral courage, an attempt to reassert the power of words to provide an accurate account of the human condition. He clinically exposes the brutality beneath the veneer of Greek enlightenment. Man in his essential nature does not change, not when fear and self-interest cause him to revert to his most basic and base instincts. By the fifth summer of the war, the sense of progress articulated in Pericles's funeral oration is long gone, and the words themselves sound hollow.

CLEON AND BRASIDAS

In its seventh summer, the war took a sudden turn in favor of Athens. With a small force, Demosthenes, the most aggressive of Athenian generals, established a fort at Pylos, on the coast of the Peloponnese. Once the Spartans learned of the fort—which could be used both as a base for raids into Laconia and as a beacon for fleeing Messenian helots—they broke off their annual raid on Athens and hurried home to deal with the threat. Sixty Spartan ships also sailed into the harbor so that the assault could be launched by land and by sea. The mouth of the harbor was largely blocked by a long, thin island, known as Sphacteria, which at one end came very close to the shore of Pylos. The Spartans landed troops on this island to keep it from being used by the Athenians to relieve the soldiers at Pylos. They also intended but failed to close the entrance to the harbor with closely packed lines of ships.

Despite overwhelming numbers, the Spartans were unable to take the fort. The Athenians, with "unflinching tenacity,"[84] fought off simultaneous assaults from land and sea until the Athenian fleet arrived, charged through both entrances of the harbor, and decisively defeated the Spartans, who managed to drag only a fraction of their ships to safety on shore. The soldiers on Sphacteria—420 in number, of whom 180 were "Spartiates," full citizens from the oldest families—were now trapped. The Spartans promptly sought an armistice that would allow them to send envoys to Athens to sue for peace. Under the terms of the armistice, all other Spartan ships were turned over to the Athenians, and fixed quantities of provisions were allowed through the Athenian cordon to feed the men on the island.

The Spartan reaction to the defeat at Pylos seems extreme. But Sparta had few full citizens to begin with, and those on Sphacteria were from its most prominent families. Perhaps even more important was the shock of a Spartan defeat on the field of battle, a shock that reverberated throughout the Greek world and suddenly made Athens seem stronger and Sparta more vulnerable. For just this reason, though, Cleon was able to convince the Athenians, who had been eager for peace hitherto, to reject the Spartan offer and counter with clearly unacceptable terms.

The armistice accordingly ended, though the Athenians, claiming Spartan violations, kept the ships. Sparta threw itself with renewed but still unsuccessful fury at the reinforced fort and looked for opportunities to rescue those on the island, which was closely patrolled and blockaded by Athenian ships. The best they could manage were risky solo efforts to bring provisions to the stranded soldiers. But these nighttime dashes enabled the men to hold out through the summer and made the Athenians repent for having rejected the offered treaty, for with the arrival of winter the Athenian ships would have to withdraw and the men would escape.

Cleon, seeing his support eroding, taunted Nicias, a well-respected general who favored peace, that it should be easy to capture the men on the island, and he claimed that if he, Cleon, were general, he would already have done it. Nicias invited Cleon to help himself and offered to resign in his favor. Cleon immediately backpedaled, but the populace supported the plan, and Cleon finally concluded he had no choice. Boasting that "he would within twenty days either bring the Spartans alive, or kill them on the spot," he sailed off with reinforcements.[85] "The Athenians could not help laughing at his empty words," Thucydides notes, "while sensible men comforted themselves with the reflection that they must gain in either circumstance; either they would be rid of Cleon, which they rather hoped, or if disappointed in this expectation, would reduce the Spartans."[86]

Yet Cleon in fact made good his boast, with a combination of luck and the tactics of Demosthenes, for which he happily took credit. Since the fort at Pylos was crowded, some Athenians cooked their dinner on the extreme edge of the island, with outposts set to prevent any surprise attack. One evening they inadvertently set fire to the woods, and the fire quickly spread, eliminating the cover and allowing the Athenians to fix the exact number and location of the Spartans. The Athenians then attacked the island, occupying the high ground on the end nearest Pylos, while archers and peltasts (lightly armed troops with javelins, darts, and slings) kept up a steady fire and then retreated behind a line of heavily armed hoplites whenever the Spartans dashed out against them. A group of Messenians landed on the other side of the island and suddenly appeared on the high ground to the rear of the Spartans. Surrounded, exhausted, and weak from want of food, the Spartans remarkably (given the ethos of Thermopylae) surrendered. "The Athenians and Peloponnesians now each withdrew their forces from Pylos and went home, and mad as Cleon's promise was, he fulfilled it by bringing the men to Athens within the twenty days as he had pledged himself to do."[87]

A total of 292 captives, including 120 Spartiates, were imprisoned in Athens pending negotiation of a peace treaty, and the Athenians made clear that the captives would be killed if the Peloponnesians invaded Attica again. But with Cleon steadfastly opposed, the negotiations went nowhere. "The Athenians . . . kept grasping at more, and dismissed envoy after envoy without their having effected anything."[88] Following additional successes in the Peloponnese at Cythera and Thyrea, the Athenians began to think that nothing could withstand them, and to "confuse their strength with their hopes."[89]

It took a series of reverses and two deaths to bring about peace at last. The Athenians were thwarted in their attempt to take Megara with the help of a prodemocracy faction. An invasion of Boeotia also ended in a narrow defeat at Delium in 424, a battle described in Plato's *Symposium* and marked by the presence of both Socrates and Alcibiades.

Meanwhile, Brasidas, the Spartans' most daring, aggressive, and effective campaigner, marched into timber-rich Thrace (critical to Athens's shipbuilding program) in an attempt to dislodge Athenian allies there. Thrace was one of the few portions of the Athenian Empire accessible by land. With "seductive arguments"—a mixture of threats, guarantees of independence, and promises of protection from the Athenians—Brasidas convinced the city of Acanthus to give way without a fight.[90] He then captured Amphipolis and Torone with the help of traitors within those cities. It was the former event that led to the exile of Thucydides, although the prompt return of his squadron did forestall a further Spartan advance on Eion.

The Athenians were now more eager to deal, if only to forestall and prepare for any further advance by Brasidas. They agreed to a one-year armistice, with each side retaining any acquisitions but refraining from further encroachments. Yet Brasidas immediately broke the armistice by receiving Scione and Mende into the Spartan alliance. Their decision to revolt would prove rash and ill-considered. Brasidas simply wanted further bargaining chips for the coming peace, "something to exchange and restore." But, Thucydides notes, "it is a habit of mankind to entrust to careless hope what they long for, and to use sovereign reason to thrust aside what they do not desire."[91]

Even as the "armistice" continued, Nicias was dispatched by the infuriated Athenians to win back Scione and Mende. Mende was readily restored, as the popular party there rebelled against the few oligarchs who had turned the city over to Sparta. A sortie from Scione was soundly defeated, and the Athenians settled in to besiege the city. When the truce ended the following year, Cleon sailed with a larger force to retake all the lost cities in Thrace. He readily recaptured Torone, but, in a preliminary reconnaissance of Amphipolis in October of 422, Cleon and his small force were caught out in the open in a surprise attack and largely slaughtered. Cleon was killed but, luckily for the Athenians, so was Brasidas, one of only seven Spartans to die in the skirmish.

With the two leading proponents of war—Cleon and Brasidas—now dead, both sides ceased to prosecute the war. Athens "had no longer that confidence in her strength which had made her before refuse to accept the offer of peace," while

Sparta had "found the actuality of the war falsify her notion that devastating their land for a few years would suffice for the overthrow of the power of the Athenians."[92] The Peace of Nicias was completed in the spring of 421, with each party to restore its conquests and its prisoners, including the Spartans from Pylos. Athens, left to deal as it pleased with the revolting Thracian cities, soon retook the city of Scione, put the adult males to death, enslaved their women and children, and gave the land to the surviving Plataeans.

THE MELIAN DIALOGUE

Ten years of war were at an end, with fifty years of peace guaranteed by the Spartans and Athenians alike. The treaty in fact lasted less than seven years, and "only a mistaken judgment," Thucydides assures us, "can object to including the interval of treaty in the war."[93] Provisions were violated or ignored from the outset, and open hostilities were common. The two principals refrained from directly invading each other's territories, but in most other respects a state of war continued.

Corinth, Boeotia, and Sparta's allies in Thrace all refused to ratify the treaty or to abide by its conditions. Amphipolis and other cities were not restored to Athens, nor would Boeotia release its Athenian prisoners. Resentment swelled, and, against the advice of Nicias but at the urging of the handsome, brilliant, and ambitious Alcibiades, Athens formed alliances with three significant cities in the Peloponnese: Argos, Mantinea, and Elis. These threatening alliances resulted in the battle of Mantinea in 418, one of the few set-piece hoplite battles of the war, which ironically took place during a period of alleged peace. Sparta won, in large part because the Athenians—not wishing to risk a decisive treaty violation— offered only limited support to its new allies, which quickly renounced their pact with Athens and again made peace with Sparta.

Further machinations ensued, usually involving proxy states. The most telling was Athens's ultimatum to Melos, a Spartan colony that had somehow managed to remain neutral through ten years of war and five years of a false peace. In 416, Athens decided it could no longer tolerate such neutrality from a tiny, unprotected island that fell within its natural sphere of influence, and sent an expedition of thirty-eight ships and more than three thousand heavily armed hoplites and archers to persuade the Melians to join their alliance.

The ensuing dialogue between Athenian envoys and Melian commissioners, as portrayed by Thucydides, is justly famous for the foolish idealism of the

Melians and the brutal realism of the Athenians. The Melians claim to have right on their side and refuse to submit to what they see as slavery. The Athenians immediately dismiss appeals to justice as irrelevant: "You know as well as we do that right, as the world goes, is only in question between equals in power, while the strong do what they can and the weak suffer what they must."[94] They urge the Melians to make the inevitable easier on themselves and on the Athenians. Yet the Melians insist that in action there is hope and that "it were surely great baseness and cowardice in us who are still free not to try everything that can be tried, before submitting to your yoke."[95] The Athenians, in words that would soon apply to themselves, are again dismissive:

> Hope, danger's comforter, may be indulged in by those who have abundant resources, if not without loss, at all events without ruin, but its nature is to be extravagant, and those who go so far as to stake their all upon the venture see it in its true colors only when they are ruined; but so long as the discovery would enable them to guard against it, it is never found wanting.[96]

The Melians allude to Athens's own seemingly hopeless but noble fight for freedom against the Persians: "We trust that the gods may grant us fortune as good as yours, since we are just men fighting against unjust."[97] But the Athenians are unmoved by the seeming parallel and tell the Melians they can no more count upon the gods than they can upon the Spartans, who are far away and will not undertake a risky expedition for the sake of Melos, whatever promises of support they might have made.

The Melians will not bend, a siege is vigorously pressed, and, "some treachery taking place inside," the familiar litany is again intoned: the Athenians "put to death all the grown men whom they took, and sold the woman and children for slaves, and subsequently sent out five hundred colonists and settled the place themselves."[98] But in this context, the coda is still shocking, and its very dryness underscores what Athens has become. Divorced from the sources of her own strength, as exemplified in the fight against Persia and articulated in Pericles's funeral oration, Athens will ruthlessly expand her power until decisively checked by still-greater forces. Pericles's claim that the Athenians respect "that code which, although unwritten, yet cannot be broken without acknowledged disgrace"[99] can no longer be taken seriously.

If this were Herodotus, the *hubris* and injustice of the Athenians would be promptly punished by the gods. This is Thucydides, and neither the gods nor justice influence events; but Athens will receive her check soon enough. Despite himself, Thucydides is presenting us with a morality tale.

THE SICILIAN EXPEDITION

Thucydides's account of the Sicilian expedition covers two full books. It is the longest sustained narrative in the work and in many respects its culmination, just as the second Persian invasion of Greece was the culmination of Herodotus's *Histories*. The comparison is apt in other respects as well. Athens was now on a distant mission of conquest, and its target was the democratic regime of Syracuse, as well as other Greek colonies on the island that more often quarreled than cooperated with one another. Athens sent a massive force that could, and probably would, have succeeded but for strategic blunders by the invaders and energetic, creative resistance by defenders temporarily united in their own fight for freedom. The result, too, was a new empire of sorts, as a victorious Syracuse came to dominate the cities within its orbit.

Pericles had warned the Athenians "not to combine schemes of fresh conquest with the conduct of the war" against Sparta.[100] But with a shaky peace still in place, that warning was pushed aside by ambition: Alcibiades's ambition for military glory and political power, and Athens's ambition to expand the scope of her empire. The pretext for invasion came in a request for assistance by the small city of Egesta, a nominal ally of Athens on the northwest coast of Sicily, and by the people of Leontini, who had been driven from their city by Syracuse. Egesta was at war with neighboring Selinus, an ally of Syracuse. The Egestaeans claimed to have great riches and promised to pay for the expedition. An Athenian delegation bore out the claim, "as attractive as it was untrue,"[101] of money in abundance in the temples and treasury there, not realizing that it was always the same money moved from place to place ahead of the visiting inspectors, and the same gold plate and other costly items moved from house to house where they dined each evening.

The cautious, pious, and well-respected Nicias argued strongly against the expedition, echoing Pericles that they must conserve and build their resources at home. Even if conquered, he explained, Sicily could not be ruled. It was too far off and the people too numerous. Any serious reverse, by contrast, would be an immediate signal for abrogation of the treaty and an opportunistic attack by Sparta and its allies. Nicias also criticized Alcibiades, though not by name, as a young man pursuing ends of his own, rather than those of his city, and living in splendor beyond his means, a young man "who seeks to be admired" and "hopes for some profit from his appointment."[102]

Alcibiades, however, carried the day. He boasted of his own ability, belittled the divided Sicilians, claimed that many barbarians would join in the attack from hatred of the Syracusans, that the Athenians could easily withdraw with their navy if difficulties arose, and most astonishingly that the Peloponnesians were sufficiently cowed to pose little threat to Athens. But his core argument (echoing Xerxes, the Persian king) was that it is the nature of empires to expand or die:

> We cannot fix the exact point at which our empire shall stop; we have reached a position in which we must not be content with retaining what we have but must scheme to extend it for, if we cease to rule others, we shall be in danger of being ruled ourselves.[103]

Nicias then made the first of a long series of mistakes that would prove fatal for Athens as well as for himself. The Athenian plan was to send sixty ships under the joint command of Nicias, Alcibiades, and a third general, Lamachus. Nicias, hoping still to dissuade the Athenians and make them understand the magnitude of the undertaking and the risks involved, argued that the force was too small and that they needed overwhelming superiority at sea, a large land army, and numerous cavalry. But the Athenians, far from being deterred, were delighted with the advice and, thinking the safety of the expedition was now assured, voted the extra resources. As a result, the armada that sailed from the Piraeus in the summer of 415—more than one hundred triremes plus transports for five thousand hoplites, as well as archers, slingers, and others (but not, unfortunately, cavalry)—"was by far the most costly and splendid Hellenic force that had ever been sent out by a single city up to that time."[104]

Yet the expedition was undermined even before it began. As the final preparations were being completed, Athens awoke one morning to find that the stone statues of Hermes that marked the doorways of private houses and temples had been disfigured. Rumors spread of a drunken frolic by a group of well-to-do young men, and Alcibiades was (probably falsely) implicated. Other allegations surfaced of mock celebrations of the initiation ceremonies in honor of the goddess Demeter, known as the Eleusinian Mysteries—allegations spread by enemies of Alcibiades who feared that a successful expedition to Sicily would make him undisputed master of the demos (i.e., a demagogue).

Alcibiades denied the charges and asked to stand trial before the expedition sailed. But his enemies, concerned that the army would support him and that his presence would sway the people, urged his immediate departure and pledged to put off any trial until after his return. Once the expedition left, however, they stirred up more serious allegations—based, as Thucydides puts it, "upon the evidence of rascals"[105]—of a planned oligarchic takeover and indicted Alcibiades and others.

When the expedition arrived in Sicily, the fraud of the Egestaeans was uncovered—they had only a tiny fraction of the money they promised. Nicias wanted to take whatever money Egesta could supply, settle matters at Selinus, see what, if anything, they could do at Leontini, and then sail around the coast, displaying the power of Athens before heading home. Lamachus urged that they attack Syracuse immediately and in full force "while the people were still unprepared, and the panic at its height."[106] Alcibiades, always one for diplomatic machinations, suggested that they first form as many alliances as possible to aid in the attack. Lamachus reluctantly supported Alcibiades, and envoys were sent to all the cities except Selinus and Syracuse. But the very size of the Athenian armada terrified the cities in Sicily and along the coast of southern Italy. Those who might have aided a more limited expedition against Syracuse and its allies feared a complete conquest by Athens, and many cities refused to support them, to allow them the use of their harbors, or even to sell them provisions.

It was at this point that a state trireme arrived to bring Alcibiades home for trial and likely execution. Alcibiades fled and eventually made his way to Sparta, under sentence of death by default, where he sought asylum with promises that he could aid them in their war against Athens. Aid them he did, and with devastating effect, though whether Alcibiades deliberately or Nicias through incompetence did more to defeat Athens is open to debate.

The Athenian armada frittered away the summer, sailing uselessly around Sicily, while Syracuse, contemptuous of Athenian inaction, gained in confidence and in allies. The two armies finally met on a plain near the city in the early winter. The Athenians won in close fighting but failed to follow up the victory out of fear of the Syracusan cavalry. Instead, they retired to winter quarters and sent a trireme to Athens asking that money and cavalrymen be sent to them in the spring.

Once the cavalry arrived, the Athenians finally moved into action. They seized the high ground outside the city at Epipolae, again defeated the Syracusans in open battle, and began to build forts and a siege wall to encircle and cut off the city. Efforts by the Syracusans to disrupt the circumvallation through cavalry attacks and counterwalls proved ineffectual. But Lamachus was killed in one of the sorties, and his death was disastrous. With the Athenian fleet coming to blockade its Great

Harbor and a wall cutting it off by land, the fall of Syracuse would be inevitable. But the timid, lethargic, and now-ailing Nicias was in sole command, and he failed to complete the last portion of the wall down to the sea on the northeast side of Syracuse, spending his time instead reinforcing the portion already completed with a second wall and negotiating for the surrender of the city.

Meanwhile, Alcibiades had succeeded in stirring up the Spartans and their Corinthian allies. He told them, with characteristic exaggeration, of a vast Athenian scheme to conquer Sicily, Italy, and Carthage, and then to use their resources to attack the Peloponnese. Alcibiades urged the Peloponnesians to aid Syracuse and also to recommence the war against Athens in order to make them fight on two fronts. Alcibiades justified his treason on the grounds that he had been wronged: "The true lover of his country is not he who consents to lose it unjustly rather than attack it, but he who longs for it so much that he will go to all lengths to recover it."[107]

Sparta sent a single general, Gylippus, and a handful of ships from Corinth and elsewhere. But it was to prove sufficient, especially as Nicias, though forewarned, made no effort to intercept them. Gylippus gathered troops from among the Syracusan allies and seized the high ground that Nicias left inexplicably unprotected. The Syracusan troops marched from the city to join him, and together they began to build a new counterwall toward Epipolae. Athens scattered the disorganized Syracusans in an initial battle, but Gylippus rallied them, made better use of their cavalry in a second engagement, and defeated the Athenians. The counterwall was completed and Athenian hopes of investing the city were at an end.

Nicias's response was to send a plaintive but self-justifying letter to the Athenians warning them that they must either recall the expedition or "send out to us another fleet and army as numerous again, with a large sum of money, and someone to succeed me, as a disease in the kidneys renders me unfit to retain my post."[108] Nicias, hoping for a recall, again misjudged his city, which promptly doubled down on the Sicilian wager, gathering ships and troops from Athens and its many allies. They were sent under the command of Demosthenes and Eurymedon, not as successors to Nicias but as two more co-commanders.

While the new armada was being assembled, the situation near Syracuse continued to deteriorate. Nicias placed his ships in a disadvantageous position at the extreme end of the Great Harbor of Syracuse, where the men had to forage far and wide for fuel and water, which made them vulnerable to the Syracusan cavalry. Worse, he gathered his spare provisions—including masts and other equipment for the ships—and left them inadequately protected in a fort that was seized in a surprise attack by Gylippus. Worst of all, democratic Syracuse, showing the same sort of adaptability that Athens had done in the war with Persia, began rapidly to assemble a navy of its own. Although they were no match for the Athenian fleet at first, they learned quickly and contested for control of the Great Harbor. They specially reinforced their ships to make them more effective at ramming in close quarters and won a critical victory before Demosthenes and his fleet arrived in the summer of 413.

These Athenian reverses emboldened the Syracusan allies and persuaded other cities to drop their neutrality. The forces Gylippus commanded grew accordingly, and Sparta and its allies, sensing the possibility of a decisive Athenian defeat, further reinforced them. At the same time, Sparta again invaded Attica and, following the advice of Alcibiades, took and fortified Decelea, which was a mere thirteen or fourteen miles from Athens. This gave Sparta a permanent base from which to launch attacks in force as well as smaller raids that kept the Athenians constantly off-balance and unable to make use of their land. All provisions now had to be imported, and the long walls and other fortifications had to be constantly manned. More than twenty thousand slaves deserted Athens to seek refuge at Decelea.

Upon his arrival, Demosthenes, the opposite of Nicias in temperament, lost no time in launching an immediate attack on the high ground at Epipolae, which was the strategic key to Syracuse, as it would enable them to complete the circumvallation. "This he took to be the shortest way of ending the war, as he would either succeed and take Syracuse, or would lead back the armament instead of frittering away the lives of the Athenians engaged in the expedition and the resources of the country at large."[109] After first failing to capture the counterwall through direct assault, Demosthenes planned a daring nighttime attack on Epipolae. Despite early success, the attack disintegrated as the Athenian forces became disorganized, lost their way, and confused enemies with allies.

Demosthenes now advocated that they leave without further loss of time and men. Nicias, fearful of being condemned at home for returning without approval from the Athenian assembly and claiming to be in contact with a faction within Syracuse that wanted to betray the city to them, sought more time. Demosthenes, joined by Eurymedon, insisted that they at least drop the siege and move to a more defensible position, with open country and open water in which their army and their fleet respectively could maneuver. Yet Nicias still objected, and "a certain diffidence and hesitation came over them."[110]

Nicias finally agreed to depart when Gylippus arrived with a large number of fresh troops mustered from the growing list of Sicilian allies. "All was at last ready, and they were on the point of sailing away when an eclipse of the moon, which was then at the full, took place."[111] Nicias, who Thucydides notes "was somewhat overaddicted to divination," steadfastly refused to depart until a period prescribed by the soothsayers of "thrice nine days" had elapsed.[112] But by then it was too late. Not content to see the Athenians sail away (as the Persians had done after Salamis), Syracuse and its allies completely blocked the Great Harbor, and an effort by the Athenian armada to break out was repulsed with great losses. The Athenians were so disheartened that they failed even to seek leave to collect their dead, among whom was Eurymedon. Demosthenes tried to rally them for another attempt, but the sailors refused to reboard the ships. Instead, they began a march overland "to the nearest friendly place they could reach, Hellenic or barbarian."[113]

Forty thousand men began that march, leaving the sick, the wounded, and their unburied comrades behind. Nicias, showing a nobility of spirit and fortitude that belied his many mistakes in leadership, did his best to rally, encourage, and comfort the men, walking through their ranks and drawing in any stragglers. But the retreating army was blocked and harried at every point. They split up in an effort to escape, but upon being surrounded and slaughtered by arrows, slings, and javelins, first Demosthenes and then Nicias surrendered. Both leaders were promptly executed. The surviving soldiers were crowded into rock quarries, where they died rapidly of disease, hunger, thirst, and exposure.

The Athenians lost more than 200 ships, 4,500 of their own citizens, and as many as 50,000 allied fighters. Thucydides ends his account by noting:

> They were beaten at all points and altogether; all that they suffered was great; they were destroyed, as the saying is, with a total destruction, their fleet, their army—everything was destroyed, and few out of many returned home. Such were the events in Sicily.[114]

ENDGAME

The Athenians reacted to the events in Sicily with anger and dismay. They now had too few ships, too few sailors, and too little money to prosecute the war. Yet they did not give way to despair. Recognizing that having the full assembly decide matters of military strategy might have been a mistake, they appointed a board of elders (including the poet Sophocles) to advise the state. They also settled down to building ships, recruiting sailors, and reducing expenses while raising revenues wherever possible. In short, they showed grit in the face of a bleak situation. The winter following the Sicilian defeat, Thucydides writes, "saw all Hellas stirring."[115] The confident Peloponnesian states redoubled their war efforts, aided now by a surging Syracuse. Longtime neutrals opportunistically joined the Spartan cause. Athenian subjects, especially in Ionia, saw their own chance and revolted. Even Persia gave the Spartans funds to build and man a powerful fleet of their own. In exchange, the Spartans secretly agreed to hand the Ionian states and islands back to Persian control—so much for their claim that they were fighting for the freedom of all Greeks from Athenian tyranny.

Despite the forces arrayed against them, and against all expectations, Athens held out for another nine years and, indeed, sufficiently gained the upper hand at certain junctures that the Spartans twice sued for peace, which the Athenians, of course, promptly rejected. Thucydides lived through these events and even returned to Athens from exile in 404. But when he died in 395 or thereabouts, his history was incomplete, ending abruptly, midparagraph in 411, the twenty-first year of the war. Rather like Nicias, who improved the existing portion of his siege wall at Syracuse rather than completing it down to the water, Thucydides doubled back and reworked his early books instead of rushing on to finish the narrative.

Fortunately, we still have his account of the *opéra bouffe* reappearance of Alcibiades, last seen in Sparta conspiring against his former homeland. Alcibiades had an affair with the wife of Agis, one of the two hereditary kings of Sparta, and she bore him a son. Thucydides only discreetly hints at this affair; it is later made explicit in Plutarch. Deciding it was time to leave, Alcibiades convinced rivals of Agis to send him to negotiate with Tissaphernes, the Persian satrap in Ionia. But Alcibiades was soon accused of seeking his own advantage rather than that of Sparta (no surprise there), and the Spartans ordered his execution. He fled to the protection of the Persians, where he urged King Darius II to drag out the struggle between Athens and Sparta, weakening both sides by promising much and delivering little.

Alcibiades simultaneously sent out feelers to certain prominent Athenians, claiming that he alone could forge an alliance with Persia that would save them from destruction. But, he explained, Darius was suspicious of the democracy and preferred to deal with a steadier, more reliable oligarchy. Since this was exactly what they wanted to hear anyway, those in Athens who favored oligarchy embarked on a campaign of assassination and terror that allowed them to seize power. They proposed rule by a Council of Four Hundred. The cowed assembly, "without a single opposing voice," ratified the new constitution and was then dissolved after a century of democratic rule.[116]

But the Athenian sailors based at the island of Samos, where they were trying to put down the Ionian revolt, would have none of it. They deposed any officers suspected of favoring the oligarchy and resolved to sail on Athens. Alcibiades then showed his nimble genius by becoming the champion of the democrats. He "extravagantly magnified his own influence with Tissaphernes," and promised to bring Persia into the war on behalf of Athens.[117] The sailors promptly elected him general. "Now it was that Alcibiades for the first time," Thucydides writes, "did the state a service, and one of the most outstanding kind."[118] He put a stop to their plans to sail immediately to Athens, thereby averting a civil war, but sent word that the democracy, or at least some broader form of representation, had to be restored.

The oligarchs had already begun to fall out among themselves, each vying for the first position, and they even unsuccessfully attempted "to make peace with Sparta upon any terms" so as to maintain themselves in power. But the Spartans launched an attack on the nearby island of Euboea, and Athens lost twenty-two ships in its defense. This defeat left the Athenians in a panic, since the fleet at Samos was in revolt and they had no ships left to protect Athens. But the Spartans did not follow up their victory by themselves sailing on Athens. Thucydides drily notes that "here, as on so many other occasions, the Spartans proved the most convenient people in the world for the Athenians to be at war with."[119] The Athenians promptly deposed the Council of Four Hundred and replaced it with an assembly of Five Thousand, of which all "who furnished a suit of armor were to be members."[120] They also voted to recall Alcibiades from exile, but he wisely stayed away until he had won (or at least claimed credit for) a victory at Cyzicus in 410 and could return to Athens in triumph.

Both the victory and the triumphant return, which was in any event short-lived, fall outside Thucydides's narrative. It was left to the prolific Xenophon (430–354) to pick up the story where Thucydides left off in the fall of 411. Xenophon starts his *Hellenika* with the words "And after this, not many days later . . ."[121] In the first two books, he tells of the continuing sea battles off the coast of Ionia; of Alcibiades's rapid fall from grace with the now fully restored democracy and his flight to the castle he had built on the Hellespont for just such an eventuality; of Athens's dramatic victory over the Spartan fleet at Arginousae in 406; of the subsequent trial and execution of most of the generals who engineered that victory but were prevented first by their pursuit of the enemy and then by a sudden storm from rescuing Athenian sailors clinging to their wrecks and from recovering the bodies of those killed; of the disastrous loss of the entire remaining fleet at Aegospotami in 405 by the inexperienced and incompetent commanders sent out to replace them; and of Athens's final surrender in 404, the dismantling of the long walls, and the installation by Sparta of the Thirty Tyrants, who were themselves driven out by the democrats within a year.

The *Hellenika* is an invaluable document, but Xenophon is no Thucydides. Thucydides sets the standard for all subsequent political, military, and diplomatic history. In the tautness of his narrative, the careful sifting of sources, and the dramatic power of the speeches he reports, Thucydides has few equals. In the complexity, the subtlety, and the lasting power of his moral vision, he stands alone. Thucydides is never simplistic. Yet his unsentimental, even clinical study of human nature in conditions of plague, war, and revolution—realistic as it is—somehow manages to retain the ideals of Pericles's funeral oration, if only as a distant, redemptive echo.

Chapter 8

ARISTOPHANES AND THE SERIOUS BUSINESS OF COMEDY

Aristotle's *Poetics* focused almost exclusively on tragedy, which he considered "of graver import" than comedy.[1] While tragedy deals with serious subjects and portrays men of greatness, comedy presents the ridiculous and offers "an imitation of men worse than the average."[2] As such, comedy undermines rather than reinforces our quest for virtue, and its poets are of a "meaner sort" than those who compose tragedies.[3]

Plato acknowledged in the *Laws* that it will be "impossible to understand the serious side of things in isolation from their ridiculous aspect."[4] Yet, like Aristotle, he stressed that, "if we intend to acquire virtue," the ridiculous must be avoided.[5] "No one must ever take [comedy] at all seriously," Plato cautioned, because "we can't be serious and comic too."[6] In the *Philebus*, moreover, he claimed that all poetic arts are "second-rate and inferior" because they offer mere imitations of a changing world of appearances, whereas philosophy gives us knowledge of things that are eternal and unchanging.[7]

Aristophanes would take exception to this philosophical indictment of comedy on both levels. First, he considered comedy to be at least the equal of tragedy. "Even comedy," he said somewhat plaintively in *Acharnians*, knows what is right.[8] Tragedy uses myth to illuminate the issues of the day. But comedy tackles them directly—the Peloponnesian War, the virtues and excesses of democracy, the jury system, the role of women, and the problem of poverty. Even cultural issues such as the rise of the Sophists and the innovations of Euripidean tragedy were fair game for Aristophanes.

Aristophanes anticipated and directly challenged Plato's later statement that "we can't be serious and comic too." Aristophanes cautions his audience, "Besides the jokes, remember, there's a lot of serious stuff."[9] Like the fool in *King Lear*,

213

Aristophanes claimed license to speak truth to power, to say "what is right" in the guise of comedy. He considered his comedies an integral part of the political, social, and intellectual discourse of his time.

In fact, Aristophanes thought that comedy can tell us as much about our true selves and our society as can tragedy. Aristotle loved tragedy for its portraits of great men. Comedy can tear down the pretentions of such men through parody and thus provide a more accurate (if less inspiring) portrayal of everyday life. Even Plato recognized as much when he recommended that Dionysius of Syracuse study Aristophanes if he wanted to understand contemporary Athens.[10] The ancient Greeks considered comedy "the mirror of life,"[11] and in Aristophanes's mirror the full richness of Athenian life was displayed and, of course, distorted for comic effect. This distortion—the puncturing of pretensions, the exposure of the ridiculous—offended Aristotle and led him to dismiss comedy as unworthy of study. But Plato's acknowledgment that it will be "impossible to understand the serious side of things in isolation from their ridiculous aspect" showed a subtler appreciation of the critical function of comedy, if only as a complement to tragedy.

Aristophanes not only placed comedy on at least the same plane as tragedy, but he thought both were superior to philosophy. Far from accepting Plato's later claim, echoed more softly by Aristotle, that the poetic arts generally are "second-rate and inferior," Aristophanes in *Frogs* dismissed philosophy as "never-ending futile chatter / In a niggling senseless game."[12] In *Clouds*, he literally burned down "the Thinkery" of his fictional Socrates and was later blamed by Plato for the climate of opinion that led to the trial and execution of the real Socrates. Leo Strauss has rightly noted that Aristophanes and Socrates were archetypal antagonists in what Plato would call "the ancient quarrel between poetry and philosophy" as to the best means to human happiness and understanding.[13] For Socrates, only abstract knowledge of the good, achieved through rational thought, could place our lives and our society on a solid foundation. For Aristophanes, only a concrete poetic portrayal of reality suffused with the poet's vision of "what is right" could "[inject] sense into a senseless race,"[14] transforming both the individual and his *polis*. Poetry, not philosophy, was the road to wisdom and self-knowledge, and Aristophanes made the journey a raucous pleasure. In his *Classical Dictionary*, John Lemprière, a British scholar from the early 1800s, with good reason pronounced Aristophanes "the greatest comic dramatist in world literature: by his side Molière seems dull and Shakespeare clownish."[15]

OLD COMEDY

Aristophanes was born in Athens around 450. He came from a prosperous landowning family but was not among the aristocracy. Little is known of his life or his politics, except what can be inferred from his plays. Aristophanes served in 390 on the Council of Five Hundred (which oversaw the administration of Athens and determined the agenda of the assembly of all adult male citizens). Otherwise, his involvement in civic life was as a dramatist rather than a direct participant. He had three sons, two of whom also wrote comedies, though without the genius or notoriety of their father.

Aristophanes's theatrical debut (*The Banqueters*) was in 427, but he did not himself produce that play or its two immediate successors. Rather, he turned to a more experienced producer, Kallistratos, because (as he explained to the audience in *Knights*) producing a comedy is the most difficult task in existence. "One must learn how to row, / before grabbing the tiller, / And one must work on deck for a bit / and study the weather / Before presuming to be a skipper."[16] Only after his third play (*Acharnians*) took first place at the Lenaea festival, when he was in his midtwenties, did he end his apprenticeship and produce a play himself (*Knights*), which also won first prize.

In all, Aristophanes wrote at least forty plays, of which eleven survive. We do not know how many total victories he enjoyed, but there were at least six (four at the Lenaea and two at the Dionysia). Only three of the extant plays (*Acharnians*, *Knights*, and *Frogs*) are known to have won first prize. *Frogs* was so popular that it enjoyed the rare privilege of a second performance, voted by the assembly. *Clouds*, by contrast, though one of Aristophanes's most important surviving plays, placed a disappointing third in a war-reduced field of three.

Most of his plays were produced during the years of the Peloponnesian War—which lasted from 431 to 404—and were deeply colored by that experience. Aristophanes relished the power and economic prosperity of the Athenian empire, which fueled Spartan jealousy and led to the outbreak of war. Whether he relished the radical democracy that oversaw that empire and conducted the war is a harder question. He lived through the Great Plague of 430–426, which killed more Athenians—including Pericles, Athens's leading statesman—than the rest of the war. He rejoiced in the Peace of Nicias in 421, which was supposed to last for thirty years but ended after a cold war of only seven. He mourned the loss of the Sicilian expedition, launched in 415 and utterly destroyed in 413. An oligarchic coup in 411 was quickly followed by the restoration of democracy in 410.

Where Aristophanes's sympathies lay, we do not know. But when Persia backed Sparta in 407, the endgame was clear. In 405, the remaining, patched-together Athenian fleet was decimated at Aegospotami, and Athens was besieged and forced to surrender in 404. There followed a reign of terror imposed by a group of Thirty Tyrants backed by Sparta, which lasted until 403. At that point, the democracy was restored and an amnesty declared. The restored democracy lasted another eighty-one years, until the Macedonians conquered all of Greece and most of the rest of the known world.

But Athens was never the same. The period of its poetic genius—so closely bound with the defeat of the Persians, the invention of democracy, and the growth of empire—had passed. Philosophy and science flourished in the ensuing years, Athens's Indian summer; but tragedy and Aristophanes's version of comedy faded away. By the time of Aristophanes's death, so-called old comedy was at an end.

The origins of this "old comedy" are obscure. The Greek word *komoidia* (comedy) combines *komos* (revel) and *oidai* (song). According to Aristotle, comedy originated in religious festivals that included phallic songs, fertility rites, and some measure of improvisation. Choruses dressed as animals may also have been included. We can only speculate as to how these rites and revels evolved into highly structured comedies.

We do know, however, that comedy received official sanction and was added to the City Dionysia festival (which took place in March each year) starting in 486, almost sixty years before the debut of Aristophanes. It was added to the Lenaea (January) around 440. Comedy was probably a fringe activity of these festivals even earlier and was also presented at other local festivals, about which little is known.

Five comedies were presented at each of the two main festivals, though for reasons of economy the number of comedies dropped to three at times during the war years. Tragedies took pride of place at the Dionysia, but comedies were featured at the Lenaea. The system worked for comedy in essentially the same way as tragedy, with an *archon* choosing the participants ("granting a chorus") and appointing for each play a *choregos* (sometimes two during the war years) to maintain, train, and provide costumes for the chorus. The state paid the principal actors, who were assigned by lot. Four actors were apparently allowed in comedy, as opposed to three in tragedy, though we know this only because some of Aristophanes's plays clearly demand four actors (and even then some very quick changes are required). The chorus was also bigger in comedy (twenty-four members) than in tragedy (originally twelve, growing to fifteen), and it had more elaborate costumes and a larger, more active role in the play.

From their introduction at the Dionysia to the time of Aristophanes's death, perhaps six hundred to seven hundred total comedies were performed at the two festivals. Only eleven of those plays survive, all by Aristophanes. For the fifty-some other writers of comedies during this hundred-year period, we have some names and titles, references by later writers, and some vase paintings that may show scenes from comic plays. But, essentially, all we know about old comedy comes from Aristophanes himself, including a few references (usually caustic) to the works of his rivals.

There are a few common features of these surviving plays that are worth noting at the outset. The plays are largely idea-driven rather than plot-driven. Tragedies and later comedies depend on tightly woven, linear plots. Old comedy presents us with a series of scenes, shticks, and song-and-dance numbers, loosely held together by a single idea—the more fantastic, the better. The principal character rides a dung beetle to Olympus to liberate Peace, who has been imprisoned there by the god of war (*Peace*); the women organize a sex strike throughout the Greek world to force the men to make peace (*Lysistrata*); the women of Athens— disguised as men—pack the assembly, vote all power to themselves, and initiate a radical form of communism (*A Parliament of Women*); Dionysus descends to the underworld to fetch Euripides and restore tragedy to the city (*Frogs*). In each case the basic idea may be fantastic, but it is logically carried through, and its comic consequences are fully exploited.

The standard (though not invariable) structure of an Aristophanes comedy includes a *prologue*, in which the stage is set for the action of the play; a *parados*, which marks the entry of the chorus; an *agon*, or formal debate, in which the main conflict of the play is presented and resolved; a *parabasis*, in which the action of the play is suspended for a direct address to the audience that may include praise for the work of the author, ridicule of his rivals, and a plea for first prize, but can also (famously in *Frogs*) be more overtly political; a series of *episodes*, in which the comic consequences of the *agon* are further exploited, with songs and dances between episodes; and the *exodus* of the chorus, often amid general rejoicing.

Aristophanes constantly plays off and mocks the theatrical conventions of tragedy. He uses the trappings of tragedy, including the costumes, the *ekkyklema* (platform), and the *mechane* (crane), for comic effect. He regularly refers to the theater setting and the audience, and often parodies the high language of tragedy, counting on at least part of his audience to recognize the literary references. Euripides—his most important influence and therefore also the subject of his mocking attacks—appears directly in three of the extant comedies (*Acharnians*,

Women at Thesmophoria Festival, and *Frogs*). Euripides was a key transitional figure between the high tragedy of his predecessors and the idea-driven plays of Aristophanes. Cratinus, an older rival, has one of his characters accuse another of being a quibbler and an idea chaser, which he sums up as a "Euripidaristopha-nizer." The term itself is worthy of Aristophanes.

Old comedy embraces matters that were inconceivable in tragedy. There is a strategic absence of sexual delicacy or inhibition. The creators of *South Park* have nothing on Aristophanes in terms of lewd, tasteless, adolescent humor and explicit, sexual language. The plays exude a carnival atmosphere, a release from daily constraints and utter freedom not just in sexual explicitness but also in polit- ical and personal satire. Even the gods are not immune from ridicule in Aristo- phanes's plays. That does not mean he was impious or an atheist. Rather, it is an indication that comedy was an occasion to mock all the powerful forces in one's life, and the Greeks expected even their gods to have a sense of humor.

The plays are generally set in modern times—a few we know from their titles were mythological burlesques, but none of those has survived—and are full of ref- erences to recent events and to individuals (politicians, fellow poets, generals, philosophers) who were likely sitting in the audience, laughing, squirming, or fuming under the ridicule. Many of the topical allusions are highly ephemeral, and scholars are still trying to track them all down. (Imagine a historian puzzling over an episode of *Saturday Night Live* in two thousand years.) But the history behind the reference is often unnecessary to understand the polemical humor, and too many footnotes can make the plays unreadable.

In keeping with the carnival atmosphere, the actors in comedy wore masks with distorted features, sometimes recognizably caricaturing a public figure being satirized in the play. The costumes were heavily padded in the belly and the but- tocks. Male characters also wore large leather phalluses that could be employed as props, as in *Wasps*, where the elderly Philocleon invites a naked flute girl climbing steps in the dark to "take this rope into your hand: / somewhat frayed perhaps, but hold on. / It's not averse to being rubbed."[17] The choruses also had elaborate costumes, as clouds, wasps, birds, or even frogs.

Yet beneath the fantastic, the exuberant, the obscene, the crude slapstick, the biting farce, and the universal irreverence, runs a serious undercurrent. Aristo- phanes's plays comment upon the most important issues and ideas of his day. The four plays generally considered his greatest masterpieces deal with the desire for peace (*Lysistrata*), the possibility of utopia (*Birds*), and the value for society of, respectively, philosophy (*Clouds*) and tragedy (*Frogs*). The beauty of the presentation, moreover, is that the serious is contained within, and only rarely under-cuts, the ridiculous. The essence of Aristophanean comedy is that wisdom and the absurd are so closely aligned and, indeed, at times indistinguishable from one another.

LIVE FROM ATHENS, IT'S SATURDAY NIGHT

Comedy in Aristophanes is always political in the broad sense of that term, meaning that it addresses issues of contemporary concern to the polis. But it is sometimes political in a narrower, more partisan sense, especially in the early plays, starting with *The Banqueters* (427), in which Aristophanes launches a series of attacks against Cleon, then the leading political figure in Athens and a strong opponent of peace with Sparta. Tina Fey's devastating impersonation of Sarah Palin seems mild in comparison.

What we know about Cleon we know largely through the abuse leveled against him by Aristophanes and Thucydides. Cleon was a tanner (a seller of hides), and he is portrayed by both writers as a vulgar flatterer who lied, bullied, and bribed his way to power, appealing to the worst elements of mob rule. They compare him unfavorably to Pericles, the aristocratic leader of Athens who died in the plague shortly after the commencement of the Peloponnesian War. Pericles had guided the assembly through force of character and intellect and a compelling vision of the greatness of Athens that kept factional politics in check.

After he was first lampooned in *The Banqueters*, Cleon made the classic mistake of trying to suppress criticism by launching an unsuccessful prosecution against Aristophanes. But the license afforded comedy was confirmed and the prosecution was dismissed. In *Knights* (424), Aristophanes's fourth play, but the first produced in his own name, Aristophanes sharpened and redoubled his attack on Cleon, then at the height of his power. "The mask makers were too jittery to make a copy" of Cleon's face, explains one of the characters, "but you spectators are smart enough to spot him."[18]

Smart enough to spot him, perhaps, but not smart enough to reject him as a political leader. In *Knights*, Demos (the people) is an elderly and intelligent but crotchety and easily swayed master. His two key servants have been Nicias and Demosthenes, named for the two generals who, in a critical turnabout during the first phase of the Peloponnesian War, defeated a Spartan force at Pylos, leading to the capture of 180 Spartan warriors on the nearby island of Sphacteria. But Demos has acquired a new servant, Paphlagon (i.e., Cleon), who lies to, flatters, cajoles, and pampers Demos, and has displaced Nicias and Demosthenes in his favor. Paphlagon has even contrived to take credit for the "cake" they baked "with Pylos in it."[19]

Nicias and Demosthenes respond by recruiting a sausage seller to out-Cleon Cleon in vulgarity, dishonesty, and brazen lies. They tell him, "You're common, pushy, and off the street," and therefore you're poised for greatness.[20] When he protests that he is unworthy to lead the people, they reassure him:

> Politics, these days, is no occupation
> for an educated man, a man of character.
> Ignorance and total lousiness are better.
> Don't jettison such god-given advantages.[21]

In a series of increasingly manic episodes, in which each tries to outdo the other in audacity and wickedness, the sausage seller does indeed outface and outmaneuver Paphlagon, ultimately convincing Demos that his seemingly loyal servant has in fact been robbing him blind. Paphlagon is banished to a remote sausage stand, and a rejuvenated Demos is restored to his proper dignity, "living again the good old times!"[22] Two thirty-year truces hidden away by Paphlagon are brought forth (embodied as beautiful young girls) and presented to Demos, who delightedly takes them home to his farm to "consummate the deal."[23]

Knights was awarded first prize at the Lenaea, but the very citizens who delighted in the discomfiture of Paphlagon continued to look to Cleon as their *demagogos* (leader of the demos). One could readily conclude that Aristophanes failed in his aim. But he was a dramatist, first and foremost, not a rival politician. The play is brilliant in its comic conceit and frenetic execution. The send-up of contemporary politics (which is still funny after 2,500 years) is both courageous (against a powerful figure in wartime) and outrageous.

Aristophanes returns to contemporary politics in *Wasps*, which placed second at the Lenaea in 422. Although the two main characters are Philocleon (love Cleon) and his son, Bdelycleon (hate Cleon), the play is less about Cleon than about the jury system and the general corruption of politics. Philocleon and his fellow jurors (the chorus of wasps) were once the "men of Marathon," who defeated the Persians and made the Athenian Empire possible.[24] But they are now old and feeble and often poor. Their one remaining passion is jury service, which allows them to feel important and to bring in a small amount of money each day. It is compensation of sorts for irrelevance and enfeeblement. The Athenian juries decided issues of much broader import than contemporary ones. There were frequent prosecutions against political rivals (a particular trick of Cleon), and important men flattered the jurors, pleaded with them, and even shed tears before them. Philocleon gleefully describes the exhilaration of casting the final vote of condemnation. Bdelycleon breaks this spell by convincing Philocleon that he is being manipulated by the politicians for a pittance ("you trail after your pay-master / like migrant olive pickers from an alien land"[25]), while they line their own pockets with the tribute from subject states. Jury service itself has become a form of humiliation, underscoring rather than correcting the jurors' diminished status. Bdelycleon (the wealthy son who consorts with aristocrats and longs for a life of luxury) may be right, but he is smug and boring. Philocleon, like Aristophanes himself, is always entertaining, even in his fervent desire to judge and condemn. He has vitality, and his frantic efforts to escape the house and join his fellow jurors are classics of stage business. His very absurdity is endearing.

Drawing upon *Knights*, *Wasps*, and other such overtly political plays, some paint a portrait of Aristophanes as politically conservative, a solid member of the middle class, longing for peace and the old ways, suspicious of new trends, and equally contemptuous of the demagogues of radical democracy and the effete aristocrats, who are entertained by flute girls at drinking parties while their city is engaged in a desperate war for survival. But assigning Aristophanes a specific political agenda is hazardous. Aristophanes was a radical innovator in the arts, wholly irreverent and ready to ridicule anyone and anything, including himself. Like Stephen Colbert or Ali G, his stage persona may itself be part of his comic shtick. Perhaps the only thing we can state with confidence is that Aristophanes believes strongly in the critical role of comedy in democracy as a means of airing issues and promoting a freedom of expression that is truly astonishing during wartime.

THE PEACE PLAYS

In early 425, when Aristophanes won first prize with *Acharnians*, Athens and Sparta had been at war for six years. Despite the devastating impact of the plague and the almost yearly incursions into the Athenian countryside by Sparta and its allies, the war was largely at a stalemate. Sparta could neither breach the long walls joining Athens with its harbor at Piraeus, nor challenge the imperial fleet, which brought regular supplies and allied tribute to the city. For their part, the Athenians did not choose to face the highly trained Spartan hoplites in a traditional set-piece land battle.

This stalemate would end dramatically later in the year, when Athens established a base at Pylos in the Peloponnese, from which to harass Spartan allies and encourage the defection of the helots. A Spartan attempt to dislodge the Athenians would end disastrously and lead to the unprecedented capture at Sphacteria of 180 elite Spartan warriors and another 240 allied soldiers. Sparta would then sue for peace, which Cleon perhaps unwisely convinced the Athenians to reject.

But these events were some months in the future when *Acharnians* was produced (one year before *Knights*). The Acharnians, who make up the chorus, were from an agricultural region that was particularly hard hit by Spartan invasions and, hence, were vociferous in their calls for revenge and their refusal even to consider an end to the hostilities. When a divine messenger appears at the assembly to offer to arrange a truce, they seize him and hound him out of the city. One citizen, Dicaeopolis (whose name means "just city"), decides to obtain his own treaty from the messenger, who offers him three vintages of wine (the Greek word for treaty and for libation is the same): a five-year, a ten-year, or a thirty-year. After rejecting the first, as smelling of "tar and caulking for men-of-war," and the second for "a vinegary smell / like squeezed allies" (i.e., allies whose increased tribute was necessary to fund the war), he settles on the one that matures in thirty years, with "a bouquet of nectar and ambrosia."[26]

His separate peace in hand, Dicaeopolis resolves to return to his country estate, free from war and destitution. But the Acharnians are furious and threaten to tear Dicaeopolis to pieces as a traitor. Dicaeopolis rushes off to visit the tragic playwright Euripides, who provides him with various rags from a lost tragedy so that he can put on "a needy and pathetic show."[27] As Dicaeopolis explains,

> I've got to act the beggar today
> and be who I am, yet not be so.
> The audience, of course, must know
> who I am, but the Chorus—dumb clucks in the making—
> must stand there gaping,
> while I bamboozle them with irony and wordplay.[28]

Dicaeopolis then proceeds with a lively parody of tragic speeches, but it is parody with a point. "Even comedy writers / can tell the truth,"[29] he tells us, as Aristophanes all but directly steps into the shoes of Dicaeopolis (indeed, some speculate that he played the part) and with great "irony and wordplay" expounds on the causes and consequences of the war. The "shocking"[30] truth he relates in the course of his comic account is that the Spartans were not wholly at fault in starting the war and that the Athenians need to "unjump"[31] some of their conclusions. Sparta and Athens are equally responsible for an internecine war among Greeks that should never have occurred. Having won his point, or at least neutralized his attackers, Dicaeopolis reestablishes his own trade with foreign enemies and enjoys the plentiful harvest of peace—food, drink, and sex—while various other characters beg him for "a piece . . . / of peace . . . say a five-year morsel,"[32] and the chorus leader resolves never again to "invite the god of war / Into my house."[33]

The play is clearly a fantastic, fantasy fulfillment. Peace in early 425 was not a realistic prospect, but peace was an object of longing nonetheless. The wise Dicaeopolis sees that war benefits the arms merchants and the politicians and the generals and all those who profit from overturning the old ways. But for the ordinary farmer, it is simply a disaster. Peace brings happiness and plenty and stability.

Aristophanes deliberately plays off the conventions and mechanics of tragic drama—wheeling Euripides out on the ekkyklema, dressing his character in tragic garb, and mimicking the speech of a tragic hero—to show that we are receptive to arguments made under the guise of tragedy that we would ignore when presented as comedy. Tragic rhetoric (like political rhetoric) can fool its listeners. It depends upon illusion and pathos. Through parody, however, comedy can penetrate that rhetoric, exposing hypocrisy and private agendas while preserving an integral dramatic structure of its own. Aristophanes asks the audience, as Helene Foley has put it, "to expect from comedy a new intellectual and artistic complexity."[34] Defying Cleon (that "creep of a coward and . . . howling bugger") and speaking the truth to the chorus of enraged Acharnians who do not want to hear it, Aristophanes clings to a simple code: "The right and the good will be my champion."[35] But humor—as both weapon and shield—never leaves his side.

Four years later, when *Peace* was performed at the City Dionysia in 421, Athens was in a very different position. Cleon and the Spartan general Brasidas—warmongers both—had been killed at the battle of Amphipolis. The Spartans—still eager to recover the elite warriors captured at Sphacteria—were ready to deal, and the Peace of Nicias, a sworn, thirty-year truce, would be signed less than two weeks after the performance.

The play is accordingly suffused with excitement about the coming end of the war. The hero, Trygaeus, decides to breed a supersized dung beetle and fly up to Olympus on its back to free Peace from a deep cave in which the god of war has imprisoned her. The ride on the dung beetle parodies Bellerophon's attempted ride to Olympus on the winged horse, Pegasus, to complain about the deaths of his children. Aristophanes employs the mechane used by the gods in various Euripidean tragedies to good effect, though his hero Trygaeus is not so sure about his wobbly journey:

> Hey there, have a heart! This isn't funny.
> Stagehands, pay attention.
> I'm feeling a breeze about my tummy.[36]

Trygaeus is in luck, though. The god of war must leave to search for new pestles (replacements for Cleon and Brasidas) with which to grind the Greek cities in the mortar of war. In his absence, Trygaeus, aided by a chorus of farmers, rescues Peace and reminds all Athens of their former way of life, which the goddess Peace made possible:

> The figs, the myrtle berries, and the new
> Raw, sweet wine, the bed
> Of violets by the well,
> The olive trees
> That we adored.[37]

The play ends with a true peace this time, for both sides, not a private peace for one man and his family. It is a celebratory play, in which the chorus exits dancing and singing, and Trygaeus takes Cornucopia, attendant to the goddess Peace, as his prize and bride.

It was not to last. The thirty-year peace was over in seven, and was in any event simply a cold war fought through surrogates. Perhaps Cleon was correct in resisting a peace that in the end resolved none of the underlying causes of the war. Aristophanes returned to the issue in 411, with *Lysistrata*. By this time, though, fifty thousand allied marines and more than two hundred ships had been lost in the botched and wholly misguided attempt to conquer democratic Syracuse. Athens was not expected to survive that loss and the consequent defection of many allies, though it miraculously did so for seven more years. It also weathered a short-lived oligarchic rebellion a few months after the play was produced.

In *Lysistrata*, no divine intervention is to be expected, yet peace is still possible through unconventional, purely human means. The young women of Greece, led by Lysistrata, engage in a sex strike to force the men either to lay down arms or to forgo lying down in their arms. Messengers come and go, always in an extreme state of priapism, as the women do their best to prevent backsliding within their own ranks. In a parallel plot, the old women, though no longer objects of sexual desire, do their part by occupying the Acropolis and blocking access to the treasury that pays for the war. The old men attempt to assault their stronghold with burning logs. But the old men cannot keep their logs up, and the women pour cold water on their fires. Sexual puns and allusions come fast and furious, and it is clear where Mae West's famous line—"Is that a pistol in your pocket, or are you just glad to see me?"[38]—had its less technological origins. At one point, the chorus leader says to a Spartan delegate, "If I were you I'd cover up. You don't want any herm dockers to spot you."[39] This reference—to the vandalism of the erect phalluses on stone statues of Hermes throughout the city on the eve of the Sicilian expedition—underscores the astonishing freedom of Aristophanean comedy, given that the event caused the questionable indictment of Alcibiades and his consequent flight to Sparta. Alcibiades's absence from Sicily almost certainly contributed to the destruction of the expedition, and his presence in Sparta caused great harm to Athenian interests, particularly when he advised the Spartans to establish a fortified base in Attica from which to despoil Athenian land and to which Athenian slaves could flee. The reference is a painful reminder of all that had gone wrong in the war (and evokes a painful image in its own right).

Lysistrata explains that, since the men have made such a mess of things, it is time for women to have a go at "saving Hellas from warfare / And folly."[40] When challenged that war is a man's affair, she responds in Euripidean fashion that war directly devastates women—mothers lose their sons, wives are parted from their husbands, and young girls "full of thwarted dreams" miss their chance to marry.[41] She advocates pan-Hellenic cooperation between Athens and Sparta and reconciliation among the classes. Using the simile of carding wool—straightening the tangles and harmonizing the strands of the disparate Athenian factions—she contends that only women have the skill to "card out the wool into a basket of goodwill, / unity, and civic content."[42] It is a theme to which Aristophanes would return in *A Parliament of Women*.

The two choruses of old men and old women join hands and unite, as Lysistrata calls for reconciliation:

> Let each husband stand beside his woman while
> each wife stands beside her husband.
> And let us celebrate this happy bond
> and thank the gods with dance.[43]

Two thousand years later, Theseus, Duke of Athens, will raise echoes of this speech at the end of *A Midsummer Night's Dream*:

> Lovers, to bed; 'tis almost fairy time.
> I fear we shall out-sleep the coming morn
> As much as we this night have overwatch'd.
> This palpable-gross play hath well beguiled
> The heavy gait of night. Sweet friends, to bed.
> A fortnight hold we this solemnity,
> In nightly revels and new jollity.[44]

Lysistrata "well beguiled / The heavy gait of night" with "revels and new jollity." But Athens would outsleep the coming morn and lose additional chances to make peace with Sparta before its final collapse. Aristophanes, the master reveler, could only shake his head with Puck: "Lord, what fools these mortals be!"[45]

UTOPIA, LIMITED

Many consider *Birds* to be Aristophanes's finest play. Certainly, there is no denying its lyric beauty or ingenious conceit. It was produced in 414, after the launch of the Sicilian expedition, when Athens was still at the height of her power, optimistically seeking to expand her already-extensive empire.

Yet the two main characters, Peisetairus and Euelpides, have abandoned Athens. Weary of constant litigation and civil strife, they seek a restful haven of communal harmony where they can live out their lives. They wander in a featureless wilderness, guided by two birds they purchased in the marketplace, looking for Tereus, former king of Thrace who, in Greek mythology and a lost play by Sophocles, was transformed into a giant hoopoe (a very colorful bird with distinctive head feathers).

Since Tereus has been both man and bird and has flown all over the world, they ask him to identify the ideal city they seek. But they reject every suggestion he makes, so he expounds instead upon the peaceful life of birds. As the chorus leader beautifully echoes,

> Happy we, the feathered race of birds:
> We need no winter coats, nor in
> The suffocating blare of summer

Do we have to roast in long rods
Of burning sun, but loll among
Fluorescent meadows in full flower,
While the cicada, insane with sun, strikes divine
Rhythms, which the noonday heats entwine
Into his song. But in wintertime
I dwell in the hollow of caves and cavort
With the Oreads, and in spring
I guzzle on myrtle berries among
Its virginal flowers, or on some fruit
From the Graces' garden.[46]

Euelpides resolves to become a bird. Peisetairus—who has "the wits of a fox: / Clever, competent, confident, subtle, the lot"[47]—goes him one better and resolves to become king of the birds. He advises the birds to found their own city, a fortified bird city to be known as Cloudcuckooland, midway between heaven and earth, with a view to controlling both. From that position the birds can block sacrifices to the gods, thereby starving them out unless they cede all power. They can also prevent the gods from passing through to commit adultery with humans.

After initial hostility to anything proposed by a man, their natural enemy, the chorus of birds enters enthusiastically into the project. It is time for them to "sprout a beak"[48] and take back the power that is rightly theirs. Peisetairus promises them "happiness, / Prosperity beyond belief. / There's nothing that you cannot have."[49] The chorus leader, in a parody of Hesiod's *Theogony*, offers a comic, revisionist mythology to demonstrate that Eros, the ur-bird, was hatched out of chaos and black night, and only then brought forth mother earth and the Olympian gods. The birds, as "manifest offspring of Eros," are "more ancient / than that bliss-given crowd" and therefore entitled to rule in their stead.[50] The parabasis evolves into a Hesiodic paean to the birds that "spell out the seasons,"[51] and the chorus leader urges the audience "to happily weave your life with the birds."[52] Among the advantages noted: if an audience member were bored with a tragic play, he could fly home for lunch and get back in time for the all-important comedy or wing off to commit adultery while the woman's husband is still seated in the front row.

Peisetairus's plan, however, has unintended consequences that completely change the life of the birds. The massive building project requires hod carriers, masons, carpenters, and sentries. It attracts all the charlatans and mountebanks of city life: a grasping poet, an oraclemonger, a geometer (who has "come to survey the air for you / and partition it into lots"[53]), an inspector, a newsagent, an informer—all seeking benefits from the new regime and threatening litigation if they are not forthcoming. There is even civil strife, as some birds are killed for trying to undermine the democracy (an ironic concept given that Peisetairus is now *tyrannos* of Cloudcuckooland) and are served up as lunch to the gods who come to negotiate a truce. Peisetairus is successful in these negotiations and brings back a divine bride who not only takes care of Zeus's thunderbolts, but also "foreign affairs, law and order, harbor dues, the shipping plan, / paymasters, jury fees, and vituperating dolts."[54] The transformation is complete. Cloudcuckooland, the idyllic land of the birds, has become . . . Athens.

The whole attraction of the life of birds was that they needed nothing and therefore had no litigation, no politics, and no distinctions between rich and poor, between slave and free, between citizen and resident alien. They lived a simple life in harmony with the seasons. The resourceful, energetic, and endlessly ambitious Peisetairus, who purports to long for such a life, promptly transforms it into the polis he left behind. There is no escape from our inherent nature. There is no utopia for us because, if we were there, it would immediately become something else. "The trickiest thing," Aristophanes tells us, "is the nature of man, / apparent in everything."[55]

Aristophanes returns to the theme of man's hopeless longing for utopia in his last two plays, produced after Athens had lost the Peloponnesian War and the empireless, shipless democracy had been restored. In *A Parliament of Women* (392), the women of Athens don boots, men's cloaks, and fake beards, and stack the assembly in order to vote all power to themselves. (The male actors were thus playing women disguised as men.) The men, they point out, have made a complete hash of things, and women at least have experience "look[ing] after our households and finances."[56] They put that experience to good use, transforming the state into a single household, in which goods, clothing, and sex all become free and shared in common. They seek to replace political strife with domestic harmony, in which there is "one level of life for everyone."[57] There will be no envy, no crime, and no lawsuits because there will be nothing to fight over—"all land, / valuables, and money" will become "public property."[58] There will be no work either. The women will manage the money, and the men are free to spend their days strutting about and dining in the common mess, as long as they do not interfere in government affairs.

The play can be read as a prescient parody of the egalitarian regime proposed in the fifth book of Plato's *Republic* and of all later communist visions of a seamless, classless society. Praxagora, the leader of the women's revolution, offers what seems like a dream of freedom, equality, and harmony but is in fact a nightmare of tyranny. There will be no work only because there are slaves to do that work (a point that would not, admittedly, have seemed either odd or unjust to a contemporary Athenian audience). "Life'll be lived from a common capital,"[59] she promises, but that "common capital" is the work of others less favored. There will be no privacy. She plans to "make the town / into a single home: all barriers would be down. / It'll be like one sole edifice / and people can wander in and out of one another's space."[60] Disobedience will be punished by starvation (i.e., exclusion from the common mess). She even seeks to regulate sexual desire in order to eliminate natural inequalities in attractiveness. Before young, good-looking persons can mate with one another, they must offer their services to the old and hideous. Two old crones accordingly drag a young suitor from his very willing girlfriend, each demanding their own satisfaction under the new regime. His protest—"It's a question of appetite, not of law"[61]—goes unheeded.

Praxagora does not abolish unhappiness; she merely redistributes it. Indeed, she seems to have augmented it. Without work or self-determination, the men's lives become aimless. And since natural inequalities cannot be eliminated, those with special gifts must have them suppressed and their very appetites must conform to law. Yet if Praxagora's solution is comically absurd, the problems of civil strife, selfishness, and inequality are nonetheless genuine.

Aristophanes approaches these problems from a different angle in *Plutus* (*Wealth*), his final surviving play from 388 (which is apparently a revision of his play by the same name produced twenty years earlier).

The central problem in *Plutus* is again raised in all seriousness in book 2 of the *Republic*: Is it better to be just and poor or unjust and rich? Put differently, is it worthwhile being just in a world in which the god of wealth, Plutus, is blind and distributes his favors without regard to moral merit?

A poor but self-avowedly just and god-fearing farmer, Chremylus, has a solution to this dilemma. He brings Plutus to Asclepius, the god of healing, and restores his sight. Chremylus then asks Plutus to make all "good, honest, sober folk"[62]—that is, all men like himself—rich. Both Praxagora and Chremylus are confronted with an initial distribution of private property that is often unfair and can depend on chance or, worse, deliberate wrongdoing. But instead of eliminating private property, as Praxagora does, Chremylus expands private property and spreads it more freely. As King Lear would later enjoin, Chremylus wants in sympathy with the poor to "shake the superflux to them, / And show the heavens more just."[63]

Yet Chremylus's cry for justice has a decidedly greedy undertone, since his object first and foremost is for Plutus to make him rich. Indeed, he admits that he loves Plutus more than his wife and son. Moreover, his plan to spread wealth to pious, hardworking farmers ensures that they will be neither pious nor hardworking any longer. Piety is the first casualty of universal wealth; no one sacrifices to the gods any longer because no one needs special favors from them. Hard work is on the same disabled list, as the outraged goddess Poverty explains:

> No one will practice the arts and crafts ever again.
> For once these have gone, who'll be at all ready
> To ply the forge, to build ships, do tailoring,
> Make wheels or shoes, do bricklaying, or come to grips
> With washing clothes or leather tanning? Who will wish
> To plow the earth and gather in the harvesting
> Of Demeter's generosity once you can
> Succumb to inactivity and do nothing?[64]

Paradoxically, it is Poverty, not Wealth, who provides men with the good things in life because she makes men work for them. Poverty also raises better men: sturdier, stronger, and less selfish. Once Wealth appears, man's lust for more becomes insatiable. Of all other things, Chremylus tells Plutus, we can grow tired and have too much, "but of you yourself no one ever has a glut. / If someone lays his hands on thirteen talents he wants sixteen. / He gets that and he hankers after forty. That goes to his head / and he wants umpteen."[65]

In these three plays, Aristophanes rejects utopian schemes while respecting the social, political, and ethical problems that prompt them. "Besides the jokes, remember," he tells us, "there's a lot of serious stuff. / Vote for me for that, and if you have a sense of fun, / vote for me, too, for the jokes."[66]

Demagogic politics brings not peace but defeat. Utopian fantasies are worse than what they would replace. What then will "save the city"?[67] For that, Aristophanes looks at philosophy and poetry.

THE CHALLENGE TO PHILOSOPHY

Most philosophers hate *Clouds*. They consider it a deliberately falsified portrait of the saintly Socrates that contributed to his condemnation in 399, and they have a point. The indictment against Socrates declared that he corrupted the youth of Athens by meddling in matters of the heavens above and the earth below, and by making the worse argument appear the stronger. That is precisely how Aristophanes portrays him in his 423 play (revised in 418 but never again performed). The Socrates of *Clouds* is a wacky professor and an unscrupulous mountebank who runs a for-profit school, rejects the Olympian gods, is engaged in fantastical scientific inquiries, and offers rhetorical tricks by which "bad arguments" can defeat "good arguments."

The real Socrates, as we all know or think we know, never accepted money, rendered the gods their due, inquired only into the good life for man, and was highly critical of the empty rhetoric of the Sophists. The martyred Socrates was a tireless searcher after the truth who prodded his fellow Athenians not to care for money or power but only for wisdom and the state of their own souls. No wonder they condemned him to death!

Yet Aristophanes has a point, too. Socrates did engage in scientific specula-tion as a younger man. Even if he did not accept money, he had a flock of youthful followers who were strongly influenced by his example (some of whom, particu-larly Alcibiades and Critias, became catalysts in Athens's downfall and the violent tyranny that followed). He rejected divine authority as a source of moral obliga-tions, and he exposed flaws in standard definitions of those obligations without (at least in the early Platonic dialogues) replacing them with any positive doc-trines of his own. He thereby appears to take "good arguments" (for traditional values) and refutes them with "bad arguments" (that lead only to skepticism, cyn-icism, and even nihilism).

Moreover, we have to remember that Aristophanes was writing a comedy. A saintly, earnest Socrates would not be very funny. (Just try reading Xenophon's plodding account of his conversations.) Comedy depends upon exaggeration and outrageous distortion within the bounds of the recognizable. (So, too, one might argue, do dramatic philosophic dialogues; the Socrates presented by Plato is as far from Xenophon's portrait in one direction as Aristophanes's is in the other.)

We also have to remember that Aristophanes was parodying not just Socrates but an entire movement in thought. All the features and beliefs of the stage Socrates were embodied in one Sophist or another, and Socrates was the most prominent and publicly recognizable member of that group. (He was also reput-edly very ugly, with distorted features easily caricatured by, and readily recogniz-able in, a mask.) By declining to acknowledge a distinction between Socrates and the Sophists, and by choosing as his foil the finest exemplar in this trend, Aristo-phanes launches a much more profound attack on philosophy than if he had ridiculed a minor figure.

The plot of the play is extremely simple. Strepsiades, a traditional farmer married to a free-spending city girl, is deeply in debt because of his horseracing son, Pheidippides. He resolves to send Pheidippides to Socrates's Thinkery to learn how to make the worse argument the better and thereby defeat his creditors. He succeeds all too well, however. Pheidippides not only defeats the creditors but, having overturned all traditional values and rejected the gods as sources of moral authority, claims the right to beat his own father since he is now wiser than the old man and can correct him as a parent would a child. Strepsiades, cursing the day he "swapped the gods for Socrates," [68] burns down the Thinkery and reaffirms his belief in "the old ways" of "the men of Marathon." [69]

The scientific inquiries of Socrates and his followers—determining whether gnats "whine from their mouths or their bottoms" [70] and "staring at the ground" to investigate the nether sphere with their "bottoms gazing at the heavens" [71] to study the stars—are portrayed as trivial and absurd. Their atheism, however, is more dangerous. They reject the Olympian gods, teaching frankly that "Zeus doesn't exist," [72] a capital offense at that time in Athens and elsewhere in the Greek world: "what we believe in: / the Void, the Clouds, the Tongue— / these three alone." [73] The Clouds, who make up the chorus, provide scientific explanations for natural phenomena, such as rain, thunder, and lightning, traditionally attributed to the gods. They can also assume any shape and are therefore, on a metaphorical level, apt symbols of the "mist / and dew and smoke" that "feed a whole tribe of sophists." [74]

It is difficult for modern readers to sympathize with Aristophanes's assault on science. The science of his day was still very primitive and highly speculative—and thus perhaps a suitable subject for ridicule. The image of Socrates, suspended in a basket so that he can "meld [his] cerebral vibrations / with the homogenous air," [75] is an apt parody of protoscientific thought. But Aristotle would shortly change that. Moreover, the replacement of divine superstition with scientific explanations for natural phenomena cannot be considered (except by the most die-hard fundamentalists) anything other than a crucial advance in man's development. Aristophanes's reactionary assault on science may be enjoyed for "the jokes," but it is not "serious stuff."

His equation of philosophy with sophistic rhetoric, however, is harder to dismiss. In the play, Socrates and his followers are masters of "the art / of logic chopping and hairsplitting." [76] They are quibblers, dealers in abstractions and overly subtle distinctions, with no concern for how their arguments might undermine morality and the life of the polis. They analyze everything, they question everything, and they believe in nothing. As Pheidippides explains, "How rewarding is the experience / of novelties and being clever! / And being able to thumb one's nose at normal practice."[77] But such nihilism leads them into the clouds of thought, and they end up choking on their own smoke.

The history of philosophy is replete with logic-chopping, hairsplitting abstractions. The Sophists in particular were certainly guilty of manipulating words so freely as to render them meaningless and devoid of all value except as pyrotechnics to confuse and overawe. (The same has been said of French deconstruction in our own day. *Le plus ça change* . . .) Aristophanes throws down the gauntlet of poetry against the use of concepts untethered from their concrete context in human life and moral traditions. (Even poetic metaphors—in fact, especially poetic metaphors—depend on this tethering.) It is precisely such a challenge that spurred Plato to create his theory of forms and to place philosophical thought on what he believed was a firm foundation. His success, or lack thereof, and hence the true nature and value of philosophy, is still disputed today. Aristophanes anticipates and encapsulates much of this debate. His indictment of philosophy, too, can be enjoyed for "the jokes," but it is "serious stuff" indeed.

Clouds placed a disappointing third when it was first produced. The following year, in *Wasps*, Aristophanes chided the audience for their "limited intelligence" and urged them in the future to "nurse and cherish poets who / Search for things to say that are new" and to "savor their thinking."[78] They did just that with his last great masterpiece, *Frogs*, which, as mentioned above, not only won first prize in 405 but received an unprecedented second performance two years later by vote of the just-restored assembly.

THE JOY OF TRAGEDY

Euripides appears as a character in three of Aristophanes's plays. We have already seen him in *Acharnians*, supplying shreds of costumes, plot devices, and speeches to Dicaeopolis. He plays a more prominent role in *Women at Thesmophoria Festival*, produced in 411. In this play, the women of Athens gather at their annual spring festival in honor of Demeter and resolve to condemn Euripides for his negative portrayals of women. As one of them explains, he is always "making out we're cock-teasers, procuresses, / whiners, traitors, gossips, lost in machinations, / essentially sick, and mankind's greatest curse."[79]

This time, accordingly, Euripides must bring his art to bear in order to save himself. He first tries to get Agathon—an effeminate tragic poet—to dress as a woman, infiltrate the Thesmophoria, and plead in Euripides's defense. Agathon wisely declines, and Euripides sends an elderly, male relative in his place, shaved, singed, and dressed in a yellow frock. But the relative rather unwisely defends Euripides by arguing that women are, in reality, so much worse than he portrays them that they should be grateful he showed restraint. The women (though they do not actually dispute the point) are outraged. The relative is subsequently betrayed, bound hand and foot, and turned over to a policeman for the sacrilege of polluting the secret rites and mysteries of the women-only festival.

Euripides makes a series of hilarious attempts to rescue the relative, all based on plot devices from his plays, with parodies of his speeches, and all utterly ineffectual. Finally, Euripides simply distracts the policeman with a naked flute girl, rescues the relative, and makes peace with the women by alternately promising never to disparage women again and threatening to "let [your husbands] know what you've been up to while they were at the / front."[80]

Aristophanes is steeped in Euripides. Every one of his plays shows Euripides's influence, whether or not he is a character in it. In *Women at Thesmophoria Festival*, Aristophanes both parades that influence and transcends it. In a camp play of cross-dressing and disguise, the devices of tragedy are so wholly out of place that they themselves become fodder for comedy. A comic dilemma requires a comic (and in this case sexual) solution. Only a naked flute girl can strip away the disguises, unleash the restraints, and give us a happy ending. Aristophanes has schooled his teacher.

But the polis still needs tragedy—drama that is morally uplifting, serious in tone, and profound in impact, and that forges a common bond and common values among citizens. That is the impetus of *Frogs*, in which, following the deaths of Euripides and Sophocles, the god Dionysus is despondent. There are no more tragic poets of consequence, "they're non-entities, all, / like swallows twittering away / and murdering their art."[81] Dionysus resolves to descend into Hades and bring back Euripides to restore drama to its rightful place in civil life.

The effeminate Dionysus disguises himself as his half-brother Heracles, donning a lion skin over his traditional yellow smock and carrying a club so huge that he can barely lift it. He stops to visit his half-brother before departing so as to learn the way (Heracles having visited Hades to retrieve the three-headed Cerberus as part of his legendary labors), but aside from telling him to take a shortcut by committing suicide, Heracles's main piece of advice is that he fetch Sophocles instead.

Dionysus is accompanied by his servant, Xanthias, a precursor of all cleverer-than-my-master servants to come. They eventually make their way to the door of Hades, where the returning "Heracles" is alternately threatened with vile punishment as a dog thief and welcomed as a hero, and Dionysus repeatedly forces Xanthias to change costumes with him, and then change back, depending on which way the winds are blowing. In the end, both are whipped in a "contest" to see who "cracks first and / gives a shriek," and therefore reveals his imposture.[82] The contest is a draw, but Dionysus is recognized as a god by his uncle, Pluto, who invites him to judge a dramatic contest between Aeschylus and Euripides.

The premier dramatist in Hades has his own throne near that of Pluto. That throne has been occupied by Aeschylus for fifty years, but Euripides laid claim to it immediately upon his arrival, supported by "cutthroats, pickpockets, thieves, assassins," and "every kind of bastard" in the underworld.[83] The "decent folks" support Aeschylus, but they are of course a minority in Hades as they are in Athens.[84] Sophocles, on his own death, deferred to Aeschylus but has vowed, if Euripides wins, to take on Euripides himself "for the sake of art."[85]

The "contest," accompanied by color commentary from Dionysus and chanted cheers from the chorus, is both funny and remarkably insightful in terms of the line-by-line criticisms the two poets level against each other. They whip each other's verses, as Dionysus and Xanthias were whipped, but neither cracks and neither is revealed as a poetic impostor. Euripides's main charges against Aeschylus are that his plays are plotless and plodding, his characters uncouth and unlettered, and his verses bombastic, repetitive, and often incomprehensible: "It's all river-Scamanders, / fosses and bronze-bossed bucklers / emblazoned with eagle-griffins / and great rough-hewn declarations / for which there are never explanations."[86] Moreover, his heroes often just "sit there mute as dummies," while "the Chorus lets go in a litany / of nonstop choral baloney."[87] Euripides, by contrast, claims to have introduced natural characters from "the workaday world we know," who engage in genuine conversations, who act and plan and scheme in ways that "are part of our living."[88] By "putting logic into art / And making it a rational thing,"[89] Euripides has taught people how to think and shrewdly manage their affairs.

The countercharges are that Euripides portrays the worst aspects of human life, "fouling our art with incestuous intercourse" and other behavior designed merely to shock. His moribund poetry is like prose, without inspiration or lift, and he teaches people "to prattle and gab,"[90] to value nothing and thereby trivialize everything. Aeschylus demonstrates how any old phrase, such as "and lost his cruet of oil,"[91] can be tagged onto Euripides's monotonous "dumdi-dumdiddidum"[92] iambic verses with devastating effect, as Dionysus acknowledges: "That cruet of oil / fixes on your prologues like cold / sores on the eyes."[93] Worst of all, Aeschylus asserts, Euripides has contributed to the general moral decay of a society now "swamped by lawyers' clerks"[94] and lying politicians. Aeschylus, by contrast, celebrated and therefore taught the citizens martial virtues and service to the state: "Just give a thought to what they were like / when they came from my hand: / six-foot heroes all of them who never shirked, / unlike your loafers and your useless jerks, / these latter-day washouts we have now."[95] His own poetry moreover is in keeping with the heroic temper of his plays: "The lofty thought and the / high ideal / call for a language to match."[96]

Dionysus, as the god of theater, is the only proper judge of this contest. But despite his initial preference for Euripides, Dionysus is unable to choose between them on grounds of dramatic excellence. "One amuses me," he notes. "The other is master."[97] He calls for scales to weigh out their respective verses "like so much cheese."[98] Aeschylus wins this particular test; his lines are much denser than those of Euripides. Yet Dionysus still cannot decide on poetic merit alone.

Accordingly, since his purpose in descending to the underworld in the first place was "to save our city and ensure / the choral festivals of drama would endure," Dionysus decides to apply a more explicitly political litmus test and choose the one who is "ready and willing / to come to the aid of the State with sound thinking." [99] He poses a series of questions—What to do about Alcibiades? Should the current slate of politicians in Athens be retained? How to deal with Sparta?—to which Aeschylus gives answers more in keeping with the explicitly political parabasis of the play, which urges a general amnesty for exiled oligarchs and aristocrats, as well as the extension of citizenship to "every man who fights in our ships," whether slave or free.[100] Dionysus, acting on intuition, chooses Aeschylus, and Aeschylus in turn urges Pluto to have Sophocles take his throne in his absence and on no account to let "that clown"[101] Euripides sit in his chair, even by accident!

Despite the comic context, the questions posed by Dionysus had an unprecedented urgency. By 405, the Athenian fleet had been largely destroyed and Athens abandoned by many of her allies. Capture of the city and its possible destruction loomed ahead. Yet Athens still rejected honorable offers of peace at the urging of its political leaders. In the parabasis, the chorus leader sadly draws the same lesson as Shakespeare's Puck: "One day it will be seen / what fools we've been."[102]

But *Frogs* still glories in the greatness of Athens and its martial and artistic heritage. And it is for that, surely, that the restored democracy—after a brief but brutal tyranny imposed by Sparta—voted to restage the play. As Aeschylus ascends toward the daylight, the chorus invokes the old gods in his support:

We beg you to inspire
Him with many a great idea
As he departs so he may shower
Our city with many a blessing to make amends
For all our sufferings in war
And bring them to an end.[103]

THE LEGACY OF ARISTOPHANES

According to the great classicist Gilbert Murray, Aristophanes died "intestate" because his brand of "old comedy" died with him and exerted little influence on the course of Western literature.[104] Aristophanes was wholly eclipsed by Menander, whose "new comedy" provided the template for comic theater from his own day through Shakespeare and Molière to Oscar Wilde and Noel Coward.

Menander was born in 342, grew up during the reign of Alexander the Great, and died circa 292. He wrote more than one hundred plays, an average of three per year, indicating that he wrote for performances outside the City Dionysia and the Lenaea. We have ninety-seven titles but possessed only fragments until the twentieth century, when scenes, acts, and two almost-complete comedies were uncovered from the Egyptian sands. But Menander is still known largely by way of Roman adaptations by Plautus and Terence, through whom he had an enduring influence on Western comedy.

His plays are intricately plotted, with many twists and turns, based on misunderstandings, unexpected encounters, and sheer coincidences. The verse is functional rather than lyrical and devoid of the puns and neologisms that characterize Aristophanes. The characters are types—young lovers, recalcitrant parents, conniving servants—but they seem alive, and the situations are realistic and suspenseful. One ancient critic (anticipating Oscar Wilde) effused: "Oh Menander! Oh Life! Which of you imitated the other?" Menander eliminated the absurd, the representation of contemporary figures (politicians, playwrights, philosophers), and the disregard for plausibility that often characterized old comedy. The tone is less bawdy and more refined. The humor is gentler and more sympathetic.

Most important, whereas Aristophanes wrote for the polis, Menander wrote for the family. His focus was on domestic life and romantic love. Menander gave birth to the situation comedy, and it has never left us since.

Yet to say that Aristophanes died intestate is wrong. There are elements of his comic genius in Cervantes and Rabelais and Joyce, and in diluted form in movies and television shows like *Animal House, Saturday Night Live*, and *The Office*. Far more important than that, however, is the intellectual stature that made Aristophanes the most formidable antagonist of Socrates and his student, Plato. In Aristophanes, it is the poet's job to safeguard the soul of the polis and to lead men to wisdom and the good life. His plays dismiss philosophy as, at best, "never-ending futile chatter / In a niggling senseless game,"[105] and, at worst, a sophistic manipulation of bad arguments over good ones that is indifferent to the claims of justice. Aristophanes appears to condemn philosophy even as practiced by Socrates and Plato because their focus on the elusive eternal, on what is true everywhere and for all people, made them indifferent to the parochial and temporal concerns of the polis. Poetry tethers us to, even as it transforms, the present and can thus make us both wiser and better citizens.

How Socrates and Plato responded to that challenge, and the way in which it changed philosophy forever, is the subject of the next chapter.

Chapter 9

PLATO—
PHILOSOPHY AND POETRY

The most important moment in all the Platonic dialogues—and hence in the history of Western philosophy—comes when Socrates asks Euthyphro a disarmingly simple question: Do the gods love piety because it is pious or is it pious because the gods love it?

Through a series of further questions, Socrates forces Euthyphro to admit, contrary to his initial impulse, that the gods love piety because it is pious; it is not pious because the gods love it. Describing an incidental affect or quality of piety (that it is loved by the gods) does nothing to advance our understanding of the essential nature of piety.

In this simple exchange, Socrates establishes philosophy as an independent discipline, with its own methodology and subject matter. It is the job of philosophy, through careful, precise analysis, to determine what is pious, what is just, what is courageous and temperate—to determine, in short, what is virtue and the good life for man. No appeal to outside authority can satisfy us. Man, through the application of *logos* (reason: what can be understood and expressed in speech), must work out these matters for himself. In the process, Socrates makes the gods irrelevant to philosophy, though not necessarily to human life, since a proper stance toward the gods is an important component of wisdom. The nature of human virtue, he concludes, is a human problem to be determined by human reason. Man must search for wisdom through his own efforts.

Socrates stresses, moreover, that there is no more important inquiry for a man to undertake. Is it not a shame, Socrates asks, for men to be concerned with any other matters—particularly with public affairs or with earning money—when they do not understand virtue or know what the good life is for man and how to attain it? Even within the realm of logos, Socrates advances the claims of philosophy above those of any other discipline. Mythology, law, science, history, and poetry may embody wisdom in some partial and accidental way. They may enter-tain, educate, promote useful knowledge, and even build character. But philosophy is the queen of all human disciplines because only philosophy can weigh human values on the scale of reason and determine how we should live. Philosophy is the ultimate judge of any and all claims to wisdom.

Paradoxically, however, Socrates himself makes no such claims. To the contrary, when the Delphic oracle announces that he is the wisest of men, Socrates concludes that the oracle is true only in a negative sense: Socrates is wise insofar as he knows that he is not. Others, by contrast, believe they are wise but are not. Hence, he infers, he is at least wiser than they. To prove his point, Socrates questions those with reputations for wisdom: lawgivers, poets, craftsmen. In each instance, he examines their beliefs about justice, virtue, and the good life, and in each case he finds them unable to give a proper account. He shows that those purporting to act with piety or temperance or courage cannot explain the basis for their claims and have not, in fact, given serious thought to the reasons or grounds for their beliefs.

Without the ability to give such an account, Socrates contends, our moral beliefs are like the famous statues of Daedalus, which were reputed to be so lifelike that they would step down from their pedestals and run off. Such ungrounded beliefs will not stand still and cannot provide a certain guide for our behavior. If we have no criteria for distinguishing between true and false beliefs on such matters, our beliefs will collide with one another and create contradictions. Worse, our beliefs will give way under the pressure of desire, or fear, or the lust for wealth and power. Only knowledge provides a solid, immovable foundation and a proof against confusion, appetite, and ambition.

The word *philosophy* is a cognate of two Greek words, *philia* (love or friendship) and *sophia* (wisdom). Philosophy, then, is the love of wisdom. But for Socrates it appears to be an unrequited love. Despite his devotion to wisdom, ignoring all personal advantage, he never claims to have attained it (except in the negative sense noted above). Yet he considers his fruitless quest to be superior to all other pursuits. The lawgivers, the generals, the poets, the masters of all the various arts and crafts that human ingenuity has devised—people who lead, delight, and benefit humankind—are all dismissed as false claimants to a wisdom they do not possess. In the end, only philosophy matters. It is an astonishing claim. Socrates in his *hubris* has set the world at naught.

We can and should challenge Socrates's claim to the transcendent status of philosophy among all the arts and sciences, among all the various activities—whether for public good or personal gain—that could occupy a man's life. Aristophanes, we saw, dismissed philosophy as "never-ending futile chatter / In a niggling senseless game."[1] Even if we do not take such an extreme view, we rightly ask: If wisdom (knowledge of virtue and the proper life for man) cannot be derived from adherence to law or custom, devotion to religion, dedication to the public good, the study of the natural world, or even from the overpowering remnants of Greek poetry, from whence does it come? What does it involve? How is it to be attained? The entire Platonic corpus is, in the end, dedicated to resolving these Socratic questions, questions that Socrates himself never claimed to resolve and yet never ceased to pursue.

Plato's response is too varied and complex in its particulars, too rich and constantly evolving, to offer a complete overview here. Alfred North Whitehead claimed that the entire history of Western philosophy may properly be viewed as "a series of footnotes to Plato."[2] We will leave the footnotes aside and focus on the immovable center of his thought and his inspiration—the life, the character, and the mission of Socrates.

The historical Socrates can never be known to us with certainty. Socrates, who was born in 469 and put to death by vote of an Athenian jury in 399, never wrote anything of his own. We know him only through the writings of Xenophon, the dialogues of Plato (in which Socrates is generally the principal character), and a few other sources. Xenophon's memoirs of Socrates have a certain charm, but they are plodding and it is difficult to envision their pedantic and rather pedestrian main character inspiring either fanatical loyalty in his followers or hatred among the populace. With Plato, we have the opposite problem. His own poetic and philosophic genius pervades the dialogues and transforms the historical Socrates into an archetype of the human spirit, an inspiration and a challenge to all future generations.

Accurate or not, Plato's portrait of Socrates is the most memorable aspect of the dialogues and exercised the most influence on later thought. It also constitutes, in itself, Plato's most convincing answer to Aristophanes. *Symposium*, Plato's own dramatic masterpiece, reverses the conceit of *Frogs* and has the god Dionysus take the crown of wisdom off the head of the prevailing tragic poet and place it upon that of Socrates. Yet, in the ultimate Socratic paradox, Socrates's claim to wisdom lies precisely in his recognition of ignorance. Knowledge of one's own ignorance is the most important sort of knowledge—self-knowledge—and hence the starting point in a quest for wisdom that transforms the character of the aspirant and our understanding of what it is to be human.

ATHENS: 416

Symposium is set in 416, shortly before the Sicilian expedition. It is a final moment of Athenian splendor. Despite sixteen years of war, Athens is planning an audacious expansion of her empire to be led by Alcibiades, the brilliant, beautiful, wildly ambitious, and charismatic ward of Pericles. The great late plays of Sophocles (*Philoctetes, Oedipus at Colonus*) and Euripides (*The Bacchae, Iphigenia in Aulis*) lie ahead. Aristophanes is still early in his career. Agathon, the young tragic poet who made a brief appearance in Aristophanes's *Women at Thesmophoria Festival,* has just won the Lenaean festival with his very first play. He is holding a *symposion* (or drinking party) to mark the event. Among the honored guests are Aristophanes and Socrates. A drunken Alcibiades makes a surprise appearance toward the end of the evening.

Yet, although the drinking party itself takes place in 416, the recounting of that event in *Symposium* takes place as much as fifteen years later. The Sicilian expedition has long since ended in disaster; Athens has lost the war, been stripped of its empire, and only just emerged from brutal tyranny to brittle democracy. Alcibiades, who embodied so many of Athens's hopes and illusions, barely even made it to Sicily. Accused in absentia of profaning (by both mocking and revealing) the Eleusinian Mysteries at a drinking party, as well as of defacing statues of Hermes throughout the city on the night before his departure, Alcibiades sought refuge in Sparta, where he provided strategic advice that proved devastating to the Athenian cause. Thus began a dizzying series of about-faces, in which Alcibiades variously helped the Spartans, returned to the Athenians, and flirted with the Persians. In 404, he was assassinated by Persian agents at his estate on the Hellespont. Two years earlier, Euripides had died in Macedon, and Sophocles in Athens. Agathon had long since been banished for allegedly espousing antidemocratic sentiments.

There is thus great intensity, even urgency, to the telling of this story, a sense of a golden age that has passed, of wisdom to be recaptured and cherished in difficult times. That sense is compounded by the knowledge that Plato wrote *Symposium* perhaps twenty years later, long after his beloved Socrates had been put to death by the Athenian assembly. Plato, born in 427 to an aristocratic family, abandoned his early interests in poetry and politics to follow Socrates. He was entranced by Socrates's insistence that we must be able to give an account of our beliefs and our values as the only sure foundation for a good life. Following the execution of Socrates, Plato withdrew to a sacred grove outside of Athens (the *academus,* hence our word *academy*) where he taught and wrote for most of the rest of his life.

Symposium is Plato's most poetic and dramatic work. It is also his most playful work, a fusion of comedy and tragedy, transmuted into philosophy by means of poetic genius. This dialogue within a dialogue within a dialogue, mixing three different eras and multiple modes of thought, is an artistic masterpiece designed to advance the claims of philosophy over art, a sincere paean to what is noble and good that proceeds largely by parody and even self-parody. It is a Rubik's Cube® to baffle and delight.

The dialogue begins when an unidentified friend asks Apollodorus, a dour young follower of Socrates, to give an account of the drinking party. Apollodorus is well prepared to offer such an account because he rehearsed it only the day before in response to an urgent request from Glaucon, who mistakenly thought that he, Apollodorus, had been present at the event. Apollodorus brusquely corrected Glaucon by pointing out that Agathon had not lived in Athens for many years, "while it's been less than three that I've been Socrates' companion and made it my job to know exactly what he says and does each day."[3] (It is significant that Apollodorus does not point to Alcibiades's absence from Athens as making the drinking party impossible; this helps with the dating of Apollodorus's recounting because Alcibiades had returned in brief triumph to Athens in 407–406 before being cast aside yet again by a democracy suspicious of his alliances and his ambitions. Thus, 403, just after the restoration of the democracy, is a reasonable date for the recounting since all the participants, except for Agathon, were present in Athens a few years earlier.)

The drinking party, Apollodorus tells Glaucon, took place when they were both still children, the day after Agathon and his troupe held their victory celebration for Agathon's first tragedy. Glaucon asks Apollodorus if he heard the account then from Socrates himself, a suggestion Apollodorus vehemently rejects: "Oh, for god's sake, of course not!"[4] Instead, he heard the account from Aristodemus, who was, Apollodorus snorts, "obsessed with Socrates—one of the worst cases at that time."[5] Aristodemus, who mimicked Socrates's dress and manners, even to the point of going barefoot year-round, was himself present at the party.

This multiple separation of the account from the event, both temporally and in narrative voice, serves at least three purposes. First, as noted, it highlights the importance of what is to be said and gives it an almost mythic aura; it is something that happened in an earlier time, when they were children, a story told to delight and instruct but also one difficult to reconstruct and perhaps even to believe. Second, it distances the account from the historic Socrates, who wrote nothing himself and is known to us only through the imperfect accounts of his imperfect followers. Third, it is a rare instance of self-parody by Plato, who doesn't just "ma[ke] it [his] job to know exactly what [Socrates] says and does each day,"[6] but in his dialogues invents (or at least re-creates) what Socrates says and does each day. Plato is a combination of the Socrates-mimicking Aristodemus and the nagging Apollodorus, who tells Glaucon that he cares only for philosophical conversation: "All other talk, especially the talk of rich businessmen like you, bores me to tears, and I'm sorry for you and your friends because you think your affairs are important when really they're totally trivial."[7] By filtering his account through the two rival followers (and perhaps winking at his own rivalry with Xenophon, the other great recounter of the conversations of Socrates), Plato shows that he himself is not immune to the parody he will bring to bear on all the other participants in the dialogue, including Socrates.

Apollodorus purports to tell "the whole story from the very beginning, as Aristodemus told it to me."[8] It begins with Socrates on his way to Agathon's house. He has bathed and put on a fresh cloak and sandals. We thus know at the outset that this will be an unusual occasion for Socrates, outside his normal way in the marketplace. When he encounters Aristodemus—unwashed, in an old cloak, and barefoot, as Socrates himself usually is—Socrates urges Aristodemus to come along despite the fact that he has not been invited. The real Socrates, in party dress, and the acolyte, in his daily attire, proceed together. But Socrates lags behind and ends up standing lost in thought on the porch of Agathon's neighbor. Aristodemus is therefore in the embarrassing position of arriving uninvited and without Socrates. Agathon plays the gracious host regardless, claiming that he looked all over for Aristodemus yesterday in order to invite him. Agathon's speech of welcome is lovely and ingratiating, but is plainly unconcerned with truth, a portent of things to come. Meanwhile, Socrates is deaf to the entreaties of Agathon's servants, who are sent to fetch him. At Aristodemus's urging, they leave him to his meditations, and he eventually shows up midway through dinner, presumably having resolved whatever issue was troubling him.

He is given the seat of honor, on the couch next to Agathon, who expresses the hope that "a bit of the wisdom that came to you under my neighbor's porch"[9] will rub off. In a deeply ironic exchange, Socrates notes that it would be wonderful indeed "if the foolish were filled with wisdom simply by touching the wise."[10] He quickly adds that he would be the winner in such an exchange since his own wisdom is of no account, while that of Agathon, attested to by "more than thirty thousand Greeks,"[11] is both radiant and splendid. The irony is not lost on Agathon—the judgment of a choice few is more important than the pleasure of the multitude—and he accuses Socrates of going too far but promises, good naturedly, that "Dionysus will soon enough be the judge of our claims to wisdom!"[12] The contest among tragic poets is over—Agathon has won—but the contest between poetry and philosophy is about to begin.

The occasion for such a judgment is established when several of the guests, badly hung-over from the night before, suggest that they send the flute girl away, go light on the wine, and spend the evening in conversation. They each agree to give a speech in praise of Eros. *Eros* in Greek indicates sexual desire or passionate love. The noun can refer either to the god Eros, or the passion, *eros*, that drives men. Since ancient Greek was written in all capital letters, and since the Greeks did not clearly distinguish between gods and the forces they inspire, the exact referent is sometimes unclear. (I will use *Eros* throughout to maintain the ambiguity of the original.)

Eros is an odd subject for praise, since it is often depicted as a destructive force in Greek tragedy, especially in Euripides (e.g., *Hippolytus*, *Medea*), who was so admired by Socrates. Even odder is that Socrates—the embodiment of rational thought—not only assents to this proposal but also claims that "the only thing I say I understand is the art of love."[13] Socrates, who repeatedly disclaims any knowledge of his own, nonetheless claims to understand Eros. We shall see, though, that his insistence on his own ignorance, his love of a wisdom he cannot attain, and his claims to understand Eros are all deeply and intimately connected.

THE FIRST THREE SPEECHES

The first speech belongs to Phaedrus, the handsome young man who initially proposed the topic. Phaedrus, the beloved of many, praises Eros for inspiring lovers to martial virtue. He quotes Homer and Hesiod and draws examples from Greek mythology to show that Eros—one of the most ancient gods—fills the lover with courage and a lust for honor, lest he feel shame before his beloved. Nothing could be more powerful, he asserts, than "an army made up of lovers and the boys they love."[14] Each will strive to be worthy of the other. But the lover is even more god-like than the beloved in his splendor and prowess.

Phaedrus's argument is homeric in its conception, stressing the value of Eros to a warrior class for whom military glory is most noble and shame most base. Yet Phaedrus focuses his discussion of Eros, as do most of the speakers, on a particular sort of homosexual love that appears to have been accepted or at least commonly recognized in fifth- and fourth-century Athens: that of older men for youths on the verge of manhood. In idealized form, the lovers mentored, befriended, and promoted the interests of their beloveds. In exchange, the youths shyly accepted the admiration of the older men and, perhaps, granted them sexual favors. Such relationships were treated, at least in many extant sources, as both natural and consistent with later heterosexual relationships. The older men were usually married, and the boys were expected to marry when they came of age. Homosexuality among adults was generally disparaged and, in Aristophanes at least, an object of ridicule. An adult male adopting the passive role in such a relationship was considered unmanly. But Phaedrus praises the love of older men for youths as itself a spur to manhood.

There is a certain amount of special pleading in Phaedrus's speech. He, the beloved boy, praises the benefits of Eros to the older lover because he wants to encourage this adulation. The next speaker, the older Pausanias, provides a mirror image, praising Eros for the benefits it bestows on the youthful beloved. Pausanias wants to encourage a favorable response from the objects of his own affection. But Pausanias has a somewhat harder task, for it was generally considered improper for youths to respond eagerly to their suitors. He therefore launches a lengthy and comically tedious disquisition on the distinction between virtuous and vicious love. Vicious love seeks only sexual gratification and is properly condemned. The vulgar have given love a bad name, leading some to think that for a youth to take *any* man as a lover is disgraceful. Virtuous love, however, seeks to benefit the beloved. Excellence of character is the "central concern" in such a relationship.[15] Where such "heavenly love" is in question, the youth may "accept a lover in an honorable way," for "the young man understands that he is justified in performing any service for a lover who can make him wise and virtuous."[16]

The self-serving nature of this speech, too, is self-evident. But Pausanias's overarching premise is unimpeachable: society must recognize the reality of physical desire and seek to channel it in useful or at least acceptable directions. Pausanias invokes the ancient Greek distinction between law or custom (*nomos*) and nature (*physis*). It is the job of properly developed nomos to guide and, where necessary, curb physis. Some countries permit sexual relationships between older men and youths without restrictions. Other countries forbid them absolutely. But reality, he argues, is more complex—because love has a dual nature—and Athenian nomos should be sufficiently nuanced to allow "virtuous" attachments.

Pausanias pays lip service to moral virtue to promote his credibility as a lover. In the end, however, he simply wants to justify pederasty. His speech receives the reception it deserves. Aristophanes is next in line, but he is overcome with an attack of hiccups during Pausanias's speech. Hiccups—along with belches and farts and other bodily noises—are stock in trade of the comedian. They are ridiculous, and subjecting Aristophanes to such a fit is obviously a bit of revenge for his portrayal of Socrates suspended in a basket. But the hiccups are also a commentary on Pausanias's hypocrisy in suggesting that the claims of the body are not really in question where "heavenly love" is concerned.

With Aristophanes indisposed, the next speaker is Eryximachus, a medical doctor who advises Aristophanes to cure his hiccups by, first, holding his breath, then gargling, and finally, failing those, tickling his nose with a feather to make himself sneeze. One must, therefore, imagine Aristophanes trying each of these remedies in turn as Eryximachus speaks. Eryximachus, the scientist, makes love a species of *techné*, of craftsmanship broadly understood as the mastery of certain techniques in the arts and sciences. He strips love of both emotion and mystery and presents it in purely clinical terms. What we call love, he explains, is simply "an attunement or a harmony" among disparate individuals driven by impulses of attraction and repulsion.[17] Where Pausanias spoke of noble and base love, Eryximachus sees only healthy or diseased constitutions. "Everything sound and healthy in the body," he tells us, "must be encouraged and gratified," and "medicine is simply the science of the effects of Love on repletion and depletion of the body."[18]

Eryximachus goes far beyond medicine, however, in his analysis of Eros. The same principles of attunement and harmony among disparate elements operate for animals and plants as well as humans. The same principles of attunement and harmony among disparate elements also govern the arts, especially music, and the motions of the planets. Indeed, these principles even govern the relations between men and gods. The goal of all techné is Eros—attunement and harmony. The nature of the techné—medicine, astronomy, music, sacrifice, and divination— depends upon the disparate elements in question, but Eros is always the same in its most fundamental nature.

Eryximachus's speech is a parody of pre-Socratic Greek natural philosophy, with its search for a single, overarching principle governing the cosmos. Yet it also seems very modern in its attempt to explain everything in scientific, materialist terms. As others have noted, Eryximachus offers us an early version of the Kinsey Report in its value-neutral attempt to reduce Eros to what can be measured and quantified and made a matter of technique.

Each of the first three speeches, then, presents only a partial and manipulable view of Eros. Phaedrus's mythic, heroic ideal; Pausanias's appeal to a political order (nomos) that recognizes the claims of nature (physis); and Eryximachus's foray into natural philosophy are all important elements of Greek thought. Yet all will be found wanting. None leads to wisdom without guidance from philosophy. Indeed, we can see that already from the speeches themselves. Phaedrus's invocation of martial virtue and Pausanias's appeal to law and morality are alike self-serving attempts to enhance their respective roles as beloved and lover. Eryximachus's understanding of Eros as a mutual relation of attraction is more balanced and less self-serving and yet is so reductionist as to seem unrelated to any true understanding of Eros. Mythology, nomos, and natural philosophy offer us important perspectives on the world in which we live. But in a contest for wisdom they fall short.

ARISTOPHANES AND AGATHON

Aristophanes begins his own speech, of course, with a joke, this one at the expense of Eryximachus. He notes that, since the sneeze treatment cured his hiccups, "the sounds and itchings that constitute a sneeze" must be part of "the orderly sort of Love"[19] that restores health and harmony in the body. Yet, despite this jibe, Aristophanes's speech is surprisingly interchangeable with that of Eryximachus, to which the fact that they were interchanged should itself alert us. Aristophanes is brilliant and poetic, where Eryximachus is clinical and scientific. But both are materialists and reductionists who see no higher value in love than mutual, unexplained physical attraction. Eryximachus tries to formulate a cosmic law governing such attraction. Aristophanes exploits its comic (and tragic) potential. "It comes with the territory of my Muse,"[20] he explains.

Aristophanes praises Eros by means of myth. "Long ago," he tells us, human beings were very different.[21] They were perfectly round, but with two sets of arms and legs, two faces and four ears on a single head and neck, and two sets of sexual organs—both male in some, both female in others, and mixed male and female (androgynous) in others. They could walk in any direction, but when they wanted to move quickly, they thrust out their eight limbs "and spun rapidly, the way gymnasts do cartwheels."[22] These ugly and fantastic beings were yet awesome in their completeness and their power. (They are a parody of the perfect spheres of ancient cosmology.) Inevitably, "they made an attempt on the gods," which was rebuffed.[23] Zeus did not want to wipe them out entirely, however—since, when not rebelling, they offered sacrifices and worship—and so instead split them in half, thereby creating the current race of men and women. In this riven state, "each one longed for its own other half"[24]—men joined to men, women to women, and, for the formerly androgynous, men joined to women. They would throw their arms around one another and wish to grow together again, and "they would die from hunger and general idleness, because they would not do anything apart from each other."[25] Zeus took pity upon them and so arranged their genitals that they could have intercourse and rediscover their connections to one another.

"Each of us, then, is a 'matching half' of a human whole," Aristophanes explains.[26] This is "the source of our desire to love each other."[27] Love draws us toward "what belongs to us."[28] Thus, when a person meets his other half, "the two are struck from their senses by love, by a sense of belonging to one another, and by desire, and they don't want to be separated from one another, not even for a moment."[29] They "cannot say what it is they want from one another,"[30] but it is not merely sex; "the soul of every lover longs for something else,"[31] even if his soul cannot say what it is. "'Love' is the name for our pursuit of wholeness, for our desire to be complete."[32] Only love holds out the prospect that it "will restore to us our original nature, and by healing us, . . . make us blessed and happy."[33]

There are numerous points worth noting about Aristophanes's brilliant speech. Both homosexual and heterosexual love are treated as perfectly natural. They stem from our original natures—with whom we were joined together—not from any disease or disharmony. Relatedly, there is no distinction between noble and base Eros. Our bodies were shaped in the image of the gods, and Eros itself is a gift of the gods necessary to our survival.

Eros, according to Aristophanes, is a cure for our deepest wound, our feeling of incompleteness. We are divided from ourselves and from one another. We are not quite sure what we need or why. But Eros is our fundamental longing for "what belongs to us"—lovers, family, friends, our *polis*, all the critical connections we forge in our lives.

Yet this longing is never satisfied, and that is the source of both comedy and tragedy. Eros is a curse as well as a blessing. Our frantic search for that unique individual who we think will complete us—the chosen one who seems inevitable but is in fact accidental, since the original pairs have long since died off—is the stuff of comedy, and its apparent realization is the happy ending that comedy requires.

Aristophanes recognizes, however, that Eros does not end with the embrace; however intense and joyful, the embrace is fleeting. The same need occurs again and again and provides, at best, only temporary distraction from the permanence of loss. What we can never have is the state of wholeness and completeness that our ancestors once knew. Indeed, our very longing for such a state is irrational because it would lead to stasis and death. Passion, paradoxically, wants an end to passion. But only endless, never fully satisfied passion keeps us alive. That is our inherent tragedy. We can never "heal" the wound of being human. What "belongs to us" is never truly our own. We accept facsimiles of our true selves. We are, in the end, strangers in a strange land, seeking what we cannot have and finding consolation where we must.

Aristophanes's image of elusive completeness in Eros has exercised a profound influence on later thinkers on love and friendship. Michel de Montaigne, the great Renaissance essayist, wrote of his friendship with Étienne de La Boétie in terms drawn directly from *Symposium*: "Our souls mingle and blend with each other so completely that they efface the seam that joined them, and cannot find it again."[34] Most interestingly, Montaigne echoes the inherent mystery and inexplicable nature of such attachments: "If you press me to tell why I loved him, I feel that this cannot be expressed, except by answering: Because it was he, because it was I."[35]

After Aristophanes, Agathon is frankly a disappointment. His speech is sweeping, poetic, and utterly empty. Agathon reproaches the others for not praising the god, Eros, so much as the good things that come to them from the god. Agathon wants to focus on "who it is who gave these gifts."[36] Eros is the happiest of the gods, he tells us, and also the most youthful because old age is abhorrent to him. Eros is beautiful and delicate, shunning ugliness and violence alike. He makes his home "wherever it is flowery and fragrant"[37] and embodies each of the classic Greek virtues: justice, moderation, courage, and wisdom most of all. He is also a great poet, as only a true artist could inspire others to art and lead them to fame. Eros is, in short, very much like Agathon, the beautiful, delicate, youthful poet. In an effusive peroration on Eros as "our best guide and guard,"[38] Agathon concludes: "Every man should follow Love, sing beautifully his hymns, and join with him in the song he sings that charms the mind of god or man."[39]

Agathon's speech is followed by a great burst of applause, "so becoming to himself and to the god did they think the young man's speech"—more becoming to himself, however, than to the god. The languid, lyrical Agathon is an epigone, a faint remnant of the greatness of classical tragedy. He himself seems aware that his speech—"part of it in fun, part of it moderately serious"[40]—is more a play of sounds and images than a substantive presentation. Yet it is applauded regardless. The portrayal of Agathon here, fresh from his victory at the Lenaea, may indicate Plato's belief that Athens is no longer capable of producing great tragedy, no longer courageous enough to face the tragic vision of its forebears. Comedy, as represented by Aristophanes, is still possible at the highest levels. But true tragedy is part of Athens's lost greatness.

Yet Agathon raises a critical point, and the fact that he gives his speech just before, and sits on the couch next to, Socrates is not accidental. Agathon is the first speaker to go beyond mere physical desire and attraction in his discussion of Eros. For Agathon, Eros is more spiritual than physical. Agathon is also the only speaker to recognize that Eros does not just lust for beauty but inspires the creation of beauty in the form of art and poetry and all other good things that men have created as part of a civilized life. For Agathon, Eros is a higher force that leads from a love of beautiful things to a desire to create beautiful things.

Leo Strauss, in his lectures on the dialogue, rightly argues that the distinction between comedy and tragedy, between Aristophanes and Agathon, is critical to understanding *Symposium*. The tragic poets, he says, created the gods, under the inspiration of beauty, by idealizing man and making him eternal and flawless. "The solemnity of tragedy" is accordingly "higher than comedy, which is a rebellion against the gods, an attempt to undo what the tragic poets did."[41] Strauss notes that whereas "tragic poetry enchants, comic poetry disenchants."[42]

Yet we must confront the fact that Aristophanes's speech is far more brilliant than Agathon's. Agathon makes no serious attempt to explain why tragedy is higher than comedy, or how the songs of the soul can soften and overcome the more urgent rumblings of the body. Aristophanes's disenchantment is more powerful than Agathon's enchantment and, hence, poses a greater challenge to Socrates and the claims of philosophy put forward by Plato. For Aristophanes, sublimation is an illusion. The spiritual is but a hypocrite's guise for the physical, as it was in the speeches of Phaedrus and Pausanias. Aristophanes disdains such disguise, as did Eryximachus. Philosophy is pointless because it cannot change our fundamental situation. Everything remains on the same, human level of frustrated fulfillment. Comedy is our only weapon against despair.

Like all good advocates, Plato states his opponent's case as powerfully as possible before proceeding to attack it. Then he incorporates its best elements in his own presentation. In this case, he will do so by enlisting comedy in particular and poetry in general in Socrates's account of how Eros, properly understood, leads us to love wisdom and to follow philosophy. Eros reveals man to himself, both his limitations and his potential. Eros, in short, teaches us how to live.

SOCRATES AND DIOTIMA

The parody suitable to a drinking party does not end with Agathon's speech. Even Socrates's usual irony is magnified as in a fun-house mirror. He first claims that he has been "struck dumb" by the "beauty of the words and phrases"[43] invoked by Agathon. Since Socrates is never struck dumb, we are primed for what follows. He then acknowledges that he should not have agreed to give a speech in praise of Eros. "In my foolishness," he says, "I thought you should tell the truth about whatever you praise."[44] But now it appears that to praise is simply to apply "the grandest and the most beautiful qualities"[45] without any concern for whether they are true or false. "I'm not giving another eulogy using that method, not at all—I wouldn't be able to do it!—but, if you wish, I'd like to tell the truth my way."[46] Socrates's "way" of praising Eros, he explains, is to "select the most beautiful truths and arrange them most suitably."[47] In other words, we will not hear any ugly truths about Eros—he will leave those to Aristophanes—but only those that are most beautiful and most suitable to the discourse at hand. It is clear that Socrates plans to transcend the base world of comedy and focus on the spiritual aspects of Eros, but without sacrificing truth to fine phrases.

Yet Socrates begins not with a speech but with his usual method of interrogation, a method suitable perhaps for the marketplace, but out of place at a drinking party among friends. Through his questioning, he gets Agathon to admit that Eros is a desire for something, rather than nothing, and that when we desire something it is because we currently lack it. A sick man desires to be well, a poor man to be rich, a weak man to be strong. To the extent we can be said to desire qualities we already have (such as health, wealth, strength), we desire to have these things in the future as well as now. The objects of a man's love and desire, therefore, are "what is not at hand and not present, what he does not have, and what he is not, and that of which he is in need."[48]

With this premise established, Socrates forces Agathon to admit that, because Eros longs for beauty, Eros must not be beautiful nor possess any of the other desirable qualities Agathon attributed to him. "It turns out, Socrates," Agathon finally and with surprising good nature admits, "I didn't know what I was talking about."[49] "It was a beautiful speech, anyway, Agathon," responds Socrates.[50]

This harsh treatment of the soft and gracious Agathon, in which Socrates's already heightened irony flows into sarcasm, is surprising. But Plato is making clear that the stakes are now high indeed and that he will use all the weapons he has at hand. Agathon is the beloved of the Athenian audience. He wears the victor's crown awarded by the same multitude that would later judge and condemn Socrates. Agathon represents not just the theater but also the democratic assembly and the jury system, the entire realm of uninformed public acclaim and public condemnation in which rhetoric and fine phrases, rather than truth, hold sway over a senseless crowd.

Yet Socrates immediately softens his criticism by noting that he too once shared Agathon's view that Eros "is a great god and that he belongs to beautiful things."[51] Socrates proceeds to describe his own instruction many years before in the art of love by Diotima, a wise woman from Mantinea. At this point, then, we are reading Plato's written record of Apollodorus's retelling of Aristodemus's report of Socrates's account of the teaching of Diotima. Why is her original teaching filtered through four separate, inevitably distorting lenses? Why, moreover, does Plato soon make clear that Diotima herself is an invention of Socrates, by having her respond directly to Aristophanes's account of Eros? In part, the indirection and misdirection is in keeping with the playful mood of *Symposium*. In part, it underscores the already-noted fact that Socrates himself left no written record of his thoughts and, hence, that such a record must be painstakingly reconstructed (or reinvented) by Plato. In part, it reflects the inaccessibility of the higher mysteries of Eros. And, in part, it is a device that allows Plato to go beyond Socrates in his exploration of these ultimate mysteries.

Diotima begins, as did Aristophanes, with myth. She leads Socrates to understand, as Socrates led Agathon, that Eros is full of longing precisely because he lacks the good things for which he longs. The beautiful and the good are objects of desire, not attributes of desire. Eros is therefore a lover, not a beloved. More surprisingly, she stresses that Eros is not a god at all. For the gods are immortal and already possess beauty and all good things. They stand in need of nothing. Eros was the child of Penia (poverty) and Poros (resourcefulness), himself the son of Metis (cunning). Eros is poor, barefoot, and homeless, but tough and resilient. He is a "schemer after the beautiful and the good."[52] Although not a god, neither is Eros human, but rather a spirit, or *daimon*, linking gods with men and serving as an intermediary between the two. He is neither beautiful nor ugly, neither rich nor wholly destitute, neither mortal nor immortal (for although he dies he is constantly reborn), but always somewhere between the two. Most important, Eros stands between wisdom and ignorance. The gods are already wise and hence do not long for wisdom. The common run of men are ignorant, but they too do not long for wisdom because they do not even recognize its absence—"of course you won't want what you don't think you need."[53] They are content in their darkness and intellectual poverty.

Eros is in love with what is beautiful, and wisdom is the most beautiful of all good things. We use the word *Eros* too narrowly, Diotima tells us, if it is limited to sexual passion. "Every desire for good things or for happiness is 'the supreme and treacherous love' in everyone."[54] Some pursue it in sports, others in making money, or through war or politics or art. Eros drives them all. Diotima broadens the context in which love holds sway to the whole spectrum of human life, within which sexual passion is but one shading. Most of us are stuck in the realm of earthly comedy: ugly, base, and ignorant. But Eros also calls us to something higher. "Everything spiritual, you see," Diotima explains, "is in between god and mortal."[55]

Socrates, however, poses the fundamental Aristophanean question: "What use is Love to human beings?"[56] For Aristophanes, love is simply an irrational compulsion, which is inescapable because it is fundamental to our natures. Diotima, as Socrates playfully recounts, anticipates Aristophanes's speech (many years before it is given); "there is a certain story," she explains, "according to which lovers are those people who seek their other halves."[57] But we do not seek simply "what belongs to us," for we would shun what belongs to us if we found it harmful, even cutting off a limb if it was diseased. "What everyone loves is really nothing other than the good."[58] We seek good things because we think they will bring us *eudaimonia*, a word usually translated as happiness, but more broadly indicating human flourishing or living and faring well. "There's no need to ask further, 'What's the point of wanting happiness?'"[59] Diotima explains, because eudaimonia is by definition what all men seek, and our task is to determine the proper components of human flourishing, of living a full and complete life.

Diotima addresses that question by noting that "mortal nature seeks so far as possible to live forever and be immortal."[60] The "real purpose of love," she explains, is "giving birth in beauty, whether in body or in soul."[61] Some seek such immortality in offspring, which is why parents, both human and animal, so fiercely defend their young. Others are pregnant in their souls and bring forth the arts and the crafts or focus upon "the proper ordering of cities and households."[62] They channel their creative urges, their desire to make beauty permanent, into works of art and craftsmanship, into laws and institutions that outlive them. We "look up to Homer, Hesiod, and the other good poets with envy and admiration for the offspring they have left behind—offspring, which, because they are immortal themselves, provide their parents with immortal glory and remembrance."[63] "This is our triumph; this is our consolation," as Virginia Woolf would later write.[64] Yet highest of all, Diotima explains, is the use of logos (reason) to strive for knowledge and understanding, and thereby to participate in what is immortal and unchanging. Logos is our greatest gift, and we must respect and nurture this gift above all others. The most important component of eudaimonia is the search for wisdom, the mastery of logos.

We see, then, yet another reason why Diotima rather than Socrates is the main speaker at this point. Diotima is necessary to allow Socrates to praise himself in praising Eros, just as Agathon indirectly praised himself in his own speech. Man's essential nature—which Socrates more than any other has realized—is Eros, poised between the ugly and the beautiful, the base and the noble, the mortal and the immortal, between ignorance and wisdom. Socrates, like Eros, is barefoot and poor, yet tough and resilient. He is effectively homeless, rejected and condemned by his own polis. He is notoriously homely yet full of spiritual beauty. Most important of all, Socrates has enough self-knowledge to recognize his own ignorance. As such, he is a lover of wisdom (i.e., a philosopher). That is why he can claim, consistent with his professions of ignorance, that he understands Eros better than anything else. His knowledge of Eros is self-knowledge, which is in turn knowledge of his own state of longing for the wisdom he does not possess. For each of the speakers, and Socrates most of all, Eros has been a mirror held up to show their deepest concerns.

But Socrates, by his own admission, falls short of "the final and highest mystery."[65] The extent of Socratic wisdom is his realization of ignorance. He needs Diotima (and Plato) to lead him any further. "I don't know if you are capable of it," she warns, but "you must try to follow if you can."[66]

THE LADDER OF LOVE

Diotima's final teaching is that "the goal of Loving,"[67] pace Aristophanes, is a constant process of sublimation, of pressing passion into the service of a higher ideal. We start out from beautiful things and use them "like rising stairs,"[68] as we move from loving a single beautiful body to loving all beautiful bodies, from loving physical beauty to loving beautiful souls, and from there to the beauty of activities, of nomos (customs and laws), learning, and the arts. At each step from the personal to the impersonal we see more, appreciate more, and understand more of what it is to be beautiful. Yet the things of this world change; they can be beautiful at one time and ugly at another, or beautiful in relation to one thing and ugly in relation to another. Our ultimate quarry is something that "always *is* and neither comes to be nor passes away, neither waxes nor wanes."[69] This thing is "the Beautiful itself, absolute, pure, unmixed, not polluted by human flesh or colors or any other great nonsense of mortality."[70] It is the form of beauty, in which all other beautiful things share, without ever adding to or diminishing the form itself.

Plato's doctrine of the forms has bedeviled readers for 2,400 years, starting with his own pupil, Aristotle. The forms are eternal, immutable, and nonphysical. They underlie and give structure to the visible world, in much the same way that Plato thinks geometry does. The forms are apprehended by thought alone. Plato believes that there is a solid, irreducible core to each concept that is intelligible to us and that, through logos, we can proceed from particular instances to a direct apprehension of that form. Once we have such a grasp of the form itself, we can proceed to give an account of it and to understand, for the first time and with a clarity hitherto impossible, the particular instances of that form in the world.

This notion of ascending and descending is captured perfectly in Plato's most celebrated metaphor from *Republic*. There he likens all of us to prisoners in a cave, with necks and legs fettered. The only light is provided by a fire burning above and behind the prisoners. Between them and the fire is a low wall, and objects of all shapes and materials are carried above the wall so that they cast shadows that the prisoners (who cannot turn their heads to look at the objects themselves) see projected on the surface in front of them. For the prisoners, these shadows are reality, and they "would in every way believe that the truth is nothing other than the shadows of those artifacts."[71] Indeed, they would honor and accord power to those among them who were sharpest at discerning and remembering the shadows and the order in which they pass.

The philosopher is the one who can break those fetters, stand up and turn around, accustom his eyes to the light of the fire, and recognize that what he has been seeing, what he has taken for reality, are mere images and shadows. Yet he must go further, up the steep path and out into the sunlight where he will at first be blinded by the dazzling light but will gradually come to know not images of things, dimly perceived, but the things themselves, and even the sun itself.

The entire visible realm and the whole of our ordinary existence, Plato says, should be likened to this prison dwelling. The upward journey is the journey of the soul in its study of intelligible things, and the equivalent of the sun in that intelligible realm is the form of the good, which orders all things and is the ultimate source of "all that is correct and beautiful in anything" and that "provides truth and understanding, so that anyone who is to act sensibly in private or public must see it."[72] At this highest level, therefore, the beautiful and the good coalesce and are known in their purest form.

Plato makes clear that he does not know whether his account is true; indeed, elsewhere he acknowledges serious problems with it. Plato is not only the greatest but also the least dogmatic philosopher, as reflected in the fact that he never speaks to us directly. He writes dialogues, not treatises; ideas are tested, never confirmed. But it is clearly for him a consistent article of faith that life is intelligible and that it must, therefore, be so ordered that our words have meaning, not in virtue of transitory, changeable appearances, but because they are tethered to fixed and immutable forms. It is this intelligible, moral order that he terms the form of the good. As Diotima explains, one who has educated his passions and spent a lifetime in study, who, led by "the mystery of Love," "goes always upwards for the sake of this Beauty," may "all of a sudden . . . catch sight of"[73] the form of the good that has somehow been beckoning him all along. It is almost a religious experience, an enlightenment won after years of toil and dedication.

Yet Socrates, like Moses, stops short of this Promised Land. That is the beauty of *Symposium*. The love of wisdom is treated as a process that, while never completed in life, nonetheless constitutes the highest form of human flourishing (eudaimonia). Even without the final vision, even without Plato's faith that such a vision is possible, the steps up the ladder of Love are worthwhile in their own right, as they lead to ever more understanding and knowledge and an ever more sensitive appreciation of what is beautiful and good. Yet this ladder is still anchored in our everyday existence. We cannot transcend our own humanity. Eros is the link between the earthly and the divine; man has a foot in each. Passion is not extirpated but pressed into the service of a higher ideal. There is a fundamental (and very modern) insight here, that sex and power are not unrelated to the love of wisdom and truth. The lower ends of *Eros* are not abandoned but controlled and fashioned into a complete human life that respects more than sensual pleasure or political power, more even than applause from the multitude.

We ourselves have gone up this ladder in the course of the dialogue. The speeches of Phaedrus and Pausanias begin and end in the realm of sex. Phaedrus invokes the heroic age of Homer, Pausanias that of the great, quasi-mythical lawmakers; but both are carrying a brief for a purely physical passion. Eryximachus mimes the great natural philosophers and their unified vision of the cosmos, but his scientific reductionism detracts from rather than expands our understanding of Eros. Techné is a means for achieving, not for choosing, ends. Aristophanes mines the worlds of sex, politics, and war for comedies that are wildly funny and yet profoundly sad in their recognition that "what belongs to us" is never, and can never be, truly our own. Agathon, the epigone representative of tragedy, emphasizes the spiritual aspects of Eros. Yet his poetic but purely emotional appeal is without rigor or even a basic respect for truth.

Neither myth nor nomos is a guarantor of wisdom. Neither science nor comedy helps us to rise above our everyday concerns. Tragic poetry transforms men into gods to make life bearable, but the poets lie. None of these can lead us to virtue and the good life for man without guidance from philosophy. Only Socrates, therefore, can embrace the full scope of our evolving human consciousness; only Socrates can master the "lesser mysteries" of myth, nomos, science, comedy, and tragedy, and incorporate them into his search for wisdom. At this highest level, the good displaces the beautiful, poetry gives way to the rigorous application of logos, and yet the good is the most beautiful of the forms and philosophy the most poetic of disciplines. Eros is love of the good and the true, as well as the beautiful; at the highest level, they coalesce.

It is a stirring vision. Yet we feel a nagging sense of unease when Socrates finally concludes Diotima's discourse. The echo of Agathon's empty rhetoric still sounds in our ears and calls into question Diotima's own resort to poetic metaphors to teach a mystery beyond the grasp of logos. Why should we accept such a vision? Why should we believe that the philosophic life is the best life for man? Those are precisely the questions raised by the arrival of Alcibiades.

ALCIBIADES

Socrates, like Agathon, ends his speech to loud applause. Only Aristophanes is clamoring to offer a response. But he never gets a chance to state his objections because Alcibiades suddenly bursts into the room with a large, drunken party. He stands in the doorway, like the god Dionysus, "crowned with a beautiful wreath of violets and ivy and ribbons in his hair."[74]

Alcibiades's entrance is a shocking coda to Diotima's soaring speech, and it rudely eclipses the vision of wisdom and perfect knowledge she has vouchsafed us. Indeed, it is Alcibiades who will give voice to what Aristophanes was surely seeking to say in response: that love is the love of a unique individual, a specific human being with a personal history, not just a set of qualities from which we abstract an impersonal form of the Beautiful and the Good.

Alcibiades announces his intention to crown Agathon with his wreath, "directly from my head to the head that belongs, I don't mind saying, to the cleverest and best-looking man in town."[75] In his drunken state and with the ribbons and ivy pushed down over his eyes, he sits between Agathon and Socrates without even noticing the latter. He is shocked when he finally sees him, claiming to have been trapped, and yet immediately announces that Socrates must be honored as well. Agathon has won a first dramatic victory, a moment of fleeting glory, but Socrates has "never lost an argument in his life."[76] He accordingly takes back from Agathon enough material to make a second wreath, with which he crowns Socrates.

Then, in the spirit of the drinking party, he proceeds to give a speech in praise not of Eros but of Socrates; not to the god of Love, but to the specific individual by whom, he admits, he has been bewitched. It is an extraordinary portrait. He likens Socrates, first, to a statue of Silenus, companion of Dionysus, ugly on the outside, but with tiny figures of the gods within. He also compares him to the satyr Marsyas, whose melodies were divine and who challenged Apollo in a contest of music. Socrates needs no instrument. All those who listen to him speak, particularly "young and eager souls," are "transported, completely possessed"[77] by his words alone.

Alcibiades notes that Socrates's conversations upset him "so deeply that my very own soul started protesting that my life—*my* life!—was no better than the most miserable slave's."[78] Socrates repeatedly cornered him and made him conclude that his political career "is a waste of time, while all that matters is just what I most neglect."[79] Socrates alone has made him feel shame and resolve to improve his character; but as soon as he leaves him, Alcibiades goes back to his old ways and his political ambitions. Thus, he stops his ears and avoids Socrates, even as he longs for his company: "My whole life has become one constant effort to escape from him."[80]

Socrates disdains precisely what Alcibiades covets. Socrates is indifferent to possessions, to fame, and even to physical beauty. He holds them, and those who value them, in contempt and, with his irony, keeps everyone and everything at a distance. "In public," Alcibiades tell us, "his whole life is one big game—a game of irony."[81] To illustrate the point, Alcibiades notes that Socrates is constantly in the company of young men, whose beauty he praises and whom he claims to love. Alcibiades, the most beautiful of the young men, naturally thought he could make just the sort of exchange Pausanias had earlier lauded: "all I had to do was to let him have his way with me, and he would teach me everything he knew—believe me, I had a lot of confidence in my looks."[82] He pursued Socrates as if he, Alcibiades, was the lover and Socrates the beloved, and yet Socrates maintained his ironic distance. Even when, one night, Alcibiades lay next to Socrates and covered them both with his cloak, Socrates spurned his beauty. "Dear Alcibiades," he said to him,

> if I really have in me the power to make you a better man, then you can see in me a beauty that is really beyond description and makes your own remarkable good looks pale in comparison. But, then, is this a fair exchange that you propose? You seem to me to want more than your proper share: you offer me the merest appearance of beauty, and in return you want the thing itself, "gold in exchange for bronze."[83]

Socrates shows the same indifference to drink, to food, to cold, to sleep, and even to danger. He drinks whatever is put before him and yet is never drunk. He enjoys a feast and yet stands up to hunger better than anyone. On winter campaign with the army, he bore the bitter cold easily, clad only in his old light cloak and walking upon the ice in his bare feet. In the summer, he would stand transfixed all through the day and night thinking through a particular problem and then, with the dawn, make his prayers and begin a new day. He saved the life of Alcibiades during one battle and then urged that a decoration for bravery be given to Alcibiades rather than to himself. In the midst of another battle that ended in disaster, "he was making his way exactly as he does around town," with such calm courage that none of the enemy dared approach him.[84]

Alcibiades claims that he "had a glimpse"[85] of the figures kept hidden inside of Socrates, in a rare moment when Socrates dropped his irony and was open like Silenus's statues. He found there something so godlike, so "bright and beautiful,"[86] as to be of the greatest importance to anyone who wants to become a truly good person. Alcibiades is echoing Diotima's proffer to Socrates of a glimpse of the eternal forms. But what Alcibiades sees is not an abstraction; it is "this utterly unnatural, this truly extraordinary man,"[87] whose ways and ideas are so seductive and unusual, whose indifference to the possessions and concerns that drive the rest of us seems so bizarre, that "the best you can do is not to compare him to anything human."[88]

Socrates responds, of course, with irony, claiming that Alcibiades is trying to make trouble between Socrates and Agathon, so that Socrates should love only Alcibiades, and Alcibiades alone can love Agathon. It is a response that provokes laughter but reinforces Alcibiades's point. Socrates rebuffs his heartfelt, anguished tribute by refusing to take it seriously. He declines to share in the humanity that Alcibiades both offers and embodies. As Martha Nussbaum puts it, "Socrates, in his ascent towards the form, has become, himself, very like a form—hard, indivisible, unchanging."[89]

This is the ultimate paradox of Socrates. We admire him, we are transfixed by him, he is an honored and cherished guest at our feast. But we do not really want to be like him—self-sufficient to the point of indifference, shielded by irony from his family, his friends, his polis, and even his own body. His inner beauty is overpowering, but his disdain of "anything human" is frightening.

No wonder Alcibiades avoids Socrates and "stops his ears" to the siren song of philosophy. Alcibiades wants martial and political glory. He wants to be revered as a god, poeticized by the likes of Agathon, whose desire to beautify and mythologize the world is unimpeded by any concern with truth. But it is too late. Alcibiades may have the love of the people, just as Agathon did, but that is fleeting, and he knows that Socrates—the only one whose judgment matters—sees through him: beneath Alcibiades's own external splendor is something small and ugly.

Alcibiades is himself a remarkable individual, an epitome of the beauty and glory celebrated by the poets. Yet this individual is deeply flawed. He has indeed profaned the mysteries offered to us by Diotima. He is too slender a reed on which to rest our hopes. Shortly after he concludes his speech, Alcibiades spins off out of control, swept up in another crowd of drunken revelers, headed to his own destruction and the destruction of Athens.

POETRY AND PHILOSOPHY

Socrates keeps Agathon close, notwithstanding Alcibiades's effort to separate them. Poetry brings beauty to human life and experience. It gives birth to noble ideals and just impulses in the soul of man. But only philosophy can cement those ideals and turn scattered impulses into a steady, determined love of the good. Otherwise, they become like the Daedalus statues; they provide no safeguard against the greed, ambition, and predation of personal Eros.

Yet there is a cost. Socrates's only loyalty is to truth and wisdom, which makes him both inhuman and superhuman. Socrates refuses to equate what is his own (family, friends, city, possessions) with what is good. We pay lip service to the good while attending to what is our own. Socrates exposes this hypocrisy, but it is a hard message.

Hence, it is a message that Plato himself enshrouds in poetry. The gods of ancient poetry are a myth to be replaced by philosophy. But philosophy itself as presented by Plato bears the trappings of a new myth, and he enlists poetry to present and sustain it. Philosophy in its highest reaches returns to poetry, but the most beautiful sort of poetry because it is based on something changeless and immortal, something that redeems all of human life.

Yet it is still an article of faith—not of logos—that there is such a realm of true knowledge. At most, we are promised a glimpse of it, shining in the distance. We strive for wisdom, but the search is never final and complete. The philosopher does not possess wisdom but longs for it and for a life in keeping with it. Is it a worthwhile quest? The answer must lie not in a mystical vision but in the life and character of Socrates, whom Plato elsewhere describes as a man who was "of all those we have known, the best, and also the wisest and the most upright."[90]

At the end of *Symposium*, all the other revelers have fallen asleep except Aristophanes, Agathon, and Socrates. A new dawn is breaking. Socrates is trying to prove to them that the most skillful tragic dramatist should also be a comic poet. Yet they are too tired to follow his reasoning and, before he can clinch his argument, first Aristophanes and then Agathon drift off to sleep. Socrates then leaves and, after washing at the Lyceum (a gymnasium just outside the city walls), spends the day just as he always does before going home to rest in the evening.

The era of Athens's greatness in tragedy and comedy—an era tied closely to Athens's defeat of the Persians and the growth of her empire—is at an end. Almost two millennia later, another such era will arise in England, following the defeat of the Spanish Armada. Great poetry and the overweening ambition of worldly Eros are closely tied. But a move up the ladder of love is essential to the survival of a defeated Athens. The philosopher is the one man who can survey and transcend the tears of tragedy and the laughter of comedy in a search for the ideal life for man. Plato, in his dialogues, is the master of both.

Yet Plato recognizes the loss. He recognizes that we want both the good and what is our own, both Socrates and Aristophanes. Indeed, it is said that when Plato died, he had under his pillow a volume of Aristophanes.

Chapter 10

ARISTOTLE AND THE INVENTION OF POLITICAL SCIENCE

F or Plato, the philosopher stands on the ladder of love, poised halfway between man and god. He seeks a life of self-sufficiency and pure *logos* (reason), divorced from the demands of his state, his family, and even his own body. Plato's image of the philosopher could not be farther from that of Aristotle, for whom those very roles—as an individual with normal appetites, as the head of a household, and as a member of a political community—define us as human beings. Aristotle seeks not an ascent, not a sublimation of desire, but a circle of ever-deeper understanding and mastery of what is already our own.

Aristotle was born in 384 in northern Greece. His father was a physician to the king of Macedon, a territory then riven by civil war and foreign invasion. When he turned seventeen, Aristotle moved to Athens to study at the Academy under Plato and quickly became his greatest pupil. When Plato died in 347, Aristotle left Athens, accompanied by a circle of friends and disciples, on an extended and productive period of travels and research.

From 343 to 341, Aristotle served Philip II of Macedon as tutor to his son, Alexander, the future world conqueror. Philip II had taken over the throne in 359 and quickly unified northern Greece. Over the ensuing two decades, he took advantage of continued fighting among Athens, Sparta, and Thebes to consolidate and expand his holdings, and in 338 he effectively ended the independence of the Greek mainland after a decisive battle against Thebes and Athens at Chaeronea. Athens maintained some of its democratic institutions, but it was now one of many subject states paying a heavy tribute to Macedon.

By the time Aristotle returned to Athens in 335 and set up his own school in the Lyceum (a gymnasium and public space just outside the city walls), Alexander the Great had already taken over from his murdered father and was preparing his campaign against Persia, a campaign that would quickly extend his empire throughout the Middle East and Afghanistan and even into India. The Hellenistic Age, which extended Greek influence and Greek power throughout the known world, was now at hand. It would last nearly three hundred years, from the death of Alexander to the beginning of the Roman Empire.

Despite his long residence there, Aristotle never became an Athenian citizen. When Alexander died suddenly in 323, at the age of just thirty-three, and anti-Macedonian feelings were at their apex, Aristotle left Athens a second time, suggesting that he wanted to spare the city that had already executed Socrates from sinning twice against philosophy. Aristotle retired to Chalcis on the island of Euboea, where he died less than a year later, at the age of sixty-two.

Aristotle was, as Dante would later dub him, the "master of those who know."[1] He wrote on every conceivable topic in mechanics, the natural sciences (including, among others, physics, astronomy, zoology, botany, and biology), psychology, medicine, poetics, rhetoric, law, politics, and all aspects of philosophy— including logic, metaphysics, epistemology, and ethics. He even wrote on dreams and divination. Of his known writings, however, barely one-third survive, and the books that do remain to us are largely compilations of lecture notes, rough in style and uneven in development.

Yet the works have a beauty of their own. In Plato, matter and manner blend perfectly as faultless prose ascends to the poetry of the forms. In Aristotle, matter and manner are equally well matched. In his extant writings we can experience the thinker at work, his tentative groping, his careful repetition, his gradual deepening of the subject matter. There is nothing finished or complete in Aristotle's work; it is a constant invitation to further thought.

This invitation is nowhere clearer than in the works that make up what he calls *practical philosophy* or the "philosophic inquiry about human things,"[2] whose end, Aristotle tells us, "is not knowing but action."[3] Practical philosophy consists of ethics (the science of character), economics (narrowly understood as the science of household management), and politics (the science of governing). His two great treatises in this area, *Nicomachean Ethics* and *Politics*, form a continuous study of man's potential for excellence, of what it means to live and fare well as an individual, as the head of a household, and as a citizen. (A partial, third treatise in the series, *Economics*, is likely spurious.)

Aristotle's practical philosophy is a reflection of the Socratic insistence that to study philosophy is to learn how to live. Plato turned that inquiry in an abstract and theoretical direction. Aristotle seeks to turn it toward science, blending empirical research and objective assumptions about the nature of man into a practical guide to the good life.

Perhaps most important, Aristotle refuses to consider the good of man in isolation from his social and political circumstances. Man is a "political animal."[4] He is by nature and capacity fitted for social relations and a political ordering of those relations. Man cannot realize his true excellence except in the context of his participation in a political community. The good life must be, in key respects, a political life.

Accordingly, the question of how best to live together is a pressing one. Aristotle and his school undertook a detailed study of 158 constitutions, including their history and evolution over time, the sources of any social unrest, and whether they proved well or badly run. All but one of these constitutional studies (the one for Athens) have been lost. But the knowledge gained from them informs almost every page of *Politics* and shows Aristotle as the inventor of political science, of the close and disciplined empirical study of the ways in which we organize ourselves into political communities and with what effects. Aristotle's *Politics* is in constant dialogue with *Republic*, where Plato outlined his own version of the ideal state, in which a small ruling class of guardians governs the populace in accordance with abstract principles of philosophy. If Plato gave us the first totalitarian utopia, Aristotle offers in contrast a pragmatic, if messy, vision of free citizens who find their fulfillment in active participation in the affairs of the state.

Aristotle never loses sight of his ultimate criterion for the ideal state: it exists not to benefit a ruling class but to secure the good life of its citizens. *Politics* thus both continues and completes *Ethics*. *Ethics* investigates the components of the good life. *Politics* investigates the political order that educates its citizens and provides them with opportunities to realize that good life. Politics is the "master art"[5] because it prescribes what the citizens should learn and how they can participate in the affairs of the state. But it must start from, and always take as its touchstone, ethics.

THE METHOD OF PRACTICAL PHILOSOPHY

Aristotle's *Nicomachean Ethics* (often shortened to *Ethics* but distinct from his *Eudemian Ethics*) is named for his son, Nicomachus, to whom he may have dedicated the work. The treatise is focused on a single question: What is the good life for man? Socrates and Plato of course ask the same question. But Socrates disclaims any knowledge on the subject and finds that those he questions are also unable to give a proper account. Plato develops his theory of forms precisely to place his own account beyond the reach of Socratic questioning and uncertainty.

Aristotle, as in so many places, strikes a middle ground. He politely but firmly (because "piety requires us to honor truth above our friends") rejects Plato's suggestion that there must be some form of the good that is present in all instances.[6] He notes that the word *good* is meant in different, if related, ways in different contexts, and he concludes "that there could not be any common good that is one and universal, for if there were it could not have been meant in all the ways of attributing being but only in one."[7] Plato insists that there *must* be such a universal concept if we are to have knowledge of such matters; Aristotle looks at actual usage and concludes that there is none. Words such as *justice* and *injustice*, he points out, are "meant in more than one sense, but since their ambiguity is between meanings that are close together, it escapes notice, and is not, as in the case of things far apart, so obvious."[8] Yet nothing but confusion will result from assimilating these various meanings to a single form.

At the same time, Aristotle rejects Socrates's insistence that we fall far short of knowledge on such matters. Ethics and politics, he explains, are not exact sciences; we must seek only as much precision as is appropriate to the subject matter. Here we are dealing with matters of character and governance, matters that are open to discussion and potential disagreement. "One ought to be content, when speaking about such things and reasoning from such things, to point out the truth roughly and in outline, . . . for it belongs to an educated person to look for just so much precision in each kind of discourse as the nature of the thing one is concerned with admits."[9] To demand proofs in ethics and politics makes no more sense than to accept probable conclusions from a mathematician.

Aristotle frequently starts his discussion of a given issue with what people ordinarily say on the subject. He quotes from poets, he cites other writers, and he reports on common beliefs. Such received opinions, he notes, are well worth considering and provide a natural starting point for any deeper inquiry. Aristotle suggests that if we are able to sort through the difficulties raised by common views without departing from them too much, we shall have dealt with the issues "in an adequate way."[10] He tests received views with real-world examples, he sorts through apparent or real contradictions, and he arrives at what appears to be the best-considered outcome. But that is often just a first sketch that is amplified after similar treatments of related issues, so that his stated views become ever deeper and ever more contextual.

Plato is deeply suspicious of common views and believes the philosopher has to transcend them, and then, based on his knowledge, radically transform human life. Aristotle is far more cautious and empirical, and his goals are correspondingly more modest. He seeks to make human life marginally more rational and thoughtful and, hence, to bring the good life closer to us. Plato wants to base ethical judgments on absolute bedrock knowledge of the forms. With such knowledge in hand, received views can simply be swept aside except insofar as they happen to correspond with the deeper knowledge provided by philosophy. Aristotle, by contrast, starts *in medias res*, as he notes good plays and epic poems do. He accepts our common discourse about ethics and seeks to understand it and to increase the rationality of the practice from within, from the perspective of a participant who wishes to improve his own activity and realize the best life for man. "Let us remember," he cautions, that we should not disregard the experience of ages, for "in the multitude of years these things, if they were good, would certainly not have been unknown."[11]

This is an inherently conservative undertaking, a point that comes out most clearly when Aristotle shifts from ethics to political science. Aristotle is inclined to accept existing practices, such as slavery and the suppression of women, and even to justify them as the product of natural inequalities. His practical philosophy incorporates rather than eliminates such discrimination. Yet, as we shall see, Aristotle does not blindly follow received wisdom. "Such things have some trustworthiness," he explains, "but the truth in matters of action is discerned from deeds and from life, since they are the determining thing in these matters. So we ought to examine the things that have been said by applying them to deeds and to life, and if they are in harmony with the deeds one ought to accept them, while if they are out of tune one ought to consider them just words."[12]

The purpose of his study of ethics and politics is practical, not theoretical. Medicine is valid only insofar as it promotes health. Military strategy is valid only insofar as it promotes battlefield success. So, too, ethics and politics alike must promote the good life for man. In this context, mere abstract knowledge, knowledge that does not inform our lives and our behavior and lead to a better social and political order, is of no use to us. "We are investigating not in order that we might know what virtue is, but in order that we might become good, since otherwise there would be no benefit from it."[13]

LIVING AND FARING WELL

Determining *the* good life for man is an inherently difficult undertaking. Some men pursue pleasure, some honor, some riches, some love, and some knowledge. The list could be expanded, and most in fact pursue a mixture of these goods. In each of these cases, however, Aristotle thinks the "good" pursued is an intermediate good. It is valued both in itself and for something in addition. "If," he explains, "there is some end of the things we do that we want on account of itself, and the rest on account of this one, and we do not choose everything on account of something else (for in that way the choices would go beyond all bounds, so that desire would be empty and pointless), it is clear that this would be the good, and in fact the highest good."[14]

Aristotle uses an umbrella term—*eudaimonia*—to specify this highest good. The word is commonly translated as "happiness," and that translation works up to a point. If pressed, we will readily say that we want pleasure or riches or honor because those things, we think, will make us happy. It makes little sense (outside of a religious context) to press further and ask to what end we want to be happy. "We choose honor and pleasure and intelligence and every virtue indeed on account of themselves (for even if nothing resulted from them we would choose each of them), but we choose them also for the sake of happiness, supposing that we will be happy by these means. But no one chooses happiness for the sake of these things, nor for the sake of anything else at all."[15]

Happiness thus seems to qualify as "something complete and self-sufficient" and "the end of actions," for which Aristotle is searching.[16] But there are two related problems with this translation. First, the term *happiness* tends to focus on feelings and emotions. In our usage, even a simpleton could be considered happy. But Aristotle would never admit that a simpleton is *eudaimon*. The eudaimon life is certainly accompanied by pleasant feelings, but eudaimonia itself is a more active, engaged concept that embraces all the virtues of which men are capable, most especially intelligence. A second, related problem is that when the word *happiness* is used to translate *eudaimonia*, the passage quoted in the previous paragraph seems false: we do not choose "every virtue . . . supposing that we will be happy by these means."[17] We choose some virtues (e.g., courage in a dangerous situation, truthfulness when the truth is not to our advantage, justice in declining more than our fair share) *despite* the threat those virtues seem to pose to our happiness, narrowly construed.

Aristotle himself paraphrases eudaimonia as "living and faring well."[18] It constitutes success in the activity of being a complete human being and living a full and rich life. For Aristotle, living and faring well encompasses what we would call happiness, but it is much more than that. A close, but quite awkward, translation is "human flourishing." The "good life" is another possibility, though the phrase is often prosaic and also potentially misleading, given its current slang connotations.

Is it correct, then, that all humans seek to live and fare well and that all intermediate goods (pleasure, wealth, virtue, honor) are sought for the sake of living and faring well? Yes, but only in the empty and circular sense that living and faring well just is, for the moment, the umbrella term that Aristotle introduces to impose order on the array of "intermediate" goods that men seek. Living and faring well is a bucket into which all those various goods are placed, pending further discussion, and Aristotle expressly recognizes it as such when he introduces the term. As soon as he gives it a more specific content, by specifying a particular mix of goods as the components of living and faring well, it will no longer be true that all men seek that particular mix; we will have moved from the descriptive to the prescriptive, from a general organizing principle to a specific recipe for the good life.

Despite its initial circularity, the centrality of Aristotle's notion of living and faring well is critical in two respects. First, it is a recognition of the complexity of human nature and the variety of ends sought by men. Unlike Plato and most later moralists, Aristotle is not interested in reducing human life to a single component or developing it along a single dimension. He is not reductionist. He recognizes the messy complexity of human life and our varied desires and values, and he does not believe that reducing or ignoring that complexity is a reflection of wisdom. A full human life is not just contemplating the forms or seeking martial glory or amassing great wealth. For Aristotle, ethics is a matter of living and faring well as a full and complete human being.

Second, the initial circularity is itself critical to Aristotle's methodology, and we see it repeatedly in *Ethics* and later in *Politics*. Aristotle introduces a term such as *eudaimonia* in the most general way imaginable in order to capture a broad agreement in our judgments. He then, through successive discussions, refines our understanding of those judgments by giving more and more specific content to the term. He does this with other key terms such as *virtue, character, citizen, polis,* and *practical wisdom.* Grappling with the way in which Aristotle gradually and steadily deepens (and changes) our understanding of these terms is the surest way to follow his argument.

Aristotle accordingly begins his account of living and faring well with a description of some of its commonly agreed-upon components, while recognizing that men will vary in their views on the relative weighting to be given to each. These include virtue and honor and intelligence, but also health and pleasure, and even good looks, reasonable wealth, and longevity. This is a highly pragmatic account. As noted, Aristotle is not interested in purifying our conception of living and faring well or shutting his eyes to the importance of the many nonmoral goods that constitute such a life. A complete human life has need of "goods of the body, and of goods that are external and from fortune, in order that [it] not be impeded on account of them."[19] Aristotle says that those who insist that the good man has no need of such things, and that even "someone who is being tortured, or someone who falls into great misfortunes," is still living and faring well as long as "he is a good person are either intentionally or unintentionally talking nonsense."[20]

That said, Aristotle immediately sets aside health, wealth, beauty, and other such external goods. They are "conditions that need to be present" for living and faring well, or things that "naturally assist" such a life, but the subject matter of ethics is the active response of the person to external conditions.[21] This is a critical point for Aristotle. Living and faring well is "something that happens, and not something that is present like some possession."[22] The proper work of a man is to make the best possible use of his moral and intellectual faculties in response to the conditions of life. This, in turn, requires the careful exercise of reason to guide and develop those faculties so that "each thing is accomplished well as a result of the virtue appropriate to it."[23]

A MEAN BETWEEN EXTREMES

Aristotle's approach raises an obvious question: Why should we consider virtue to be necessary to living and faring well? Wealth, pleasure, honor, and even intelligence all seem critical components of the good life. But couldn't a bad person enjoy all those goods? Indeed, in *Republic*, the Sophist Thrasymachus argues that the bad man is more likely to enjoy them because he will not be impeded in his pursuit by any scruples about virtue.[24]

In considering this question, we have to remember two things. First, Aristotle is taking our standard ethical judgments for granted. He is not trying to provide foundations or arguments for those judgments that will compel acquiescence by a confirmed skeptic like Thrasymachus. He is writing for those who already assume that virtue is a critical component of a good life and want a better understanding of its nature. Second, Aristotle is not using the word virtue (*arête*) in a narrowly moral sense, but rather in the sense that we might speak of the virtues of a good horse. The word is often translated as "excellence," and it connotes whatever makes something an outstanding example of its kind. For Aristotle, the virtues are ideals of character and behavior that are beautiful (noble) in and of themselves. The man of excellent character will disdain to lie, cheat, and steal not because some moral theory tells him it is wrong to do so but because those are base and ignoble actions. In this sense, a person without virtue could not be eudaimon because "no one would maintain that he is happy who has not in him a particle of courage or temperance or justice or practical wisdom, who is afraid of every insect which flutters past him, and will commit any crime, however great, in order to gratify his lust for meat or drink, who will sacrifice his dearest friend for the sake of half a farthing, and is as feeble and false in mind as a child or a madman."[25]

In his analysis, Aristotle adheres closely to traditional Greek values such as courage, temperance, justice, and liberality. Each of these virtues of character, he explains, is "of such a nature as to be destroyed by deficiency and by excess," [26] while "the mean is praised and gets them right."[27] His point is not that we must always act with moderation or be moderate in our feelings. Some circumstances (e.g., a threat to one's family) may call for bold action and extreme anger. Other circumstances (e.g., a minor, unintentional slight) will properly be brushed aside with no action taken and no feelings of anger. Being moderately angry in both circumstances would not be the mark of an excellent character. A man of excellent character will feel and react appropriately to the circumstances.

Thus, courage is a "mean condition" between two vices, cowardice and foolhardiness, "one resulting from excess and the other from deficiency."[28] Temperance is a mean condition between dissipation and insensibility. Having an even temper is a mean condition between irascibility and impassivity. Liberality is a mean condition between stinginess and wastefulness. Again, this is not to say that the man of courage will be only moderately courageous. Rather, he will be courageous in all circumstances, some of which will place him at extreme peril, others of which may expose him to very little peril. His feelings and actions will be calibrated accordingly. Similarly, the temperate man may enjoy food, drink, and sex in appropriate circumstances, but he will not live a life of dissipation or the life of an anchorite. He will disdain the pleasures of the dissipated person but, at the same time, will appreciate "pleasant things that are not impediments to health and good condition, and are not contrary to what is beautiful, and not beyond his resources."[29]

The mean condition is a bull's-eye struck by an expert archer. It is a mark of true excellence, not of an average condition. At the same time, there is no mean condition of cowardice or foolhardiness or of dissipation or insensibility because "however one does them one is in the wrong."[30] The same is true of certain feelings, "such as joy at others' misfortunes, shamelessness, and envy."[31] There are no "right conditions" under which such feelings should arise. Whichever way one moves from the bull's-eye, one has missed the target. Aristotle's doctrine of the mean recognizes that "it is possible to go wrong in many ways," but "there is only one way to get something right."[32] Irascibility may manifest itself as "getting angry at people one ought not to get angry at," or "in circumstances in which one ought not," or "more than one ought," or "more quickly, and for a longer time."[33] Impassivity will likewise manifest itself as a failure to get angry at people with whom one should be angry, in circumstances where anger is warranted, or, if anger is aroused, it may not be sufficient to the occasion or too slow to manifest itself or be dissipated too quickly. Only the man of excellent character strikes exactly the right balance in each case.

Calibrating that balance is far from easy in the midst of constant wrong signals from those who lack the virtues in question. The people at each extreme will justify themselves by accusing the person at the mean of being at the other extreme. Thus, "the coward calls the courageous person rash while the rash person calls him a coward, and analogously in the other cases."[34] The man of practical judgment will make use of the extremes in calibrating his own character and feelings. In determining how to improve one's character, Aristotle tells us, "one ought to consider what we ourselves are carried away toward."[35] If we have a tendency to timidity, we ought to affect boldness. If we are too rash, we should err toward circumspection in our actions. Similarly, if we have a tendency toward stinginess, we should force ourselves even to be excessively generous, and vice versa. "We ought then to drag ourselves over toward the opposite side, for by pulling far away from going wrong we will come to the mean, the very thing that people do who straighten warped pieces of lumber."[36] In all such cases we must guard against what seems to us the most comfortable and pleasant action, since pleasure can warp judgment until, through habit, pleasure is aligned with virtue. "In everything the pleasant or pleasure is most to be guarded against; for we do not judge it impartially."[37]

TRAINING IN VIRTUE

The most secure route to virtue, then, is to train ourselves "to be pleased and pained at what one ought and as one ought."[38] A man who feels excessive fear but still stands his ground is not, in Aristotle's view, as courageous as a man with steadier feelings. Similarly, a man who must struggle to master his temptation to drink too much is less temperate than the man who has no desire to drink excessively. This inversion may seem odd to us. After all, is not courage precisely the overcoming of fear and temperance the overcoming of temptation? The man who is not afraid or not tempted does not seem to require either courage or temperance. We are inclined to think (prompted by modern psychology) that we cannot help our feelings, and that virtue lies in what we do *despite* those feelings.

Aristotle would strongly disagree. He believes that with proper education and good habits one's feelings become aligned with and reinforce one's actions. One becomes naturally disposed toward virtuous actions and feels no internal tension that must be overcome. "By refraining from pleasures we become temperate, and once having become temperate we are most capable of refraining from them; and it is similar in the case of courage, for by habituating ourselves to disdain frightening things, and by enduring them, we become courageous, and having become courageous we shall be most capable of enduring frightening things."[39] Excellence of character for Aristotle is a settled disposition, a stable equilibrium of the soul that naturally perceives and embraces what is fine and beautiful. "What is most conducive to virtue of character," he explains, "is to enjoy what one ought and hate what one ought."[40]

We learn to enjoy what we ought and to hate what we ought through training and habit, and so too the opposite. Just as virtue can become a settled disposition of the soul, so too can baseness become fixed in our characters. "By acting in our dealings with people some of us become just, others unjust, and by acting in frightening situations and getting habituated to be afraid or to be confident, some of us become courageous and others become cowards."[41] Once a disposition becomes fixed through habit, moreover, it becomes extremely difficult to change. Argument and teaching alone will not suffice. "It makes no small difference, then, to be habituated in this way or in that straight from childhood, but an enormous difference, or rather all the difference."[42] Even when people reach adulthood, moreover, they still must practice and habituate themselves to virtue, lest pleasure and weakness lead them astray.

Thus, even as *Ethics* draws to a close, Aristotle makes clear that his "philosophic inquiry about human things" is far from over.[43] He must move from an analysis of the components of a life of excellence to an analysis of education and the political order that makes such a life possible. Laws, both written and unwritten, are needed for that task, "for most people are more obedient to compulsion than to argument, and are persuaded more by penalties than by what is beautiful." [44]

Such a critical matter as the proper training in excellence cannot simply be left to the head of each individual household. In an era in which public education was largely unknown, Aristotle finds it surprising that only the Spartans and a few others have taken care with upbringing and exercise, while other cities are "utterly careless about such things, and each person lives the way he wants, 'laying down the law for his children and wife' in the manner of a Cyclops."[45] This is not the best way for a society to ensure the excellence of its citizens.

Obviously, parents will contribute to the proper upbringing of their children. And there is much to be said for "educations tailored to each person," focused on the talents and skill and disposition of the individual, rather than those given in common.[46] But "it is surely not in the power of just anyone to get whoever is put in front of him into a beautiful condition."[47] The head of a household has neither the expertise nor the compulsory authority of the state at his command. Thus, the inquiry must now focus on what sort of laws are best suited to educate citizens in excellence and to provide them with an opportunity to live and fare well. This, in turn, requires a discussion of the nature and origins of the state.

A POLITICAL ANIMAL

The word *polis*, which is usually translated as "state," refers to the many autonomous city-states that flourished throughout Greece and the eastern Mediterranean during the sixth and fifth centuries. The polis, for Aristotle, is necessary to the good life in three respects. First, we cannot flourish except within the context of a relatively secure and stable social order. Second, as noted, we will not become good unless we are properly trained from a young age in accordance with the laws and customs of our community. Third, and most interesting, participation in government is itself one of the components of a good life. In other words, we realize our potential and fully exercise our natural capacities only as citizens actively engaged in the affairs of our state.

This third point is what Aristotle largely means by calling man a "political animal." Nature does nothing without purpose, and man is the sole animal with "the gift of speech" and a "sense of good and evil, of just and unjust."[48] Speech is inherently communal; it draws men together in bonds of cooperation and trust and some degree of mutual concern. The guarantor of those bonds is justice, which must be "the principle of order in political society."[49] Such a society is not just a pact for mutual survival and protection but also a means for exercising our moral and intellectual virtues as part of a shared enterprise in which all are invested and from which all benefit.

"A social instinct is implanted in all men by nature";[50] only a beast or a god lives in isolation from his fellows. Men and women join together to perpetuate themselves with offspring. Households cluster together into villages, and villages into larger units. "When several villages are united in a single complete community, large enough to be nearly or quite self-sufficing, the state comes into existence, originating in the bare needs of life, and continuing in existence for the sake of a good life."[51] This development is as natural as that of an acorn growing into a small tree and then into a fully mature oak. The state is, in this sense, "a creation of nature."[52] Since no one is self-sufficient, moreover, "the state is by nature clearly prior to the family and to the individual."[53] In other words, since the individual and the family cannot exist in isolation, they exist "in relation to" the state.[54] They find their natural fulfillment as part of this larger whole because "excellence of the part must have regard to the excellence of the whole."[55]

This is a profound, if potentially troubling, observation. The point is largely foreign to modern political theory, which starts from the primacy and integrity of the individual and treats the state as a regrettable if necessary restraint on individual freedom. Modern political theory at least since Rousseau has tended to view *physis* (nature) as artificially constrained by *nomos* (law and custom), which ought to be strictly limited and always stands in need of justification. Yet Aristotle sees no such disharmony. Proper nomos is in fact an outgrowth of physis because it is an essential part of our nature to band together in political communities. Political life is necessary not just to our survival but also to our fulfillment and eudaimonia. The legitimacy of political authority (why individuals are bound by the laws)—which is the focus of so much modern political theorizing—is simply not an inquiry undertaken by Aristotle. For Aristotle the question is not whether or when civil disobedience is justified but how best to realize our full potential as part of a political community.

Yet, as noted, Aristotle's teleological focus—his tendency to view the parts in light of the whole—also leads him to reason backward from existing social conditions to tendentious assumptions about the nature of the men and women subject to those conditions. If the state is a natural outgrowth, it is easy to succumb to the temptation to assume that relationships found across a variety of states—particularly those between men and women, and masters and slaves—must themselves be natural. Thus, he concludes, "the male is by nature superior, and the female inferior; and the one rules, and the other is ruled; this principle, of necessity, extends to all mankind."[56] He also justifies slavery as "both expedient and right"[57] because "the lower sort are by nature slaves"[58] and need to be ruled, as men rule children or even domestic animals.

"Political science," Aristotle tells us, "does not make men, but takes them from nature."[59] Yet he elsewhere recognizes that political science can indeed have a significant role in "mak[ing] men" through habit and training, and that many traits considered natural (part of physis) are in fact conventional (a product of nomos). Aristotle himself questions whether slavery is a "violation of nature."[60] Yet his views on the inherent inferiority and incapacity of women and slaves were so deeply embedded in his time that he failed to exercise his own moral and intellectual capacities to transcend them.

PUBLIC AND PRIVATE

The household is for Aristotle the critical economic unit of the state. Indeed, the Greek term for household management, *oikonomike*, is the origin of our term *economics*. A man rules his wife, his children, and his slaves, as a king rules his people, so as to ensure sufficient prosperity to support and sustain the household. Yet the household is not independent; it is part of the state. Therefore, the proper organization of the household is an appropriate and important subject for political science and must be considered with an eye to the good of the state.

Plato sought to ensure harmony between households (private interest) and the state (public interest) by abolishing the household as a separate unit. In *Republic*, the guardians—the ruling class of warriors from which the leaders of the state are chosen—hold women, children, and property in common. They live in barracks, dine in a common mess, and parents do not even know who their children are (nor children their parents). The state itself becomes a family, and all children refer to grown men and women as father and mother, respectively. Plato compares the state to a single organism in which each part is wholly dependent upon the others. The goal is for the state to be as unified as possible.

Aristotle disagrees. He finds the strongest unity, as did our founders, in plurality. "The state . . . is a plurality, which should be united and made into a community by education . . . by philosophy [and] by customs and laws."[61] The goal of the good state is not the greatest unity possible, but a unity consistent with the eudaimonia of its constituent elements. This is an uneasy mix perhaps but, for Aristotle, a critical one nonetheless. Individual autonomy and family integrity are maintained, but as parts of a greater whole. The community of the polis should not seek to displace the more intimate relationships of family and friends. "Of the two qualities which chiefly inspire regard and affection—that a thing is your own and that it is precious—neither can exist in such a state as [Plato's]."[62] The regard and affection to be found in familial and other close relationships are critical to the good life. "How much better is it," Aristotle wryly notes, "to be the real cousin of somebody than to be a son after Plato's fashion."[63]

Private property is also important to the good life. Having all property held in common would eliminate the perfectly legitimate desire of men to safeguard themselves and their households. "How immeasurably greater is the pleasure, when a man feels a thing to be his own."[64] Such feelings may stem from "the love of self," but that, too, "is a feeling implanted by nature and not given in vain," because people will attend to their own business and their own interests most of all.[65] An unbounded pursuit of personal wealth is a perversion of man's highest nature. But "there is the greatest pleasure in doing a kindness or service to friends or guests or companions, which can only be rendered when a man has private property."[66] Anticipating modern economic theory by more than two millennia, moreover, Aristotle explains that common property would be a source of more frequent disputes than private property.

At the same time, Aristotle rejects the view of many Sophists that self-interest alone should rule men's actions. The state is not a mere association for mutual protection and economic exchange (the so-called night-watchman state of modern political theory), within which individuals pursue only their own narrow interests. It is a community with a shared purpose to realize a vision of the good in all three spheres of human activity: the personal, the familial, and the political.

In *Ethics*, Aristotle taught that one can only understand a human life in terms of the excellence at which it aims. So, too, with the state, but the inquiry is exponentially more complicated. The state exists for the good of its citizens. Yet the good of the citizens is not divorced from that of the state. Individuals and households do not reach their own ends apart from the state. Law educates and trains the citizens and allows them to fulfill their capacities, to live and fare well in the full range of human activities and human interactions. The good life is achieved only in the context of a state and only through active participation in the political life of the state.

Accordingly, Aristotle turns his attention to existing states, to their varied constitutions, and to the many ways in which they depart from this end and fail to realize their own excellence. He will then use this study as a means for developing his views on the ideal state.

CONSTITUTIONS AND THE CAUSES OF SOCIAL UNREST

Having studied 158 constitutions in detail, Aristotle speaks with some authority when he states that "all the constitutions which now exist are faulty."[67] In *Politics*, he looks with special care at the constitutions of Sparta, Crete, Carthage, and Athens, pointing out for each their strengths and weaknesses.

All states, he explains, have three basic components: a legislative and deliberative component that fashions law and policy, an executive and administrative component that enforces laws and implements policies, and a judicial component that adjudicates disputes and administers justice. Yet how these various components overlap and relate to one another, whether they are in one or many hands, and, if the latter, how the offices are filled depends upon the particular constitution at issue. There are, moreover, numerous essential classes within the state, including farmers, artisans, traders, laborers, military men, administrators, adjudicators, and rulers. The rights and responsibilities assigned to each of these classes, and in particular the question of who qualifies as a citizen, further defines the constitution.

Within this endless potential variety, however, there are three main types of state, depending upon whether "the supreme authority... [is] in the hands of one, or of a few, or of the many."[68] Here Aristotle's love of classification, so evident in his biological writings, comes into play. Monarchy is the rule of one person, aristocracy is the rule of the best, and what he calls polity or constitutional government is the rule of the many. These forms of government are all classified as "healthy" insofar as the ruler or rulers govern with a view to the common interest. By contrast, "governments which rule with a view to the private interest, whether of the one, or of the few, or of the many, are perversions"[69] of the state, "for they are despotic, whereas a state is a community of freemen."[70] All the members of a state, "if they are truly citizens, ought to participate in its advantages."[71]

Yet each of the three healthy forms of government frequently collapses into its defective or perverted counterpart. True monarchy—in which a single individual is not only so markedly superior to his fellows as to be a natural and inevitable ruler but also exercises his power for the benefit of all—is so unlikely that Aristotle spends little time discussing it. Such a king would have to be as a god among mortals, and even then the problem of succession arises, for sons are not necessarily the equal of their fathers. Kingship is the oldest form of government, but it either evolves toward aristocracy and constitutional democracy or degenerates into tyranny. "This tyranny is just that arbitrary power of an individual which is responsible to no one, and governs all alike, whether equals or betters, with a view to its own advantage; not to that of its subjects, and therefore against their will. No freeman willingly endures such a government."[72]

Aristocracy, too, is unlikely because true excellence is both rare and difficult to identify; those who have merit and those who are thought to have merit are not necessarily the same (as disappointed voters so often discover). Wealth is in any event more common and often proves more persuasive than merit, and hence oligarchy is a more likely form of government than aristocracy. In an oligarchy, the wealthy control the power of the state for their own aggrandizement, while the rest of the citizens suffer impoverishment in both their property and their civil rights, "for the weaker are always asking for equality and justice, but the stronger care for none of these things."[73]

Democracy is the "most tolerable" of the three perverted forms of government. But Aristotle is not comfortable with extreme democracy either, which he notes (perhaps with a nod to Athens) can also become both lawless and despotic. "Men always want more and more without end; for it is of the nature of desire to be unlimited, and most men live only for the gratification of it."[74] Accordingly, when the many take power in the state they tend to vote for measures to equalize not just the rights of citizenship but also the distribution of property and honors. Such measures have no apparent end point; "the poor are always receiving and always wanting more and more, for such help is like water poured into a leaky cask."[75] Aristotle acknowledges that "the encroachments of the rich are more destructive to the constitution than those of the people."[76] But if the many are to rule the state, it must be not just for their own benefit but "in accordance with strict principles of justice" and the rule of law.

None of the three "healthy" types of government (or even their perverted counterparts) is commonly found in its purest form; there are variations on each type. Even absolute rulers (whether kings or tyrants) need ministers and advisors invested with substantial power; and most other states have a pragmatic mix of aristocratic, democratic, and autocratic elements. The state is a delicate balance among these conflicting class interests, and when those interests are pressed out of proportion, social unrest and even revolution result. In a useful reminder against current political polarization, Aristotle remarks: "Those who think that all excellence is to be found in their own party principles push matters to extremes; they do not consider that disproportion destroys a state."[77]

In the Greek city-states of the fifth century, a constant struggle raged between democracy and oligarchy, with individual states, including Athens, oscillating from one to the other. Aristotle notes that "poverty is the parent of revolution and crime."[78] But such struggles are fostered by (or at least carried on under the rubrics of) justice and equality. The democrats believe that, because they are equal as free citizens, they should also be equal in wealth and power. The oligarchs believe that, because they are unequal in wealth, they should also be unequal in power and the perquisites of citizenship. "For the one party, if they are unequal in one respect, for example wealth, consider themselves to be unequal in all; and the other party, if they are equal in one respect, for example free birth, consider themselves to be equal in all."[79]

Aristotle includes in book 5 a detailed, empirical analysis of class conflict, revolution, and the methods for preserving existing regimes. Using historical examples, he highlights the importance of psychological factors—anger, fear, and slighted honor—not just economic ones. "In revolutions the occasions may be trifling, but great interests are at stake."[80] By and large, democracy is "safer and less liable to revolution than oligarchy."[81] But revolutions can still occur when demagogues incite the masses, thereby provoking the rich in fear and compelling them to combine. Or an increase in power and renown of certain magistrates may more naturally tip democracy into oligarchy. But the pendulum is likely to shift back when power breeds insolence and avarice or when the oligarchs may fall out among themselves. In democracies, Aristotle cautions, the property and income of the rich should be preserved. In oligarchies, "great care should be taken of the poor, and lucrative offices should go to them."[82] In these ways, the balance of the existing regime will be preserved.

Aristotle's advice to tyrants is even more Machiavellian. In words that seem very modern indeed, he notes that tyrants preserve themselves by sowing fear and mistrust among the citizens by means of spies, by distracting them with foreign wars, by eliminating men of spirit who might lead a revolution, by humbling the people and making them incapable of decisive action, by forbidding "common meals, clubs, education and the like"[83] in order "to prevent people from knowing one another (for acquaintance begets mutual confidence)."[84] In other words, no

Facebook®, no Twitter® accounts, and no others means by which citizens can share their dissatisfaction and conspire together. For the tyrant intent on retaining his position, Aristotle explains, "there is no wickedness too great for him."[85]

But there is also another method a tyrant might employ, "which proceeds upon an almost opposite principle of action."[86] He should pretend a concern for public revenues and render a strict account of what is received and what is spent. He should collect taxes only for state purposes and moderate any indulgence in pleasure and luxury, or at least he "should not parade his vices to the world."[87] He should also maintain the appearance of being a great soldier, even if he is not, and "appear to be particularly earnest in the service of the gods."[88] He should personally honor men of merit, while leaving punishments to be inflicted by others. In short, he should show himself to the people "in the light, not of a tyrant, but of a steward and a king."[89] In this way, "his power . . . will be more lasting," and "he will not be wicked, but half wicked only."[90]

THE IDEAL STATE

In turning from the flaws of actual states to his discussion of the ideal state, Aristotle's approach is thoroughly pragmatic. He is driven not by theoretical preconceptions but by a close consideration of what is possible in light of human nature and existing circumstances. We must not assume a standard of excellence above that of ordinary persons. Our search is for the best state, not simply as an aspiration, but "having regard to the life in which the majority are able to share, and to the form of government which states in general can attain."[91] Thus, Aristotle would start from existing constitutions and introduce changes that improve the state without exceeding what is feasible. Starting from scratch, as Plato did in *Republic*, is not only unrealistic but also dangerous insofar as it departs too readily from human nature and existing practice. As Oliver Wendell Holmes Jr., the great American jurist, would later write, "the life of the law has not been logic; it has been experience."[92] It is upon this experience that Aristotle seeks to build his state.

Yet Aristotle never loses sight of his ethical touchstone: the goal of the state is to ensure the best possible life, the eudaimonia, of its citizens. The ideal state is one in which a good man finds moral, intellectual, and political fulfillment, and the rest of the citizens share in that fulfillment as much as they are capable of doing. Realistically, the state "cannot be entirely composed of good men, and yet each citizen is expected to do his own business well," and therefore have his own form of excellence.[93] Aristotle accordingly seeks a constitution that recognizes that the excellence of the citizen need not necessarily coincide with that of the good man. The good citizen varies with the constitution. The good man does not. Aristotle wants to ensure that, in his proposed state, the good man can also be a good citizen, and that all others are at least good citizens, even if they are not fully good men in the sense outlined in *Ethics*. The excellence of all is the care of the state, and "that form of government is best in which every man, whoever he is, can act best and live happily."[94]

Aristotle is far from naive. He recognizes that many, if not most, citizens will struggle over wealth and honors. These goods must be sufficiently distributed to provide the necessities of life and to avoid class warfare and social unrest. But they are not, for Aristotle, the critical components of eudaimonia. The goods that matter, excellence of character and intellect, are not limited even if they are rare. Accordingly, the production and distribution of material goods is an essential first step for a self-sufficient state. But we must not confuse what is necessary for life with the true purpose of life. The goal of the state is "to make the citizens good and just" so that they realize, as best each of them can, a perfect and self-sufficing life.[95]

The constitutional form such a state will take is a fusion of democracy and oligarchy, subject to the rule of law. Democratic elements must predominate, for not only are democracies "safer and more permanent"[96] than oligarchies, but "none of the principles on which men claim to rule and to hold all other men in subjection to them are right."[97] Self-determination is a critical component of any just regime, and "no government can stand which is not founded upon justice."[98] Yet the rights and property of the rich, and their desire for honor within the state, must also be respected in order to avoid a backlash against the democracy. Aristotle sensibly notes that, "if a constitution is to be permanent, all the parts of the state must wish that it should exist and these arrangements be maintained,"[99] or, if that is not possible, at the very least "the portion of the state which desires the permanence of the constitution ought to be stronger than that which desires the reverse."[100]

This last point leads to perhaps the most surprising aspect of Aristotle's pragmatic "ideal state," and shows how far we are from Plato and later utopias.[101] Aristotle believes that the most critical component of such a state is a secure and stable middle class, meeting together on terms of friendship and equality, sympathetic with the poor, yet not inclined to attack the rich. If the middle class is stronger and more numerous than either extreme, has sufficient means, and a full share in government, it will be invested in the success of the state and prevent either of the extremes from becoming dominant.

A city ought to be composed, as far as possible, of equals and similars; and these are generally the middle classes.... And this is the class of citizens which is most secure in a state, for they do not, like the poor, covet other men's goods; nor do others covet theirs, as the poor covet the goods of the rich; and as they neither plot against others, nor are themselves plotted against, they pass through life safely.[102]

Too much wealth in the hands of a few is as destructive to the good of the state as too little wealth in the hands of the many. All disparities in wealth cannot and should not be eliminated, but they can be mitigated by means of payments for jury service and attendance at the assembly, and by common meals, gymnasiums, religious festivals, and public education, in which all share on terms of equality. In keeping with the schemata of his *Ethics*, the middle class is the mean between the extremes of wealth and poverty and hence will be "most ready to follow rational principle."[103]

Plato would concentrate political power in the hands of a few wise men. Aristotle recognizes not only that such men are difficult to identify, but more fundamentally that the many can, collectively, be wiser than the few. "For the many, of whom each individual is not a good man, when they meet together may be better than the few good, if regarded not individually."[104] In other words, the very process of collective deliberation and judgment is likely to reach a better result than the isolated judgments of individuals, even if those individuals are, by hypothesis, the best and wisest in the state. This is perhaps the most profound (and optimistic) endorsement of democracy ever made.

Moreover, the participation in such an exercise of collective judgment is itself a critical aspect of the good life. The fulfillment of our human logos (our capacity for speech and reason) requires active participation in the administrative, judicial, and policy affairs of the state. Aristotle is critical of representative government as removing the citizen too far from the decision-making process and hence impoverishing his exercise of practical reason. The democracy he advocates, and that he experienced in Athens, is direct: the citizens meet together in the assembly to make key decisions and regularly participate as jurors in administering justice.

The right to hold administrative offices is also open to all citizens. Many such positions are to be chosen by lot, others by elections in which all have an equal vote. In the ideal state, citizens take turns ruling and being ruled: "the good citizen ought to be capable of both; he should know how to govern like a freeman, and how to obey like a freeman—these are the excellences of a citizen."[105] The younger men will mainly provide security through military service, while the older men mainly administer the state, but all will serve in varying capacities throughout their lives as citizens.

This ideal state seems more radical than any democracy we know today. But, for Aristotle, the exercise of democratic freedom must occur within a constitution and background laws that provide structure and stability to the state and impose limits upon the decisions of the majority. The rule of law is critical to ensure that the disparate citizens who compose the state—despite differences in merit and ability—are able to function as a unity and act for the benefit of the entire state, not just of a popular majority. "Men should not think it slavery to live according to the rule of the constitution; for it is their salvation."[106]

Laws established in tranquility must rule in times of passion and upheaval. "The law is reason unaffected by desire."[107] Nothing is more important in a state than to habituate citizens to obey the laws and temper their own passions. In an early version of the "broken windows" theory, Aristotle writes that this spirit of obedience is especially important in small matters, "for transgression creeps in unperceived and at last ruins the state, just as the constant recurrence of small expenses in time eats up a fortune."[108] He also counsels against lightly changing the laws, even if minor improvement can be made, for "the citizen will not gain so much by making the change as he will lose by the habit of disobedience."[109]

Yet the law, he recognizes, is an imperfect instrument. "It is impossible that all things should be precisely set down in writing; for enactments must be universal, but actions are concerned with particulars."[110] Thus, good laws *and* good magistrates alike are necessary to good government. In Aristotle's view, this fact confirms the need for a well-constructed state to be small in size. For "if the citizens of a state are to judge and to distribute offices according to merit, then they must know each other's characters; where they do not possess this knowledge, both the election to offices and the decision of lawsuits will go wrong."[111] Aristotle is willing to sacrifice the military security of a larger state for the personal relationships and knowledge of one another that are critical to a well-governed state. The citizens must know each other's merits and flaws, and they must be able to meet together in the assembly to decide their own destiny. Overpopulation can also create practical problems and lead to civil unrest. Greek city-states regularly sent their excess population off to found new colonies throughout the Mediterranean.

Only a favored fraction of the community, however, is allowed the eudaimonia that is otherwise the purpose of the state. Athens at its height had perhaps fifty thousand male citizens, but at least four times that number of slaves, resident foreigners, women (who, technically, counted as citizens but had minimal rights), and children. The state may exist for the sake of the citizens, but the citizens are a minority of the state who depend upon the labor of others. Aristotle brutally states that "no man can practice excellence who is living the life of a mechanic or laborer."[112] Citizens perform political, military, religious, and cultural functions. They require leisure to do so, which means that others must devote themselves to production and cultivation so as to ensure for citizens a good life that they cannot realize themselves. It seems odd that Aristotle, as a resident foreigner in Athens, was willing to exclude himself from the full rights of citizenship and hence from the best life, as he conceived it. It seems even odder that his account of eudaimonia should depend on the exploitation of so many others.

A LIBERAL EDUCATION AND THE ENDS OF LIFE

In addition to the nature and division of offices, Aristotle deals with many other aspects of the ideal state, such as its proximity to the sea, the proper layout of its streets, the establishment of separate gymnasia for boys to be watched over by magistrates (apparently Aristotle did not share Plato's tolerance for pederasty), and the proper age for marriage (eighteen for women, thirty-seven for men). But, of all such things, the most important is education. "The best laws, though sanctioned by every citizen of the state, will be of no avail unless the young are trained by habit and education in the spirit of the constitution."[113] All arts, including excellence, require training and practice to become habitual. It is up to the state, therefore, to ensure the moral and political excellence of its citizens. Education should be the same for all citizens and should be public rather than private. A citizen belongs to the state, not just to himself, and the care of each citizen is inseparable from the care of the whole.

The primary purpose of education is to develop reason and enforce good habits and thereby fill up "the deficiencies of nature."[114] The state must inculcate in each person a sense of responsibility to others, "for where absolute freedom is allowed there is nothing to restrain the evil [that] is inherent in every man."[115] Education must therefore, above all, teach the moral virtues. "There is clearly nothing which we are so much concerned to acquire and to cultivate as the power of forming right judgments, and of taking delight in good dispositions and noble actions."[116]

Aristotle suggests that any focus on the useful in education should be strictly limited, because the point of education is not to "mak[e] mechanics" of future citizens. Youths should not be trained for employments that either "deform the body" or "degrade the mind."[117] They should learn to read and write, and they should take gymnastic exercise for the health and strength of the body. Such skills will certainly be useful to them in business and politics and war; but those are not the ends of education. "Men must be able to engage in business and to go to war, but leisure and peace are better."[118]

The branches of study that matter most are valuable in themselves, regardless of their practical use. This point is best illustrated in Aristotle's discussion of music, which "can form our minds and habituate us to true pleasures."[119] The study of music provides education, amusement, and intellectual enjoyment. Music "has a power of forming the character"[120] and "a natural sweetness"[121] that makes it ideal in the education of the young. It also purges, as does poetry, the darker emotions of passion and fear, and thereby softens the character and "conduces to excellence."[122] The study of music thus makes one a better man and a better citizen. Shakespeare, as he expressed in *The Merchant of Venice*, would agree.

> The man that hath no music in himself,
> Nor is not mov'd with concord of sweet sounds,
> Is fit for treasons, stratagems and spoils;
> The motions of his spirit are dull as night,
> And his affections dark as Erebus:
> Let no such man be trusted.[123]

An education in music, in poetry, and in philosophy is justified "not as being useful or necessary, but because it is liberal or noble."[124] Aristotle's ideal of a liberal education as the refinement of sensibility and of moral and intellectual reasoning—a sound mind in a sound body—has held sway for more than 2,300 years, despite the increasing preprofessionalism in our colleges and universities. In words that should be inscribed above the entrance to every campus, he writes: "To be always seeking after the useful does not become free and exalted souls."[125] There is considerable elitism in such a view—in keeping with Aristotle's contention that not all men are capable of eudaimonia—yet there need not be. Just as the benefits of democracy and citizenship can be extended to all adults, so too can the benefits of a liberal education be extended to all who stand willing to avail themselves of the opportunity. Aristotle's deepest insights in *Politics* can be removed from the limitations of their historical context to form a broader, more inclusive vision of the best life and the most just community.

Yet the historical context reveals a deep irony in *Politics*. In it, Aristotle presents a vision of the ideal polis just as the era of the polis is coming to its end. Internecine warfare among the ever-contentious Greeks had so weakened them as to make them an easy target for Philip II and his son Alexander. Even after the death of Alexander, when his vast domain was broken into three huge fragments, the Greek peoples remained largely quiescent under continued Macedonian domination. Their city-states survived in form at least, but their democratic autonomy was largely gone.

In both *Ethics* and *Politics*, Aristotle weighs the merits of two lives: that of the statesman and that of the philosopher. He offers arguments in favor of each before concluding that "the active life will be the best, both for every city collectively, and for individuals."[126] Yet he cannot but qualify this judgment, noting that "to a reflecting mind it must appear very strange that the statesman should be always considering how he can dominate and tyrannize over others, whether they are willing or not."[127] Those who feel no need to exercise their excellence through the domination of others, but "desire pleasures which depend on themselves," will find their true satisfaction in a quiet, largely private life of contemplation, softened by music and friendship.[128] Such a life, he tells us, is as self-sufficient, pleasurable, richly fulfilling, and close to the divine as any human being can attain.

The Hellenistic period saw the birth of several new schools of philosophy, particularly Epicureanism and Stoicism, which built on Aristotle's vision of the self-sufficient life. Their focus is largely personal and apolitical, in keeping with the increasing centralization of power and the diminished role of free citizens in determining their own fate. These schools carried through into Roman times and found a ready audience at all levels of the Roman Republic, from slaves to emperors. The Romans had a genius for adaptation, and it is with their adaptations of Greek comedy and Greek philosophy that I hope to begin my exploration of the Roman search for wisdom.

CHRONOLOGY

Minoan Civilization	2200–1400
Mycenaean Palace Culture	1600–1100
Fall of Troy	ca. 1125
Dark Ages	1100–800
Phoenician Alphabet Adopted	ca. 800
First Olympic Games	776
Lycurgus: Spartan Constitution	ca. 750
Homer	ca. 725
Hesiod	ca. 700
Draco's Code of Laws in Athens	621
Solon's Reforms in Athens	594
Aeschylus	525–456
Pindar	522–443
Establishment of Democracy in Athens	507
Ionian Revolt Aided by Athens	499
Sophocles	496–406
Persian Wars	490–479
Battle of Marathon	490
Battles of Thermopylae and Salamis	480
Battle of Plataea	479
Herodotus	484–425
Euripides	480–406

Thucydides	460–395
Aristophanes	450–386
Peloponnesian War	431–404
Peace of Nicias	421
Sicilian Expedition	416
Fall of Athens	404
Xenophon	430–354
Plato	427–347
Death of Socrates	399
Aristotle	384–322
Philip II of Macedon	382–336
Pyrrho	360–270
Alexander the Great	356–323
Menander	342–292
Epicurus	341–270
Battle of Chaeronea	338
Zeno of Citium	334–262
Euclid's *Elements*	ca. 300

SUGGESTIONS FOR FURTHER READING

GENERAL BOOKS ON
GREEK HISTORY AND CULTURE

Two classic introductions to ancient Greece are H. D. F. Kitto, *The Greeks* (1951; repr., Harmondsworth, UK: Penguin Books, 1991), and Edith Hamilton, *The Greek Way to Western Civilization* (1942; repr., New York: New American Library, 1948). Two more comprehensive treatments are Finley Hooper, *Greek Realities* (1967; repr., Detroit: Wayne State University Press, 1978), and John Boardman, Jasper Griffin, and Oswyn Murray, eds., *The Oxford History of Greece and the Hellenistic World* (Oxford: Oxford University Press, 2001), which contains synoptic essays on all aspects of Greek history and culture. Werner Jaeger's three-volume work, *Paideia: The Ideals of Greek Culture*, 2nd ed. (New York: Oxford University Press, 1943–45), translated by Gilbert Highet, is still a treasure of valuable insights and stirring commentary.

Histories of ancient Greece that will interest general readers include Robin Lane Fox, *The Classical World: An Epic History from Homer to Hadrian* (New York: Basic Books, 2006); Thomas R. Martin, *Ancient Greece: From Prehistoric to Hellenistic Times* (New Haven, CT: Yale University Press, 2000); Michael Grant, *The Rise of the Greeks* (New York: Charles Scribner's Sons, 1987); W. G. Forrest, *The Emergence of Greek Democracy, 800–400 B.C.* (New York: McGraw-Hill, 1970); and Victor Ehrenberg, *From Solon to Socrates: Greek History and Civilization During the 6th and 5th Centuries BC*, 2nd ed. (London: Methuen, 1973). Useful books on more specialized topics include Edith Hamilton, *Mythology* (Boston: Little, Brown, 1942); Robert Graves, *The Greek Myths* (London: Penguin Books, 1992); Jules Cashford, trans., *The Homeric Hymns* (London: Penguin Books, 2003); E. R. Dodds, *The Greeks and the Irrational* (Berkeley: University of California Press, 1951); George Sarton, *A History of Science*, vol. 1, *Ancient Science through the Golden Age of Greece* (New York: W. W. Norton, 1970); Marshall Clagett, *Greek Science in Antiquity* (1955; repr., Mineola, NY: Dover Publications, 2001); Victor Davis Hanson, *Wars of the Ancient Greeks* (Washington, DC: Smithsonian Books, 2004); and Anthony Gottlieb, *The Dream of Reason: A History of Philosophy from the Greeks to the Renaissance* (New York: W. W. Norton, 2000).

Quotations from the lyric poets in the text are from Andrew M. Miller, *Greek Lyric: An Anthology in Translation* (Indianapolis, IN: Hackett, 1996). Quotations from the pre-Socratic philosophers are from Patricia Curd, *A Presocratics Reader: Selected Fragments and Testimonia* (Indianapolis, IN: Hackett, 1996).

An indispensable reference guide is John Roberts, ed., *The Oxford Dictionary of the Classical World* (New York: Oxford University Press, 2005).

HOMER

We are blessed with three excellent pairs of translations of the *Iliad* and the *Odyssey*, each with its own special virtues. Those of Richmond Lattimore are the most faithful to the Greek original, both in meter and matter, and have a stately grace that is unforgettable but sometimes a bit leaden. Those of Robert Fitzgerald are the most poetic but also the freest, and they employ an off-putting spelling of names that are simply too familiar to us in their Romanized forms to support a more accurate phonetic transliteration. My favorites are the recent translations of Robert Fagles, which I use in the text and which appear to me to marry the best aspects of the other two. As a bonus, Bernard Knox, the supreme classical scholar, has written indispensable introductions to both translations.

The secondary literature on Homer is so vast as to stymie even the most dedicated scholar. For the general reader who wants to sample the best of it, I recommend, in addition to the Bernard Knox introductions, two collections of essays, the first edited by Harold Bloom as part of the Modern Critical Views series published by Chelsea House, and the second edited by George Steiner and Robert Fagles, as part of the Twentieth Century Views series published by Prentice Hall. For a more in-depth treatment of the *Iliad*, try Mark W. Edwards, *Homer: Poet of the Iliad* (Baltimore, MD: Johns Hopkins University Press, 1987). Also, I highly recommend Eva Brann's thoroughly charming *Homeric Moments: Clues to Delight in Reading the* Odyssey *and the* Iliad (Philadelphia, PA: Paul Dry Books, 2002). Finally, there is a fine set of lectures on the *Iliad* by Elizabeth Vandiver produced by the Teaching Company.

HESIOD

In the text, I use the translations of Apostolos Athanassakis, *Hesiod:* Theogony, Works and Days, Shield (Baltimore, MD: Johns Hopkins University Press, 2004). Athanassakis's notes and introductions are invaluable and decipher the many allusions in the text. Also quite useful are the notes to the translation by R. M. Fraser, *The Poems of Hesiod* (Norman: University of Oklahoma Press, 1983).

There are very useful articles or chapters on Hesiod in Bernard Knox, *Essays Ancient and Modern* (Baltimore, MD: Johns Hopkins University Press, 1989); Werner Jaeger, *Paideia: The Ideals of Greek Culture*, 2nd ed., vol. 1 (New York: Oxford University Press, 1945); and John Boardman, Jasper Griffin, and Oswyn Murray, eds., *The Oxford History of Greece and the Hellenistic World* (Oxford: Oxford University Press, 2001). The two book-length treatments I found most helpful are Stephanie Nelson, *God and the Land: The Metaphysics of Farming in Hesiod and Vergil* (New York: Oxford University Press, 1998), and Jenny Strauss Clay, *Hesiod's Cosmos* (Cambridge: Cambridge University Press, 2003).

AESCHYLUS

For the translations in text, I have used the Penguin Classics version of *Prometheus Bound and Other Plays* (1961), translated by Philip Vellacott, and the wonderful translation of the *Oresteia* by Richmond Lattimore, in *Aeschylus I* (1953), which is part of the University of Chicago's Complete Greek Tragedies series. Lattimore's introduction is also very good.

The best general introductions to Greek tragedy are Ian C. Storey and Arlene Allan, *A Guide to Ancient Greek Drama* (Malden, MA: Blackwell, 2005), and Eric Csapo and William J. Slater, *The Context of Ancient Drama* (Ann Arbor: University of Michigan Press, 1995). Friedrich Nietzsche's discussion in *The Birth of Tragedy: Out of the Spirit of Music* is still eminently worth reading, despite the strong overlay of Schopenhauer and Wagner, which he later repudiated. There is also a useful chapter on ancient drama in John Boardman, Jasper Griffin, and Oswyn Murray, eds., *The Oxford History of Greece and the Hellenistic World* (Oxford: Oxford University Press, 2001), and an excellent discussion of the use of mythic material in tragedy by Peter Burian, "Myth into *Muthos*: The Shaping of Tragic Plot," in *The Cambridge Companion to Greek Tragedy*, edited by P. E. Easterling (Cambridge: Cambridge University Press, 1997). There is also a good set of lectures on Greek tragedy in Elizabeth Vandiver's *Greek Tragedy*, produced by the Teaching Company.

On Aeschylus in particular, I recommend the following: *Aeschylus* (Broomall, PA: Chelsea House, 2002), which is part of the Major Dramatists series edited by Harold Bloom; the first ten chapters of *Oxford Readings in Greek Tragedy* (Oxford: Oxford University Press, 1983), edited by Erich Segal; chapter 1 of the second book (but still first volume) of Werner Jaeger, *Paideia: The Ideals of Greek Culture*, 2nd ed. (New York: Oxford University Press, 1945); and part 2 of Bernard Knox, *Word and Action: Essays on the Ancient Theater* (Baltimore, MD: Johns Hopkins University Press, 1986). Finally, the most compelling reading of the *Oresteia* is to be found in the first three chapters of H. D. F. Kitto, *Form and Meaning in Drama* (London: Methuen, 1956).

SOPHOCLES

For the translations in text, I have used the Robert Fagles version of *The Three Theban Plays* (Harmondsworth, UK: Penguin, 1984) and the various translations in *Sophocles II* (1957), which is part of the University of Chicago's Complete Greek Tragedies series.

The foremost interpreter of Sophocles is Bernard Knox. His two books—*The Heroic Temper: Studies in Sophoclean Tragedy* (Berkeley: University of California Press, 1964) and *Oedipus at Thebes: Sophocles' Tragic Hero and His Time* (New Haven, CT: Yale University Press, 1957)—his essays in part 3 of *Word and Action: Essays on the Ancient Theater* (Baltimore, MD: Johns Hopkins University Press, 1986), and his introduction to Fagles's translations are all invaluable. I also recommend *Sophocles* (Broomall, PA: Chelsea House, 2003), which is part of the Major Dramatists series edited by Harold Bloom; chapters 11 through 18 of *Oxford Readings in Greek Tragedy* (Oxford: Oxford University Press, 1983), edited by Erich Segal; chapter 2 of the second book (but still first volume) of Werner Jaeger, *Paideia: The Ideals of Greek Culture*, 2nd ed. (New York: Oxford University Press, 1945); and chapters 4, 5, and 6 of H. D. F. Kitto, *Form and Meaning in Drama* (London: Methuen, 1956).

EURIPIDES

I have used in the text the various translations in the five volumes on Euripides that are part of the University of Chicago's Complete Greek Tragedies series.

Among the secondary literature, helpful sources include part 4 of Bernard Knox, *Word and Action: Essays on the Ancient Theater* (Baltimore, MD: Johns Hopkins University Press, 1986); *Euripides* (Broomall, PA: Chelsea House, 2003), which is part of the Major Dramatists series edited by Harold Bloom; chapters 19 through 29 of *Oxford Readings in Greek Tragedy* (Oxford: Oxford University Press, 1983), edited by Erich Segal; chapter 4 of the second book (but still first volume) of Werner Jaeger, *Paideia: The Ideals of Greek Culture*, 2nd ed. (New York: Oxford University Press, 1945); and *Euripides* (Oxford: Oxford University Press, 2003), part of the Oxford Readings in Classical Studies series and edited by Judith Mossman.

HERODOTUS

In the text, I have used the new translation by Andrea L. Purvis in *The Landmark Herodotus: The Histories* (New York: Anchor Books, 2009), edited by Robert B. Strassler. The book contains an excellent introduction by Rosalind Thomas as well as twenty-one scholarly appendices and numerous maps and explanatory footnotes. *The Landmark Herodotus* is an invaluable resource, but general readers may find that the scholarly apparatus detracts from the sheer pleasure of reading Herodotus, in which case a good translation of *Histories* by Aubrey de Sélincourt is available from Penguin Books (1954).

Excellent secondary sources include James Romm, *Herodotus* (New Haven, CT: Yale University Press, 1998); Peter Green, *The Greco-Persian Wars* (Berkeley: University of California Press, 1996); and *The Cambridge Companion to Herodotus* (Cambridge: Cambridge University Press, 2006), edited by Carolyn Dewald and John Marincola.

THUCYDIDES

In the text, I have used the revised translation of Richard Crawley in *The Landmark Thucydides: A Comprehensive Guide to the Peloponnesian War* (New York:

Free Press, 1996), edited by Robert B. Strassler. The book contains an excellent introduction by Victor Davis Hanson as well as eleven scholarly appendices and numerous maps and explanatory footnotes. For readers who prefer to skip the scholarly apparatus, there is a good translation of *The Peloponnesian War* by Rex Warner (Harmondsworth, UK: Penguin Books, 1972). Quotations in text from Xenophon's *Hellenika* are from *The Landmark Xenophon's* Hellenika (New York: Anchor Books, 2010), translated by John Marincola and edited by Robert B. Strassler.

Excellent secondary sources include Victor Davis Hanson, *A War Like No Other* (New York: Random House, 2006); Donald Kagan, *The Peloponnesian War* (New York: Penguin Books, 2004); Donald Kagan, *Thucydides: The Reinvention of History* (New York: Viking, 2009); and W. Robert Connor, *Thucydides* (Princeton, NJ: Princeton University Press, 1984).

ARISTOPHANES

A wholly satisfactory translation of Aristophanes is impossible. There are too many puns, too many neologisms, and too many topical allusions for a seamless transition to English. For the translations in text, I have used Paul Roche's excellent one-volume version of *Aristophanes: The Complete Plays* (New York: New American Library, 2005). The plays are also well (if unevenly) translated in a three-volume edition published by Penguin Books.

As background reading, I recommend K. J. Dover, *Aristophanic Comedy* (Berkeley: University of California Press, 1972); Leo Strauss, *Socrates and Aristophanes* (Chicago: University of Chicago Press, 1980; first published 1966 by Basic Books); Douglas M. MacDowell, *Aristophanes and Athens: An Introduction to the Plays* (Oxford: Oxford University Press, 1995); chapter 5 of the second book (but still first volume) of Werner Jaeger, *Paideia: The Ideals of Greek Culture*, 2nd ed. (New York: Oxford University Press, 1945); *Oxford Readings in Aristophanes* (Oxford: Oxford University Press, 1996), edited by Erich Segal; and Paul Cartledge, *Aristophanes and His Theatre of the Absurd* (London: Bristol Classical Press, 1990).

PLATO

The best contemporary translations of Plato are by Hackett Publishing, also reproduced in a four-volume, leather-bound set by Easton Press. Hackett's translation of *Symposium*, by Alexander Nehamas and Paul Woodruff, is available separately in paperback.

For a broader introduction to Plato's thought, I recommend chapter 1 of my earlier book, *Three Questions We Never Stop Asking* (Amherst, NY: Prometheus Books, 2010). The secondary literature I found most helpful in dealing specifically with *Symposium* includes chapter 14 of Alexander Nehamas, *Virtues of Authenticity: Essays on Plato and Socrates* (Princeton, NJ: Princeton University Press, 1999); chapter 6 of Martha C. Nussbaum, *The Fragility of Goodness: Luck and Ethics in Greek Tragedy and Philosophy* (Cambridge: Cambridge University Press, 1986); Leo Strauss, *On Plato's* Symposium (Chicago: University of Chicago Press, 2001); and part 3 of Allan Bloom, *Love and Friendship* (New York: Simon and Schuster, 1993).

ARISTOTLE

Most quotations from *Nicomachean Ethics* are from the translation by Joe Sachs as part of the Focus Philosophical Library (2002). All quotations from *Politics* are from *The Complete Works of Aristotle* (Princeton, NJ: Princeton University Press, 1984), edited by Jonathan Barnes. Cambridge University Press has published a paperback edition of this version of *Politics* along with *The Constitution of Athens*, edited by Stephen Everson.

As secondary works, I recommend J. O. Urmson, *Aristotle's Ethics* (Oxford: Blackwell, 1988); part 3 of Martha C. Nussbaum, *The Fragility of Goodness: Luck and Ethics in Greek Tragedy and Philosophy* (Cambridge: Cambridge University Press, 1986); *The Cambridge Companion to Aristotle* (Cambridge: Cambridge University Press, 1995), edited by Jonathan Barnes; R. G. Mulgan, *Aristotle's Political Theory* (Oxford: Clarendon Press, 1977); and chapter 5 of my earlier book, *Three Questions We Never Stop Asking* (Amherst, NY: Prometheus Books, 2010).

NOTES

PREFACE

1. Francis Steegmuller, ed. and trans., *The Letters of Gustave Flaubert: 1830–1857* (Cambridge, MA: Harvard University Press, 1980), p. 81.
2. Matthew Arnold, *Culture and Anarchy: An Essay in Political and Social Criticism* (London: Smith, Elder, 1869), p. viii.
3. Gloria L. Cronin and Ben Siegel, eds., *Conversations with Saul Bellow* (Jackson: University Press of Mississippi, 1994), p. 145.
4. Friedrich Nietzsche, *Thus Spoke Zarathustra*, in *The Portable Nietzsche*, trans. Walter Kaufmann (New York: Viking Press, 1968), p. 152.
5. Steegmuller, *Letters of Gustave Flaubert*, p. 23.

INTRODUCTION: THE GLORY THAT WAS GREECE

1. Quoted in Werner Jaeger, *Aristotle: Fundamentals of the History of His Development*, trans. Richard Robinson, 2nd ed. (Oxford: Clarendon Press, 1948), p. 321.
2. Andrew M. Miller, trans., *Greek Lyric: An Anthology in Translation* (Indianapolis, IN: Hackett, 1996), p. 9.
3. Ibid., p. 15.
4. Ibid., p. 28.
5. Ibid., p. 22.
6. Ibid., p. 52.
7. Patricia Curd, ed., and Richard D. McKirahan, trans., *A Presocratics Reader: Selected Fragments and Testimonia* (Indianapolis, IN: Hackett, 1996), p. 36.
8. Ibid., p. 87.

CHAPTER 1: HOMER AND THE HEROIC IDEAL

1. Arthur K. McComb, ed., *The Selected Letters of Bernard Berenson* (London: Hutchinson, 1965), p. 294.
2. Homer, *Iliad*, trans. Robert Fagles (New York: Penguin Books, 1998), 14.102–04.

3. Ibid., 1.106–107.
4. Ibid., 1.143, 174, 188.
5. Ibid., 1.165.
6. Ibid., 1.280–87.
7. Ibid., 9.238.
8. Harold Bloom, ed., *Modern Critical Views: Homer* (New York: Chelsea House, 1986), p. 3.
9. Homer, *Iliad*, 1.206.
10. Ibid., 9.127–28.
11. Ibid., 9.145.
12. Ibid., 9.192–93.
13. Ibid., 9.361–62, 365.
14. Ibid., 1.586.
15. Ibid., 9.228.
16. Ibid., 9.378–79.
17. Ibid., 9.412.
18. Christopher Marlowe, *Doctor Faustus*, in *The Complete Plays*, ed. Frank Romany and Robert Lindsey (London: Penguin Books, 2003), p. 390, 13.90–92.
19. Finley Hooper, *Greek Realities* (1967; repr., Detroit, MI: Wayne State University Press, 1978), p. 53.
20. Homer, *Iliad*, 9.413–17.
21. Ibid., 9.386–87.
22. Homer, *Odyssey*, trans. Robert Fagles (New York: Penguin Books, 1996), 11.556–78.
23. Homer, *Iliad*, 1.586.
24. Ibid., 9.781, 783, 785.
25. Ibid., 2.927.
26. Ibid., 12.280–81.
27. Ibid., 8.141–45.
28. Ibid., 6.482–83.
29. Ibid., 3.17–22.
30. Ibid., 3.24–25.
31. Ibid., 3.36–41.
32. Ibid., 3.52.
33. Ibid., 3.58–59.
34. Ibid., 3.526–27.
35. Ibid., 24.908.
36. Ibid., 6.430–31.
37. Ibid., 6.435–39.
38. Ibid., 6.474–75.

39. Ibid., 6.509–12.
40. Ibid., 6.543–44.
41. Ibid., 6.577–84.
42. Ibid., 17.755.
43. Ibid., 16.50–55.
44. Ibid., 16.105–106.
45. Ibid., 16.115–19.
46. Ibid., 17.143–46.
47. Ibid., 18.123.
48. Ibid., 18.126–27.
49. Ibid., 18.143–47.
50. Ibid., 19.271–76.
51. Ibid., 22.1.
52. Ibid., 18.359–60.
53. Ibid., 22.237–41.
54. Ibid., 23.418–19.
55. Ibid., 24.268–71.
56. Ibid., 24.561.
57. Ibid., 24.590–91.
58. Ibid., 24.610–11.
59. Ibid., 24.728–30.
60. Ibid., 24.794.
61. Ibid., 1.2–3.
62. Ibid., 1.6.
63. Erich Auerbach, *Mimesis: The Representation of Reality in Western Literature* (Princeton, NJ: Princeton University Press, 1973), p. 6.
64. Homer, *Iliad*, 11.12–16.
65. Eva Brann, *Homeric Moments: Clues to Delight in Reading the* Odyssey *and the* Iliad (Philadelphia, PA: Paul Dry Books, 2002), p. 40.
66. Bruno Snell, *The Discovery of the Mind in Greek Philosophy and Literature* (Mineola, NY: Dover, 1982), p. 22.
67. Homer, *Iliad*, 4.62–64.
68. William Shakespeare, *King Lear*, in *Tragedies*, vol. 1 (London: J. M. Dent, 1906), 4.1.36–37.
69. Brann, *Homeric Moments*, p. 3.
70. Homer, *Iliad*, 3.187–90.
71. Auerbach, *Mimesis*, p. 7.
72. Ibid., p. 3.
73. George Steiner and Robert Fagles, eds., *Homer: A Collection of Critical Essays* (Englewood Cliffs, NJ: Prentice-Hall, 1962), p. 9.

74. Homer, *Iliad*, 18.64–65.
75. Ibid., 12.32–40.
76. Ibid., 6.171–75.

CHAPTER 2: HESIOD—POET OF EVERYDAY LIFE

1. Gregory Nagy, *Greek Mythology and Poetics* (Ithaca, NY: Cornell University Press, 1992), p. 47.
2. Hesiod, *Works and Days*, in *Theogony; Works and Days; Shield*, trans. Apostolos N. Athanassakis, 2nd ed. (Baltimore: Johns Hopkins University Press, 2004), ll. 639–40.
3. Hesiod, *Theogony*, in Athanassakis, *Theogony; Works and Days; Shield*, ll. 22–23.
4. Hesiod, *Works and Days*, in Athanassakis, *Theogony; Works and Days; Shield*, ll. 654–59.
5. Ibid., l. 39.
6. Hesiod, *Theogony*, ll. 1–4.
7. Ibid., ll. 36–40.
8. Ibid., l. 32.
9. Ibid., l. 33.
10. Ibid., ll. 27–28.
11. Hesiod, *Works and Days*, l. 10.
12. Ibid., l. 2.
13. Hesiod, *Theogony*, ll. 27–28.
14. Andrea L. Purvis, trans., and Robert B. Strassler, ed., *The Landmark Herodotus: The* Histories (New York: Anchor Books, 2009), 2.53.2.
15. Hesiod, *Theogony*, ll. 96–103.
16. Hesiod, *Works and Days*, l. 86.
17. Hesiod, *Theogony*, ll. 108–13.
18. Ibid., ll. 176–77.
19. Ibid., ll. 459–60.
20. Ibid., l. 500.
21. Ibid., l. 636.
22. Ibid., ll. 717–21.
23. Ibid., ll. 884–85.
24. Ibid., ll. 892–93.
25. Ibid., l. 47.
26. Ibid., ll. 60–61.
27. John Boardman, ed., et al. *Oxford History of Greece and the Hellenistic World* (Oxford: Oxford University Press, 2001), p. 84.
28. Hesiod, *Works and Days*, ll. 42–46.

29. Ibid., ll. 113–14.

30. Ibid., l. 140.

31. Ibid., ll. 153–56.

32. Ibid., l. 166.

33. Ibid., ll. 195–96.

34. Hesiod, *Theogony*, l. 535.

35. Hesiod, *Works and Days*, ll. 79–80.

36. Hesiod, *Theogony*, ll. 590–93.

37. Hesiod, *Works and Days*, ll. 97–102.

38. Werner Jaeger, *Paideia: The Ideals of Greek Culture*, vol. 1, *Archaic Greece: The Mind of Athens*, trans. Gilbert Highet, 2nd ed. (New York: Oxford University Press, 1986), p. 63.

39. Hesiod, *Works and Days*, l. 225.

40. Ibid., ll. 40–41.

41. Ibid., ll. 265–66.

42. Ibid., ll. 270–73.

43. Ibid., ll. 207–11.

44. Ibid., ll. 211, 262, 267.

45. Ibid., l. 279.

46. Ibid., l. 273.

47. Bernard Knox, *Essays Ancient and Modern* (Baltimore, MD: Johns Hopkins University Press, 1989), p. 18.

48. Hesiod, *Works and Days*, l. 42.

49. Ibid., ll. 702–705.

50. Ibid., ll. 347, 371–72.

51. Stephanie Nelson, *God and the Land: The Metaphysics of Farming in Hesiod and Vergil* (New York: Oxford University Press, 1998), p. 134.

52. Jaeger, *Paideia*, p. 57.

53. Hesiod, *Works and Days*, l. 14.

54. Ibid., l. 20.

55. Ibid., ll. 314–16.

56. Ibid., l. 288.

57. Ibid., ll. 381–82.

58. Ibid., l. 398.

59. Ibid., ll. 289–90.

60. Hesiod, *Theogony*, ll. 902–03.

61. Hesiod, *Works and Days*, l. 393.

62. Nelson, *God and the Land*, p. 57.

63. Hesiod, *Works and Days*, l. 503.

64. Ibid., ll. 493–97.

65. Ibid., ll. 486–87.

66. Ibid., l. 569.
67. Ibid., l. 492.
68. Ibid., l. 558.
69. Ibid., ll. 513–14, 518, 529–33.
70. Ibid., ll. 554–56.
71. Ibid., ll. 582–84.
72. Ibid., ll. 589–94.
73. Ibid., ll. 673–75.
74. Ibid., ll. 700–701.
75. Ibid., l. 711.
76. Ibid., ll. 714, 719.
77. Ibid., ll. 826–28.
78. Ibid., ll. 651–53.
79. Ibid., ll. 660–62.
80. Ibid., l. 653.

CHAPTER 3: AESCHYLUS AND THE INSTITUTION OF JUSTICE

1. Richard S. Dunn, ed., et al., *The Journal of John Winthrop, 1630–1649* (Cambridge, MA: Harvard University Press, 1996), p. 10.
2. Richard Crawley, trans., and Robert B. Strassler, ed., *The Landmark Thucydides: A Comprehensive Guide to the Peloponnesian War* (New York: Free Press, 1996), 2.22.1.
3. See Bernard Knox, *Word and Action: Essays on the Ancient Theater* (Baltimore, MD: Johns Hopkins University Press, 1986), p. 64.
4. Werner Jaeger, *Paideia: The Ideals of Greek Culture*, vol. 1, *Archaic Greece: The Mind of Athens*, trans. Gilbert Highet, 2nd ed. (New York: Oxford University Press, 1986), p. 259.
5. Friedrich Nietzsche, *The Birth of Tragedy*, in *Basic Writings of Nietzsche*, trans. and ed. Walter Kaufmann (New York: Modern Library, 1968), p. 73.
6. Aeschylus, *The Persians*, in Prometheus Bound *and Other Plays*, trans. Philip Vellacott (London: Penguin Books, 1961), l. 242.
7. Ibid., l. 243.
8. Friedrich Dürrenmatt, *Plays and Essays*, ed. Volkmar Sander (New York: Continuum, 1982), p. 236.
9. Aeschylus, *Persians*, in Vellacotts, Prometheus Bound *and Other Plays*, ll. 10–11.
10. Ibid., l. 748.
11. Ibid., ll. 531–32.

12. Ibid., ll. 265–66.
13. Ibid., ll. 824–25.
14. Ibid., ll. 818–20.
15. Jaeger, *Paideia*, p. 262.
16. Aeschylus, *Prometheus Bound*, in Vellacott, Prometheus Bound *and Other Plays*, l. 110.
17. Ibid.
18. Ibid., l. 454.
19. Ibid., l. 449.
20. Ibid., l. 502.
21. Ibid., l. 450.
22. Ibid., ll. 236–37.
23. Ibid., ll. 264–66.
24. Ibid., ll. 176–77.
25. Ibid., l. 103.
26. Ibid., ll. 374–75.
27. Aeschylus, *Agamemnon*, in *Aeschylus I: The Complete Greek Tragedies*, trans. Richmond Lattimore (Chicago: University of Chicago Press, 1953), ll. 10–11.
28. Ibid., ll. 36–38.
29. Ibid., l. 20.
30. Ibid., ll. 74–75.
31. Ibid., l. 61.
32. Ibid., l. 220.
33. Ibid., ll. 227–30.
34. Ibid., l. 217.
35. Ibid., ll. 160–66.
36. Ibid., l. 340.
37. Ibid., ll. 371–72.
38. Ibid., ll. 453–54.
39. Ibid., ll. 527–28.
40. Ibid., ll. 606–607.
41. Ibid., ll. 903–904.
42. Ibid., ll. 371–72.
43. Ibid., ll. 954–55.
44. Ibid., l. 1290.
45. Ibid., ll. 1325–26.
46. Ibid., l. 1371.
47. Ibid., l. 1375.
48. Ibid., ll. 1401–1404.
49. Ibid., ll. 1525–29.

50. Ibid., ll. 1564–65.

51. Ibid., ll. 1575–76.

52. Ibid., l. 1604.

53. Ibid., ll. 1673–75.

54. Ibid., l. 1565.

55. Aeschylus, *The Libation Bearers*, in Lattimore, *Aeschylus I*, ll. 140–41.

56. Ibid., ll. 299–301.

57. Ibid., l. 422.

58. Ibid., ll. 311–12.

59. Ibid., ll. 49–53.

60. Ibid., ll. 692–95.

61. Ibid., l. 830.

62. Ibid., l. 902.

63. Ibid., l. 930.

64. Ibid., l. 1017.

65. Ibid., ll. 1053–54.

66. Ibid., ll. 1074–76.

67. Aeschylus, *The Eumenides*, in Lattimore, *Aeschylus I*, l. 52.

68. Ibid., l. 428.

69. Ibid., l. 489.

70. Ibid., ll. 583–84.

71. Ibid., l. 592.

72. Ibid., l. 494.

73. Ibid., ll. 518–19.

74. Ibid., l. 502.

75. Ibid., l. 526.

76. Ibid., ll. 698–99.

77. Ibid., l. 895.

78. Ibid., ll. 1000–1002.

79. Aeschylus, *Agamemnon*, l. 160.

80. Robert Fagles, ed., introduction to Aeschylus, *Oresteia* (Norwalk, CT: Easton Press, 1999), p. 19.

CHAPTER 4: SOPHOCLES—THE THEBAN PLAYS

1. Bernard Knox, *The Heroic Temper: Studies in Sophoclean Tragedy* (Berkeley: University of California Press, 1983), p. 5.

2. Patricia Curd, ed., and Richard D. McKirahan, trans., *A Presocratics Reader: Selected Fragments and Testimonia* (Indianapolis, IN: Hackett, 1996), p. 98.

3. Ibid.

4. Ibid.

5. Andrew M. Miller, trans., *Greek Lyric: An Anthology in Translation* (Indianapolis, IN: Hackett, 1996), p. 110.

6. Sophocles, *Ajax*, trans. John Moore, in *Sophocles II: The Complete Greek Tragedies*, ed. David Grene and Richmond Lattimore (Chicago: University of Chicago Press, 1957), ll. 365–68.

7. Ibid., ll. 517–19.

8. Ibid., ll. 669–77.

9. Ibid., l. 690.

10. William Shakespeare, *King Lear*, in *Tragedies*, vol. 1 (London: J. M. Dent, 1906), 5.3.323–24.

11. Sophocles, *Ajax*, in Grene and Lattimere, *Sophocles II*, ll. 123–26.

12. Ibid., l. 349.

13. Ibid., ll. 479–80.

14. Ibid., l. 777.

15. Virginia Woolf, *The Common Reader* (New York: Harcourt, Brace, 1984), p. 26.

16. Sophocles, *Electra*, trans. David Grene, in Grene and Lattimore, *Sophocles II*, ll. 94–95.

17. Ibid., ll. 230–31.

18. Ibid., ll. 170–72.

19. Ibid., ll. 133–38.

20. Ibid., ll. 1414–15.

21. Ibid., ll. 1485–90.

22. Ibid., l. 140.

23. Ibid., ll. 218–19.

24. Ibid., ll. 381–82.

25. Ibid., ll. 304–305.

26. Sophocles, *The Women of Trachis*, trans. Michael Jameson, in Grene and Lattimore, *Sophocles II*, ll. 32–33.

27. Ibid., ll. 538–42.

28. Ibid., ll. 1276–77.

29. Ibid., ll. 943–46.

30. Ibid., ll. 1278–79.

31. Sophocles, *Philoctetes*, trans. David Grene, in Grene and Lattimore, *Sophocles II*, ll. 55–56.

32. Ibid., ll. 79–85.

33. Ibid., ll. 1319–21.

34. Ibid., ll. 1445–47.

35. Ibid., ll. 534–36.

36. Edmund Wilson, *The Wound and the Bow: Seven Studies in Literature* (Athens: Ohio University Press, 1997), p. 240.

37. Sophocles, *Philoctetes*, in Grene and Lattimere, *Sophocles II*, ll. 1048–52.

38. Ibid., ll. 1245–46.

39. H. D. F. Kitto, *Form and Meaning in Drama* (London: University Paperbacks, 1960), p. 137.

40. Sophocles, *Philoctetes*, l. 537.

41. Aeschylus, *Seven against Thebes*, in Prometheus Bound *and Other Plays*, trans. Philip Vellacott (London: Penguin Books, 1961), ll. 695–96.

42. Ibid., l. 712.

43. See George Steiner, *Antigones* (New Haven, CT: Yale University Press, 1984), p. 4.

44. Sophocles, *Antigone*, in *The Three Theban Plays*, trans. Robert Fagles (Norwalk, CT: Easton Press, 2000), l. 174.

45. Ibid., l. 180.

46. Ibid., ll. 210–14.

47. Ibid., ll. 238–39.

48. Ibid., ll. 74–75.

49. Ibid., l. 104.

50. Ibid., ll. 328–35.

51. Ibid., ll. 504.

52. Ibid., ll. 521.

53. Ibid., ll. 541–42.

54. Ibid., ll. 615–16.

55. Ibid., l. 835.

56. Ibid., l. 790.

57. Ibid., ll. 749–51.

58. Ibid., l. 823.

59. Ibid., l. 825.

60. Ibid., l. 1112.

61. Ibid., ll. 1000–1001.

62. Ibid., l. 1185.

63. Ibid., ll. 1202–1203.

64. Ibid., ll. 1462–63.

65. Ibid., l. 1446.

66. Ibid., ll. 377–78.

67. Ibid., l. 414.

68. Ibid., ll. 406–409.

69. Ibid., ll. 136–38.

70. Ibid., ll. 912–13.

71. Ibid., ll. 377–78.

72. Bernard Knox, introduction to Sophocles, *Oedipus the King*, in Fagles, *Three Theban Plays*, p. 143.

73. Ibid., l. 41.

74. Ibid., ll. 270–73.

75. Ibid., ll. 413–18.

76. Ibid., ll. 476–78.

77. Ibid., l. 805.

78. Ibid., l. 934.

79. Ibid., l. 1285.

80. Ibid., ll. 1678–84.

81. Ibid., l. 1068.

82. Ibid., l. 894.

83. Ibid., ll. 1467–71.

84. Ibid., ll. 1168–69.

85. Sophocles, *Oedipus at Colonus*, in Fagles, *Three Theban Plays*, ll. 18–21.

86. Ibid., ll. 1873–76.

87. Knox, *Heroic Temper*, p. 144.

88. Sophocles, *Oedipus at Colonus*, ll. 1396–98.

89. William Wordsworth, "Ode on Intimations of Immortality from Recollections of Early Childhood," in *Norton Anthology of Poetry*, ed. Alexander W. Allison et al., 3rd ed. (New York: W. W. Norton, 1983), pp. 551–55.

90. Sophocles, *Oedipus at Colonus*, l. 1727.

91. Ibid., ll. 1396–98.

92. Ibid., ll. 1778–79.

93. Ibid., ll. 783–86.

94. Ibid., ll. 686–89.

95. Ibid., l. 1718.

96. Ibid., ll. 1999–2001.

CHAPTER 5: EURIPIDES AND THE TWILIGHT OF THE GODS

1. Aristotle, *Poetics*, 1460a32–34, trans. Ingram Bywater, in *The Complete Works of Aristotle: The Revised Oxford Translation*, ed. Jonathan Barnes, 2 vols. (Princeton, NJ: Princeton University Press, 1984), 2:2316.

2. Ibid., 1453a29.

3. Euripides, *Iphigenia in Aulis*, trans. Charles R. Walker, in *Euripides IV: The Complete Greek Tragedies*, ed. David Grene and Richmond Lattimore (Chicago: University of Chicago Press, 1958), ll. 175–76.

4. Ibid., ll. 303–304.

5. Ibid., l. 396.

6. Ibid., l. 459.

7. Ibid., ll. 512–13.

8. Ibid., l. 512.

9. Ibid., l. 499.

10. Ibid., ll. 1272–73.

11. Ibid., l. 961.

12. Ibid., l. 598.

13. Ibid., ll. 1218–19.

14. Ibid., l. 1377.

15. Ibid., ll. 1398–99.

16. Friedrich Nietzsche, *The Dawn*, in *The Portable Nietzsche*, trans. Walter Kaufmann (New York: Viking Press, 1968), p. 91 (sec. 557).

17. Euripides, *Iphigenia in Aulis*, in Grene and Lattimere, *Euripides IV*, ll. 1185–86.

18. Ibid., l. 1525.

19. Ibid., ll. 1034–36.

20. Ibid., l. 808.

21. Euripides, *Hecuba*, trans. William Arrowsmith, in *Euripides III: The Complete Greek Tragedies*, ed. David Grene and Richmond Lattimore (Chicago: University of Chicago Press, 1958), l. 56.

22. Ibid., l. 80.

23. Euripides, *The Trojan Women*, trans. Richmond Lattimore, in Grene and Lattimore, *Euripides III*, ll. 83–86.

24. Euripides, *Hecuba*, in Grene and Lattimere, *Sophocles II*, ll. 256–57.

25. Ibid., ll. 800–804.

26. Ibid., ll. 488–92.

27. Euripides, *Electra*, trans. Emily Townsend Vermeule, in *Euripides V: The Complete Greek Tragedies*, ed. David Grene and Richmond Lattimore (Chicago: University of Chicago Press, 1959), l. 1008.

28. Ibid., ll. 184–85.

29. Ibid., ll. 57–58.

30. Ibid., l. 1034.

31. Ibid., l. 1035.

32. Ibid., l. 779.

33. Ibid., ll. 842–43.

34. Ibid., ll. 1105–1106.
35. Ibid., l. 1244.
36. Ibid., ll. 1178–79.
37. Ibid., l. 1109.
38. Euripides, *Orestes*, trans. William Arrowsmith, in Grene and Lattimore, *Euripides IV*, l. 356.
39. Ibid., l. 1654.
40. Ibid., l. 1679.
41. Ibid., p. 110.
42. Ibid., ll. 720–21.
43. Ibid., l. 1050.
44. Ibid., ll. 298–99.
45. Henry James, *Hawthorne*, in *Essays on Literature, American Writers, English Writers* (New York: Library of America, 1984), pp. 351–52.
46. Euripides, *The Medea*, trans. Rex Warner, in *Euripides I: The Complete Greek Tragedies*, ed. David Grene and Richmond Lattimore (Chicago: University of Chicago Press, 1955), ll. 250–51.
47. Ibid., ll. 257–58.
48. Ibid., ll. 265–66.
49. Ibid., ll. 564–65.
50. Ibid., ll. 886–88.
51. Ibid., ll. 1242–47.
52. Ibid., ll. 809–10.
53. Ibid., ll. 1049–51.
54. Ibid., l. 165.
55. Ibid., l. 1362.
56. Ibid., ll. 1323–24.
57. Euripides, *Hippolytus*, trans. David Grene, in Grene and Lattimore, *Euripides I*, l. 1007.
58. Ibid., l. 14.
59. Ibid., ll. 47–50.
60. Ibid., l. 1409.
61. Euripides, *The Bacchae*, trans. William Arrowsmith, in Grene and Lattimore, *Euripides V*, ll. 1008–10.
62. Ibid., l. 861.
63. Ibid., l. 299.
64. Ibid., ll. 335–37.
65. Ibid., l. 344.
66. Ibid., l. 232.
67. Ibid., ll. 217–18.
68. Ibid., l. 214.

69. Ibid., ll. 1122–23.

70. Ibid., l. 1137.

71. Ibid., ll. 1144–45.

72. Ibid., ll. 1303–1304.

73. Ibid., ll. 505–506.

74. Ibid., l. 507.

75. Ibid., ll. 201–204.

76. Bruno Snell, "From Tragedy to Philosophy: *Iphigenia in Aulis*," in *Oxford Readings in Greek Tragedy*, ed. Erich Segal (Oxford: Oxford University Press, 1988), p. 400.

77. Euripides, *Bacchae*, in Grene and Lattimere, *Euripides V*, ll. 201–22.

78. Ibid., l. 910.

79. Euripides, *Heracles*, trans. William Arrowsmith, in *Euripides II: The Complete Greek Tragedies*, ed. David Grene and Richmond Lattimore (Chicago: University of Chicago Press, 1956), ll. 104–106.

CHAPTER 6: THE INQUIRIES OF HERODOTUS OF HALICARNASSUS

1. Andrea L. Purvis, trans., and Robert B. Strassler, ed., *The Landmark Herodotus: The Histories* (New York: Anchor Books, 2009), 1.1.

2. Ibid., 1.87.

3. Ibid., 2.29.

4. Ibid., 7.152.3.

5. Ibid., 4.30.1.

6. Homer, *Odyssey*, trans. Robert Fagles (New York: Penguin Books, 1996), 1:4.

7. Purvis and Strassler, *Landmark Herodotus*, 3.106.3.

8. Ibid., 2.73.4.

9. Ibid., 2.2.

10. Ibid., 2.86–89.

11. Ibid., 3.38.1.

12. Ibid.

13. Ibid., 4.104.1.

14. Ibid., 4.172.2.

15. Ibid., 4.117.

16. Ibid., 1.93.4.

17. Ibid., 1.196.3.

18. Ibid., 1.197.5.

19. Ibid., 1.199.

20. Ibid., 2.123.1.
21. Ibid., 1.140.
22. Ibid., 2.99.
23. Ibid.
24. Ibid., 1.182.
25. Ibid., 2.121.1.
26. Ibid., 2.131.3.
27. Ibid., 1.12.2.
28. Ibid., 4.195.2.
29. Ibid., 3.122.1.
30. Ibid., 2.125.
31. Ibid., 2.156.
32. Ibid., 2.131.3.
33. Ibid., 4.42.4.
34. Ibid., 1.23.
35. Ibid., 2.121.
36. Ibid., 3.130–37.
37. Ibid., 5.92.
38. Ibid., 1.60.3.
39. Ibid., 8.106.
40. Ibid., 2.174.
41. Ibid., 2.162.4.
42. Ibid., 2.172.3–5.
43. Ibid., 1.5.3.
44. Ibid., 1.5.4.
45. Ibid., 1.30.2.
46. Ibid., 1.30.3.
47. Ibid., 1.31.4.
48. Ibid., 1.32.1.
49. Ibid., 1.32.9.
50. Ibid., 3.40.3.
51. Ibid., 7.10.
52. Ibid., 7.14.3.
53. Ibid., 7.16.2.
54. Ibid.
55. Ibid., 1.131.
56. Ibid., 2.53.1.
57. Ibid., 2.53.2.
58. Ibid., 2.3.2.
59. Ibid., 4.205.

60. Ibid., 1.32.1.
61. Ibid., 1.53.3.
62. Ibid., 7.6.4.
63. Ibid., 1.86.6.
64. Ibid., 1.136.2.
65. Ibid., 3.80.6.
66. Ibid., 3.81.3.
67. Ibid., 3.81.1.
68. Ibid., 3.82.5.
69. Ibid., 1.5.3.
70. Ibid.
71. Ibid., 1.6.3.
72. Ibid., 5.48.3.
73. Ibid., 5.105.2.
74. Ibid., 6.21.2.
75. Ibid., 6.44.1.
76. Ibid., 6.101.3.
77. Ibid., 6.105.1.
78. Ibid., 6.109.3–5.
79. Ibid., 6.112.1.
80. Ibid., 6.114.
81. Ibid., 6.116.1.
82. Ibid., 6.120.
83. Ibid., 7.22.1.
84. Ibid., 8.30.2.
85. Ibid., 7.41.1.
86. Ibid., 7.46.2.
87. Ibid., 7.35.2.
88. Ibid., 7.174.1.
89. Ibid., 7.200.1.
90. Ibid., 7.206.1.
91. Ibid., 7.223.4.
92. Ibid., 7.229.1.
93. Ibid., 8.3.1.
94. Ibid., 7.139.5.
95. Ibid., 7.190.
96. Ibid., 7.191.2.
97. Ibid., 7.142.2.
98. Ibid., 8.98.1.
99. Ibid., 8.62.2.

100. Ibid., 8.68.2.

101. Ibid., 8.96.1.

102. Ibid., 8.100.5.

103. Ibid., 9.38.2.

104. Ibid., 9.62.3.

105. Ibid., 9.90.1.

106. Ibid., 9.100.2.

107. Ibid., 8.144.2–3.

108. Ibid., 5.78.4.

CHAPTER 7: THUCYDIDES—POWER AND PATHOS

1. Richard Crawley, trans., and Robert B. Strassler, ed., *The Landmark Thucydides: A Comprehensive Guide to the Peloponnesian War* (New York: Free Press, 1996), 1.1.

2. Ibid., 1.20.

3. Ibid., 1.22.2.

4. Ibid., 1.22.4.

5. See Harold Bloom, *The Anxiety of Influence: A Theory of Poetry*, 2nd ed. (New York: Oxford University Press, 1997).

6. Thomas Gray, "Elegy Written in a Country Churchyard," in *Norton Anthology of Poetry*, ed. Alexander W. Allison et al., 3rd ed. (New York: W. W. Norton, 1983), pp. 463–66.

7. Crawley and Strassler, *Landmark Thucydides*, 1.22.4.

8. Ibid., 3.82.2.

9. George Santayana, *The Life of Reason*, vol. 1, *Reason in Common Sense* (New York: Charles Scribner, 1905).

10. Crawley and Strassler, *Landmark Thucydides*, 3.82.2.

11. Ibid., 1.76.2.

12. Ibid., 3.82.4.

13. Ibid., 5.26.5.

14. Ibid., 1.22.2.

15. Ibid., 1.22.3.

16. Ibid., 1.22.1.

17. W. H. Auden, "September 1, 1939," in *Selected Poems*, ed. Edward Mendelson, 2nd ed. (New York: Vintage Books, 2007), p. 95.

18. Crawley and Strassler, *Landmark Thucydides*, 1.1.3.

19. Ibid., 1.23.1.

20. Ibid., 1.23.2.

21. Ibid., 1.95.3.
22. Ibid., 4.80.2–3.
23. Ibid., 1.138.3.
24. Ibid., 1.138.6.
25. Ibid., 1.70.2–5.
26. Ibid., 1.70.9.
27. Ibid., 1.33.3.
28. Ibid.
29. Ibid., 1.42.2.
30. Ibid., 1.44.2–1.45.
31. Ibid., 1.72.1.
32. Ibid., 1.74.3.
33. Ibid., 1.75.2.
34. Ibid., 1.76.2.
35. Ibid., 1.78.2.
36. Ibid., 1.81.4.
37. Ibid., 1.88.
38. Ibid., 1.140.1.
39. Ibid., 1.143.5.
40. Ibid., 1.143.4.
41. Ibid., 1.144.
42. Ibid., 1.78.1.
43. Ibid., 2.16.2–2.17.
44. Ibid., 2.21.2.
45. Ibid., 2.22.1.
46. Ibid., 2.37.1.
47. Ibid., 2.37.3.
48. Ibid.
49. Ibid., 2.38.1.
50. Ibid., 2.39.1.
51. Ibid., 2.40.1.
52. Ibid., 2.40.2.
53. Ibid., 2.39.1.
54. Ibid.
55. Ibid., 2.40.3.
56. Ibid., 2.43.1.
57. Ibid., 2.41.1.
58. Ibid., 2.48.3.
59. Ibid., 2.49.
60. Ibid., 2.47.4.

61. Ibid., 2.52.3.
62. Ibid., 2.53.2.
63. Ibid., 2.53.4.
64. Ibid., 2.59.3.
65. Ibid., 2.61.2.
66. Ibid., 2.63.2.
67. Ibid., 2.64.3, 2.64.6.
68. Ibid., 2.65.4.
69. Ibid.
70. Ibid., 2.65.8.
71. Ibid., 2.65.10.
72. Ibid., 3.36.2.
73. Ibid., 3.36.4.
74. Ibid., 3.37.2.
75. Ibid., 3.46.
76. Ibid., 2.71.2.
77. Ibid., 3.68.1.
78. Ibid., 3.58.2.
79. Ibid., 3.74.1.
80. Ibid., 3.81.4.
81. Ibid., 3.81.5.
82. Ibid., 3.84.2.
83. Ibid., 3.82.4.
84. Ibid., 4.12.2.
85. Ibid., 4.28.4.
86. Ibid., 4.28.5.
87. Ibid., 4.39.3.
88. Ibid., 4.41.4.
89. Ibid., 4.65.4.
90. Ibid., 4.88.1.
91. Ibid., 4.108.4.
92. Ibid., 5.14.
93. Ibid., 5.26.2.
94. Ibid., 5.89.
95. Ibid., 5.100.
96. Ibid., 5.103.
97. Ibid., 5.104.
98. Ibid., 5.116.3–4.
99. Ibid., 2.37.3.
100. Ibid., 1.144.1.

101. Ibid., 6.8.2.

102. Ibid., 6.12.2.

103. Ibid., 6.18.3.

104. Ibid., 6.31.2.

105. Ibid., 6.53.2.

106. Ibid., 6.49.1.

107. Ibid., 6.92.4.

108. Ibid., 7.15.1.

109. Ibid., 7.42.5.

110. Ibid., 7.49.4.

111. Ibid., 7.50.4.

112. Ibid.

113. Ibid., 7.60.2.

114. Ibid., 7.87.6.

115. Ibid., 8.2.

116. Ibid., 8.69.

117. Ibid., 8.81.2.

118. Ibid., 8.86.4.

119. Ibid., 8.96.5.

120. Ibid., 8.97.1.

121. John Marincola, trans., and Robert B. Strassler, ed., *The Landmark Xenophon's Hellenika* (New York: Anchor Books, 2010), 1.1.1.

CHAPTER 8: ARISTOPHANES AND THE
SERIOUS BUSINESS OF COMEDY

1. Aristotle, *Poetics*, 1451b5, trans. Ingram Bywater, in *The Complete Works of Aristotle: The Revised Oxford Translation*, ed. Jonathan Barnes, 2 vols. (Princeton, NJ: Princeton University Press, 1984), 2:2316.

2. Ibid., 1449a32–33.

3. Ibid., 1448b26.

4. Plato, *Laws*, 7.816e, trans. Trevor J. Saunders, in *Plato: Complete Works*, ed. John M. Cooper, 4 vols. (Norwalk, CT: Easton Press, 2001), 4:1318.

5. Ibid.

6. Ibid.

7. Plato, *Philebus*, 59c, trans. Dorothea Frede, in Cooper, *Plato: Complete Works*, 1:398.

8. Aristophanes, *Acharnians*, in *The Complete Plays*, trans. Paul Roche (New York: New American Library, 2005), p. 27.

9. Aristophanes, *A Parliament of Women*, in Roche, *Complete Plays*, p. 661.

10. See Ian C. Storey, introduction to Aristophanes, *Clouds*, trans. Peter Meineck (Indianapolis, IN: Hackett, 2000), p. x.

11. Werner Jaeger, *Paideia: The Ideals of Greek Culture*, vol. 1, *Archaic Greece: The Mind of Athens*, trans. Gilbert Highet, 2nd ed. (New York: Oxford University Press, 1986), p. 358.

12. Aristophanes, *Frogs*, in Roche, *Complete Plays*, p. 607.

13. Leo Strauss, *Studies in Platonic Political Philosophy* (Chicago: University of Chicago Press, 1985), p. 20.

14. Aristophanes, *Frogs*, p. 607.

15. Roche, *Complete Plays*, pp. x–xi.

16. Aristophanes, *Knights*, in Roche, *Complete Plays*, p. 92.

17. Aristophanes, *Wasps*, in Roche, *Complete Plays*, p. 262.

18. Aristophanes, *Knights*, p. 77.

19. Ibid., p. 69.

20. Ibid., p. 75.

21. Ibid.

22. Ibid., p. 127.

23. Ibid.

24. Aristophanes, *Clouds*, in Roche, *Complete Plays*, p. 176.

25. Aristophanes, *Wasps*, p. 235.

26. Aristophanes, *Acharnians*, in Roche, *Complete Plays*, p. 15.

27. Ibid., p. 26.

28. Ibid., p. 25.

29. Ibid., p. 27.

30. Ibid.

31. Ibid., p. 34.

32. Ibid., p. 53.

33. Ibid., p. 51.

34. Helene P. Foley, "Tragedy and Politics in Aristophanes' *Acharnians*," in *Oxford Readings in Aristophanes*, ed. Erich Segal (Oxford: Oxford University Press, 1996), p. 142.

35. Aristophanes, *Acharnians*, p. 36.

36. Aristophanes, *Peace*, in Roche, *Complete Plays*, p. 282.

37. Ibid., p. 299.

38. *She Done Him Wrong*, dir. Lowell Sherman (Paramount Pictures, 1933).

39. Aristophanes, *Lysistrata*, in Roche, *Complete Plays*, p. 469.

40. Ibid., p. 434.

41. Ibid., p. 446.

42. Ibid.

43. Ibid., p. 477.

44. William Shakespeare, *A Midsummer Night's Dream*, 5.1.366–72, in Sylvan Barnet, ed., *Comedies*, vol. 1 (New York: Knopf, 1995), p. 602.

45. Ibid., 3.2.115.

46. Aristophanes, *Birds*, in Roche, *Complete Plays*, p. 388.

47. Ibid., p. 356.

48. Ibid., p. 359.

49. Ibid., p. 356.

50. Ibid., p. 370.

51. Ibid.

52. Ibid., p. 372.

53. Ibid., p. 383.

54. Ibid., p. 405.

55. Ibid., p. 357.

56. Aristophanes, *Parliament of Women*, p. 623.

57. Ibid., p. 637.

58. Ibid.

59. Ibid., p. 638.

60. Ibid., p. 641.

61. Ibid., p. 654.

62. Aristophanes, *Plutus*, in Roche, *Complete Plays*, p. 682.

63. William Shakespeare, *King Lear*, 3.4.35–36 in Sylvan Barnet, ed., *Tragedies*, vol. 1 (New York: Knopf Doubleday, 1992), p. 362.

64. Aristophanes, *Plutus*, p. 688.

65. Ibid., p. 675.

66. Aristophanes, *Parliament of Women*, p. 661.

67. Aristophanes, *Frogs*, p. 607.

68. Aristophanes, *Clouds*, p. 197.

69. Ibid., p. 176.

70. Ibid., p. 140.

71. Ibid., p. 142.

72. Ibid., p. 151.

73. Ibid., p. 154.

74. Ibid., p. 148.

75. Ibid., p. 144.

76. Ibid., p. 139.

77. Ibid., p. 194.

78. Aristophanes, *Wasps*, p. 250.

79. Aristophanes, *Women at Thesmophoria Festival*, in Roche, *Complete Plays*, p. 498.

80. Ibid., p. 531.

81. Aristophanes, *Frogs*, p. 544.

82. Ibid., p. 569.
83. Ibid., p. 576.
84. Ibid.
85. Ibid.
86. Ibid., p. 581.
87. Ibid.
88. Ibid., p. 583.
89. Ibid., p. 584.
90. Ibid., p. 588.
91. Ibid., p. 594.
92. Ibid., p. 593.
93. Ibid., p. 565.
94. Ibid., p. 589.
95. Ibid., p. 585.
96. Ibid., p. 587.
97. Ibid., p. 603.
98. Ibid., p. 601.
99. Ibid., p. 603.
100. Ibid., p. 573.
101. Ibid., p. 608.
102. Ibid., p. 573.
103. Ibid., p. 609.
104. Gilbert Murray, *Aristophanes: A Study* (Oxford: Clarendon Press, 1933), p. 199.
105. Aristophanes, *Frogs*, p. 607.

CHAPTER 9: PLATO—PHILOSOPHY AND POETRY

1. Aristophanes, *Frogs*, in *The Complete Plays*, trans. Paul Roche (New York: New American Library, 2005), p. 607.

2. Alfred North Whitehead, *Process and Reality: An Essay in Cosmology*, ed. David Ray Griffin and Donald W. Sherburne (New York: Free Press, 1985), p. 39.

3. Plato, *Symposium*, 173a, trans. Alexander Nehamas and Paul Woodruff, in *Plato: Complete Works*, ed. John M. Cooper, 4 vols. (Norwalk, CT: Easton Press, 2001), 2:457.

4. Ibid., 173b.
5. Ibid.
6. Ibid., 173a.
7. Ibid., 173c.

8. Ibid., 174a.

9. Ibid., 175d.

10. Ibid.

11. Ibid., 175e.

12. Ibid., 176a.

13. Ibid., 177e.

14. Ibid., 178e.

15. Ibid., 185c.

16. Ibid., 184d, 185b.

17. Ibid., 187a.

18. Ibid., 186c, 187a.

19. Ibid., 189a.

20. Ibid., 189b.

21. Ibid., 189d.

22. Ibid., 190a.

23. Ibid., 190b.

24. Ibid., 191a.

25. Ibid., 191b.

26. Ibid., 191d.

27. Ibid.

28. Ibid., 192c.

29. Ibid.

30. Ibid.

31. Ibid., 192d–193a.

32. Ibid., 192e.

33. Ibid., 193d.

34. Donald M. Frame, trans., *The Complete Essays of Montaigne* (Stanford, CA: Stanford University Press, 1976), p. 139.

35. Ibid.

36. Plato, *Symposium*, in Cooper, *Plato*, 194e.

37. Ibid., 196b.

38. Ibid., 197e.

39. Ibid.

40. Ibid., 198a.

41. Leo Strauss, *On Plato's* Symposium, ed. Seth Benardete (Chicago: University of Chicago Press, 2001), p. 169.

42. Ibid.

43. Plato, *Symposium*, 198b.

44. Ibid., 198d.

45. Ibid., 198e.

46. Ibid., 199a–b.
47. Ibid., 198d.
48. Ibid., 200e.
49. Ibid., 201c.
50. Ibid.
51. Ibid., 201e.
52. Ibid., 203d.
53. Ibid., 204a.
54. Ibid., 205d.
55. Ibid., 202e.
56. Ibid., 204c–d.
57. Ibid., 205e.
58. Ibid., 206a.
59. Ibid., 205a.
60. Ibid., 207d.
61. Ibid., 207e.
62. Ibid., 209a–b.
63. Ibid., 209d.
64. Virginia Woolf, *The Waves* (Orlando, FL: Harcourt, 2006), p. 118.
65. Plato, *Symposium*, 210a.
66. Ibid.
67. Ibid., 210e.
68. Ibid., 211c.
69. Ibid., 211a.
70. Ibid., 211e.
71. Plato, *Republic*, 515c, trans. G. M. A. Grube, rev. C. D. C. Reeve, in Cooper, *Plato*, 3:971.
72. Ibid., 517c.
73. Ibid., 210e, 211c.
74. Ibid., 212c.
75. Ibid., 212e–213a.
76. Ibid., 213e.
77. Ibid., 218a.
78. Ibid., 215e.
79. Ibid., 216a.
80. Ibid., 216b–c.
81. Ibid., 216e.
82. Ibid., 217a.
83. Ibid., 218e–219a.
84. Ibid., 221b.

85. Ibid., 221e.
86. Ibid.
87. Ibid., 221c.
88. Ibid., 221d.
89. Martha Nussbaum, *The Fragility of Goodness: Luck and Ethics in Greek Tragedy and Philosophy* (Cambridge: Cambridge University Press, 1986), p. 195.
90. Plato, *Phaedo*, 118a, trans. G. M. A. Grube, in Cooper, *Plato*, 1:49.

CHAPTER 10: ARISTOTLE AND THE INVENTION OF POLITICAL SCIENCE

1. Dante, *The Divine Comedy: Inferno*, canto 4, trans. Allen Mandelbaum (Norwalk, CT: Easton Press, 2001), l.131 (*"il maestro di color che sanno"*).
2. Aristotle, *Nicomachean Ethics*, 10.1181b16, trans. Joe Sachs (Newburyport, MA: Focus Publishing, 2002).
3. Ibid., 1.1095a6.
4. Aristotle, *Politics*, 1.1253a3, trans. Benjamin Jowett, in *The Complete Works of Aristotle: The Revised Oxford Translation*, ed. Jonathan Barnes, 2 vols. (Princeton, NJ: Princeton University Press, 1984), 2:1986.
5. Aristotle, *Nicomachean Ethics*, 1.1094a29, trans. W. D. Ross and J. O. Urmson, in Barnes, *Complete Works of Aristotle*, 2:1729.
6. Ibid., 1.1096a16.
7. Ibid., 1.1096a27–29 (Sachs translation).
8. Ibid., 5.1129a26–29.
9. Ibid., 1.1094b18–25.
10. Ibid., 7.1145b7.
11. Aristotle, *Politics*, in Barnes, *Compete Works of Aristotle*, 2.1264a1–2.
12. Aristotle, *Nicomachean Ethics*, in Barnes, *Compete Works of Aristotle*, 10.1179a18–24 (Sachs translation).
13. Ibid., 2.1103b27–30.
14. Ibid., 1.1094a18–23.
15. Ibid., 1.1097b3–8.
16. Ibid., 1.1097b20–21.
17. Ibid., 1.1097b3–6.
18. Ibid., 1.1098b21–22 (Ross/Urmson translation).
19. Ibid., 7.1153b17–18 (Sachs translation).
20. Ibid., 7.1153b19–21.
21. Ibid., 1.1099b27–28.

22. Ibid., 9.1169b30–31.

23. Ibid., 1.1098a16–17.

24. *The Republic of Plato*, trans. Allan Bloom, 2nd ed. (New York: Basic Books, 1991), 343b–44c.

25. Aristotle, *Politics*, 7.1323a26–34.

26. Aristotle, *Nicomachean Ethics*, 2.1104a13 (Sachs translation).

27. Ibid., 2.1106b27–28.

28. Ibid., 2.1108b11–13.

29. Ibid., 3.1119a17–19.

30. Ibid., 2.1107a25.

31. Ibid., 2.1107a11–12.

32. Ibid., 2.1106b28–31.

33. Ibid., 4.1126a9–12.

34. Ibid., 2.1108b26–28.

35. Ibid., 2.1109b2.

36. Ibid., 2.1109b5–7.

37. Ibid., 2.1109b7–8 (Ross/Urmson translation).

38. Ibid., 4.1121a4–5 (Sachs translation).

39. Ibid., 2.1104a35–2.1104b4.

40. Ibid., 10.1172a22–24.

41. Ibid., 2.1103b15–18.

42. Ibid., 2.1103b25–27.

43. Ibid., 10.1181b16.

44. Ibid., 10.1180a5–7.

45. Ibid., 10.1180a27–29.

46. Ibid., 10.1180b8.

47. Ibid., 10.1180b27–28.

48. Aristotle, *Politics*, 1.1253a10.

49. Ibid., 1.1253a39.

50. Ibid., 1.1253a30.

51. Ibid., 1.1252b28–30.

52. Ibid., 1.1253a3.

53. Ibid., 1.1253a19–20.

54. Ibid., 1.1253a27.

55. Ibid., 1.1260b14.

56. Ibid., 1.1254b13–15.

57. Ibid., 1.1255a2.

58. Ibid., 1.1254b19.

59. Ibid., 1.1258a21–22.

60. Ibid., 1.1254a18–19.

61. Ibid., 2.1263b36–41.
62. Ibid., 2.1262b21–23.
63. Ibid., 2.1262a13–14.
64. Ibid., 2.1262a40–2.1263b1.
65. Ibid., 2.1263b1–3.
66. Ibid., 2.1263b4–6.
67. Ibid., 2.1260b35.
68. Ibid., 3.1279a27–28.
69. Ibid., 3.1279a29–30.
70. Ibid., 3.1279a21.
71. Ibid., 3.1279a30–31.
72. Ibid., 4.1295a20–23.
73. Ibid., 6.1318b4–5.
74. Ibid., 2.1267b2–4.
75. Ibid., 6.1320a30–32.
76. Ibid., 4.1297a11–13.
77. Ibid., 5.1309b22–23.
78. Ibid., 2.1256b12.
79. Ibid., 3.1280a22–24.
80. Ibid., 5.1303b18–19.
81. Ibid., 5.1302a9.
82. Ibid., 5.1309a20–21.
83. Ibid., 5.1313b1.
84. Ibid., 5.1313b5–6.
85. Ibid., 5.1314a14.
86. Ibid., 5.1314a31.
87. Ibid., 5.1314b34.
88. Ibid., 5.1314b40.
89. Ibid., 5.1315b1–2.
90. Ibid., 5.1315b8–10.
91. Ibid., 4.1295a29–31.
92. Oliver Wendell Holmes Jr., *The Common Law* (Cambridge, MA: Harvard University Press, 2009), p. xxiv.
93. Aristotle, *Politics*, 3.1276b38–39.
94. Ibid., 7.1324a22–23.
95. Ibid., 3.1280b11–12.
96. Ibid., 4.1296a12–13.
97. Ibid., 3.1283b27–28.
98. Ibid., 7.1332b28–29.
99. Ibid., 2.1270b20–22.

100. Ibid., 4.1296b15–17.
101. Ibid., 4.1295a29.
102. Ibid., 4.1295b25–32.
103. Ibid., 4.1295b6.
104. Ibid., 3.1281b1–2.
105. Ibid., 3.1277b14–16.
106. Ibid., 5.1310a34–35.
107. Ibid., 3.1287a31–32.
108. Ibid., 5.1307b34–35.
109. Ibid., 2.1269a16–17.
110. Ibid., 2.1269a10–12.
111. Ibid., 7.1326b14–17.
112. Ibid., 3.1278a20–21.
113. Ibid., 5.1310a14–16.
114. Ibid., 7.1337a1.
115. Ibid., 6.1318b40–6.1319a2.
116. Ibid., 8.1340a15–18.
117. Ibid., 8.1337b11–12.
118. Ibid., 7.1333b1–2.
119. Ibid., 8.1339a22–23.
120. Ibid., 8.1340b11.
121. Ibid., 8.1340b16.
122. Ibid., 8.1339a22.
123. William Shakespeare, *The Merchant of Venice*, 5.1.83–88, in *Comedies*, ed. Sylvan Barnet, vol. 1 (New York: Knopf, 1995), p. 92.
124. Aristotle, *Politics*, 8.1338a32.
125. Ibid., 8.1338b2–3.
126. Ibid., 7.1325b14–15.
127. Ibid., 7.1324b22–25.
128. Ibid., 2.1267a11.

INDEX